ETHNIC IDENTITY IN NAHUA MESOAMERICA

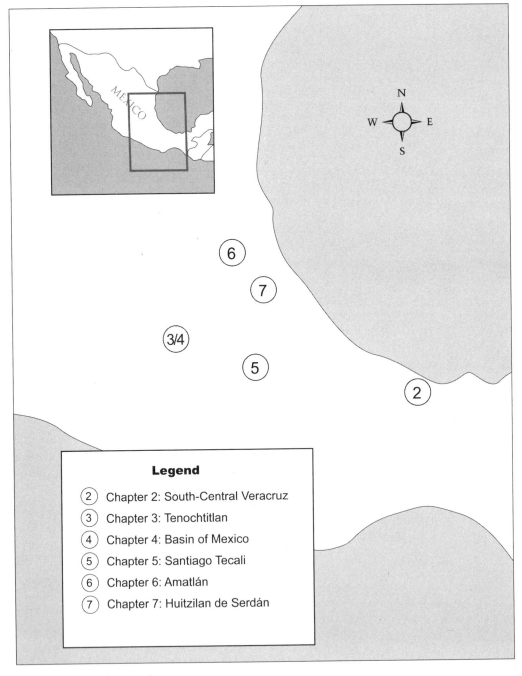

Mexico: locations of case studies.

Ethnic Identity in Nahua Mesoamerica:

The View from Archaeology, Art History, Ethnohistory, and Contemporary Ethnography

By
Frances F. Berdan, John K. Chance,
Alan R. Sandstrom, Barbara L. Stark,
James M. Taggart, and Emily Umberger

The University of Utah Press
Salt Lake City

The Defiance House Man colophon is a registered trademark
of the University of Utah Press. It is based upon a four-foot-tall,
Ancient Puebloan pictograph (late PIII) near Glen Canyon, Utah.

11 10 09 08 07   1 2 3 4 5

LIBRARY OF CONGRESS CATALOGING-IN-PUBLICATION DATA

Ethnic identity in Nahua Mesoamerica : the view from archaeology, art
history, ethnohistory, and contemporary ethnography / by Frances F.
Berdan ... [et al.].
    p. cm.
  Includes bibliographical references and index.
  ISBN 978-0-87480-917-6 (cloth : alk. paper)   1. Nahuas—Ethnic
identity.   2. Nahuas—History.   3. Nahuas—Social conditions.
4. Ethnicity—Mexico—History.   5. Mexico   History.   6. Mexico—
Social conditions.   I. Berdan, Frances.
  F1221.N3E84   2007
  972'.00497452—dc22   2007038026

Contents

Figures

Tables

Preface

EVERY BOOK HAS ITS UNIQUE BEGINNING, SOME SMALL SPARK THAT ignites it. For this book, it was the 68th Anglo-American Conference of Historians, hosted by the Institute of Historical Research at the University of London in 1999. The theme of this conference was "Race and Ethnicity": the organizers were interested in broad and tricky questions of ethnicity and race, with substance deriving from any part of the world. That would, of course, include Mesoamerica. So I submitted an abstract on Aztec ethnicity, only to find that I was the only Mesoamericanist to do so. Happily, though, Debra Birch, one of the conference organizers, liked the idea of a Mesoamerican component and encouraged me to find additional presenters to constitute a session. The idea of a view of ethnicity through time seemed intriguing, so I enlisted John Chance of Arizona State University and Alan Sandstrom of Indiana University–Purdue University Fort Wayne to offer their insights and data on ethnicity in colonial Mexico and the contemporary Huasteca Nahua, respectively. The conference organizers persuaded Peter Wade of the University of Manchester to serve as a discussant, and he offered many valuable and encouraging comments.

One nice thing about a small session is the amount of time allotted to each presentation. With just the three of us, we each had a good forty-five minutes to get our teeth into issues of ethnicity as they pertained to these different time periods in central Mexico. To all of us who have become accustomed to squeezing our massive data sets and complex thoughts into fifteen minutes of podium time, this was paradise. It also meant that we had composed presentations considerably beyond the usual. We had, in essence, produced article- or chapter-length works. With these as a foundation, the next step was almost inevitable: the production of a book on the topic.

Ethnicity is a tricky topic, especially when approached from archaeological remains and ethnohistorical documentation. Yet we all recognized that there was (and is) cultural diversity during the long train of Mesoamerican prehistory and history. How does this translate into ethnic identity, ethnic relations, ethnogenesis, ethnic maintenance, and ethnic "fade-out"? Where does ethnicity fit into state and imperial strategies and goals? What about ethnicity and class? What role does ethnicity play in economic, social, and political relations among groups and individuals, both horizontally and vertically? What are the definitions, dimensions, and dynamics of these complex and often volatile relationships? Perhaps it was time to grapple with such questions.

While maintaining our focus on the central highlands and Gulf lowlands of northern Mesoamerica, and on a long time frame, we thought it would be ideal to have a balance of contributors who dealt with ancient material remains, ethnohistory (pre- and post-hispanic), and contemporary Nahua peoples. We were fortunate to have Barbara Stark (archaeologist) and Emily Umberger (art historian), of Arizona State University, and James Taggart (ethnographer), of Franklin and Marshall College, enthusiastically join the project. With this enriched authorship, we then forged ahead. The goal was to produce an integrative volume about Mesoamerican ethnicity that addressed a spectrum of ideas and changes from precolumbian to modern times. The unique strengths of the book would be its multidisciplinary approach and the application of ethnicity to a long time trajectory.

But these things take time, and it became apparent that the project needed a boost. Under the enthusiastic and expert leadership of Barbara Stark, a four-day research session was organized for February 2005 at Arizona State University (ASU). This conference, titled "Ethnicity in Mesoamerica," was generously sponsored and funded by the ASU Division of Graduate Studies, College of Liberal Arts and Sciences, School of Human Evolution and Social Change, and Center for Latin American Studies. The School of Human Evolution and Social Change and the Herberger College of Fine Arts, ASU, supported the completion of Emily Umberger's chapter through a visiting interdisciplinary appointment (fall 2005). Pamela Effrein Sandstrom also attended the conference, and we express our particular gratitude to her for expertly compiling our individual bibliographies into a single, unified, and coherent whole.

As a prelude to the conference, in fall 2004 Chance and Stark taught a graduate and undergraduate seminar at ASU on the topic of Mesoamerican and comparative ethnicity. Based on their work in this seminar, they drafted essays on concepts of ethnicity, ethnicity and the state, and ethnicity and class, which served as a springboard for conference discussions as well as a foundation for the introductory chapter of this book and the themes of the book as a whole. During the conference Sarah Clayton, Christopher Garraty, Lars Krutak, Neil Miller, and Alanna Ossa, all graduate students at ASU who were involved with questions of social identity or class in their own research, participated in one or more of the discussion sessions and contributed valuable ideas. The guest conference participants (Berdan, Sandstrom, and Taggart) presented public colloquia, and at the close of the conference all the members and graduate students held a roundtable discussion with lively audience participation. Both the contributors' discussions and the public events for the university community were the matrix of give-and-take that moved the contributors' thinking forward. This work was further refined through constructive and helpful comments by Elizabeth Brumfiel and an anonymous reviewer.

The conference itself gave the project a dynamic, creative energy—the type of energy that derives from the intellectual stimulation of several minds wrestling with the same problem from different directions. We all left the conference reinvigorated and well focused. We also developed new and more polished ideas, a better sense of the bigger picture, a deeper appreciation of one another's unique methods, and a sense of how each chapter related to the others. In addition, it was particularly gratifying when Stark and Chance volunteered to write the introductory chapter. They were especially well equipped for this task, being heavily immersed in the conceptual aspects of ethnicity and having already coauthored an encyclopedia article on the topic. The final chapter, "Some Finishing Thoughts and Unfinished Business," reflects our recognition that this book is far from the last word on the topic. In many ways, it is barely the first. We look forward to seeing numerous improvements in the future.

Frances F. Berdan

1

Diachronic and Multidisciplinary Perspectives on Mesoamerican Ethnicity

Barbara L. Stark and John K. Chance

IDENTITY CONSTITUTES A BROAD TOPIC OF SOCIAL SCIENCE INVESTIGA-tion into which ethnicity fits as one among many inquiries. Even so, ethnicity forms a seemingly limitless domain in the literature. Sandstrom (this volume) notes Cohen's (1981:307) observation that "ethnicity has already become the subject of such an extensive literature that there can hardly be any conceptual formulation about it not made by someone before." We chose to complicate this daunting subject even more by asking secondarily about relationships between ethnicity and states and ethnicity and class. The case studies in subsequent chapters and the theoretical and conceptual discussion in this chapter span prehispanic, colonial, and modern contexts, encompassing a series of dramatic and profound political, economic, and cultural changes. Mesoamerica, as a precolumbian "cultural area" with multiple complex societies, became a Spanish colony and then several modern states. The primary periods of concern among the chapters are the Postclassic period (A.D. 900–1521), Colonial period (A.D. 1519–1810), and recent times. To address this temporal panorama, we draw on multiple disciplines: archaeology, art history, ethnohistory, and ethnography.

Even though ethnicity and its relations to states and classes are unmanageably broad topics, it is precisely because we address the relationships among diverse topics and times that we gain greater insights into Mesoamerican ethnicity. Our emphasis is on the dynamic qualities of ethnicity seen through various spatial and temporal scales. We do not wish to exaggerate the importance of ethnicity in relation to states and classes. As we discuss below, ethnicity is variably salient and can be expressed in a variety of ways. In view of the scope of topics, perhaps the only eminently practical decision that guides the book is confinement of the case studies to areas with Nahua languages in central and eastern Mexico.

The heterogeneous area of Nahua languages in late prehispanic times encompassed a range of social forms, from large (by Mesoamerican standards) city-states to small villages. The case studies fall within the geographic area absorbed into the Aztec Triple Alliance empire just prior to the Spanish Conquest. Although political conquests, migration, and the spread of Nahua languages after A.D. 900 created some cultural uniformities, speakers of Nahuatl and Nahuat (two closely related languages) have never, as far as we know, imagined themselves to be single ethnic categories. Nor have central and eastern Mexico today given rise to large ethnicized political phenomena comparable in scope with those of the Maya-speaking south: the Mexican Zapatistas of Chiapas and the Guatemalan pan-Maya movement. This book focuses on the strategically important Nahua heartland, an area where an assortment of ancient states, the Aztec Empire, the colony of New Spain, and the capital of the Mexican nation were born, highlighting a variety of ways in which ethnicity has been expressed over the past thousand years. Nevertheless, discussions in this chapter and others draw on wider Mesoamerican investigations in order to situate the Nahua region and its scholarly literature in their proper contexts.

We begin in the Postclassic period (A.D. 900–1521) with Stark's study of an ethnic enclave in the western lower Papaloapan basin of Veracruz and Berdan's and Umberger's analyses of ethnic factors in the Aztec Empire on the eve of the Spanish invasion. Then we move with Chance to the Colonial period (A.D. 1519–1810), particularly in the Valley of Puebla, and finally to Sandstrom's and Taggart's ethnographic accounts of communities in northern Veracruz and northern Puebla.

In this chapter we consider a series of conceptual and substantive matters from comparative literature to provide a framework for the chapters that follow, and we do so in a conscious effort to articulate the interpretive perspectives of the contributors, which have informed our thinking. Specifically, we consider (a) concepts of ethnicity, (b) ethnicity and the state, and (c) ethnicity and class. We do not attempt to resolve the ways in which individual contributions differ, but we place some of these differences in a wider framework, with abundant thanks to the contributors and to Arizona State University seminar students for their insights, commentaries, and contributions to our thinking. ASU colleagues James Eder, Michelle Hegmon, and Michael Winkelman assisted in our explorations of comparative literature. Michael Smith and Lori Wright also pointed us toward some key sources.

CONCEPTS OF ETHNICITY

The concept of ethnicity (like the concept of culture) can be slippery because of the dynamic qualities of ethnic categories, varying associated cultural "content," the shifting strategies of people employing ethnic categories, and the myriad cooperative, exploitative, and aggressive encounters among individuals and groups (e.g., Kuper 2003:esp. 392–395). We do better to shift the focus to ethnogenesis, ethnic maintenance, and ethnic "fade-out" rather than to hinge our thinking entirely on the concept of ethnicity. This dynamic perspective requires appropriate time-depth, however, and a scale of information that is often difficult to obtain. A larger time scale involves shifts in sources of information from ethnographic to historic to archaeological (below we address how different disciplines approach ethnicity). These shifting spatial scales quickly outstrip the traditional arenas of archaeological, art historical, ethnohistorical, and ethnographic research, as administrative districts and states set economic and social policies and programs affecting local communities and as people and governments alike grapple with processes beyond their borders. Currently, international commerce and political actions are increasingly pervasive in their effects.

Ethnicity is aptly characterized as part of a set of dimensions involving human "difference" and identity, constructed in cultural categories and forged and adjusted through life actions (Anthias 1998; Durrenberger and Pálsson 1996: 19–20; Grillo 1998). A section of *Current Anthropology* in 2004 titled "Identity, Temporality, and Moral Geographies" highlights the conceptual difficulties of addressing ethnic identities in dynamic circumstances today. Holtzman (2004) particularly highlights multiple spatial and temporal scales in Kenya, as does Metcalf (2001) for upland Sarawak. Metcalf (2001) speaks of "cultural cohesions" and "upriver People" rather than traditional longhouse identities; both are broader terms folding in considerable cultural diversity. Despite the swiftness of changes in multiple domains (e.g., media, economy, environment) and considerable local refiguring of identities, the notion of ethnicity remains apt, if less fixed than once imagined. In Mesoamerica changing Mam economic ventures in Chiapas create contrasts with Mam in Guatemala (Hernández Castillo and Nigh 1998), an example of change swift enough that it, like many others, can be charted in the course of an ethnographer's career.

Ethnicity as Common Heritage

Particularly since the appearance of Barth's (1969:13–14) influential work, ethnicity is commonly conceived as cultural membership that presumes something about the members' origin and background. Ethnic identity thus involves references to a presumed common heritage. The content of this common heritage varies widely, and theorists themselves have taken different positions. The "hard" position uses a kinship model to define the common heritage, with a biological slant that emphasizes descent. Emberling (1997:302), for example, states that by positing a common ancestry, ethnicity effectively extends the kinship idiom. Keyes (1981:5–6) is also quite explicit on this point, arguing that ethnicity is a form of kinship reckoning and amounts to "a cultural interpretation of descent." The notion of shared descent leads to the overlap of ethnicity and racial categories in some cases, especially in the case of race as an attributed identity. Yet any consistent biological content may be virtually nonexistent. Sandstrom's and Chance's discussions (this volume) of race in Mexico provide examples of ambiguous cross-cutting biological categorizations unreliably related to ethnic categories.

Other investigators take a "softer" position about heritage and make allowance for ethnic claims to common ancestry and origin that are not necessarily kinship based (De Vos 1982:9). Sometimes the common elements may be rather slender, vague threads indeed. Postclassic Mesoamerica appears to support the "soft" version of ethnicity as common heritage. In this world of small, stratified polities, ethnic identities were often shared by nobles and commoners alike, and ethnicity seems not to have been phrased in terms of descent or other kinship idioms. Brumfiel (1994a:90), for example, contrasts ethnicity with kinship and political patronage and defines ethnic identity as based on a shared history and cultural inheritance. In Late Postclassic central Mexico, she argues, this more open-ended version of ethnicity provided a fluid environment for various populations to engage in political factionalism. Place and history, rather than kinship, seem to inform Mesoamerican ethnic sensibilities—hence the importance of migration stories, sacred places of origin, and strong identification with particular city-states or communities, either ancestral or based on current residence. Although community-linked identities continue to play an important role in the modern states that occupy the Mesoamerican area (e.g., Monaghan 1995; Watanabe 1992), economic opportunities and exigencies, religious changes related to organizations operating internationally (e.g., Sandstrom, this volume), and other aspects of current affairs are challenging these community orientations.

In Mesoamerica and beyond, recent studies of ethnogenesis and changes in ethnic relations address the effects of historical conditions (e.g., Adams 1997). Dominating the literature are considerations of precolonial to colonial to postcolonial transitions and the travails of modern states. Many modern states are highly polyethnic and many exhibit instability, a condition challenging to scholars steeped in Western traditions of states with long (although tumultuous) histories reaching into medieval times and exhibiting enough of a dominant ethnicity to constitute "nation-states" (e.g., Geertz 2004 and commentators in Kaufmann, ed. 2004). Often ignored is the historical and archaeological panorama of states forming, expanding, reconfiguring, being defeated and incorporated, and collapsing. Van Beek (2001) notes an underlying philosophical bias that permeates categorization of cultural life and groups; the bias involves an essentialist enterprise, an endeavor to cement an assumption that social categories have captured a natural reality when in fact they recognize a socially contingent reality. Ethnic group members themselves often make primordial claims. It is for this reason that we note the utility of a focus on ethnogenesis and ethnic maintenance rather than just on ethnicity (see especially Chance and Sandstrom, this volume). Next we discuss naturalizing tendencies in identity claims.

Self, Within-Groups, Others, and Boundaries

Barth (1969:13–14) defined ethnic group membership as both self-ascribed and attributed by others, relying on selected diacritical symbols in social communication. Various authors have used alternate terms to capture the self-defined aspect of identity versus identity applied by others. Cohen (1978a:387) refers to subjectivist (by self) and objectivist (by others) categorizations (with the unfortunate terminological effect of implying that outsider concepts are more objective than insider concepts). He builds on Kunstadter (1978) to focus on the process of assignment to ethnic categories, which proceeds on the two fronts of self-definition and outside ascription. The interdependent, or interactive, quality of these two poles is stressed by Jenkins (1994), who notes that for a range of contexts, from individual to collective, the categories that people manipulate can be defined internally within groups and external to the group, for all social identities. Differentials in power and control of resources create some of the constraints, impositions, tensions, and resistance between (or among multiple group) poles of action, leading Toland (1993:12), for example, to see ethnicity as a defense mechanism against inequality. A perspective on the history of relations is critical. Jenkins (1994:198) notes that historical events and constraints merit more attention in the examination of self-ascribed versus attributed poles of action.

This dynamic situation of negotiated or contested relations is essential for analysis of ethnic groups as elements of a society or state. It is also critical for analyses of ethnic groups in relation to classes. Ethnicity is not the only important social identity with the qualities Barth defined, as class (or estate) identities may converge in important ways with these qualities, as we explore below. Much less common, at least in the modern world, is a heritable aspect to occupational identities, which we do not discuss here.

Barth (1969:15–17) stresses that ethnicity implies boundary maintenance. Such social boundaries may have territorial implications, but many societies are polyethnic, with ethnic groups that interfinger in the social order without strict adherence to districts or areas. In fact, ethnicity is a concept used instead of "culture" because of situations within a single state or polity in which culturally distinct groups fitting the ethnic criteria above are part of the social composite. The distinction is one of degrees: neighboring societies with different cultural practices normally have some range of interaction and may maintain boundaries in various respects. From some analytical perspectives, formalized interactions of culturally different neighboring groups may be best conceived as forming a nonstate socioeconomic unit. Barth originally was especially interested in ecologically interdependent or complementary societies. Nevertheless, as a general rule the concept of ethnicity is more useful for important identity distinctions within a multicultural society than among societies that differ culturally.

As Jenkins (1994) observes, the anthropological emphasis subsequent to Barth's work has been more concerned with self-ascription than with attribution of ethnicity, but at times the severe limitations on the latitude afforded recipients of attributed identities has been acknowledged (De Vos and Romanucci-Ross 1982:50). The differences in power and resources within states and empires create circumstances in which ethnic attribution can override self-ascription in the larger social arena. Analyses of state and institutional "programs" for minority groups, such as those discussed by Spicer (1962) for Native American groups in northwestern Mexico and the U.S. Southwest during the Spanish, Mexican, and U.S. histories of conquest and administration, show that assumptions and goals of members of a more powerful majority can have cumulative and often devastating effects despite considerable successful resistance by minorities. Symbolic practices in statecraft may capitalize on ethnic stereotypes, as discussed in the chapters by Berdan, Stark, and Umberger. States and empires provide a crucial backdrop for analyzing ethnic relations, both today and in the past.

Much written about ethnicity examines modern or ancient states or empires and focuses on minorities. The concept of ethnic minorities implies an ethnic majority, although some states are dominated by ethnic minorities rather than majorities (Kaufmann 2004:2). Researchers interested in ethnic minorities have paid attention particularly to disadvantaged groups and patterns of discrimination. Less common are ethnic arrays in which no ethnic group is strongly in the majority and group differences form a social fabric without pejorative relationships (Wimmer 2004:46); this condition is often held as an ideal rather than a fact. States typically create and sustain power and wealth differentials that advantage or could advantage particular groups or classes, with the result that contested relations are inherent. Of course, the scale and form of negotiations may vary widely. States and other centralized societies have a capacity to mobilize and control resources, including forms of public proclamation and information flow that, apart from affecting more narrowly defined economic resources, may constitute a basis for shaping cultural reproduction. They also command central resources for the application of force.

In sum, because self-identified ethnicity is counterposed against others who differ, it is a concept especially suited to multicultural societies. In the modern world, labor, refugee, and other migration has reached extremes, along with the incorporation of groups into wider economies and "media" information flows; nevertheless, there are many similarities with the economic and political circumstances of the ancient and colonial worlds.

Primordial and Instrumental Views

Barth's view of ethnicity countered traditional assumptions that ethnicity means shared fundamental cultural values, with members communicating and interacting within the group or population, which is largely biologically self-perpetuating. In this traditional view, ethnicity is closely modeled on normative views of culture. So-called primordialist emphases in concepts of ethnicity stress its formation through enculturation and are compatible with this traditional view; instrumentalist approaches are more focused on social boundary transactions and flexibility in actors' strategies and identities, including ethnic ones (Emberling 1997:306). Among the contributors in this volume, Taggart particularly highlights how personal values and self-conceptions entwine with cultural/ethnic values, and he observes how emotional attachments enter into interethnic actions. Chance and Sandstrom, in contrast, stress the role of competition and an instrumentalist perspective. A focus on context that involves an instrumentalist stance also underlies Berdan's and Umberger's contributions because of their attention to imperial statecraft and the symbolic and stereotypic aspects of ethnicity.

Research within the primordialist framework may place great weight on a "direct historical approach" with respect to the continuity of a core of cultural values and language extending back into the past. For example, the latter perspective conditions aspects of Flannery and Marcus's (1983) treatment of long-term divergent evolution of the Zapotecs and Mixtecs, their discussion of Zapotec ethnogenesis (Marcus and Flannery 1996:23–32), and Wilkerson's (1972:890–920) consideration of the ethnogenesis of Huastecs and Totonacs in northern Veracruz. Primordialist and instrumentalist dimensions of ethnicity are not exclusive of each other and may be aspects of a dynamic history. For example, Stark's argument (this volume) for an intrusive highland enclave in Middle Postclassic times in the Gulf lowlands may signal a "nahuatization" that provided a historical precedent shaping some of the later interactions in that region with the Aztec Triple Alliance. In this Gulf area, Aztec cultural practices gained a greater foothold than in many other distant provinces.

Psychological and Within-Group Dimensions

Some ethnic behaviors may be directed internally among group members to communicate and reinforce solidarity. Thus Barth's outwardly directed boundary maintenance is not the only process of interest. Group membership may be communicated and sanctioned through daily or ritual practices. How individuals maintain themselves in social groups, including ethnic groups, leads to consideration of a psychological dimension of ethnicity. Some authors (e.g., De Vos 1982; Jenkins 1994; Winkelman 2001) emphasize an individual's dependence on cultural contexts and on others for their sense of self and their engagement with key values, some nearly unconsciously built into everyday life (Bourdieu 1977), along with other values that are consciously championed or at least acceded to. This psychological dimension of ethnic identity is one of the underpinnings of the primordialist view of ethnicity. The emotional quality of ethnic identity seems to be highly variable and contextually sensitive, just as ethnicity is variously salient in different circumstances.

In a number of modern studies a "triumphant" ethnicity (Adams 1997:175) or "new ethnicity" (Anthias 1998:525) adopts a celebratory view of qualities of group life and shrugs off attributed negative stereotypes. This may be in part a reaction to negative attributions, but it is also a positive strategy for solidarity in a situation where mobilization of support for change in social conditions is possible or sought. Hall's (1992a) concept of a "new ethnicity" differs somewhat; he notes shifting self-ascriptions and attributions that move from essentialist and biological/racist views relating to blacks in England to recognition of variations among blacks. In all these cases renegotiation and redefinition of identities are highlighted.

Ethnic and Other Identities

In Barth's view, ethnicity is one of the social criteria that tends to constrain other social statuses for members. There is no consistent evidence of this last characteristic in precolumbian Mesoamerica, perhaps due to the degree of tolerance of ethnic differences, at least in the late Basin of Mexico (Zantwijk 1973:24).

Although Barth did not emphasize the hierarchical or nested character of ethnic identities, his definition of ethnicity can accommodate sliding scales of ethnic affiliation that are contextual in application (see Moerman 1965 for an example of shifting, nested scales of ethnic affiliation in Thailand). As proposed by Anthias (1998) and in keeping with observations by many scholars (e.g., Cohen 1978a:387), a multidimensional set of identities can intersect and interact with ethnic identity (Anthias [1998] discusses gender particularly). Medina (1997), for example, points out the intersections of class and ethnicity in Belize. Anthias (1998) uses the concept of positioning to represent the effects of such intersections.

Challenges to received notions of ethnicity have come from ethnographic research. Pacific Islanders, for example, are said to fashion their group identities *not* on notions of shared ancestry or history—basic elements of "ethnic" identities, as we have seen—but rather on the basis of common environments and experience. According to Linnekin and Poyer (1990:8), in Oceanic societies identity is a matter of behavior and performance, and "shared identity comes from sharing food, water, land, spirits, knowledge, work, and social activities." Not only do people change their social identities and maintain multiple identities simultaneously, but the cultural criteria often taken as symbolic of ethnicity, such as residence, language, dress, and so forth, become "effective determinants of identity" (Linnekin and Poyer 1990:9). Thus Linnekin and Poyer (1990:10–11) argue that ethnicity was not significant in precontact Oceania and further that the concept itself, if viewed as shared ancestry, may ignore significant distinctions made by the people themselves. Astuti (1995:465) makes much the same point for the Vezo of Madagascar. The Vezo ethnotheory of group identity

> is not an ethnic theory. The Vezo maintain that they are not what they are because they were born to be so. Their alternative model of identity and difference stresses instead that Vezo become what they are through what they do; both identity and difference result from activities that people perform in the present rather than from a common or distinct origin they acquired at some point in the past.

These examples suggest that even in modern stratified, state settings, group identities need not take an ethnic form that involves a shared history or ancestry. Why this is so and the factors that promote these different sorts of identities remain unclear. We suspect the relatively egalitarian nature of many pre-contact Oceanian societies helped shape the "non-ethnic" group identities in that region. Howard (1990:273) notes that identities of the ethnic type are important in Oceanian politics but argues that they resulted from the imposition of ethnic categories by Western colonialism. Although a "performance" criterion of cultural identity is different from the criteria traditionally invoked for ethnicity, the two bases for group identity may enter into the dynamics of class and state relationships similarly. Taggart (this volume) also demonstrates quite clearly that "performance" and "shared heritage" are not mutually exclusive bases for identity formation. The Nahuat of Huitzilan in the Sierra Norte of Puebla place the accent on doing, but they also have a significant sense of shared ancestry.

As the identity concept becomes increasingly popular among academicians and the number and kinds of identities proliferate, there is a danger that the term may lose some of its analytical power. Part of the problem is that *identity* is used to designate at least three things: a collective sense of being, externally imposed categories, and more open forms of self-understanding (Brubaker and Cooper 2000:19). As noted above, ethnographic analyses of ethnic identity have tended to focus on group or self-identification at the expense of external categorization or attribution. The relationship between the actors' perceptions of group identity and the social contexts in which they occur remains an unresolved issue (Jenkins 1994:219; Jones 1996:67–71).

We would do well to heed Jenkins's (1994:218–219) reminder that ethnic identities are not static forms but "practical accomplishments." Group identification cannot be isolated from external categorization, and "identity is the practical product of the ongoing interaction of processes of internal and external definition" (Jenkins 1994:219). This does not mean that those who hold an ethnic identity and external others who categorize them need agree, even if all use the same terms. There are many extant examples to the contrary, and there will always be different points of view between in-groups and out-groups. Thus Hendrickson (1991) has shown that in Guatemala the ethnic category of Indian imposed by ladinos and the government is at odds with the various Indian self-identifications adopted by Maya-speaking villagers. Yet both internal and external definitions feed off each other in complex ways.

In some contexts ethnic identities may be virtually indistinguishable from national or state identities. Truly monoethnic states are rare, if they have ever existed at all. A dominant ethnic group that controls a state politically may successfully impose its identity on the rest of the inhabitants, who come to subordinate (though not lose completely) their own identities to that of the state. This was often the case in the Basin of Mexico in Postclassic times. Brumfiel (1994a:100–101), for example, has suggested that the Otomí residents of the city-state of Xaltocan came to identify with the ruling Nahua family as protectors and benefactors of the entire community. Ethnicity could thus serve as a unifying ideology at the state level, despite a historically diverse ethnic composition.

"National" identities are created when ethnic groups collectively develop feelings of broad identity rivaling state identity and come to conceive of themselves as a group with a shared agenda (Maybury-Lewis 2002:108). In today's world many nationalist groups are challenging the authority of the states in which they live. The Zapatistas of Mexico and the pan-Maya activists in Guatemala are just two examples of a prevalent form of "ethnonationalism" in which ethnic groups resist state hegemony and seek to create their own regional and local sociopolitical formations (Tambiah 1996:128–129). To an undetermined extent, both causes have been fostered by population movements, repression, and hardships that were consequences of the Guatemalan civil war and neoliberal political and economic policies in Mexico. These factors had broad though differential geographic effects in Guatemala and the Mexican state of Chiapas. No comparably broad geographic and social dislocation has affected modern Nahua communities. This divergence in history contributes to the contrast in Maya and Nahua nationalist activity.

In sum, state, national, and ethnic identities are all founded on perceptions of a shared heritage. They are differentiated by the degree to which they involve control of the state apparatus, aspiration to such control, or attempts to obtain other forms of recognition or benefits (such as economic ones) outside the political arena.

Regional Identities

In several contexts investigators mention regional identities, sometimes without clearly discussing them vis-à-vis ethnic identities (e.g., Brumfiel 1994a; Jonsson 2005; Lieberman 1978:461–462). These regional identities are part of ethnogenesis and often exhibit variation in scale. In Mesoamerica the notion of regional identities captures a less specific kind of identity than community, city-state, or polity but shares a geographic component. This notion of regional quasi-ethnic identity seems to emerge from the expansion of states or empires and, at least as suggested by Brumfiel (1994a) for the Aztec Basin of Mexico, is partly engineered by state-level discourse that simplifies a mosaic of city-state or small-polity loyalties and organization.

We suspect that regional identities commonly reflect state-scale (if not state-initiated) conceptualizations, dependent on a large frame of reference in which decisions are executed and alliances are established. In some modern cases they grow from the effects of international economic processes (e.g., Metcalf 2001). Whether regional identities are further forged through alliance and resistance to state control, as with "Jumas" in southeastern Bangladesh (van Schendel 1995) and with a "Southern" identity in the United States following the Civil War, is dependent on a variety of historical factors and the time frame

across which events transpire. The utility of the term *regional identity* in particular cases is exceptionally dependent on the geographic scale and context. One
could view modern "Maya" ethnic identity attributions as a language-inspired
ethnic attribution with a regional context (southeastern Mexico and parts of
Guatemala). In some cases this usage initially exhibits an attributional quality, but an outside origin does not prevent local leaders and their rhetoric from
embracing or manipulating broad attributions for self-identification in political movements.

Apart from regional identities per se, many investigators have explored the
ways that a connection to a place contributes to ethnic identities. For example,
Holtzman (2004:esp. 69) considers how a locality identity overlaps traditional
cultural identities (and less capitalized economies) for Samburu in Kenya.
Lowland versus highland Samburu identities likely became salient with the
establishment of state boundaries, grazing controls, greater highland governmental investments, and declining pastoral mobility (Holtzman 2004:73–74),
illustrating the importance of state- and global-scale processes.

Causes of Ethnicity: Competition and Violence

As Cohen (1978a:395) observes, we have much to gain by understanding the
conditions that trigger ethnicity. In the most general sense, as Sandstrom (this
volume) argues, ethnicity can be seen as "a creative response on the part of
the members of one group to domination by, or competition with, members
of another group." Competition for resources and power is critical for ethnic
maintenance. Viewed as a tool to advance a group's welfare, ethnicity may be
expected to be more salient in contexts or periods where power disparities are
great, and less so when they decrease (McGuire 1982). As we noted above, class
differences in state societies create conditions ripe for elaboration or persistence of ethnic identities, and today, as in the past, international contexts (e.g.,
world systems) provide a further dimension of competition.

The primordialist and instrumentalist perspectives for ethnicity converge
in respect to some of the causes and outcomes of ethnicity. Taggart (this volume) observes that the underlying values and world view wrapped into cultural identities have an emotional attachment and underwrite judgments of
self and others that can fuel a sense of justified violence in competition between or among ethnic groups. Economic exploitation and oppression can
constitute "slow violence" in stratified societies. Despres edited a volume in
1975 devoted to studies of intergroup competition, and the importance of competition continues to be regarded as a fundamental reason that groups stress
ethnicity. Sandstrom (this volume) notes several studies in Mesoamerica that
demonstrate, paradoxically, a stronger emphasis on traditional identities in
communities closer to modern urban centers than in those farther removed, a
fact he views as directly supporting the idea of ethnic identity as a response to
competition. To grasp the nature of competition frequently requires a relatively
long temporal perspective in which particular episodes of disenfranchisement,

violence, or exploitation are situated. For example, Stark's (this volume) intrusive archaeological ethnic enclave likely reflects a new superordinate group, although it remains unclear whether much of a local population remained in the immediate vicinity.

Methodological Considerations:
From Ethnographic Methods to Studies of the Past

The great majority of anthropological work on ethnicity has relied on interviews and participant observation, sometimes supplementing the ethnographic present with recent historical background. Yet constraining historical conditions may have much deeper roots in time. Significantly, much of the variety of ethnic situations and relations falls within archaeological and historic periods quite different from modern industrial and capitalist conditions. For this reason it is useful to consider the advantages and constraints of ethnography and of investigations using non-ethnographic methods. These non-ethnographic approaches remain poorly integrated with the bulk of ethnic studies. For example, whereas ethnographic studies of ethnicity in Mesoamerica have concentrated overwhelmingly on rural communities, archaeological studies have been more concerned with ethnic enclaves in urban settings (see below and Stark, this volume). Our choice to examine Mesoamerica in a multidisciplinary perspective requires attention to the variety of methods and sources of data for the study of ethnicity. Such a perspective also will be fruitful in other disciplines that have a major stake in the study of ethnicity, such as political science and sociology (see, for example, Kaufmann, ed. 2004)

ETHNOGRAPHY
John K. Chance

Matters of ethnic identity and ethnic relations have formed a major part of Mesoamerican ethnography since its beginnings in the 1920s. Mexican anthropology in particular has a long tradition of *indigenismo* (indigenism), which focuses attention on indigenous cultures and identities and their place in national development, whether from an assimilationist point of view, as in earlier studies, or a pluralistic one, more characteristic of post-1968 generations. Many classic studies, such as Redfield's (1941) portrait of the folk-urban continuum in Yucatán, Caso's (1948) early attempt to define the parameters of Mexican Indian identity, Wolf's (1955) model of closed and open communities, Fuente's (1965) pioneering work on ethnic relations, Aguirre Beltrán's (1979) refuge region hypothesis, Stavenhagen's (1975) work on ethnic and class relations in the Maya Highlands, and Bonfil Batalla's (1996) provocative treatise on the national significance of Mexican indigenous culture, to name but a few, are concerned with issues of ethnicity in whole or in part. Indian-mestizo relations (or Indian-ladino relations in Chiapas and Guatemala) have also attracted much attention from ethnographers over the past 70 years (see Fuente 1967; Hewitt de Alcántara 1984:42–69; and Sandstrom 1991 for useful reviews).

It is fair to say that most of our models and much of our substantive data on Mesoamerican ethnicity are derived from interviews and participant observation in rural localities and other small-scale settings. Much of what we have learned about ethnicity depends directly or indirectly on insights from ethnography, yet the limitations of the ethnographic approach to issues involving space and time have also been the subject of considerable discussion in anthropology. Earlier generations grappled with the problem of how to place local community ethnography in national contexts (e.g., Lewis 1951; Redfield 1941). The development of dependency and world systems theory in the 1960s and 1970s raised the spatial stakes even higher as anthropologists confronted—and continue to confront—the difficulties of relating the worm's-eye insights of local ethnography to the far-flung capitalist world economy (Hewitt de Alcántara 1984:97–130; Nash 1981). The 1980s brought the postmodern critique of ethnographic representation (Marcus and Fischer 1986), and the related explosion of "identity" studies has had a major impact. As Monaghan (2000a:4) observed in a recent review of Mesoamerican ethnography:

> Given the late-twentieth-century obsession with identity, the increasing bureaucratization of rural life, and the intense pluralism of Middle America, it is perhaps not too surprising that ethnicity is at the top of the list [of gatekeeping concepts].... For social scientists concerned with meaning in social life, it is surprising how dominant instrumental notions of ethnicity continue to be in our theorizing. If in earlier work indigenous people were passive and traditional, today they are highly active and possessed of an extra-cultural rationality. Even the terms we use—"indigenous," which connotes a freely chosen identity, versus the now discouraged "Indian," suggesting an outside and colonialist imposition—incorporate this difference.

Although most Mesoamerican ethnography continues to be locally focused, few would disagree that much of the dynamic of contemporary life is linked to ethnic processes originating at regional, national, and international levels. As Kearney (1996:180) points out, ethnicity is independent of space and nationality. The forces commonly grouped under the concept of "globalization"—particularly the world domination of finance capital, the impact of electronic media and communications, and increased transnational migration—have reinforced "a growing concern among anthropologists that our material was rapidly outrunning our methods" (Metcalf 2001:165). The best "site" for the ethnographic study of ethnicity is no longer clear, if it ever was. Just as anthropologists of the 1960s followed their peasant informants to the cities and observed how they often exchanged indigenous for mestizo or ladino identities (e.g., van den Berghe 1968), recent studies of international migration have shown how transnationalism can transform identities at both ends of the migrant circuit (e.g., Nagengast and Kearney 1990). Postmodernists have argued that transnational changes since the 1970s, with migration chief among them, have enveloped us all in a new kind of "postmodern hyperspace" (Rouse

2002:158, citing Jameson 1984:83). Many anthropologists, whether they identify as postmodernists or not, would agree with Marcus (1995) that taking the modern world system seriously as a concept points ethnography in the direction of a multisited research strategy. Metcalf (2001:180) goes a step further and argues that ethnographic field sites of any kind cannot be derived a priori from theory but are culturally located and must be empirically discovered.

Ethnographers also have become acutely aware that the inherently synchronic nature of participant observation does not, by itself, adequately address questions of historical process. The temporal dimension of inquiry is especially important in areas such as Mesoamerica that have traditionally invoked a sense of common history as an ethnic criterion, as we have seen. There are thus fertile possibilities for collaboration between ethnography and ethnohistory, yet these two fields remain uneasy bedfellows in Mesoamerican studies. With a few notable exceptions (see Chance, this volume), ethnohistorical studies have concentrated on precolumbian and early colonial societies of the fifteenth and sixteenth centuries. Although work on these periods is of fundamental importance (see Berdan, Stark, and Umberger, this volume), this deep temporal perspective has tended to isolate Mesoamerican ethnohistory from many concerns of contemporary ethnography. To a large degree, the two fields have gone their separate ways. Lacking the time or the inclination to supplement their work in the present with historical sources on the past, many ethnographers over the years have fashioned a schematic and idealized "ethnographic past" from historical hypotheses constructed at a distance, often on the basis of secondary or tertiary sources or by extrapolation from ethnographic data (Chance 1996c:381, 385). This is not necessarily bad as long as such works are taken as starting points for inquiry (see Bricker 1981, Hill and Monaghan 1987, and Monaghan 1995 for exceptional attempts to avoid the "ethnographic past" by integrating ethnographic and documentary analysis).

Thus the analysis of ethnicity in space and time, as is the case with so many other topics in contemporary anthropology, continues to pose methodological challenges for ethnographers. Although this volume does not address methodology specifically, it takes a diachronic approach and brings researchers concerned with past and present manifestations of Nahua ethnicity into open dialogue (as Bartolomé and Barabas [1990] did earlier for Oaxaca). We hope our effort here will encourage others to explore these issues further.

Archaeology and Bioarchaeology
Barbara L. Stark

The importance of internally reinforcing social behaviors within ethnic groups, especially within families, is one of the practical keys to archaeological investigations of ethnicity. Archaeological studies have limitations, sometimes severe, in detecting diacritical symbols that helped define ethnic groups, since not all material culture is preserved and many behaviors leave no material trace. Thus archaeological studies typically provide no evidence of how group members defined themselves. Nevertheless, there is an advantage in long-term observations that can address both varied scales and the intermittent and cumulative effects of state-generated or other institutionally based interventions in local practices that affect identities.

In archaeological studies, enculturated practices or meanings are a recurrent element of approaches to ethnicity, despite Barth's (1969) radical departure from traditional views. A rapprochement between intrinsic versus instrumentalist approaches to ethnicity draws on Bourdieu's (1977) concept of *habitus* to envision a reflexive dynamic between historically based, unconscious cultural assumptions and changing social interactions involving "others" that require tactical responses and new self-conceptualizations (Banks 1996:45–47; Bentley 1987; Hegmon 1998:271–274; Jones 1996:67–76). Recurrent cultural differences, especially as expressed through family-scale rituals and practices, are important in several archaeological case studies of enclaves, discussed below. Differences in enculturation, values, and systems of meaning that are fundamental in daily and family life establish differences in content, not just differences in symbolic boundaries. Familial or daily rituals are internally directed communications that reinforce membership (Spence 1996:333).

Issues of enculturation affect the ways archaeologists approach ethnicity through material evidence. McGuire (1982:163), writing about historic archaeology, suggests that ethnicity may channel social life and thus affect socialization and behavior. A range of material effects of separately organized behaviors may result. He singles out food remains, ceramics, and architecture as frequent archaeological bases for recognizing ethnicity. Similarly, Burmeister's (2000) method for detecting migrants with a different cultural background focuses on private home activities because more visible actions may be subject to change through economic or practical considerations.

A parallel stream of analyses in archaeology, not focused on ethnicity in particular, has addressed "technological style." Technological style represents habitual fabrication practices that are not part of more overt, negotiated symbolic behavior. Technological style may disclose the learning history maintained within groups of closely interacting people and provide a basis for distinguishing social and cultural differences, such as group boundaries and social identities, which could include ethnicity (Hegmon 1998).

Overall, archaeological studies of ethnicity in Mesoamerica have been successful in mounting strong arguments for certain enclave situations in which boundaries, persistence, and family-linked rituals can be detected. Ethnic groups within a region have likewise been proposed only where multiple lines of evidence can be marshaled to avoid simplistic assumptions, such as the idea that "pots mean people," that is, that the ubiquitous ceramic styles studied by archaeologists equate with ethnic groups. Sugiura (2005), for example, uses a combination of linguistic, historical, ceramic, and settlement pattern data to argue for ethnogenesis during the Postclassic period in the Toluca area in central Mexico. Multiple lines of evidence and an adequate spatial scale of resolution for data mean that relatively intensive survey, surface collection, and mapping play an unusually critical role in detecting ethnic groups. Certainly traditional excavations have often had a vital part in understanding enclaves as well. Excavations play an even greater role in charting elite affiliations expressed in remains from palaces and tombs, which may involve ethnic, class, or polity "quotations" of valued styles and raise the possibility of intrusive rulers or elites who were ethnically distinct.

Most enclave ethnic studies in archaeology address a community or "barrio" scale that affords a social cross section. In comparison, dynastic or elite ethnicities are investigated at a smaller scale and have proved exceptionally tricky to interpret. One form of ethnogenesis involves ruling classes distancing themselves from subjects by claiming outside (i.e., "privileged") cultural and biological descent (e.g., Brown 1973). This situation need not involve privileged ethnic migrants. For example, Stone (1989) argues that Late Classic Maya elites employed historic Teotihuacan-derived insignia to establish a disconnection from commoners, a process that Braswell (2002) likens to ethnogenesis in the case of earlier Teotihuacan-related evidence at Kaminaljuyú. Much Mesoamericanist debate about the presence of elite foreigners hinges on objects in alien styles, reproduced with varying degrees of faithfulness, often combined with some imports from the distant center (see Helms 1993 on the symbolic role of prestigious centers).

Increasingly, isotopic biological assessments are providing independent evidence about buried individuals' histories with which to evaluate the implications of foreign styles and imports. Isotopic analyses of bone and teeth utilize oxygen, responsive to water sources, and strontium, responsive to geology. These isotopic studies assess localities inhabited at different times in an individual's life, in some cases allowing detection of immigrants. Bone is continually remodeled during an individual's lifetime and can indicate locality of residence during recent years before death, but teeth form during particular childhood episodes. Identification of immigrants complements comparison of associated material culture that may derive from or symbolize a different society. The detection of movement of individuals in bioarchaeology is an important step forward for analysis of migration, provided the distances involved encompass a sufficient shift geographically to affect isotopic dietary profiles and sufficient time was spent in locations so that metabolic effects can be registered. Migration in turn is an important issue for understanding the origins of enclaves, intrusive dynasts, sacrificed captives from distant lands, and communities with foreigners. Studies at Tikal (Wright 2004, 2005), Copán (Buikstra et al. 2004), Teotihuacan (Price et al. 2000; Spence et al. 2004; White et al. 1998, 2004), and Kaminaljuyú (Valdés and Wright 2004; White et al. 2000; Wright et al. 2002) have identified likely immigrants and foreigners, as well as discredited proposed elite or rulers' foreign origins.

Obviously, we confront a number of circumstances in which ethnicity may have been recognized or manipulated in the Mesoamerican past, but with a delicate interface conceptually and practically with archaeological studies of style, imitations, and trade, especially as orchestrated in elite versus commoner lives. It is important to underscore the complexity of ethnicity versus other expressions of identity or actions. Despite these challenges, archaeologists arguably have been successful in detecting some enclave situations using suites of evidence.

Enclaves are detected either as a portion of a city occupied by people culturally affiliated with a distant society or as an enclave settlement in a region with a different local culture. Identification of enclaves implies a concern with migration, which raises broader questions about motivations, constraints, and opportunities (Burmeister 2000). The four best-published cases are Tlaitlotlacan, Teotihuacan, a barrio within the city (Spence 1989, 1992, 1996); the "Merchants'" or Gulf Lowland Barrio at Teotihuacan (Rattray 1987, 1988, 1989, 1990); Matacapan, a Teotihuacan enclave settlement in the Tuxtla Mountains (Ortíz and Santley 1998; Pool 1992; Santley et al. 1987); and part of Kaminaljuyú in the Valley of Guatemala (Sanders 1978; Sanders and Michels 1977), thought by many to show an enclave of Teotihuacanos within the settlement, although newer bioarchaeological evidence lends no support to this idea. Spence (1996) reviewed these instances and that of Tikal, grouping them into ambassadorial state representation versus diasporas, perhaps related to trade. I note briefly the information from Tlaitlotlacan, Matacapan, and Kaminaljuyú as informative examples.

At Tlaitlotlacan, tomb style, extended interments, some grayware sherds (rarely, creamware [Spence 1989:86]), funerary urns and fragments, and a stone door jamb of a tomb bearing glyphs are closely patterned on practices in the Valley of Oaxaca and different from the rest of Teotihuacan (Spence 1989, 1992). The Oaxacan-style grayware was predominantly produced at Teotihuacan, but a few vessels were imported from Oaxaca (Spence 1989:81). Despite the range of stylistic ties to Oaxaca, residents dwelled in typical Teotihuacan apartment compounds, and most of the pottery was like that of other Teotihuacan residents. This is a good example of a case that partially matches Barth's concept of ethnicity, in that only a few homeland traits were maintained over multiple generations at Tlaitlotlacan—symbolic, presumably, of a sense of identity or common origin different from that of other Teotihuacanos. The enclave as a whole is recognizable, even at the level of surface collections, because of a persistently different material culture, especially certain ceramics. Excavation showed that the enclave endured for several centuries and became anachronistic in its adherence to homeland styles long after they had changed in Oaxaca. Near the Oaxaca barrio or possibly part of it were burials, pottery, and figurines similar to those in West Mexico (Gómez 1998), along with Oaxacan-style items, so the ethnic character of inhabitants in that part of the city may be more diverse than first thought. More distant settlements in the Teotihuacan domain also have evidence of "barrios" of Oaxaca-linked inhabitants, such as at Chingú, in the Tula Valley (Díaz 1980, 1981), and two smaller settlements nearby (Crespo and Mastache 1981).

Matacapan, in the Tuxtla Mountains of Veracruz, was first interpreted as containing a barrio of Teotihuacanos, but later work revealed that material diagnostics were not sufficiently localized within the settlement to warrant the term (Arnold et al. 1993:186). The settlement as a whole is now described as an enclave dominated by Teotihuacanos within the region. Pool (1992) suggests that locals were drawn into the growing settlement because of economic opportunities. The range of Teotihuacan-related evidence includes a pyramid facade, cooking vessels, serving vessels, ritual items, burial practices, and figurines (Ortíz and Santley 1998; Pool 1992; Santley et al. 1987). Most such artifacts, although stylistically related to Teotihuacan, represent local products that also show stylistic reinterpretation. Survey showed that Teotihuacan stylistic traits were concentrated at Matacapan, although not exclusively (Santley and Arnold 1996).

At Kaminaljuyú, starting with excavations by Kidder et al. (1946), an area was identified where Teotihuacanos were present (Sanders and Michels 1977), although new data undermine this interpretation. Kaminaljuyú was one of the centers with Teotihuacan state representatives in Spence's (1996) analysis. Pyramids in the proposed Teotihuacano area have facades and construction techniques similar to those at Teotihuacan. Tombs there show a mix of Maya- and Teotihuacan-style vessels (some of the latter imported, such as Thin Orange). This mix of items in tombs led Sanders (1978:40) to suggest that men from Teotihuacan married local women, because no residential areas were found with Teotihuacano material culture. Once isotopic assays of burials were accomplished, lack of a recognizable Teotihuacan residential area proved to have been a crucial but underappreciated clue undermining the idea of a long-term presence of powerful outsiders.

Demarest and Foias (1993) and Braswell (2002) do not accept the idea of a foreign enclave and focus instead on indications that Teotihuacan was a source of prestigious styles and exotic items that were manipulated by local elites. Recent isotopic analyses of Kaminaljuyú burials did not identify Teotihuacanos, although one individual from Kaminaljuyú may have spent time in central Mexico (Valdes and Wright 2004; White et al. 2000; Wright et al. 2002). It may be argued that the buried individuals were not the first Teotihuacano arrivals but rather descendants who grew up in Kaminaljuyú and who thus do not display homeland isotopic values. So far, however, Kaminaljuyú increasingly does not fulfill expectations for an enclave of powerful Teotihuacanos; instead, elite stylistic affiliations appear to fit the evidence better. Kaminaljuyú underscores the important role of persistent boundaries in the patterns of daily life for reliable archaeological detection of enclaves.

Other Mesoamerican ethnic interpretations have been suggested from a contrast in ceramics from one area of a settlement (e.g., at Tula [Healan et al. 1989:241, 248]) or a new ceramic inventory in the Basin of Mexico at the time of historically recorded migrations (Smith 1984). These instances are certainly worth noting and may represent clues to ethnicity, but further investigation is required before we can identify possible symbols of ethnicity as opposed to some other forms of economic or social boundaries.

Significantly, some archaeological studies have *failed* to find noncontroversial material indicators of ethnic differences even where late documents indicate intrusive groups who had a different language and diverse polities of origin (see Hegmon 1998:279). The Postclassic immigration of Mixtecs into the Valley of Oaxaca, already occupied by a variety of Zapotec communities, has not been detected archaeologically because alternative explanations of ceramic and architectural changes fit most of the data (Marcus and Flannery 1983).

As Stark remarks (Chapter 2), Mesoamerican archaeological work shows a potential for recovery of data very likely to represent ethnic enclaves, but the number of archaeological successes in analyzing likely ethnic enclaves is low. Rather than a discouraging sign, it is a positive one because the successes mainly derive from intensive urban or regional surveys, a relatively recent and still uncommon archaeological field investment. It remains to be seen whether additional fieldwork using appropriate methods will reveal more of the ethnic diversity recorded in later documents and anticipated for Mesoamerican states and empires. This requirement of a broad context for archaeological investigation contrasts with the community focus prevalent in ethnography, discussed above. The everyday practices of family life in respect to food and rituals contrast with the publicly manipulated state imagery discussed next.

Art History
Emily Umberger

Studies of art objects can contribute to discussions of ethnicity in native Mesoamerica. Like objects that are the province of archaeologists, art objects can be analyzed in many ways—in their technology, materials, and archaeological contexts—but they differ in their more complex imagery and their depiction of ideas that can be considered conscious projections of native thought.

What do complex visual images have to offer? Images depicting anthropomorphic figures, in particular, may show personal dress, gear, physical differences among people, and even actions signifying distinct cultures. Some of these ways of depicting people may be inherent in local ethnic identity, especially when markers of local affiliation are included, whereas others may refer to a foreign "homeland," of which they are typical signs, at least in the eyes of the culture that represents them. References can be to older cultures as well as contemporary ones, and they may involve imitations of style traits, that is, the *way* things are represented, as well as iconography, that is, *what* is represented. Further, artworks, by showing how identity and difference were conceived in particular cultures, provide emic views of prevailing notions about ethnicity. In this respect, they show how identity is manipulated by the local patrons and artists, especially in cases where a contrast is set up between the local and the foreign—between self-ascribed identities and attributed identities—and they show how the different categories of identity may overlap.

The manifold aspects of artworks mean that the act of interpretation is correspondingly difficult. In order to analyze references to ethnicity, we must first define the corpora of both local and foreign territories. Once these are defined and separated, we can use models from both inside and outside Mesoamerica to help form hypothetical explanations for different types of foreign references. In research elsewhere many such models are accompanied by better documentation than Mesoamerican artworks and give a range of expressive possibilities from which the researcher can suggest likely scenarios (e.g., Onians 1988).

Often style and meaning are seen as separable components of artworks, but the two categories usually overlap in complex ways. Style when defined broadly may include an artwork's motifs as well as the way in which they are depicted. But even defined more narrowly as referring just to the way things are depicted, style can communicate further messages. Works rendered in foreign styles are recognizable as foreign, and this was part of their connotative meaning for the original viewers (Winter 1998). So to separate style and meaning is to misunderstand the visual arts: form is an important part of the message. Another assumption leading to misunderstanding is that visual images can be read literally as representing reality. Even when individual parts represent real things, however, they may be combined and arranged in ways that create fictions that do not correspond with social or political realities. In other words, art manipulates images.

Art historians working on Mesoamerica offer much material relevant to discussions of ethnicity in the form of style and image analysis. On a basic level, they formulate an understanding of the oeuvres corresponding with different cultures. However, as a rule they do not discuss the relationship of their data to questions of ethnicity. One exception that contributes much is Nagao's (1989) study of the public artworks of the Epiclassic period sites of Cacaxtla and Xochicalco. Her main point is that despite the Maya appearance of these artworks, in the proportions, apparel, and poses of figures and in other aspects of content and style, there is no evidence that the local patrons and artists were ethnically Maya. This conclusion was based on a comparison of the images with the archaeological remains of trade goods at the site. Nagao's assumption was that these remains might reveal the presence of an intrusive group or close economic relations with the distant Maya, but she found that they did not indicate such relationships. She suggests thus that the Maya style might have been evoked to distance people at the site from the culture of nearby Teotihuacan, which had fallen from power in recent years, and to make an affiliation with the Maya, who still held power in various centers. Whatever the reasons, Nagao's most important point about notions of identity in art is that the presence of a style does not necessarily identify it as the product of the group associated with the style.

Nagao does not address ethnicity directly or use the vocabulary of ethnicity studies. I am aware of only one art historian of Mesoamerican art, Pasztory (1989), who does, and she bases her ideas on the same seminal work that archaeologists use: Barth's influential statement of 1969. In contrast to the earlier Preclassic cultures, Pasztory notes the existence in Classic period Mesoamerica of styles distinctive of broad regions, which she calls ethnic styles (see also

Kubler 1973). That the people of the time were very conscious of these differences among group artworks and that they manipulated and maintained such
differences is manifested especially in the objects on which Pasztory focuses.
In some notable examples the artists juxtaposed people of different origins,
rendered in the styles of their areas of origin without the stylistic blending that
is usual in artworks. Most are representations of Teotihuacanos visiting foreign
places, peacefully interacting with the local people rendered in their own styles
(e.g., the Bazán Stone from Oaxaca and Stela 31 at Tikal).

Pasztory also noted examples of competition among rival societies. Although the Classic period was one of long-distance trade and peaceful interactions, it was also a period of warfare and ritualized enactments of conflict
(such as the ball game). Her example is an image generated from rivalry on
a small scale between two Maya cities, an image first analyzed by Schele and
Miller (1986). In this relief, artists from Tonalá rendered an image of the defeated ruler of Palenque in the distinctive graceful figure style of his home city
but prone and stripped of most of his regalia. Here the purpose of stylistic emulation was the humiliation of the enemy and his culture. Pasztory notes that
the functions of the group styles of the Classic period affirm Barth's hypothesis
about the formation and maintenance of ethnic boundaries. These were tools
used during cultural interaction; they were not created in isolation.

As both Nagao and Pasztory point out, there are many possible objectives
when one group "copies" the style traits of another (see also Baxandall 1985;
Stone-Miller 1993; Umberger 1996a; and Winter 1977). In addition to emulation to make statements about alliance or parody to make statements about
dominance—scenarios involving contemporary cultures—copying was done
to archaize or revive ancient forms (Umberger 1987a). Since claims of shared
ethnicity are based on claims about the past, references to past groups may take
the form of archaisms, and they may be used to bolster contemporary claims
by people in one group over those of another.

The group styles of the Classic and Epiclassic are called ethnic styles above,
but there are problems with this use of the word *ethnic*. Since the artworks were
produced for states for political purposes and have meaning at the state level,
they seem not to represent ethnic groups as something separate from the polities in which they lived. In many societies the basis of ethnic identity is usually
different from the basis of citizenship, and the two categories are often not contiguous. However, in Mesoamerican societies like these, it can be very difficult
to ascertain to what extent the distinction of citizenship vis-à-vis ethnicity applies. The distinction needed here is analogous to that between citizenship and
ethnicity in polycultural states in the modern world.

Only in the case of peoples who are known through a combination of artworks and other types of evidence can one tease out these differences. Theoretically, such information might be extractable from the hieroglyphic inscriptions that cover Maya artworks, as in the case of the Tonalá relief for which the
ruler's identity is known from hieroglyphs. However, these texts have not yet

been tapped for evidence relating to notions of ethnicity. Nagao used archaeo-logical evidence to question the evidence of the public monuments at her two sites, but because of blanks in the available information, she could not draw further conclusions. Neither of her data sources provided people's actual bio-logical identity or verbal statements about ethnicity. To date, questions about the intermeshing of ethnic, class, and political identities are left unanswered by the archaeological information. As we see in Chapter 3, in the Aztec case it is the postconquest colonial writings that make possible hypotheses about how different identities overlapped, interacted, and were evoked to forward the purposes of a state. The study of Aztec notions of ethnicity is enlightening and suggestive. Yet they cannot be applied to other Mesoamerican societies without sensitivity. There were probably differences among these societies. As Pollard (1994) has demonstrated, the Tarascan contemporaries of the Aztecs thought about ethnicity and the state's incorporation of ethnic groups in very different ways.

In the end, the researcher must keep in mind many caveats when attempting to interpret the imagery and style of artworks, whether they are accompanied by other threads of data or not. Artists often combined local conventions with those of the foreign people referenced, and the modern researcher has to have multiple lines of evidence to separate the two. Imagery is highly manipulated in public monuments, especially conquest monuments, in which the elevation and degradation of different individuals are usually projected through actual or implied contrasts. In addition, artistic manipulations may go beyond the depiction of ethnic markers such as gestures and costume parts to conventions of style. Finally, the researcher has to determine the intentions behind cul-tural mimicry—whether it was to mock, degrade, elevate, or create alignment —and understand how various group identities operated at different levels of interaction in the complex political scenario of ancient Mesoamerica.

Sometimes the "directions for reading" are in the image itself, but the most valuable aids for interpreting the visual expressions of Mesoamerican thought are written sources about cultures dating to just before the Spanish Conquest. Of course, like all sources of data, these too must be used carefully, as they were addressed to a very different society and responded to very different agendas.

Documents
John K. Chance

Documentary sources have particular limitations. They may be classified in a general way as those that consciously intend to inform their readers (e.g., chronicles, histories, newspapers) and those that provide "evidence of wit-nesses in spite of themselves" (Bloch 1953:61), such as court testimony. Even though either type of document may categorize ethnic identities, each reflects the author's, news agency's, or, often, state authority's views. Or the documen-tary context may channel commentary (as in court records) in institutionally defined ways far different from the testimonies elicited by ethnographers or drawn from observation of daily discourse and other actions. Court records and wills, however, represent individuals' statements, constrained by formal circumstances. A colonized area such as Mesoamerica presents additional problems. Most of the available documentation is in Spanish, not in the indigenous languages of the region. Furthermore, most of these Spanish documents were written by colonists or other nonindigenous peoples who usually possessed little understanding of the culture of the people they were writing about. For this reason, documentary-based historical studies of ethnicity for post-1519 Mesoamerica are as scarce as the archaeological ones for previous periods. Reliable indications of ethnic self-ascription are often beyond the grasp of the investigator.

But there is also cause for optimism. As Mesoamerican ethnohistorians have become more conversant with documents (mainly colonial) written in indigenous languages by indigenous people, the prospects of penetrating the veil of ethnic self-ascription have improved significantly. Even here the information is often indirect, but insights can be obtained, for example, from a will written in Nahuatl in which the testator declares his or her place of residence and political affiliation. Of the few studies available that touch on ethnicity in colonial Mexico, the most illuminating are those based on indigenous sources (Lockhart 1991; Restall 1997; Terraciano 2001). Chance (this volume) discusses this vein of scholarship for the Nahua-speaking area of colonial central Mexico. Likewise, chronicles written in Nahuatl, such as the Florentine Codex (Sahagún 1961:165–197 [1575–1580]), along with native pictorial sources, provide the best clues for ethnic identity in prehispanic central Mexico. As researchers become more adept at using these sources, the potential will grow for learning more about ethnicity in the past.

Concepts and Methods

For Mesoamerica and more broadly, we have taken note of the thread of historical origins that runs through ethnic categories and the importance of individual and group self-attribution and of outsider ascriptions of identity. Each is a part of active social relations, and the "boundary" that is signaled and negotiated is not, therefore, quite as steady in this dynamic context as Barth conveyed. "Imagined" and "inventive" identities likely seem troublesome only to tourists and analysts unprepared for change and seeking "authentic" identities. Several investigators have grappled with the challenge of how to think about degrees of historical conservatism in the constitution of ethnic identities (e.g., Eder 2004) and how to address activist treatments of identities. In Mesoamerica today, pan-Maya activism and ethnogenesis contrast with Nahua identities more commonly organized with a community focus. There are numerous examples of nested scales of ethnic identity and shifting analytic frames of contrast and inclusivity; this feature must be accommodated as part of ethnicity in many societies. Likewise, the extent to which affective values and behaviors accompany accepted ethnic categories is also situationally variable. Ethnicity is a useful concept for understanding important identities in plural or multicultural societies, and we apply it to states or "complex society" situations.

Different disciplines address distinct data sources and afford contrastive opportunities and liabilities in the study of ethnicity. Indigenous Mesoamerica requires insights from all of them, and in combination they show an enduring manipulation of cultural heritage and place as a basis for ethnic identities rather than race, despite the colonial experience.

Particularly because of (1) the wide range of variation in the extent to which cultural practices and values associate with ethnicity, (2) the shifting nature of nested ethnic and other identities, and (3) the highly variable symbols of ethnicity, the subject of ethnicity at times seems too wide-ranging and variable to offer a manageable domain of analysis. Nevertheless, it is clear that in many situations ethnicity has political and economic consequences, with strategies that people pursue dependent on affiliational notions about the heritage of groups. Consequently, the successful study of states and empires and of class relations partly relies on also paying attention to any effects of ethnic identities.

ETHNICITY AND THE STATE

The Notion of States

We define archaeological, historical, and modern states as societies with a central governing authority and a complex internal division of labor that includes differentiated internal hierarchies (e.g., religious, civil) (Wright 1977:383). States normally come into being and function in a web of surrounding complex polities (see Renfrew 1986), not as isolated social forms. *Statecraft* refers to the cross-culturally recurrent and locally contingent strategies directed internally at the subject population and externally at neighboring societies, ostensibly promoting the longevity and strength of the state itself (or at least the current ruling cadres). These strategies represent a combination of calculated innovative and traditional practices that (1) promote governmental legitimacy, sacred authority, and loyalty; (2) at times promote state demographic or territorial growth; (3) concentrate and increase power and wealth in ruling cadres and among elites; (4) balance different interest groups and appease or mitigate factionalism; and (5) foment economic and military strength against neighbors and promote internal prosperity, especially to benefit ruling and elite groups and encourage subject loyalty. Activities that feed into these domains of statecraft include oppression, repression, aggression, expropriation, appeasement, alliances, clientage, modifications of the environmental-ecological infrastructure affecting agriculture, resource extraction, transport, health, and defense, and, at times, maintenance of a (seemingly) successful status quo. Many practices and postures in statecraft are as much the concern of petty states and "city-states" that form part of the historical and geographic complex of polities as they are of the big states that better exemplify all the defining features. Smaller polity sizes preclude expression of some of the internal complexity that helps define states. Claims of legitimacy and sacred authority frequently are intertwined, and several aspects of statecraft react to and manipulate ethnic identities. Examples include fomenting regional identities, glorifying the ruling majority or minority ethnicity, stereotyping ethnic identities to advantage state interests, and forging a new level of state or national identity. States, as multicommunity political forms, inherently imply the subordination of subject settlements and populations, a process that changes aspects of peoples' identities.

There is a shadowy distinction between states and expansionist states that incorporate independent neighboring societies. Eventually, a sufficient scale implies an empire, if we define empires as large states that control, directly or indirectly, formerly independent and often culturally different societies (Doyle 1986:45; Schreiber 1992:3). Cohen (1978a:381) noted that expansive chiefdoms and ancient states both incorporated neighboring groups and may often have included groups self-conceived as distinct in origin or history and perhaps so labeled by others. In the past, therefore, larger-scale societies, which existed seemingly always in complex relations with similar neighbors, provided an arena in which social identities and actions may have been organized partly in terms of ethnicity. The frequent instability of states (contra Cohen 1978b:35–36), their internal division of labor that includes different districts and ecologies, and their competitive relationships create many of the circumstances in which cultural differences and population movements and contacts lead to recognition of cultural differences and ethnic categorizations. Viewed in a historical and comparative perspective, states do not necessarily tend toward ethnically monolithic polities—"nation-states" (see Geertz 2004 and commentaries in Kaufmann, ed. 2004).

A continuing difficulty in studies of states is reification. Some authors define states in comparison with chiefdoms as polities that overcome tendencies to fission (Cohen 1978b:35–36). This conceptualization is highly inconvenient in historical perspective and masks many of the struggles encompassed in statecraft. As Eisenstadt (1963) ably analyzed, states have contested political and economic relations, with central authority (or "the crown") vying with established interests among the nobility or other powerful institutions such as religious and commercial organizations. Modern states offer numerous examples of the diversity of interest groups, values, and goals that affect political and economic action within states and among them. States are more of a cauldron than a cake, more like activity at a bird feeder than in a beehive. With an ample historical perspective, they divide, reorganize, and collapse, so that there is tremendous variation in their trajectories and longevities. Geertz (2004) puzzles about the uncertain nature of modern states, but even ones that endured a considerable time often did so through an astonishing internal dynamic, with different groups, especially ruling dynasties, succeeding one another in the appropriation of the symbols of office and power, often without a dissolution of the fundamental class system.

It is useful, even necessary, to distinguish some conditions in ancient states from those prevailing more recently. The political economy of ancient agrarian states provides many incentives to settle clients beholden to the state or ruler for their lands. A desire for loyal clients for food production, a labor force, taxation, and military mobilization made rulers prone to settle new people, especially if additional lands were seized through expansion. Eisenstadt (1963) noted the importance of what he called "free floating" resources not subject to traditional claims, which include lands and other valuables seized during expansion or the institution of new tribute or taxation on the heels of expansion. Except for gains through expansion or internal divestiture, we can expect many lands to be tied up with traditional claims by communities or in elite or institutional holdings. Legitimacy through historical precedents is difficult to overcome except through expansionist force because undermining legitimate claims within a cultural system likely undermines state authority itself, which typically is engineered through adroit manipulations and redefinitions of traditional symbols and rights to resources.

Absorbing new clients was possible because state expansion and political factionalism are powerful engines for creating refugees and landless minorities. Neighboring complex polities encompassing their own share of factions, winners, and losers may generate exiled groups or émigrés seeking advantage. Despite the growth of population within many states, conditions of ancient health and mortality considerably checked population increase, and an "oversupply" of citizens was measured more through crop reversals than by political aims in wealth generation. Accepting new immigrant clients to guarantee state production or loyal subjects is well attested for the Late Postclassic Basin of Mexico (see Stark, this volume). In modern parallel, many states today accept or encourage transnational labor migrations or allow commercial or state institutions (e.g., military) to "outsource" work to achieve either economically or politically convenient projects. The spread of capitalism, however, creates forms of economic, political, and class power grounded on manufacture, fossil fuel–based mechanized transport, communication technology, military technology, and monetary capital far different from ancient agrarian states and animal or human transport; consequently, there were different implications for successful statecraft, even though promotion of state identities and preservation of class advantages can be charted for both ancient and modern states.

Urbanism and States

Urban centers in many forms are part of state societies. Urbanism represents physical aggregation of a range of service functions for a surrounding region that includes subsidiary settlements and population (e.g., political, economic, ritual functions) but with great variation in the mix of functions and the degree of demographic aggregation. Highly nucleated cities contrast with dispersed "garden cities," for example, depending on ecological, political, and economic conditions. Many ancient urban centers, as seats of political power, grew relatively rapidly, fueled by immigration (both state imposed and voluntary) as people sought access to opportunities in urban environments or sometimes were forcibly resettled. Both ancient Teotihuacan and Tenochtitlan in Meso-america are good examples of rapid urban growth, along with Mexico City in recent times. Urban centers offered a range of opportunities and brought people in diverse cultural groups in closer proximity in a context of changing relationships that could foment use of ethnic categories.

The modern world has demographic growth that, with exponential effects, creates in many states a problem of slower economic and service expansion than population growth, with unprecedented transnational migration and striking international and regional shifts in labor opportunities due to capital-ist efforts to reduce labor costs. Moreover, urbanization is so profound a trend that an unprecedented proportion of the world's population dwells in settle-ments large enough to accommodate a range of different ethnic groups (and other identities, such as occupational ones).

Although modern capitalist economies entail market interdependence that was unmatched in the ancient world, with its more agrarian focus, there are important urban and state economic factors in common that contributed to peoples' recognition and manipulation of ethnic identities in the past. Contact with "others" is one of the key steps in ethnogenesis and in the competitive in-teractions that establish and maintain ethnic boundaries. The precolumbian Mesoamerican market system, like the colonial and modern ones, had market-places situated in cities and towns. Market exchanges provided settings in which differences could be observed and built on in ethnic relations. Moreover, tribute demands, especially by the expansive Aztec Triple Alliance empire, at times required people in provinces to trade beyond the empire to obtain trib-utary items (Berdan 1980). Aside from these economic considerations, urban environments afford opportunities for public ritual and communication using monumental displays and performance panoplies. Arguably, the city itself be-comes a powerful state symbol. Ancient states particularly relied on symbolic practices in urban environments to manipulate and communicate about iden-tities and legitimacy.

State Legitimacy

Ancient and modern statecraft share one set of challenges, those of establishing legitimacy on a long-term basis. Force is costly to apply, especially as subject populations increase with territorial expansion, although modern technolo-gies of communication, information monitoring, and weaponry make forcible suppression more feasible on a larger scale than in the past. Ancient agrarian states faced the dilemma that deadly force applied too zealously or flights of refugees would begin to undermine the agrarian production on which they ul-timately depended. With expansionist states and empires, legitimacy is a sub-stantial challenge, as power is mainly obtained through force or threat of force. Often legitimacy is an issue of class power as well as dynastic power. Ancient states did not commonly operate with an abstract nation-state concept linked to shared culture, or with Enlightenment-derived concepts of the representation of citizens' rights. Instead, the legitimacy of the ruling dynasty and the ruling group (possibly conceived in ethnic terms) is more the concern of statecraft. Legitimacy was particularly important in dynastic successions (Goody 1966).

Within states, upper-echelon decision makers juggle a variety of interest groups, with classes prominent among them. Some scholars define states as societies with economic stratification, organized to institutionalize and maintain those differences (Fried 1967:186, 230). Successful placation of powerful class interests is one of the factors in the longevity of states and critical in the political economy. Blanton and Feinman (1984) see the Mesoamerican "world system" in Postclassic times as keyed to acquisition of luxury or wealth items in the core in part because of their utility in satisfying and retaining loyal clients.

Grillo (1998:11–13, 54, 72–73) asserts that ethnicity was not a particularly salient identity in ancient ("patrimonial") states compared with modern ones. His reasoning is that government was bent on tribute extraction, with personalized patron-client relationships predominating. Correspondingly, there was scant concern with subjects' way of life or cultural identity. In particular, he asserts, there was little emphasis on establishing a shared overarching national identity and unified moral order. There are some respects in which Grillo's generalization seems apt and others in which it neglects important processes in the Aztec case and others. Part of the problem is the simple one of applying a classificatory typology rather than focusing on the processes under way. Statecraft is not a "thing" but a series of strategies varying over time and by context, and for which goals are often seen to be contradictory when different contexts and actions are compared—part of the juggling act that sustains states.

The Mexica, as the most powerful segment of the Triple Alliance, manipulated ascriptive ethnicities to denigrate subject populations and correspondingly glorify their own ethnicity, especially their own mythic history legitimizing their imperial position. The explicit recognition of ethnic variety in the empire (some of it bogus in respect to self-identification by subject groups) had the effect of placing the central state government as the adjudicating and overarching authority. The state has particular power and resource advantages in controlling public cultural production and proclamations (or attempting to).

Grillo (1998:11–16) contrasts ancient and modern states, noting that both have a political economy but that modern states include rhetoric and actions in a moral economy. In the moral economy, legitimacy is partly underwritten by adherence to a set of values and goals for promoting the well-being of citizens and favoring rationalist bureaucratic measures. He argues that in ancient states a political economy prevailed in which the government and ruling class sought to obtain and retain material and power advantages. Again, there is merit in this observation, but it obscures elements of ancient statecraft that foment a moral economy and overarching positive identity of the state. During a famine, for example, the Aztec emperor is said to have opened his storehouses to feed the people of Tenochtitlan (Smith 1996:52–53). Public works such as aqueducts and dikes provided general benefits as well as a more stable economic base in the Basin of Mexico (Berdan 2005:27–28; Smith 1996:74). Laws and judges reflected some aspects of a moral economy (Townsend 1992:84–85).

Naturalizing Properties of Ethnic Rhetoric and Emblems

A concern with legitimacy fuels a naturalizing bent in both statecraft and ethnicity. Language is one of a range of emblems that, because of the frequent limitations of approximating native-speaker proficiency with later learning, often comes to signify a seemingly intrinsic quality. The Aztecs appear to have used language-based labels that covered much larger populations than were organized as self-defined identity groups. Naturalizing ethnic identity is a trap for solely "primordialist" approaches to ethnic groups. Ironically, ethnic self-attributions and ascriptions often gravitate to naturalizing rhetoric and physical traits to imply an intrinsic quality to a socially engineered category—hence the frequent recourse to language or speech patterns that incorporate unconscious learned behaviors. Similarly, physical or racial traits are often adduced with the implication of biological inheritance. Other lasting phenotypic modifications such as foot binding, cranial deformation, or dental inlays may play a role in ethnic (or class) signaling. Often, however, generalized behavioral traits are simply alleged in a stereotypic way that does not admit variation. Why? These recurrent elements of identity and signaling posit fixed forms to create an impression of intrinsic qualities; this in turn can cement unequal social relationships. Ethnic resistance to ascriptive restrictions may lead to strong internal sanctions to promote group conformity and solidarity, partly as a cooperative protection and also as an alternate internal system of values and accomplishment (McGuire 1982). The same manipulation of naturalizing rhetoric and assumptions enters into the promotion and protection of class differences in access to resources and power, as discussed below.

The State, Ethnicity, and Globalization

Modern states in a rationalist ideal differ from older ones in that defined subjects within their borders are presumed to be in some measure equal before the law if they accept their states' principles and foundation myths. This view contrasts with the medieval Christian notion that people have different social statuses and correspondingly different rights and privileges in a hierarchical society. Variants of this ideology were widespread throughout the world in the past and can still be found in the present. An ideal model of the modern state, in contrast, derives historically from the French and American revolutions of the eighteenth century and has since diffused widely around the globe. One dominant idea is that the modern state is a nation-state that rules directly over all inhabitants within its borders and seeks to impose the same legal, institutional, and bureaucratic arrangements over all its subjects. It is ideally homogeneous and seeks a common identity and a uniform loyalty among its citizens. As Durkheim and Weber observed, the modern state does not just collect taxes and provide for its rulers but seeks to intervene directly in the affairs of its citizens in order to change the world for the people's benefit (Collier et al. 1995:2, 5; Grillo 1998:3, 13–15).

Such ideals tell only part of the story, however, for at the root of the nation-state lies a series of contradictions. Collier et al. (1995:2) argue that modern national legal systems (what they term "bourgeois law," the body of legal concepts developed since the eighteenth century in Europe and its colonies and diffused widely since then), by requiring equal treatment for all citizens, ignore differences that exist outside the law and in doing so help create such differences. Furthermore, bourgeois law demands difference by enforcing the right of people to express their differences, and by "treating those who share an identity as equals, law casts as unequal those who do not share that identity" (Collier et al. 1995:2). Grillo (1998:3, 13) points to a similar founding contradiction in the history of France, Britain, and the United States. On the one hand, the modern nation was to be a homogeneous association of like-minded people, but on the other, in the view of many citizens, it was a community related by blood and kinship "to which certain peoples by reason of race and culture were thought incapable of assimilating," such as the Jews in France or southern and eastern European immigrants in the United States at the beginning of the twentieth century (Collier et al. 1995:3). Thus by simultaneously creating and denying difference and insisting on a governmental right to interfere in citizens' everyday lives, modern nation-states provide settings in which ethnicity (whether construed as ties of "blood and kinship" or invoked as a common heritage) is more prone to politicization and may assume greater importance than it did in ancient or "patrimonial" states, where inequalities of all kinds were viewed as unremarkable and accepted as natural (see Wimmer 2004:47).

In the early twenty-first century, however, a major point of contention lies in the ethnic implications not so much of the rise of the nation-state but rather, as some would have it, of its fall. Globalization and the rise of supranational economic and political forces have altered the relationships between states and their peoples, and today's "postmodern" state (Grillo 1998:216–235) is commonly perceived to be weakening. Borders between some countries are increasingly contested: witness the European Union and attempts to open the United States–Mexico border. Agreements such as GATT and NAFTA and efforts to create an international court system appear to be eroding national sovereignty. Appadurai (1996:39–40), for example, argues that deterritorialization and the separation of labor, finance, and technology have the effect of separating state and ethnic-nation from each other. Separatist ethnic (national) movements, such as those of the Sikhs, Tamil Sri Lankans, Basques, Puerto Ricans, Moros, and Quebecois, can be transnational and seek to create states of their own. The world is headed, Appadurai (1996:168) claims, toward a new "postnational global order," a course of change that is apparently irreversible. This is at root a causal argument. Globalization, beginning in the 1970s, has brought about a crisis in the nation-state. As the state weakens, identity politics and ethnonationalism surge to fill the power vacuum, invoking the rhetoric of alternative modernities (Comaroff 1996:167). With this logic the state eventually will wither away.

The predicted demise of the state may be premature, however. As Grillo (1998:1) points out, the nation-state has arguably been in perpetual "crisis" since it became dominant in the nineteenth century. Wimmer (2004:54–46) notes some cyclic aspects to exclusionary versus permeable state boundaries, and Kaufmann (2004:8) remarks on expansionist versus restrictive state strategies in respect to state-linked ethnicity. Indeed, the defining characteristics of modern states, including territoriality, sovereignty, the monopolization of violence, and citizenship, have always been suspect to some degree (Baker-Cristales 2004:24). It is widely accepted that globalization today contests the core identities of national cultures, pluralizing them and making identities more positional and political (Hall 1992b:309). But must this necessarily occur at the expense of state sovereignty? We think not.

In her study of transnationalism in Malaysia, Singapore, and Hong Kong, Ong (1999:2, 15, 210) argues that political borders in this part of the world are not becoming insignificant, but rather the state is refashioning its relationship to international capital and to citizens and noncitizens alike. In this region, states continue to define and regulate diverse populations even as citizenship becomes more flexible and increasing numbers of middle- and upper-class people hold multiple passports. These states are pursuing a "postdevelopmental" strategy of seeking multiple links with global capital and multilateral agencies, a kind of "communitarian capitalism" aimed at helping the middle and upper classes participate in global capitalism. These Asian "tiger" countries are not relinquishing sovereignty but learning how to manage it in a more flexible manner. Ong (1999:217–219) suggests that here globalization has induced a kind of "graduated sovereignty" whereby states retain control over their territories but allow corporations to regulate some domains. In Malaysia, for example, Malays are granted rights and benefits that are largely denied to Chinese and Indian minorities. Many immigrants from other countries come to work for transnational companies, but they face limited rights of employment and cannot apply for citizenship. In this situation state sovereignty and ethnicity, rather than compete with each other, appear to go hand in hand, and "ethnicity often becomes a sorting mechanism for defining the meaning of and the claims on sovereignty" (Ong 1999:220).

Baker-Cristales (2004) makes a parallel argument in her study of predominantly working-class migrants from El Salvador in California. Despite the fact that one-third of El Salvador's population lives in the United States, the Salvadoran state is not weakening in the face of massive transnationalism but reforming itself to accommodate global capital accumulation and the exigencies of transnational labor migration. It continues to occupy a central place in migrants' lives and to shape their identities. Baker-Cristales reminds us that the state can be thought of as not just a bureaucratic and administrative apparatus but a cultural form—like ethnicity—by which people imagine their collective identities.

Rather than see ethnic nationalism and the state as adversaries and declare the former the winner and the latter the loser, it is more productive to understand their relationship in dynamic, historical, and dialectical terms. Just as the relationship between the state system and the capitalist world economy has fluctuated over the past several centuries, so has the relationship between the state and ethnicity. In the present moment we are witnessing a decline of the classic model of the nation-state as the locus of a national economy, a national culture, and a fixed population. But this is a decline during one particular period in time, not an irreversible erasure. Today's ethnonationalist movements are one sign that far from being obsolete, the idea of the national state is still a powerful force in the world (Baker-Cristales 2004:28). Other ethnic movements are not separatist in nature but seek to reform the states in which they are located. In the Mesoamerican region, for example, one of the notable characteristics of contemporary Maya cultural activism is its location in two contrasting national contexts: the Zapatistas in Mexico and the pan-Mayan movement in Guatemala. These are different kinds of movements with different goals, but they are alike in that neither is separatist. In each case their adherents seek not to deny or transcend national borders but to improve their position and increase their autonomy within their respective countries. Although both movements make full use of transnational tactics to achieve their ends, their goals are to reform the nation-states of Mexico and Guatemala.

The variability in modern states, especially in relation to ethnicity, is part of a historical panorama extending back into the colonial and precolumbian eras. In these past contexts, too, states were dynamic, unstable, and both responsive and at times unresponsive to internal and external changes that dramatically affected their organization and longevity. Highly variable in size, organizational complexity, economic enterprises, and cultural traditions, ancient and modern states alike have faced internal factions, unstable and aggressive neighbors, and economic arrangements transcending their own borders. From a long-term perspective, complex societies with multiple social hierarchies seem to be an enduring feature, reconstituted and changeable but with no signs that they are giving way to a different economic and political form.

ETHNICITY AND CLASS

The Notion of Class

There are diverse definitions of class, some focused on economic advantages such as control of the means of production and/or control of the means of distribution (Smith 1976). Authors differ regarding whether strict economic criteria or a combination of economic and social considerations should be the basis for class membership. In either case a social system in which economic advantage is acquired and retained almost always entails consideration of additional cultural factors such as inheritance and restriction of opportunities to acquire wealth (via access to appropriate training, jobs, marriages, capital, etc.). The behaviors and attitudes to act effectively in upper-class social environments are part of the education that differentially favors descendants of advantaged class members.

Consequently, it is not surprising that even in capitalist economies there is a strong heritable element to class membership, which is also consonant with sociobiological expectations. In ancient states with precapitalist economies, usually with an agrarian emphasis, class membership was strongly influenced by descent, despite periodic upsets due to warfare and conquest, among other factors. In fact, one of the challenges for ancient statecraft was the institution of avenues of social mobility to enlist wider support and engage appropriate talents to staff key offices and undertake tasks. Some researchers have preferred to use the term *estate* to recognize the ascribed rather than achieved positions, rights, and duties of people in a distinct class (Eisenstadt 1963; Hicks 1999; Nutini 1995; Tönnies 1953). Class membership, then, becomes a profound, salient identity, perhaps more so in ancient than modern contexts, but important in both. *Class* seems to be a more widely recognized term than *estate*, and we employ it here to indicate social strata with an economic advantage or disadvantage, recognizing that the means by which membership is obtained and the related cultural values, rights, obligations, and symbolic communications of class membership vary in different social systems.

Participation in an established elite class usually involves participation in a subculture, with associated education, speech, comportment, skills, and a myriad of distinct daily practices from those pertaining to lower classes. In many ancient states, elite class membership was likely to be conceived in terms of descent or origin. In elite class culture, access to and use of power to commission works of great technical artistry, ones that commemorate historical glories or symbolize sacred authority, represents a sharp divide from the powers of commoners. Baines and Yoffee (1998) note the "aestheticization" of elite life in ancient civilizations, often through training in and mastery of esoteric lore, elaborate forms of speech, writing, painting, music, and martial arts. These practices yield differences as profound as any ethnic group contrasts, with the exception that an elite class in states is usually considerably involved in widely understood public ceremonies and religious rituals; this is not the case for ethnic groups, which may practice different rituals from the majority. Helms (1993) stresses the substantial ritual and symbolic qualities of elaborate crafting, often done for ritual performances and sacred contexts of use and commissioned by leaders or rulers.

At times, ruling classes have claimed separate origins from commoners (e.g., Brown 1973). In Mesoamerica, Toltec descent was sought (through marriage alliances) and claimed by elite classes particularly (Berdan, Umberger, this volume). To be Toltec was to be civilized, and a transformation from Chichimec (northern, "uncivilized") was a mark of historical accomplishment. A naturalizing claim of difference was inserted into ethnic discourse. Places as well could serve as touchstones for a claim to intrinsic differences and rights. In Mesoamerica caves and mountains are among such sacred places. Thus Chichimec origins from one of seven caves, or visiting the caves or other key places, established a legitimate history. The Mexica historical narrative of migration, ostensibly including lands to the northwest of the Basin of Mexico, others to the southeast, along the Gulf, and to the northeast, represented a claim of precedence and historical connection, forming an imperial charter (Sahagún 1961:189–197 [1575–1580]). Because places such as mountains and caves had sacred connotations and gave access to supranatural domains (more directly accessible than the sacred celestial sphere), claims of visits or origins were not simply a history of migration but a claim of supernaturally charged legitimate differences and rights.

In the modern world, elite distinctions are maintained by restricted access to places and social contexts (e.g., exclusive, usually expensive membership clubs; private, usually expensive educational institutions; "refined" social and cultural events; international travel and acquaintance with exotic, usually expensive locales; use of exclusive, expensive residential real estate; use of personal staffs; and often access to opportunities for powerful economic or political positions, such as boards of directors). In the tug of war between descent and wealth, in capitalist economies access to privilege can be affected by wealth more than birth, compared with the ancient world, where birth often determined access to wealth.

The Intersection of Class and Ethnicity

We regard class and ethnicity as distinct concepts, neither of which can be reduced to the other. The relationship between them is highly variable, and it is complicated by several factors. First, whereas ethnicity is an inherently subjective concept and always implies an identity (or identities), class has both objective and subjective characteristics and can be viewed either way, as Marx recognized when he distinguished between a "class in itself" and a "class for itself." Thus objective economic analysis may justify the use of the class concept even where class consciousness is lacking. The same cannot be said for ethnicity. Second, class and ethnic group membership can overlap empirically in complex ways, from colonial situations in which they may be virtually isomorphic (though rarely for long), to extremely fluid social formations in which classes may exhibit ethnic heterogeneity and ethnic groups may be class stratified. Third, these empirical overlaps make it possible for people to interpret one in terms of the other if it suits their purposes. Thus in the eighteenth century in the colonial city of Oaxaca, Mexico, where the elite maintained a rigid hierarchy of socioracial or ethnic distinctions (the *sistema de castas*), some individuals were able to parlay their mobility in the economic class system into higher locations in the sistema de castas, such as exchanging a mulatto for a white Spanish identity (Chance 1978:158). Similarly, ethnic stratification of Indians and ladinos in mid-twentieth-century Chiapas, Mexico, was manipulated by the latter to bolster their class position (Stavenhagen 1975:195–213).

In both these examples dominant elites tend to conceptualize class differentiation in ethnic terms, a very common phenomenon that obfuscates class interests and makes it easier to assign praise or blame where competition for resources is at issue. The examples also illustrate how an ideology of ethnic stratification with deep colonial roots may persist for centuries, even as competing class distinctions gradually become more important (Schryer 1990:23). Thus in colonial Mexico one elite response to growing class differentiation was to add new categories to the sistema de castas to make mobility in the ethnic stratification system more difficult (Chance 1978:175). For Chiapas in the 1950s, Stavenhagen (1975:207–211) stresses how classes were very slowly gaining importance but still not fully formed and still intertwined with ethnic (he calls them "colonial") categories in complex ways. Though other earlier studies were concerned with how ethnic stratification might be modified by or give way to class distinctions (more on this below), there are also circumstances in which a class may change into an ethnic group, with a corresponding change in identity, as in situations of ethnogenesis (see Chance and Sandstrom, this volume).

In today's world the old modernist assumption that "primordial" ethnic loyalties would give way to class stratification has long since been turned on its head. Various sorts of identity politics, based on ethnicity, gender, or myriad other "new social movements," vie for attention around the globe, while class and class analysis, for some, has become increasingly irrelevant, at least as a basis for political strategy (Laclau and Mouffe 1985). Though it is indeed the case that class consciousness (class for itself) is not a primary catalyst of political movements today, to eschew class analysis (class in itself) altogether would be a major mistake and rob us of one of our most powerful analytical concepts (Kearney 1996:154). As recent ethnography has shown, class continues to shape people's identities in significant ways (e.g., Lem 2002; Medina 1997). Even where class identities are vague and subordinate to ethnic and other ones, growing class inequality (class in itself) is often an important ingredient in political mobilization. To return to Chiapas, the class differences already manifest in the 1950s have now penetrated further into many Maya communities, widening the gap between rich and poor. Far from muting Indian ethnic identity in the region, class stratification has instead helped bring about the new pan-Maya ethnicity embodied in the Zapatista rebellion (Collier and Quaratiello 1999:123).

The relationship between class and ethnicity is, if anything, extremely fluid and dynamic, much like the relationship between state sovereignty and ethnicity discussed in the previous section. Many polemics about class and ethnicity to the contrary, it is difficult to argue that one is inherently more fundamental than the other. Sweeping generalizations about the relationship between the two remain suspect, and we lack a convincing general theory. As Schryer (1990:42) has suggested, class and ethnicity vary independently and their boundaries can vary widely, even in different communities within a single region.

RETROSPECT AND PROSPECT

We examined the concept of ethnicity, which we grounded in Barth's (1969) perspective, but with revisions to accommodate concurrent nested scales, considerable historical change, processes of internal ethnic group reinforcement, and a varying balance of primordialist and instrumentalist factors. With respect to the criterion of common heritage, we observed that through a long time depth, indigenous Mesoamerican concepts emphasize more the notion of common history than common descent, despite colonial efforts to introduce racist biological concepts; Taggart (this volume) notes additionally the role of common activities. Our observations and commentaries about ethnicity have been tempered by the long perspective of our Mesoamerican case materials and the methodological achievements of diverse disciplines that marshal pictorial, material, spatial, written, and direct observational and interrogative data.

We considered the state contexts affecting ethnic group competition and ascription and the associated urban, exchange, resettlement, and expansionist processes that bring groups into new situations where ethnogenesis may occur. Statecraft often includes ethnic rhetoric and symbols, coordinated in an effort to establish the legitimacy of ruling cadres. State "propaganda," public rituals, and ethnic discourse frequently employ stereotypic and naturalizing principles.

State (and imperial) societies provide the contexts for ethnicity, and class relationships become one of the important intersections of identities and interests. Class membership, especially for elites, can incorporate the cultural differentiation, heritage assertions, and boundary maintenance characteristically defining ethnicity. Although class and ethnicity may converge, they also may diverge, requiring case-by-case analysis.

We find ethnicity, state, and class in indigenous Mesoamerica to be more intelligible in a comparative sense across time (and disciplines) than from any one period or discipline. We do not find rapid reformulations of modern ethnic identities to be as surprising as most analysts because a long-term perspective highlights change. Moreover, we do not find the contexts of modern states and classes entirely alien to ancient and colonial contexts, and differences that are contingent on particular circumstances are more comprehensible through comparison than for any one period in isolation.

From our long-term comparisons, we can see the interplay of cultural difference, class advantage/disadvantage, and the engineering and maintenance of political power as an enduring contested arena, the essence of "complex societies." We see a recursive aspect to the intersections of cultural values, changing social and economic circumstances, and the active decisions individuals and groups make. In this fashion we situate ethnicity in a theoretical spectrum that Giddens (1984) and Bourdieu (1977) especially have explored. Past configurations drastically changed by a series of world-scale events lead to the question of what drastic changes may reorder (or are reordering) the present configuration of modern states that divide the ancient geography of indigenous Mesoamerica. Is the extension of direct and indirect hegemony by one or more capitalist core states the crucial change afoot? Are environmental impacts and demographic increase likely to profoundly alter the political and economic organization of the modern world and the ethnic configurations we see? If the history of Mesoamerican ethnicity, class, and states is a guide, we can be assured of eventual profound changes. Ethnic and other identities surely will remain in play, however, as they are part of the fundamental fabric of social life.

2

Archaeology and Ethnicity in Postclassic Mesoamerica

Barbara L. Stark

IN THIS CHAPTER I CONSIDER HOW ETHNICITY WAS CONCEIVED AND expressed in Mesoamerica during the Late Postclassic period (A.D. 1350–1521) in order to evaluate a case of a proposed intrusive ethnic enclave from the Middle Postclassic period (A.D. 1200–1350) in south-central Veracruz, Mexico. The case illustrates the smaller of two scales of ethnicity in Postclassic Mesoamerica, the fluid nature of ethnic expression, and the later, indirect effect of a major state power, the Aztec Triple Alliance, in reducing some expressions of ethnicity. I also comment on some of the conditions that affected precolumbian Mesoamerican ethnicity in a more general fashion.

South-central Veracruz is depauperate in documentary coverage for the Postclassic period (A.D. 900–1521). Particularly for the central highlands, Mesoamerican archaeological case studies of ethnicity incorporate documents with native and Spanish emic perspectives (Brumfiel 1994a; Brumfiel et al. 1994; Smith 1984), but this advantage applies primarily to the Late Postclassic period. For eras without documents or for which documentary mentions are mythic claims about a distant past, researchers apply material and spatial criteria, along with consideration of the persistence of cultural differences and, in some instances, cultural similarities to possible homelands, as noted in Chapter 1. In the case considered here, a much stronger than usual suite of evidence indicates a Middle Postclassic ethnic enclave in south-central Veracruz.

Two scales of ethnicity are observable in Late Postclassic Mesoamerica on the basis of documentary materials. One is a broad, usually linguistic level combined with culturally stereotypic traits. Another level concerns polity or "city-state" affiliation or origins. We see the linguistic scale mainly through "Aztec" perceptions and policies, that is, those of Basin of Mexico Nahuatl speakers who were integral members of the Aztec Triple Alliance, dominated by Tenochtitlan. This level of ethnicity was ascribed, but it is unlikely that ethnicity was also self-attributed at the same broad scale. Colonial documents such as the Florentine Codex by Fray Sahagún (1961 [1575–1580]) describe some groups with names that reflect language and, usually, a set of cultural traits. Examples are the "Totonaque," who "spoke a barbarous tongue"; the Matlazinca (or Toloque), about whom the same remark is made; and the Olmeca Uixtoti and Mixteca (Sahagún 1961:182, 184, 187 [1575–1580]). At the close of Sahagún's chapter on kinds of people, many Nahua speakers are characterized as "Chichimecs" because they came from lands to the north or west, while other groups to the east, not Nahua speakers, are remarked as non-Chichimec. In other contexts Chichimec is opposed to Toltec, representing a contrast of "barbarian" and "civilized" mores.

Thus language and place of origin interfinger in the native comments from the imperial core in regard to large-scale frameworks. Basin of Mexico documents show considerable variation in how location and language figured in ethnic ascriptions. Smith (1984:162) notes a case in which locality affiliation and a dominant language overrode multiple languages in an account that referred to the Toluca Valley inhabitants as Matlazinco. Brumfiel (1994a:95–96) comments on a similar phenomenon in which sectors of the Basin of Mexico were categorized by group or polity names that masked considerable internal variation in ethnicity as expressed at a smaller scale.

I suspect that broad linguistic (and spatial) scales of ethnicity were a recurrent feature of expansionist states and empires in Mesoamerica whenever distant neighbors were incorporated or confronted at political boundaries or simplification of complicated ethnic divisions was administratively useful. Some stereotypic and somewhat derogatory identities seem to be part of the rhetoric that glorified the Mexica and the Aztec state. For Thailand, Moerman (1965:1219) notes that states may serve as organizing poles regarding interaction and identity, which counteracts diversity in ethnic categories in large, politically decentralized, unstable regions. Ethnogenesis in expanding states is at times a feature of policies to divide, demote, and organize subjects, as well as a form of resistance to state control (Gailey and Patterson 1987:9; Patterson 1987:122). The latter implies self-identification by groups, which seems more evident in the smaller scale of ethnicity discussed next.

A smaller scale of ethnicity in colonial documents is city-state or polity origin or affiliation, critical in many day-to-day economic and political affairs. In the Postclassic Basin of Mexico many cities and towns had new arrivals and refugee groups who were granted lands, creating mosaics of ethnic affinity on the basis of the polity or city-state of origin (e.g., for Texcoco, Bray 1972:163; Hicks 1982:236–237; Offner 1979:232–236; for Tenochtitlan, Calnek 1976:289; Zantwijk 1985:82–83; for Xaltocan, Brumfiel 1994a:92). Because of their complex history of migration, political change, and royal intermarriage, Bray (1972:162–163) thinks central Mexican states were typically multiethnic, and he notes several examples. Zantwijk (1973:25) suggests that governments at times tied ethnicity to complementary institutions, thus providing an accommodation of potentially conflicting interests in a "balancing act." Incomers granted lands might form calpolli or teccalli corporate groups (Brumfiel

1994a:91–92; Lockhart 1992:15-28). (Chance, this volume, treats the calpolli scale as separate from and smaller than that of polities, but for my purposes I group them; however, such scale variations are crucial for recognizing nested levels of ethnicity).

Small-scale ethnic affiliations were not immutable, however. Brumfiel (1994a:100–101) calls attention to evidence that diverse groups that had been accommodated or recruited into polities became known by their new polity affiliation rather than their polity of origin. Whether we can distinguish ethnicity and residency (or citizenry) as contrastive native concepts is partly terminological and situational (see Umberger, this volume, for discussion of differences in how polity affiliations were rendered in documents). In any case, the smaller polity scale of ethnicity was subject to fairly fluid adjustments in respect to ascription and self-identification.

CAUSES OF MESOAMERICAN SCALES OF ETHNICITY

As Cohen (1978a:395) notes, "much less attention has been given to understanding what conditions tend to evoke ethnic identities of particular scale and intensity than to describing what ethnicity is as a phenomenon." Different conditions bear on each of the scales I identified.

Languages and Related Cultural Attributions

A basis for the broader of the two scales for ethnicity is the importance of languages for communication. Although multilingual people and societies existed in Mesoamerica, maintenance of separate languages requires their perpetuation in frequent interactions. From the perspective of nonspeakers, language groups are a basis for ascription of cultural affiliation, even though such categories may be poor representations of those people's social or ethnic affiliations. Cook and Joo (1995:37) note similar issues for Oaxaca today, as well as the importance of Zapotec language with respect to ethnicity. It is not surprising, then, that most of our information about linguistically based ascriptions of identity comes from the imperial core and refers to others within the far-flung empire. Ossa (2000) shows that central Mexican references to the Huastec masked a mosaic of language, cultural, and political differences.

Brumfiel (1994a:94) notes Aztec unfavorable stereotyping of broad linguistic and cultural categories, which suggests an active state effort to enhance the dominant group's political and social role by denigrating others; such efforts affirm the broad scale of ethnicity I am discussing. The Aztec evidence is multidimensional, however. At times vital qualities are built into stereotypes, such as the hunting and warfare prowess of the Otomí (Sahagún 1961:179 [1575–1580]; 1981:98, 109 [1575–1580]) or the license of the Huastecs (Sahagún 1961:186 [1575–1580]; 1969:34 [1575–1580]), but with the unspoken implication that Mexica or centrist values moderate and rule over such fundamental but potentially disruptive qualities (Brumfiel 1994a:95). Apparently, ethnic impersonators donned clothing for performances based on stereotypes (Sahagún 1954:45 [1575–1580]), and the manipulation of identities was part of public rituals in the capital. Likewise, in war, the capture of distant "barbarians," such as Huastecs, did not net warriors the same rewards as captives from the nearer polities in the core (Sahagún 1954:77 [1575–1580]), thereby explicitly devaluing distant peoples. Such communications could not be directed with any reliable frequency to distant Huastecs themselves and thus seem aimed more at inculcating a superior attitude validating imperial dominion. Key political interactions with polities of Huastec speakers would likely be conducted in a fashion permeated by such assumptions of superiority, however.

Pollard (1994) sees a state role in forging and expanding Tarascan ethnicity at the expense of other groups, except in frontier areas, where more variability was tolerated for strategic reasons.[1] Just as the Aztec Empire and the Tarascan expansionist state manipulated ethnicity to favor dominant groups and promote the virtues of "centrist" culture, so, too, past expansionist states may have contributed to ethnic stereotypes, ranking, and competition among ethnic groups or suppression of local ethnicities.

Small Polities

The smaller scale of Late Postclassic ethnicity involving city-state or polity origins is affected by long-term historical processes in Mesoamerica, despite its intensely situational nature. I comment on these long-term conditions and then focus on their expression in the region of the case study. Two other factors in Mesoamerica—transport and military technology—contributed to the prominence of small polities, and each is discussed briefly. Mesoamerica encompassed a wide range of social forms: significantly, at any one time the region included a range of societies, never all politically unified. From this synchronic and diachronic diversity flow some of the fundamental political conditions affecting ethnicity. Substantial urbanization and the growth of expansionist states and empires were two factors that promoted structural juxtaposition and integration of different polities and populations likely representing diverse cultural interests and practices. Juxtaposition of different interests was also due to the continued existence of independent small polities that I term *small states* (although in some respects they do not fit state definitions constructed with larger polities in mind). For many Mesoamerican peoples, these small states formed a basis for self-identification according to origins.

Large states, although often surprisingly stable in Mesoamerica for centuries, all eventually collapsed or transformed, decomposing into constituent districts that formed small independent states or city-states.[2] One Postclassic precondition was the Late Classic (A.D. 600–900) breakdown of two large states or empires in the Mexican highlands, resulting in more competing centers. The decomposition of both Monte Albán and Teotihuacan in the Late Classic period produced a proliferation of polities and unsettled conditions across the central and southern highlands for over half a millennium, followed

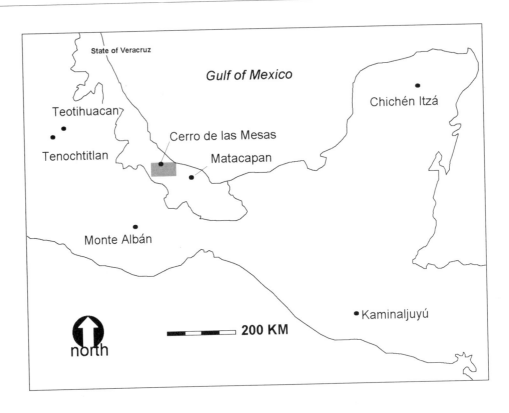

FIGURE 2.1.
Mesoamerica: selected
centers named in the text.
Shaded box indicates the
case-study region.

eventually by the Aztec Triple Alliance empire, which forged the largest political unit in Mesoamerica in prehispanic times.

Another precondition to Postclassic times was the proliferation of centers in
geographic areas that traditionally exhibited small states. The extensive Maya
Lowlands were consistently characterized by multipolity organization, with
considerable variation in polity sizes and with fluctuations in their extent and
integration (Marcus 1989). The Late Classic period witnessed a multiplication
of competing polities in the southern lowlands, where eventually many centers
were abandoned (the Maya "collapse"); however, the northern lowlands continued the history of political cycles and multipolity organization.

Data from the western lower Papaloapan basin in the Gulf lowlands of
Veracruz indicate a pattern similar to the Maya proliferation of centers in the
Late Classic period (Figures 2.1, 2.2). In this region the Early Classic settlement
hierarchy was dominated by Cerro de las Mesas (Drucker 1943b; Stark 1991),
located in the Blanco River delta. The full extent of the Cerro de las Mesas polity remains unknown, but Daneels (1997) has documented a separate settlement hierarchy with multiple Early Classic centers in the lower Cotaxtla basin,
the next drainage to the west, which therefore seems to have been substantially
independent of Cerro de las Mesas. To the east, at the lower edge of the Tuxtla
Mountains, Tres Zapotes was a substantial center in the Early Classic period
(Drucker 1943a; Pool and Ohnersorgen 2002; Weiant 1943). The Cerro de las
Mesas realm was probably concentrated in the western lower Papaloapan ba-

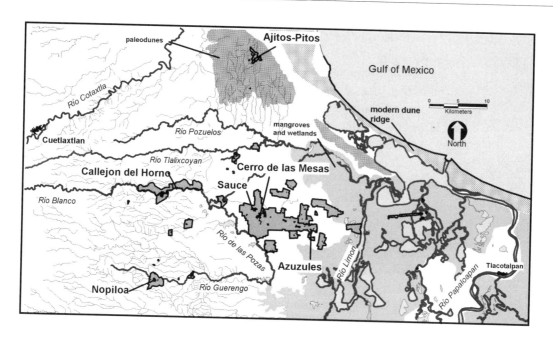

sin, perhaps encompassing the lower Guerengo, Acula, Papaloapan, Tlalix-coyan, and Blanco rivers.

FIGURE 2.2.
Major landforms in the western lower Papaloapan basin. Survey blocks are shaded and outlined.

The settlement hierarchy changed in the Late Classic period, and the western lower Papaloapan basin area was broken up politically. There were at least three large centers of approximately similar size. Azuzules, slightly east of Cerro de las Mesas, was the major complex along the Blanco River. Nopiloa dominated the lower Guerengo. Ajitos-Pitos dominated the paleodunes and may have controlled the lower Tlalixcoyan River. Each of these centers differed slightly in its architectural characteristics, but ceramic differences among the three localities were modest, and they participated in the same obsidian distribution network. In pottery, figurines, and obsidian they continued traditions from the earlier Classic period, although not without innovations. In part because of their possibly more defensive layouts, these centers imply a more competitive political situation than in the Early Classic period.

Even though the Cerro de las Mesas polity was larger spatially than these later ones, all represented relatively small polities, akin to the range of state sizes found in the Maya Lowlands. It is against the backdrop of a long, continuous cultural tradition in the Classic period that the remarkable changes in the Middle Postclassic period stand out, as discussed below.

In sum, these "small-state regions," such as the central and southern Gulf lowlands and the Maya Lowlands, represent a persistent situation in an extensive portion of Mesoamerica. Combined with the "break-up states" succeeding Monte Albán and Teotihuacan in the Mexican Highlands, the regions mentioned present a widespread situation of competing small states. The political landscape was punctuated by some larger regional states, such as Tajín (Wilkerson 1987), Xochicalco (Hirth 2000), and Tula (Smith and Montiel 2001).

Nevertheless, these large regional states did not endure as long as Monte Albán and Teotihuacan, usually lasting only 200–300 years. Even these successfully expansionist regional states were susceptible to the highly competitive conditions that fostered shifting alliances and political upsets.

Given the proliferation of Late Classic and Early Postclassic polities across Mesoamerica, elites were necessarily active in a volatile situation of alliances and contests with neighbors, in territorial expansion, or in protecting traditional lands. These polities were hierarchically organized and typically split along vertical cleavages that reflected dynastic, elite, or other competition. The disaffected factions had an "out"—migration and affiliation with another rival polity. Nalda (1981) entertains the idea that Mesoamerican migrations might often reflect groups in class struggles expressing resistance to a social hierarchy, but the importance of elite leadership in documentary cases suggests that they more commonly represented vertically organized factions than classes when they departed. Hicks (1994) provides an example of vertically organized cleavage involving the ruling dynasty of Texcoco. The archaeological case considered below also exhibits vertical organization.

Successful states had incentives to incorporate groups of clients, settle them on lands internally, or pacify new holdings by settling loyal enclaves in distant areas. Both these political strategies, incorporation via land grants and enclave formation, were important in guaranteeing supporters and in holding territories for tribute. In turn, commoners necessarily would have to affiliate strategically to guarantee community longevity and land rights as well. The volatile political histories meant elites and commoners alike had every reason to pay attention to their polity origins or affiliations, partly as an expression and reinforcement of their own solidarity in changing contexts, whether they were disaffected émigrés, refugees, colonists, or entrenched community/polity members. Migrants may have retained social ties to their polity of origin, at least for a time. Ethnic mosaics may be a widespread feature of situations with considerable population movement among multiple competing states as well as ones involving conquest states (LeVine and Campbell 1972:86, 92).

I suggest that there was escalation of an ethnic mosaic by Postclassic times rather than a difference in kind from earlier times. For example, in the Early Classic period (A.D. 300–600), Nalda (1981) notes two instances of small Teotihuacan groups within local cultures in Querétaro and Guanajuato, and other researchers have discussed examples in Hidalgo and Veracruz (e.g., Crespo et al. 1981; Díaz 1980, 1981; Ortíz and Santley 1998; Pool 1992; Santley et al. 1987). There were ethnic barrios within the capital of Teotihuacan as well, mentioned below.

In modern studies of ethnicity, internal competition for power (and hence resources) and competition among societies for resources is often underscored as the context that explains both ethnic members' stake in ethnic affiliation and the recognition of their ethnicity by outsiders (Despres 1975b:199; Hodder 1979; McGuire 1982). Comaroff (1987) suggests that economic disadvantage generally underlies ethnic social disadvantage, and Toland (1993) argues that states are vehicles for dominant groups that categorize ethnicity and values, with subordinate ethnic groups contesting such relations. Some individuals within ethnic groups may advance their own interests through vertical differentiation within the ethnic group (Brass 1991:247, 254). Thus competitive relations may occur internally in ethnic groups as well as externally to them. It is worth noting that "competition" remains somewhat indistinct as a concept without further specification of its context and possible outcomes, but I do not address that problem here.

In some ethnic contexts, ecological and economic complementarity have been observed in fluid ethnic relations (Leach 1954), and this situation may have archaeological expressions as well. In Mesoamerica there are some indications that immigrant groups occasionally constituted occupational classes that had an ethnic identity (e.g., for Aztec times, Calnek 1976:289; Lockhart 1992:192), but economically differentiated ethnic communities have not been identified that were organized by altitude, as suggested for the Andes. In the Andes, Goldstein (2000) discusses diasporic communities that take advantage of different resource zones tied to altitude, in both Tiwanaku and Inca times (Murra 1972), with the result that resource localities are multiethnic. The most prominent context of Late Postclassic Mesoamerican ethnicity seems to have involved movements of groups that were disaffected, disadvantaged in political struggles, or perhaps politically or economically entrepreneurial, seeking opportunities in other city-states or polities. These circumstances created an ethnic mosaic in many late polities. The case discussed below supports the picture of Postclassic population movements, but it is not yet clear if the enclave reflects an independent effort or instead results from arrangements mandated by an overarching state.

Transport Technology

A multitude of polities with uncertain or shifting relations is particularly striking in Mesoamerica because of the strictures on land transport in a region with substantial mountainous terrain. Lacking pack, riding, or other transport animals, Mesoamerican people hauled goods and moved themselves on foot or by canoe (Hassig 1985). High costs were associated with long-distance interactions that involved moving many people or large quantities of supplies (Drennan 1984), affecting the reach of armies and administrators and shaping the content and extent of trade. Choke points for control of trade were not as exclusive with foot travel as with wheeled transport.

These transport and spatial conditions meant that many centers and polities were not so differently endowed, compared with their neighbors, that they could count on a competitive advantage to bolster their hold on clients and allies. Improved lands, more lands, and more clients were recurrent goals for political and economic success, but there were few guarantees for the long-term fortunes of ruling groups and polities. Such conditions make the willingness of rulers to accept newcomers and grant them lands more intelligible. Forging Mesoamerican power required lands and people. One interpretation of the case study below is the granting of land to an intrusive enclave.

Military Technology

A situation with multiple competing polities also depended on modest differentials in control of the "means of destruction." Mesoamerica does not display a revolutionary technological history in warfare, although access to cotton armor, defensive installations, and tactical acumen were important in military history (Hassig 1988:75–109). Successful military expansion was often as much a function of larger forces than the enemy (or political alliances to mobilize such forces) as it was of technological advantage. Successful opponents to the Aztec Triple Alliance, for example, consisted of relatively large regional states (the Tarascans) or sets of allies (the Tlaxcalans). Since all states face internal challenges to central power (Cowgill 1988; Eisenstadt 1958, 1964), the additional difficulties in achieving economic or military advantage created conditions in which multiple polities in relatively close interaction were a recurrent circumstance before the Late Postclassic period and the success of the Aztec Triple Alliance.

Discussion

Brumfiel (1994a) asks why ethnicity was so important for corporate groups in Aztec times rather than kin-ordered groups or more personal clientage. She argues that ethnicity allowed nobles to maintain an indirect affinity to their subjects, rather than direct kin ties, and thus did not erode their claimed intrinsic right to rule. Clientage, she contends, was simply more efficiently arranged with ethnic groups than negotiated on a more individualistic basis. As outlined above, I suggest also that there was a strong historicity to the predominance of small-scale, polity-of-origin ethnicity. This scale of ethnicity was fomented by a long history of small states and highly competitive polities that made state expansion particularly challenging, as coalitions could arise in opposition. Indeed, the Aztec Empire itself depended at its inception on alliances. Rulers' claims to land allowed them to accommodate and settle new clients typically known by their polity of origin—where they might continue to have contacts and alliance prospects.

   In certain respects the changeable history of polities prior to the Aztec Empire parallels the unstable history of polities in eighteenth-century Burma described by Lieberman (1978). In that context, ethnicity cross-cut polities, was treated flexibly by individuals, and was generally tolerated governmentally in multiethnic polities. Although ethnicity shifted to some extent to favor dominant polities (Lieberman 1978:458), it was not a primary issue in statecraft and political clientage. I suspect that similar conditions concerning ethnicity were in effect in Postclassic central Mexico. In this respect the subdued role of ethnicity in political and economic activities corresponds to Grillo's (1998:11–13,

27–36) contention that rulers in ancient states were little interested in ethnic groups or in countervailing ethnic diversity by inspiring affiliation with central state values. Instead, extraction of tribute and maintenance of client loyalties were the primary focus. Nevertheless, Grillo overlooks the fact that Aztec statecraft did manipulate ascribed ethnicity as part of a symbolic program to glorify the state, or at any rate, the ruling ethnic group. Likewise, it is clear that ethnic groups formed part of the relationships through which people organized political actions.

I suggest that polity of origin was a crucial but not unvarying factor in the constitution of ethnicity. It likely was being eroded by a degree of stabilization afforded by the Aztec Triple Alliance, by the use of larger-scale ethnic categories and stereotypes to enhance and demote populations in accord with state aims, and by the co-optation of local elites to both vest them in the Aztec state and defuse factionalism and alliance that ran along ethnic lines (Brumfiel 1994a; see Brass 1991:270–298 for a more general discussion of the roles of leaders in ethnic groups). A tension between polity/place loyalties and class loyalties for elites was surely one of the key dynamics in the Late Postclassic Aztec realm.

The many centuries through which Monte Albán and Teotihuacan thrived as the heads of major polities during the Classic period (and earlier) constitute a contrastive situation to the Late Postclassic. Pasztory (1989, 1993) remarks on the proclivity of these and other Classic states to have a recognizable stylistic stamp on public monuments and "art," including the emblematic attire of individuals. These emblematic characteristics may show the cumulative effects of strong state authority in forging a dominant ethnic identity or a state identity. Such identities were recognizable vis-à-vis independent polities and largely overrode whatever internal divisions may have existed during the polities' founding and early growth. Early Monte Albán, for example, had three discernible spatial segments that later were not identifiable (Blanton 1978:37–40, 44–46, 75–98). Later social divisions existed but were not suggestive of ethnicity and might represent administrative sectors.

Teotihuacan was unusual among Classic centers in the presence of "foreign barrios" (at least two), but Teotihuacanos "abroad" or in provinces are recognizable through the state stylistics Pasztory remarks on. Immigration also has been identified at Teotihuacan, with indications in the Tlajinga 33 compound that incomers were assimilated and generally did not underscore their origins through material remains, at least not in those recovered archaeologically (White et al. 2004). The likely state-sponsored program to construct apartment compounds is perhaps one clue to a series of projects that promoted considerable commonality across the city in access to goods, built space, and ritual gear emblematic of life in both the city and the state.

Mesoamerican work has shown that archaeology *can* recover data that are extremely likely to represent ethnic affiliation in the case of enclaves, as reviewed in Chapter 1, but this accomplishment does not guarantee that the archaeological record discloses all such instances or even many of them. Symbolic boundaries may signal identities even if no contrasts are preserved from daily life. The most convincing archaeological enclave cases, however, demonstrate spatial patterns reflecting persistent cultural and social boundaries, with a recognizable "homeland" affiliation and with cultural differences reflected in more than one aspect of daily life, particularly including family rituals, mortuary practices, and cuisine—contexts crucial to enculturation and internal group solidarity.

Perhaps the most striking point to emerge from the review of archaeological cases in Chapter 1 is how few there are—yet on the basis of my discussion above we would expect considerable ethnic diversity in Mesoamerican states and urban centers. We should keep in mind, however, that few systematic surface collection and residential testing programs have addressed variations in material culture in cities and smaller settlements in their vicinities. The intensity of the Teotihuacan mapping project and its attendant surface collections are not replicated by most settlement mapping projects or survey of support zones where immigrant communities might have been settled. The Veracruz case considered next as an intrusive enclave is also a result of systematic surface collections, with a resolution at the level of individual domestic mounds.

A MIDDLE POSTCLASSIC ENCLAVE
IN THE WESTERN LOWER PAPALOAPAN BASIN

A suite of evidence points to an intrusive enclave in the delta of the Blanco River. Although my main focus is presentation of the evidence, I consider the issue of identifying non-enclave inhabitants in the immediate area and examine publications concerning culturally distinct neighbors in adjacent areas who shared, for example, the same imported obsidian network. The study of interactions with neighbors is handicapped by problems in detecting Postclassic occupations, especially in the Tuxtlas area to the east (Pool 1995). The ethnic enclave interpretation better suits current evidence, which provides no indication that the enclave was established by a foreign power (a key defining characteristic for colonies) (e.g., Stein 2005:10–11). Instead, ceramic ties are less specific, suggesting a highland origin but not a specific locale or site.

As observed above, the antecedent history of the western lower Papaloapan Basin in Veracruz shows considerable cultural continuity from the Late Preclassic period (600–100 B.C.) to the end of the Classic period (A.D. 900). The exact span during which this tradition disappears is unknown, possibly postdating A.D. 900, and the cause of its cessation is also unknown. A drastic alteration is noticeable in material culture in the Middle Postclassic period (A.D. 1200–1350, based on ceramic cross-dating). The new ceramics have their closest counterparts in southern Puebla and the Basin of Mexico. Previously, I shied away from treating these changes as necessarily indicating an ethnic intrusion (Curet et al. 1994; Stark 1995). Although the intrusion of outsiders with highland cultural affiliations was a strong possibility, I argued that imperial takeovers also might lead to a considerable reorientation of material culture and economic networks. In the view here, based on additional data, emulation is inadequate to account for all the evidence. Although emulation may have some applicability, the evidence points to a broad range of traits that were part of commoner daily life, not an elite-skewed emulation process. As an example of emulation, people in the enclave produced "Complicated Polychrome" as a version of Choluteca polychromes, a ceramic that is one characteristic of the "Mixteca-Puebla" Horizon (Smith and Heath-Smith 1980).

Additional data collected in four more years of survey make an interpretation of an enclave of outsiders more likely than local imitation of highland pottery styles. I now can describe the persistent spatial localization and boundaries maintained by the intrusive group. The interpretation of a Middle Postclassic intrusion is based on (1) changes in family-scale rituals as seen through new figurines, (2) new food preparation techniques involving tortilla griddles (comales), (3) new styles of serving and storage vessels, (4) a marked change in settlement pattern, and (5) a marked change in obsidian importation. Each category of evidence is discussed in more detail below. Family-scale rituals, food preparation, and service ware involved habitual daily life and are likely to have been part of enculturation and continuing reinforcements of social group membership. Service dishes may additionally form part of wider social settings for hosting, thus reinforcing group membership but also communicating wealth or status distinctions. A new center at Sauce, with much less investment in monumental structures than earlier centers, shows a disruption in local political authority. Long-distance economic networks for clear gray obsidian replaced the dominant Classic period source of black/dark gray obsidian. There is no reason to believe that this new network was engineered by Sauce, which was modest in size. Rather, Sauce inhabitants took advantage of a new network that covered a much larger area in south-central Veracruz.

The changes in material culture show a variety of stylistic affinities with the central highlands, particularly southern Puebla and Tlaxcala (Curet et al. 1994) but including the Basin of Mexico as well. In comparison, ceramic data from the lower Cotaxtla drainage (Daneels 1997) and from the western Tuxtla Mountains (Pool 1995) do not show the highland-related complex that appears in the Middle Postclassic period in the western lower Papaloapan basin. Therefore, at a very broad scale, we can envision an intrusive highland group, but my survey data show that it was localized in the Blanco River delta. Demonstration of the spatial evidence of persistent boundaries requires a series of thematic maps to show the distribution of the material culture categories.[3]

In assessing changes within the western lower Papaloapan basin, at times I draw on a dataset created by Christopher Garraty, who used regression analysis for "unmixing" collections (Garraty and Stark 2002). The 1998 and 1999 survey collections from a Late Postclassic center, Callejón del Horno, created a possibility of better discrimination of Late from Middle Postclassic components

TABLE 2.1. Figurine Occurrences in Middle and Late Postclassic Collections.

	DRUCKER'S TYPE II	DRUCKER'S TYPE III	TOTAL
Middle Postclassic	147	57	204
Late Postclassic	46	0	46
Total	193	57	250

Note: Collections identified in Garraty and Stark 2002 using unmixing and inspection techniques; $p = 0.0000$ using Fisher exact probability test.

in the region. The Middle Postclassic was defined in terms of collections from the center of Sauce. Garraty took advantage of the relatively "pure" materials from the Sauce and Callejón del Horno centers and their immediate vicinities to distinguish other Late versus Middle Postclassic collections. Garraty and Stark's (2002) distribution maps show that the Middle Postclassic component is concentrated in the delta of the Blanco River whereas the Late Postclassic component is more widely distributed, including upriver along the Blanco and in adjacent drainages.

After evaluating changes in figurines, settlement patterns, and food preparation, I test the localization of Middle Postclassic remains by examining selected pottery distributions to show their localization in the Blanco delta. For the pottery distributions, I go beyond the unmixed data set and plot all occurrences of the diagnostic pottery types for the Middle Postclassic period. Last, I examine the distribution of the clear gray obsidian, which is not restricted to the Blanco delta, as it has a wider distribution in south-central Veracruz. The obsidian distribution affords us a basis to see if "locals" who had a material culture different from that of the new Middle Postclassic people can be detected in the areas surrounding the Blanco delta, although the results are not conclusive. After presenting evidence for an intrusive enclave, I consider an ecological and a political factor that could help explain the presence of the enclave.

Ceramic Figurines and Household Rituals

Changes in family-scale rituals are indicated by the introduction in the Middle Postclassic period of a completely new suite of flat, "cookie-cutter" figurines, that is, Drucker's (1943b:64) Type II and Type III categories. The larger Type III figurines are associated with the Middle Postclassic occupation rather than the Late Postclassic one (Table 2.1). Type II figurines, however, are found with both occupations. Figurine occurrences in the unmixed collections from the Middle versus the Late Postclassic periods are significantly different using a Fisher exact probability test ($p = 0.0000$) (Siegel 1956:96–104). Type III figurines were recovered only in collections from the delta area of the Blanco River (Figure 2.3).

These two types of Postclassic figurines are mold-made, exhibiting hair styles or headdresses different from earlier examples. Earlier Classic period figurines were highly varied but included near-life-sized idols, medium-sized

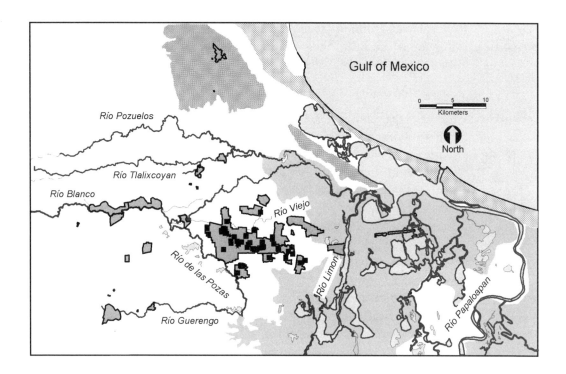

and small "smiling-face" figures, and a broad range of whistles and animal figurines (Gutiérrez and Hamilton 1977; Medellín 1960; Stark 2001:179–226). Molding was employed in the Classic period, but figurines were not flat, "cookie cutter" styles. Styles of clothing on Drucker's Type III figurines are different from Classic period styles and clearly show the introduction of a triangular *quechquemitl*. In native documents representations of triangular quechquemitl are widespread in regions examined by Anawalt (1981:38, 128, 164–165, 187, 213), including highland areas, but I have not located examples among the Classic period figurines from the western lower Papaloapan basin prior to the Postclassic period, despite Anawalt's (1981:212) suggestion that this garment originated in the Gulf lowlands.

FIGURE 2.3. Distribution of Type III figurine fragments (a square represents a collection, a star represents an isolated find).

Settlement Patterns

Settlement patterns show a considerable change from the Classic tradition, which featured large buildings around formal plazas, ball courts at the centers, and outlying monumental buildings, including massive rectangular platforms (Stark 1999). The numerous Classic formal complexes are abandoned, and the single known center, Sauce, shows a different layout. Monumental platforms are few and much less imposing. No ball court has been located, although a modern *ejido* has substantially affected part of Sauce. The center seems to have had relatively nucleated habitation, but not to the exclusion of dispersed occupation in the countryside. The settlement pattern consists of a head town (Sauce) and dispersed rural habitations in the surrounding delta. Although inhabitants continued to live in and around Classic period monumental centers (as is true today), these centers were no longer foci of new construction incorporating Middle Postclassic pottery.

Food Preparation

Food preparation changed with the widespread introduction of buff paste tortilla griddles (comales). Buff comales were abundant in both the Middle and Late Postclassic occupations. They probably were produced at rural households southeast of Sauce in Middle Postclassic times (Curet 1993). Previously, maize, the carbohydrate staple, would have been ground and prepared in foods such as tamales or drinks rather than toasted in tortillas. The degree to which tortilla preparation was new requires further discussion, however. A change in food preparation begins slightly earlier in the Blanco delta with the appearance of brown paste comales in scattered collections, especially at the east end of the delta near the Late Classic center of Azuzules. This shift occurred toward the end of the Late Classic period but does not constitute a strong case for new arrivals with different domestic practices because other associated cultural changes cannot be identified.[4]

Serving and Storage Vessels

Styles of serving and storage vessels change with the Middle Postclassic complex. New polychrome bowls feature cholutecoid designs (Drucker's [1943b:48] Complicated Polychrome), and many bichromes and some polychromes pertain to a "guinda" complex—bowls and rarely jars with a polished red slip and black painted designs, including an engraved variant, and also polychrome variants with black-and-white-on-red designs. Black-on-orange bichromes became abundant, sometimes involving complicated designs on vessel exteriors. None of these ceramic types appeared in the Late Classic complexes, which featured serving bowls in several categories: fine paste ceramics in orange or gray, negative resist and false negative resist decoration, and metallic-appearing slips and washes. Also new were Hard Ware and Buff Ware; these two types include unslipped, polished small jars and bowls, respectively, in distinctive new pastes and surface finishes. Dull Buff Polychrome bowls were new, as were Fondo Sellado (stamped base) bowls.

Cholutecoid, guinda, and black-on-orange ceramics—sometimes in variant styles and proportions—are found in Puebla and the Basin of Mexico during the Postclassic period (Curet et al. 1994). Fondo Sellado is common in Puebla. Not all the Middle Postclassic ceramics have readily apparent highland inspiration, however. No analogue to Dull Buff Polychrome bowls has been detected elsewhere. These varied new ceramics have not yet been tested regarding source clays, but it is likely that they were predominantly locally produced.

The localization of the Middle Postclassic ceramic complex in the Blanco delta, indicated by Garraty's unmixing analysis (Garraty and Stark 2002), can be further examined by plotting the occurrences of seven pottery categories al-

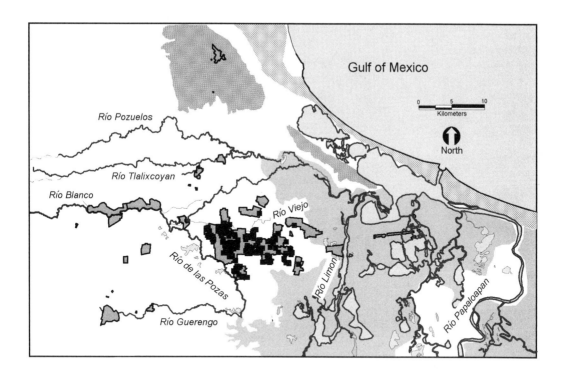

FIGURE 2.4.
Distribution of Dull
Buff Polychrome rims
(code 45a).

most exclusively associated with the Middle Postclassic in Garraty's reference collections: Dull Buff Polychrome (Figure 2.4), Black-on-red Incised (Figure 2.5), Black-and-white-on-red Polychrome (Figure 2.6), Interior Banded bowls (Figure 2.7), Buff Ware (Figure 2.8), Hard Ware (Figure 2.9), and vessels with the frieze motif (Figure 2.10). These plots augment Garraty and Stark's analysis because they include additional collections, not just those that could be assigned to the Middle Postclassic period through unmixing. Plots of these seven ceramic categories show an extremely localized distribution in the delta of the Blanco River. Extremely rarely, Black-on-red Incised and Interior Banded bowls occur upriver along the Blanco. Otherwise, every example of these sherds is confined to the delta.

Obsidian Importation

By the Middle Postclassic period, imported obsidian for the prismatic blade industry changed in respect to source materials (Stark et al. 1992). Pico de Orizaba clear gray obsidian predominates in Middle Postclassic collections (Table 2.2), and striking platforms are often ground on the polyhedral cores from which the prismatic blades were struck. Previously, ground platforms were absent or rare in the region. Green obsidian, presumed to derive from Pachuca, Hidalgo, increases slightly compared with the Classic period. Green obsidian is even more plentiful in the Late Postclassic period than in the Middle Postclassic, however, and clear gray obsidian is present in reduced amounts. Previously, the Classic period obsidian assemblage was dominated by black to dark gray

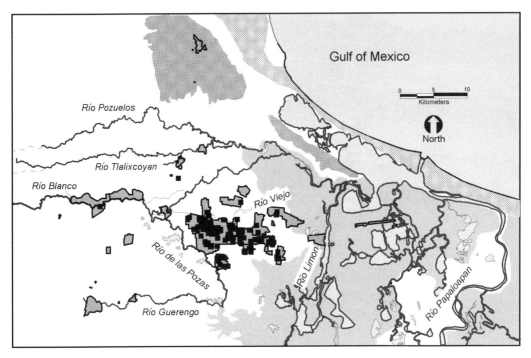

FIGURE 2.5. Distribution of Black-on-red Incised rims (code 7g).

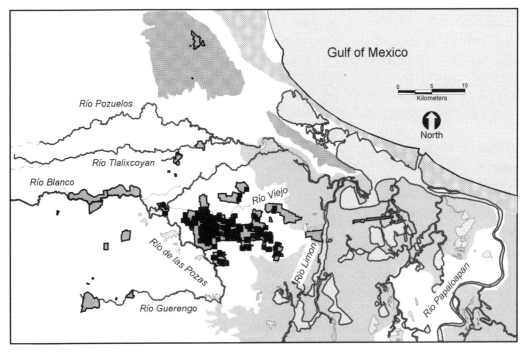

FIGURE 2.6. Distribution of Black-and-white-on-red Polychrome rims (codes 24, 26).

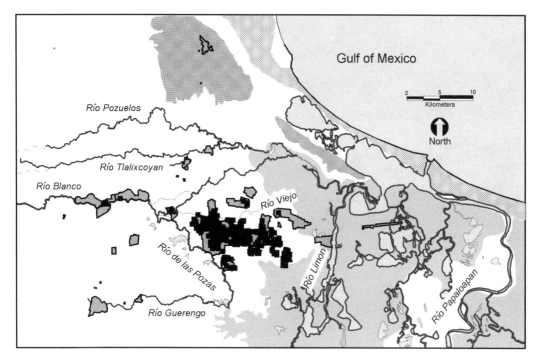

FIGURE 2.7. Distribution of Interior Banded bowl rims (codes 9n,o, 10n, 11p,u, 23n, 45h,i).

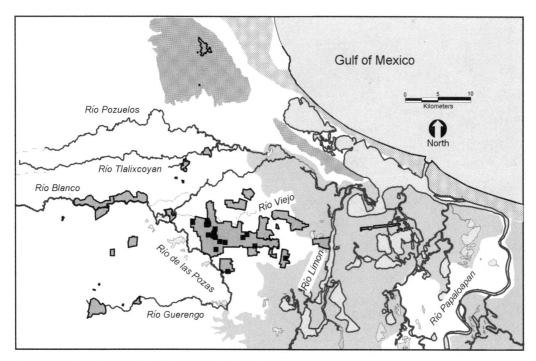

FIGURE 2.8. Distribution of Buff Ware rims (code 41a).

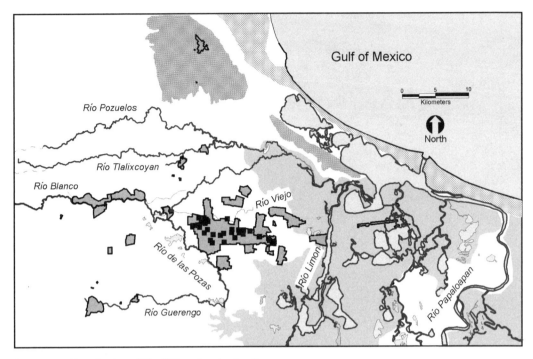

FIGURE 2.9. Distribution of Hard Ware rims (code 58).

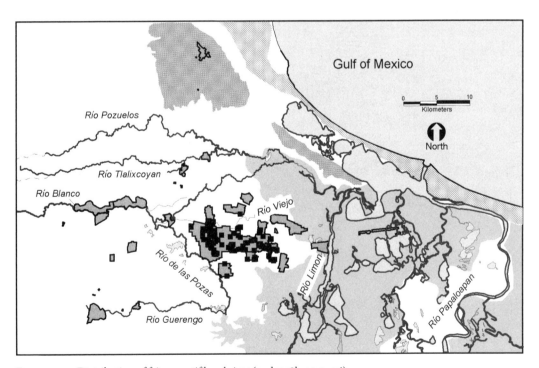

FIGURE 2.10. Distribution of frieze motif bowl rims (codes 18b, 30 0, 45j).

TABLE 2.2. Summary of Counts for Obsidian Colors at Sauce and Callejón del Horno.

	BLACK/DARK GRAY	GREEN	CLEAR GRAY	RATIO OF GREEN TO CLEAR GRAY
Sauce center and periphery reference collections[a]	163	40	1,145	.035
Callejón center and periphery reference collections	69	589	273	2.16

[a] Feature 1756 was excluded because it has an unusual concentration of prismatic blade production debris, probably representing a workshop in the vicinity. Sauce's position in an area with prior Classic occupation may be responsible for some of the black/dark gray obsidian.

obsidian from Zaragoza-Oyameles, Puebla (Stark et al. 1992; Heller 2001). Because obsidian distribution networks are typically much broader than individual communities or polities, clear gray obsidian should have reached any local inhabitants in the vicinity who did not share ethnicity and material culture with the proposed Sauce enclave.

Were people in the Sauce enclave intrusive within a surrounding Postclassic local population or did they settle in a locally depopulated area, selecting the delta and taking advantage of the largest patch of highly productive lands for double-cropping (Stark and Ossa 2007)? At first it might seem surprising to consider the possibility that the enclave was intrusive into a local Middle Postclassic culture, when none has been identified from the material evidence. However, exactly this problem with recognizing Postclassic occupants characterizes the archaeology of the western Tuxtlas region (Pool 1995), and continuity in Late Classic pottery would make Postclassic occupations "invisible" analytically. In the next section I use the new clear gray obsidian to look for these possible local inhabitants. The presence of local inhabitants has a bearing on the likelihood of the two explanations of the enclave that are mentioned in the concluding discussion.

Enclave Intrusion into an Occupied or an Abandoned Region?

To evaluate whether an unrecognized continuity or subtle change not recorded in our ceramic typology might characterize a local Middle Postclassic occupation, I examine whether the distinctive Postclassic clear gray obsidian prismatic industry is found in collections that lack what we currently recognize as Postclassic pottery. I consider only the prismatic blade industry because, much earlier in Preclassic times, clear gray obsidian was used with a flake technology.[5] When prismatic blade technology became characteristic near the close of the Preclassic period in the western lower Papaloapan basin, black–dark gray obsidian gained greater importance, and the Classic period obsidian assemblages are almost entirely composed of black or dark gray prismatic materials.

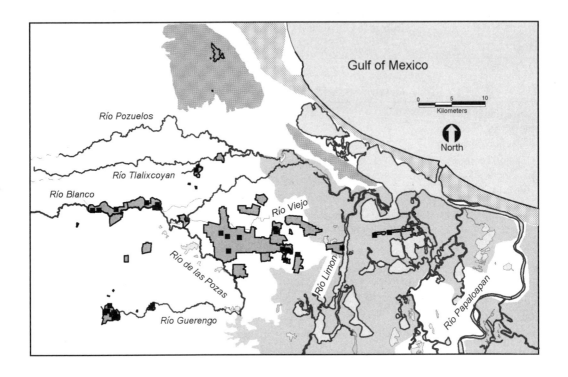

FIGURE 2.11.
Distribution of
collections with clear
gray prismatics but
lacking Postclassic
ceramic diagnostics
(only collections at or
above the median for
rims, 68, are considered).

If no clear gray prismatic blades occur apart from what we recognize as Postclassic ceramics, there is no case for a remnant local population since it is likely the same imported obsidian would reach them as the people in the Sauce area. If, instead, clear gray prismatics occur apart from known Postclassic ceramic diagnostics, two inferences are possible. One interpretation is that this obsidian reached local people who did not use the new Sauce enclave artifacts. The other interpretation is that clear gray prismatic obsidian began to trickle into the region before the Sauce enclave appeared. In either case, instances of clear gray obsidian apart from the new ceramic complex should have a high percentage of Late to Terminal Classic diagnostic pottery (thus perhaps lingering into the Postclassic period).

Figure 2.11 shows collections that meet a series of criteria designed to identify users of clear gray prismatic obsidian who lacked the new Middle Postclassic pottery: (1) the number of rims is at or above the median (68) for rims to ensure a more robust sample size for more reliable inferences; (2) the percentage of Postclassic diagnostic rims (both Middle and Late Postclassic types) is zero; and (3) there are one or more clear gray blades. Figure 2.11 shows that there *may* have been local people who acquired clear gray obsidian but did not use what we recognize as Postclassic pottery.

Further investigation is required, however, to ensure that these are not occupants pertaining to the Late Postclassic period rather than the Middle Postclassic, since clear gray prismatics were available in both periods. For this analysis, the ratio of green to clear gray prismatic counts is an added criterion.

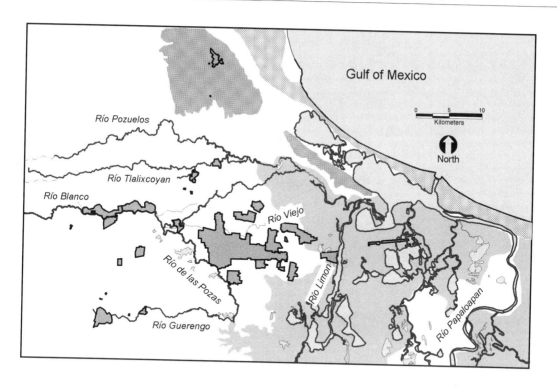

The average value for this ratio during the Late Postclassic period in collections at and near the center of Callejón del Horno is 2.16; earlier, within and around Middle Postclassic Sauce, the average ratio is 0.035 (Table 2.2). Figure 2.12 shows the single case from the previous analysis in which the ratio is above 1, located upriver along the Blanco River, not far from Callejón del Horno. This collection likely reflects Late Postclassic occupants who had a considerable amount of green obsidian in addition to clear gray even though no Postclassic pottery co-occurs in the collection.

In contrast to the pattern for ratios above 1, we can examine the ratios below 0.03, which are more likely to represent Middle Postclassic collections. In Figure 2.13 the 37 collections with a ratio of green to clear gray obsidian prismatics less than 0.03 are distributed both in the delta (where the possible new enclave is situated) and in other surveyed localities that had occupation in the preceding Late Classic period. In these collections clear gray obsidian prismatics were available despite the absence of any recognized Postclassic pottery, and there was very little or no green obsidian. Therefore, a Middle Postclassic date is more likely than a Late Postclassic date. The occurrence of several of the collections in the Blanco delta raises the strong possibility that sample error led to a lack of Middle Postclassic pottery in these collections and that people represented by the delta collections were also part of the enclave. It is the collections *outside* the delta that provide an indication of local people following different cultural practices but with access to clear gray obsidian blades. If the few non-delta collections represent continuing occupation and not effects of sample

FIGURE 2.12. Distribution of collections with clear gray prismatics, no Postclassic ceramic diagnostics, and a ratio of green to clear gray prismatics of greater than 1 (only collections at or above the median for rims, 68, are considered).

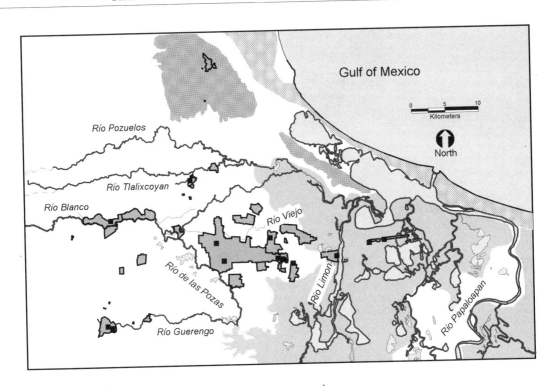

FIGURE 2.13.
Distribution of
collections with clear
gray prismatics, no
Postclassic ceramic
diagnostics, and a ratio
of green to clear gray
prismatics of less than
0.03 (only collections at
or above the median for
rims, 68, are considered
and collections with
Late to Terminal Classic
percentages above the
median of .026).

error or the beginning of clear gray prismatic blade distribution at the end of the Late Classic period, then these collections point to an extreme dislocation and reduction of prior population.

Discussion

Not only did family practices regarding food preparation and rituals change with the Middle Postclassic period complex (called Upper I by Drucker [1943b]), but so too did serving vessels that would have been used in more public display, such as feasts and other social obligations. Finally, economic arrangements altered, and different obsidian sources served the area. The Middle Postclassic complex is localized in the Blanco delta with persistent boundaries.

The Middle Postclassic intrusion is one of the most marked cases of material culture and settlement change documented archaeologically in Mesoamerica. Unfortunately, we do not know enough about the archaeology of neighboring parts of the Gulf lowlands and adjacent areas in the highlands, such as Puebla and Tlaxcala, to trace the origins of the intrusive people exactly. They are undoubtedly part of the "nahuatization" that occurred in the central Gulf lowlands. At the time of early Spanish documents, many communities are reported as having inhabitants who spoke "mexicano" (Scholes and Warren 1965:780), but these reports probably reflect a combination of the imposition of Aztec control and any earlier events, such as the arrival of an intrusive enclave.

The Sauce enclave may represent an independent group from adjacent highland areas that sought its fortunes in the western lower Papaloapan basin, seizing control of part of an area in political disarray. Their choice of the Blanco delta is expectable if they sought the largest patch of the most productive farmlands allowing double cropping. If the newcomers arrived as an independent group from the central highlands, there was an elaboration of material culture associated with their local identity, including innovations such as Dull Buff Polychrome. A diminished local population (an idea supported by the obsidian analysis) would offer little opposition to a group selecting some of the best farmlands.

Rather than an ecological explanation for their localization in the Blanco delta, we can consider a political alternative. The small size of the Sauce enclave suggests that these people may have owed allegiance to some outside, larger center. We cannot safely assume that a small town such as Sauce was an independent polity. In view of the modest size of the Sauce enclave, these people may have been granted lands by a ruler of an outside head town. Immigrant groups are often recorded in documents as being accepted as new clients and granted lands as part of political aggrandizement by city-state polities in the Late Postclassic Basin of Mexico (e.g., Offner 1979), as mentioned in Chapter 1. A grant of lands in exchange for allegiance would also account for the remarkable concentration of Middle Postclassic remains in the delta at a time when we can document few signs of non-enclave contemporary occupation outside the delta.

Whatever its history, the Sauce enclave was a small-scale polity (or a subordinate town under an as-yet-unidentified polity). This is a context of ethnic affiliation that was particularly volatile in Late Postclassic times in central Mexico. The localized cultural practices of the Sauce enclave did not endure long. In the Late Postclassic period substantial changes again occurred in the western lower Papaloapan basin, although they were not as profound as those during the Middle Postclassic. Late Postclassic changes represent dislocation of Sauce political authority and establishment of a new center, Callejón del Horno, and new economic arrangements linked to the Aztec Triple Alliance. The Aztecs conquered head towns to the west and east which became part of tributary provinces (Garraty and Stark 2002).

The Middle Postclassic Sauce enclave was suppressed in terms of its distinctive material culture in later Aztec times, as much of the distinctive pottery and the Type III figurines did not carry forward in the Late Postclassic period. It appears likely that the broader integration of populations into the Aztec Empire, whether directly through political action or indirectly through economic and political changes nearby (as proposed by Garraty and Stark [2002]), sometimes had profound impacts on distant local groups, such as the likely western basin enclave. Social and economic changes related to the Aztec Empire are explored further by Skoglund et al. (2006).

In sum, although the spatial and cultural distinctness of the proposed Sauce enclave is nearly unmatched in current Mesoamerican literature, this distinctness was transient and points firmly to concepts of ethnicity that stress the situational character of ethnic negotiations rather than an unyielding cultural heritage. The case supports Lieberman's (1978) observation that stronger state authority may reduce some ethnic expressions: the Aztec Empire was associated with a disappearance of a discrete Sauce enclave even though some practices, such as the use of buff comales, continued in the region.

Indications that ethnic immigrant groups in the Basin of Mexico were vertically organized are echoed in the Sauce case. Garraty and Stark (2002) show that collections from Sauce and its immediate vicinity were the highest ranking in elaborate, higher-labor-investment ceramics compared with collections from the countryside. The presence of a single head town at Sauce compared with a dispersed rural population in the enclave also suggests a social hierarchy. The western basin evidence matches documentary indications from central Mexico that small-scale polity affiliation was important in ethnicity, and the Sauce enclave extends the geographic distribution of the small-scale ethnic phenomenon beyond central Mexico.

Unlike the archaeological enclave situations I reviewed in Chapter 1, the Sauce Middle Postclassic enclave is headed by a town and includes a surrounding pocket of delta farmlands with a rural dispersed population. Both the Oaxaca barrio and the Sauce enclave are more crisply defined than the Matacapan enclave in the Tuxtlas, proposed as a settlement with intrusive Teotihuacanos that was swelled with local immigrants. Teotihuacan-related stylistic traits were concentrated at but not confined to Matacapan, as they also occurred at other settlements in the Tuxtlas region. This lack of clear boundaries may be due to Teotihuacan's unusual political and economic power, which led to more emulation and expansive trade compared with the Oaxaca barrio or with the small Sauce town: the former was not part of the elite stratum of urban Teotihuacan, and the latter likely owed allegiance elsewhere.

A broad chronological perspective reveals marked differences among the archaeological cases with respect to the duration of enclaves. With Matacapan, not only are there less distinct spatial boundaries for enclave traits, but these traits also fade very gradually over time in the Tuxtlas, apparently lasting during the Late Classic period long after Teotihuacan itself lost power. In the Maya Lowlands some Teotihuacan imagery continued in use by elites in public art after the fall of the city, generally confined to war symbols. In contrast to Matacapan and the Maya cases, the Oaxacan barrio has not been documented as surviving the fall of Teotihuacan, and Sauce did not continue as a center under Aztec hegemony, nor did most of the distinctive material culture traits endure into Aztec times. The temporal duration of enclave-related traits seems to have been extraordinarily sensitive to the prestige of the homeland, to the strategies adopted by local elites, and to the activities of any new major superordinate power that might suppress or replace styles. In the next chapter Umberger shows how complex the manipulation of symbols of identity was in an expansionist state and empire as she considers the case of the Aztec Triple Alliance.

ACKNOWLEDGMENTS

Suggestions from Elizabeth Brumfiel, John Chance, George Cowgill, Rosemary Joyce, Christopher Garraty, Hjorleifur Jonsson, Michelle Hegmon, Tom Patterson, Christopher Pool, and Michael Smith were quite helpful, but these colleagues are not responsible for any shortcomings in this chapter. The Proyecto Arqueológico La Mixtequilla was made possible by support from the National Science Foundation (BNS 85–19167, BNS 87–41867, and SBR-9804738), the National Geographic Society, and Arizona State University, and permission from the Instituto Nacional de Antropología e Historia. Any success in the project is entirely dependent on the excellent fieldwork participation of a number of students and archaeologists over the several seasons of survey. I thank the local communities for their kind welcomes and cooperation. The students and guests in my joint seminar with John Chance and my ethnicity conference colleagues provided essential stimulating ideas that helped sharpen and broaden my background on this subject.

3

Ethnicity and Other Identities in the Sculptures of Tenochtitlan

Emily Umberger

THE STONE MONUMENTS THAT DECORATED THE CEREMONIAL CENTER of Tenochtitlan, the Aztec imperial capital, provide prehispanic views of human identity, among them allusions to ethnicity, but their imagery is difficult to interpret.[1] Ethnohistorians use written and pictorial evidence from the colonial period, collected and recorded after the Spanish Conquest in 1521, to talk about ethnicity. Archaeologists use these plus the material remains of architecture and artifacts. Art historians use the same resources to explicate visual imagery, but they rarely explore aspects of society and politics (however, see Klein 1987, 1993, and 1994). Only one art historian has addressed ethnicity directly, Pasztory (1989), who did a Barthian (1969:9–38) analysis of the functions of the group art styles distinctive to four large culture areas of the Classic period. She called these *ethnic styles* (see discussion in Chapter 1, this volume).

Pasztory's study was limited in scope by the nature of the data available from this early period. In contrast, more information exists to reconstruct the societal structures of the Late Aztec phase at the end of the Postclassic (1325–1521). The data enlighten us about notions of ethnicity both inside and outside units of different scales—from individual *calpolli* (small territories held by social units also called *calpolli*) to *altepeme* (plural of *altepetl*, the Aztec word for an urban settlement and its dependents),[2] to empires of different sizes. These additional data are in the form of colonial alphabetic and pictorial sources, the latter being accompanied by alphabetic texts and presenting prehispanic ideas. They provide both the broad contexts of prehispanic activities and other lines of evidence to complement, add to, contrast with, or even contradict the information derived from archaeological and artistic remains. Some aspects of these sources resulted from the altered situation brought about by the conquest, but if examined critically, other aspects can be identified as relics of the past and invaluable for its reconstruction (see Umberger 2007). Nothing like this body of written and pictorial evidence exists for the Classic period. Maya hieroglyphic inscriptions are comparable in some ways, but the information conveyed by them is thematically narrow, and their usefulness for the analysis of ethnicity has not yet been demonstrated. Classic period specialists have contrasting sources of archaeological data, such as the contrasting evidence of public art and smaller artifacts (e.g., Nagao 1989 and sources cited in Emberling 1997:320), but they are difficult to use to discuss ethnicity. Also important is Nagao's (1989) warning that style does not equal ethnicity.

Three exemplary articles exploring Aztec ethnicity—Berdan's chapter in this volume, Brumfiel 1994a, and Brumfiel et al. 1994—together form the background for this study. In the following, like Berdan, I use colonial sources to reconstruct ideas from late prehispanic times, but like Brumfiel and her colleagues, I combine these with archaeological remains. Post-Barthian ideas on ethnicity emphasize its dual aspects of self-ascription and attribution of identity to others (Barth 1969:9–38; Brumfiel 1994a; Comaroff 1987; Chapter 1, this volume). In relation to these two sides of ethnicity the evidence provided by the archaeological remains that Brumfiel studies is very different from that provided by monumental objects with complex imagery from Tenochtitlan. Brumfiel's relics are Otomí labrets found in archaeological surveys at Xaltocan. The wearing of these labrets was a matter of self-ascription, but they could have been involved in attributed ethnicity too, as Brumfiel and her coauthors recognized from the evidence of colonial pictorials. However, neither archaeological remains nor colonial documents reveal much about the contextualization of these labrets in prehispanic discourses. Nor can questions involving the Otomí specifically be answered easily by prehispanic images.

Fortunately, there exist two monuments from the imperial capital that reveal Tenochca views of groups other than the Otomí and their own claims of difference from all non-Tenochca groups. On both monuments identity is based primarily on political affiliation, which is indicated in the hieroglyphs next to the conquered people. Apparently, the affiliation of the victors, the Tenochca Mexica, did not need to be indicated because the monuments were located in their city. In contrast to the information given in the hieroglyphs, class is indicated by contrasts between the costumes of the victors, who are depicted as being of the Toltec-descended noble class, and those of the losers, who, although likewise members of a noble class, are depicted symbolically as demoted to a lower position through Chichimec costumes. These costumes made them comparable to commoners, as dependents or tributaries. References to ethnicity appear only in cases where the polity name was derived from an ethnic name. It also is possible that a polity's patron god bore an ethnic name other than that of the place but this name is not referred to in the hieroglyphic labels.

This chapter has two parts. The first considers the concept of ethnicity in late Aztec times, using colonial written and pictorial sources and setting the stage for the prehispanic visual evidence. It begins with a review of what is known about the nature and distribution of the named enclaves in the Basin of Mexico and the complex interactions among ethnicity, polity membership,[3] and

FIGURE 3.1.
Tizoc Stone, andesite, diameter 265 cm, made ca. 1484 for the ruler Tizoc of Tenochtitlan (Museo Nacional de Antropología, Mexico City). This sacrificial stone, called a "great stone of the sun" in Spanish colonial sources, features a solar disc on top and fifteen pairs of victor and captive figures around the sides. The whole represents the expanse of the empire. Photograph and permission to publish courtesy of the Instituto Nacional de Antropología e Historia, Mexico City.

class in the basin. Next is an examination of the gentile nouns of Nahuatl (Aztec language) that designate and sometimes conflate different types of identity. The term *gentile noun* is used by Nahuatl scholars (e.g., Andrews 1975:331–333; 2003:503–511) for a word naming a person from a particular place or a person of an ethnicity not linked to a place. Usage, however, shows a more complex picture. Other nouns of identity are formed in the same way, and even among those that refer to place of origin, the place may be generic and nonspecific (for instance, gentile nouns that refer to people who come from wetlands or live in houses). Gentile nouns are represented hieroglyphically in colonial pictorials, too. I call them *gentile glyphs*. Finally, I discuss colonial evidence on generic categories of identity, notably the categories that identify people as either Toltec or Chichimec. These two categories have ethnic as well as class implications and obvious metaphorical dimensions.

The second part of the chapter deals with the material remains found in Tenochtitlan. The two monuments mentioned above are great sacrificial stones of the sun, dating from the reigns of Motecuhzoma I and Tizoc, respectively. My primary foci are the glyphic labels that identify the captives, who represent the rulers of different places, dressed in the garb of patron deities. The glyphs, although derivative from place glyphs, are not place glyphs. They are also not personal name glyphs, so the figures must be interpreted as generic representatives of places rather than specific personages. I call them *title glyphs* to differentiate them from the gentile glyphs in manuscript versions.

Although the two monuments are similar in many respects, I describe the later Tizoc Stone (Figure 3.1) in detail because it has more information relevant to the consideration of identity in prehispanic times. In addition to having more conquest scenes and thus glyphs, it bears the Tenochca ruler Tizoc, who is named by a personal hieroglyph, among the victors. The earlier monument has four fewer scenes and lacks a figure with a personal name (see Padilla et al. 1989).

A final section presents examples of figures on Tenochca monuments that reveal further aspects of the fluidity of Aztec ideas about categories. Especially instructive examples are images of the defeated Tlatelolcatl-Huitzilopochtli on a series of artworks from the time of the fall of his polity in 1473, as well as his image on the Tizoc Stone, which was made ten years later. The Tlatelolca and Tenochca considered themselves of the same (Mexica) ethnic group that traveled from a mythic homeland under the directives of Huitzilopochtli. Thus representations of Tlatelolca-Huitzilopochtli are alternative images of the god, but seen in defeat. Although none of the images is accompanied by the name glyph of the losing ruler, Moquihuix, his persona and dynastic line are implied referents. The altered images that reveal his demoted state indicate that ethnic gods did not have just images corresponding to seasonal or cosmic changes on Tenochca political monuments. The Tlatelolcatl figure, in turn, leads to further questions about the other defeated images on the Tizoc Stone, most of which cannot be answered with current data.

In addition, the symbolic use of costumes on the Tizoc Stone cannot be extended even to other Tenochca monuments, as indicated by the Teocalli of Sacred Warfare of 1507. On this sculpture the Chichimec identity depicted on the Tizoc Stone for negative reasons is claimed by a Tenochca ruler, Motecuhzoma II, for positive reasons.

In the Aztec world ethnicity was one of many social identities (Emberling 1997:299–306), and it could be invoked in flexible ways and manipulated for various reasons during public rituals and on commemorative monuments. To us, the variations among these symbolic usages appear arbitrary and inconsistent. We wonder if there were permanent social realities or if all aspects of identity were subject to change according to context and the needs of particular times, places, and calendrical rituals. Preliminary investigations indicate the possibility that an individual had a permanent identity related to claimed origin in the distant pre-basin past, what we would call ethnic identity, and that this was something different from his or her class and polity membership. However, distinguishing actual/fixed from symbolic/mutable identities and distinguishing individual from group identities can be difficult because the different terms in colonial sources are, in fact, unexplained in these respects.

ETHNICITY AND THE BASIN OF MEXICO REGIONS

Most of the ethnic names used by the inhabitants of the Basin of Mexico were invented during the imperial period and were derived from the area they occupied (Brumfiel 1994a; see also Boone 1991). Nevertheless, following the lead of colonial authors, some scholars still accept Aztec claims that these areas bore the names of migrant groups (or they avoid the issue altogether). The numbers and names of the groups vary, but there is a general consensus on the principal ones. Gibson (1964:9) listed fourteen in the basin that he considered important. The first five were extinct groups that figured in the past (to be discussed below), but more relevant to his study of the postconquest basin were the nine surviving groups that occupied it in late Aztec times: the Culhuaque (or Culhua), Cuitlahuaca, Mixquica, Xochimilca, Chalca, Tepaneca, Acolhuaque (or Acolhua), Mexica, and Otomí.

Eight of these groups are said to have migrated from unknown places in the north and west, most from a mythical place called Aztlan or its environs.[4] The names of the eight groups came from imperial-period regions in the basin. Whatever the real histories of these regions, their names, and their populations, the people who dominated them in late Aztec times were Nahuatl-speakers and had only minor cultural variations in clothing patterns (see Anawalt 1981, 1985:5, and 1990; Berdan 1987). It is obvious in the best-documented of these regions, the Acolhua and Mexica areas, that some ancestors did migrate to the basin but that they did not call themselves by these names, that they did not speak Nahuatl, and that their cultural practices were very different from those of their descendants.

A case in point is the most prominent person of early basin history, Xolotl, the ancestral figure of the Acolhua dynasty. Little exists but modern speculation concerning his origin and language (e.g., Offner 1983:19–21). He is labeled by the generic term Chichimec, not a specific group name, and certainly not Acolhua, the name of a small city-state within the later region that took this name (see below). Colonial sources such as Durán's and Alva Ixtlilxochitl's histories document the transformation of these people from wandering migrants (barbarian Chichimecs) into civilized urban dwellers (Neo-Toltecs). The Nahuatl language, gods, ritual practices, and governmental forms of the late basin residents were acquired after they settled and intermarried with descendants of the ancient Toltecs, who occupied settlements in the southern part of the basin when the wanderers arrived (Bray 1972; Calnek 1978).

The members of the ninth group, the Otomí, are different. In contrast to the invented nature of the ethnic migration histories of the eight Nahuatl-speaking groups, the Otomí seem to be an ethnic group with a deeper history. Otomí were found in the basin regions dominated by the Nahuatl groups in late Aztec times, and they were (and are) still found in enclaves outside the basin, especially in areas to the north and west (P. Carrasco 1950). Although some became Nahuatized, others retained ancestral linguistic and cultural differences. All this implies a pre-basin history as a group. The Otomí also differ from the Nahua groups in that they did not control any of the basin territories during the century before the Spanish Conquest. Their elite had ruled the northern city-state of Xaltocan, but that was before its defeat by Tepanec Azcapotzalco in about 1395, more than thirty years before that city fell in turn to the Aztec Empire (Brumfiel 1994a; P. Carrasco 1950:257–268).

Clearly, the idea that the eight basin regions were settled by groups of the same names was a projection of late imperial, political geography on the past. The final consolidation of these regions was accomplished incrementally as the Triple Alliance empire conquered each. After conquest a region was reorganized to form part of basin-wide economic and political networks focusing, eventually, on the city that became preeminent, Tenochtitlan (Hodge 1984:especially maps on p. 27; 1996). I call these eight areas basin regions to differentiate them from the provinces of the empire's tributary system (for which, see Barlow 1949; Berdan et al. 1996).

At the time of the Spanish Conquest each basin region was dominated by a principal city-state, or capital, and included lesser city-states that in turn dominated villages and detached settlements, called *estancias* in Spanish. The smallest units were communities called *calpolli*. Otherwise there were great differences among the regions. Some calpolli and larger sections had names derived from the basin regions (and are generally considered to contain those ethnicities) and from other places, plus group names that, although also treated as ethnicities, were based on other criteria. Calpolli names such as Huitznahuac, Nonoalco, and Tlailotlacan, for instance, refer to mythic enemies, foreign-language speakers, and codex painters, respectively. These calpolli are found in different city-states and regions, and their occupants are sometimes said to be descendants of a migrating group, as in the case of the Tlailotlaque (Alva Ixtlilxochitl 1975–1977:2:32–33 [1600–1640]). Needless to say, these group names are problematic when considered to be ethnicities.

Some well-documented basin regions and altepeme had sections whose variant names indicated differences in group heritage, but other communities that are less well known may not have had such variety. Whichever situation pertained to an individual region, one might say that the basin in general was multiethnic and that groups claiming different identities dominated the respective regions and projected their corporate history back to an area of origin. Hodge (1984:18, 139) has stated that these territories were not held together by ethnicity, in the sense of a truly common past among their residents, because of the many other factors involved in their consolidation, but this sort of identity played a role in regional politics and needs to be considered for that reason.

The general name for the basin regions in the Aztec language appears in no written source. Carrasco's (1999:20) observation (derived from Molina's dictionary) that the territory of an altepetl was called *altepeianca* might be combined with his observation that a province was named for its capital, *hueialtepetl*, to yield the term *hueialtepeianca* for the regional territory itself. As for their specific names, under the same principle, five of the ethnic regions bear the same name as the head town in late imperial times: Culhuacan, Cuitlahuac, Mixquic, Xochimilco, and Mexico.

In the other three regions, all of which are larger, the political capitals at the time of the conquest seem not to have borne the regional name, and the scenarios differ in each. In the 1420s, after defeat by the powers that were soon to form the empire, the Tepaneca capital was transferred from Azcapotzalco to Tlacopan. The region itself was probably called Tepanecapan, the term given to sections occupied by Tepaneca in some cities. In the 1460s, after the Chalco region's defeat and incorporation into the empire, its capital was changed from the city-state of Chalco to Tlamanalco, but the region was still called Chalco. The late prehispanic capital of the Acolhua region, which was called Acolhua-can (Berdan and Anawalt 1992:2:40 n. 1; Motolinía 1950:32–33 [1536–1543]), was Texcoco, and if this city replaced a previous capital, the transfer was in the deep past and not recorded in historical texts.

From evidence about this region's history, a circumstantial case can be con-structed to argue that the regional name, Acolhuacan, was appended to a se-quence of cities as each became prominent. Texcoco's history as a head town is documented back to Quinatzin, a descendant of Xolotl, the founder of the dynasty that ruled in imperial times (Hicks 1982:231). Where the name Acol-huacan comes from is a matter of hypothesis. No city in the region bears it as a primary sobriquet, but according to Alva Ixtlilxochitl (1975–1977:1:299 [1600–1640]), Xolotl gave a small domain and its city-state center, Coatlichan, to one of his lieutenants, and it was then called Acohuatlychan (his spelling) Acolhuacan. The name may have been derived from the lieutenant's personal name.[5] Coatlichan still had importance at the time of the conquest as an early seat of rulers of Toltec descent. From this it might be hypothesized that the dynasty of the city was somehow ancestral to the later rulers of Texcoco, who valued its Toltec connections, that the name Acolhuacan became that of the whole territory, and that it was attached to their capital.

Hieroglyphs and their glosses in the Codex Mendoza indicate either that Texcoco was called Acolhuacan on occasion or that Acolhuacan was attached to it as a second name. The evidence is the labeling of almost identical place glyphs as Texcoco *ciudad* (city) and Acolhuacan *pueblo* (town) (Figures 3.2A and B). Such double names, combining territorial/ethnic and city names, are not unknown, as in the case of the capital itself, which was called Mexico-Tenochtitlan. As will be seen, a late capital of the Tollocan Province was called Tollocan-Matlatzinco, with Matlatzinco meaning "place of the Matlatzinca," the name of the ethnic group that dominated the area. It is possible that the same was true of the capitals of other basin regions, such as the Tepanec and Chalco areas.

Ethnicity, Polity Membership, and Class

When the ethnic terms were used to refer to people in late Aztec times, they were most often the terms of polity membership. However, it wasn't this simple: polity membership and ethnicity were intricately interrelated and difficult to separate. It is obvious, as Calnek (1976:290) and Berdan (this volume) state, that the politics of place took priority over the politics of ethnicity. The idea that polity membership was a person's primary affiliation is supported by a state-

FIGURE 3.2.
Hieroglyphs in the Codex
Mendoza (1541–1542,
Bodleian Library, Oxford)
for places with the root
consisting of a bent arm
dismembered at the
shoulder to indicate *acol-*.
(A) As part of a place
glyph glossed Tezcuco
ciudad on folio 3v. (B) As
part of an almost identical
place glyph glossed
Acolhuacan *pueblo* on
folio 5v. (C) As part of
a place glyph glossed
Acolhuacan *pueblo* on
folio 21v with additional
gloss *acolmecatl calpixqui.*
This last gloss indicates
that the tax collector of
the Acolhua Tributary
Province was located in
the town of Acolman.
(D) The place glyph for
Acolman *pueblo* on folio
3v. Drawings by the author
after Berdan and Anawalt
1992, vol. 4.

ment of the early seventeenth-century writer Chimalpahin (1965:66 [1606–1631]), first noted by Smith (1984:162): "It was the custom that when a person moved from his town and went to settle in another already established town, such a person would assume as his own name that of the town to which he had moved." Brumfiel et al. (1994:110) conclude from this quotation that "despite the historically diverse composition of Central Mexican communities, *ethnicity* [their word] served [as] a unifying ideology at the community level" (see also Smith 1984:162). I suggest that this community-level identity might be classified by modern scholars as polity membership rather than ethnicity, or at least that it may have referred to political "communities" of different scales, from calpolli to basin regions.

But this viewpoint does not answer all questions. In what ways was ethnicity in the basin something different from present or former polity membership? Did a person have a permanent ethnic identity, pointing to an origin in the past, or was his identity based solely on present residence? There is some evidence supporting an identity different from class and place of residence. In the case of the person who lived in the Mexica half (Mexicapan) of the urban center of Azcapotzalco after its downfall in 1428 (see especially Barlow 1952; Gibson 1964:38, 189, 476; and Lockhart 1992:26), his designation as Mexica was a type of permanent ethnic identity, since he no longer resided in the Mexica region. His community-level identity seems not to have eliminated this other one.

The best-studied Aztec city is, of course, Tenochtitlan,[6] the imperial capital whose rulers and gods were at the top of the imperial hierarchy. Tenochtitlan in its final form had a plural society in which different groups lived together in separate enclaves (Calnek 1976; Zantwijk 1985), and this ideal of differentiated sections is evident in the instructions Motecuhzoma I gave to the governor who led colonists from the Basin of Mexico to distant Oaxaca. He ordered that the colony be organized into barrios of Mexica, Texcocans, Tepanecs, Xochimilcas, and other groups, as in Mexico (Durán 1984:2:238 [1581]). In the colonies the ideal of division into districts based on different origins seems most apparent in the capital and in the empire's second city, Texcoco, and may not have been the rule for other cities.

Another ideal, equally important and seemingly found throughout the basin, was that of contrasting ethnic heritages of commoners and nobility. Whereas the commoners were in enclaves of separate ethnicities, theoretically descended from ancestral migrants (Chichimeca), the nobles were the result of marriages between high-status Chichimeca and Neo-Tolteca in the basin. In Tenochtitlan and Texcoco it is possible that the arrangements dominating the two classes overlapped—in other words, it is possible that the nobles also occupied calpolli in groups that were related ethnically—but this is not known. Whatever degree of multiethnicity existed in an area, the two systems of identification worked together to unite Aztec polities both vertically within a community and horizontally with other communities (Brumfiel 1994b:8; see also De Vos 1975:5–6). Within the city-state there was unity among members of the dominant ethnic group—in Tenochtitlan the Mexica ethnicity—and unity among all members of the society in terms of citizenship. Outside, unity was created among the nobility of different city-states in the basin and its near environs based on common Tolteca blood. Obviously, a dynamic situation was set up by the varying possibilities of changing loyalties according to political and economic exigencies, and this situation determined "the course of political development" (Brumfiel 1994b:8).[7]

Whatever one's level in the social hierarchy, one's identity was flexible and "situational" (Nagata 1974; Okamura 1981; Sandstrom, this volume; Stark and Chance, this volume), but class determined the number and nature of identities one could adopt. A commoner could assume the identities derived from ethnicity and polity membership, and the commoner head of a calpolli could probably take on the guise of the neighborhood patron god. However, commoners were barred from claiming other identities that pertained to beings higher in the hierarchy, just as they were barred from wearing the associated clothing.

In contrast, a noble had a large pool of guises, and the higher he was in a political hierarchy, the more identities he could assume without challenge. The ruler, as a city-state's most powerful noble, could take the identities of the city's patron god and many others. He could also adopt the garb of ancient people of both strains of his heritage, the Chichimeca as well as the Tolteca. The only restraints were imposed by those above him, either more powerful persons or the deities themselves, whose judgments were interpreted by religious specialists. Nobles could also adopt the identities of those with less political power, such as women, if it suited them to appropriate these because of other, valued associations. Or, in an inversion, they could attribute the identities of women and commoners to those under their political power, including conquered foreigners, for negative reasons. In other words, the objects of defamation, whatever their actual/original social identities, could be demoted symbolically, and their demotions were meant to contrast with the image of successful, dominant male nobles. This was true also of foreign gods; they were demoted and their images manipulated in various ways.

Specific and Generic Categories

In his list of ethnic groups important to the Basin of Mexico, Gibson (1964) named five extinct groups, the best known being the Tolteca and Chichimeca (singular Toltecatl and Chichimecatl). Although occasionally used as though they referred to specific ethnicities, as in Gibson's list, these terms and their derivatives (e.g., Teochichimeca) were also generic terms grouping together people with more specific ethnic names (on the Tolteca, see especially Davies 1977, 1980, and 1984 and D. Carrasco 1982; see also Smith's 1984 distinction between generic and specific ethnicities). The terms generalized commonalities among groups and often organized their symbolic associations in contrasting dualities. The term Tolteca symbolized civilization based on settled agricultural life, and it was often used in contrast to Chichimeca, which symbolized barbarity and the wandering life of migrants. Both terms had class implications, since the noble class was descended from marriages between the Neo-Tolteca of the basin and newly arrived Chichimeca whereas the commoner class was descended only from Chichimeca ancestors. Tolteca was also used to designate those skilled in the various arts inherited from older societies. In this last respect it was a term of occupation rather than class or ethnicity.

Sahagún's Florentine Codex makes distinctions between the Teochichimeca and other Chichimeca, with the Teochichimeca being totally unacculturated barbarians who wore animal skins and lived in caves and the other Chichimeca being partially acculturated to the basics of Tolteca life. The more acculturated Chichimeca were called also Nahuachichimeca, "those who understood, who also therefore spoke, the Nahuatl language and a barbarous tongue" (Sahagún 1950–1982:Book 10:175 [1575–1580]). It was most likely the lack of political ascendancy and the wealth that accompanied power, as well as some less civilized traits, that made the Nahuachichimeca different from true Tolteca. Chichimeca, then, was probably used for commoners and those who lacked or lost power in the Aztec present, in contrast to the more mythic and distant connotations of the wild Teochichimeca (Sahagún 1950–1982:Book 10:171–173 [1575–1580]). I say this even though Chichimecatecuhtli, "Chichimeca lord," was a title of supreme power sought by both Acolhua and Tepaneca rulers in a previous time; I do not think it was one to which the Tenochca of late imperial times aspired.

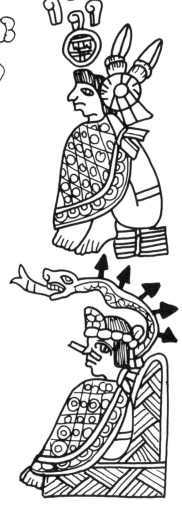

FIGURE 3.3. (*above*) Illustration in the Codex Xolotl (sixteenth century, Bibliothèque Nationale, Paris) of the thirteenth-century marriage of a parvenu Acolhua husband, in fur cape and carrying a bow and arrow (accoutrements of Sahagún's Teochichimeca), to a noble Toltec-descended wife, in cotton clothing, from one of the Neo-Tolteca basin city-states. Drawing by the author after Dibble 1980:Plate 2.

FIGURE 3.4. (*right*) Change in Tenochca regal costume symbolizing change from subordinate to independent status, as represented by Sahagún's native artists in the *Primeros Memoriales* (Códice Matritense), folio 51r (ca. 1559–1561, Real Academia de la Historia, Madrid). Chimalpopoca, the Tenochca ruler before the 1428 overthrow of his overlords, the Tepaneca of Azcapotzalco, wears a rosette of yellow parrot feathers and a brown leather cape as he sits on a bundle of reeds (probably Sahagún's Chichimeca accoutrements). Itzcoatl, the ruler after the war, wears a turquoise headdress and nose rod and a blue cape edged with red circles. He sits on a woven seat with backrest. These are all Neo-Toltec royal accoutrements. Drawing by the author after Sahagún 1997 [1559–1561].

Two very different types of non-Tolteca garb are depicted in the Codex Xo-lotl and *Primeros Memoriales*, respectively. They represent two different types of Chichimeca groups, and context explains their differences as a matter of time and acculturation. The Codex Xolotl depicts people during the early, postmi-gration period of basin history, wherein newly arrived barbarian leaders (Sa-hagún's Teochichimeca) became Toltecized through generations of intermar-riage with females from Tolteca-descended lines (Figure 3.3). The change in their culture through time is signaled by a change in costume from fur to cotton capes, the garb of the basin's Neo-Tolteca rulers. The *Primeros Memoriales* shows a similar symbolic contrast in later Aztec history, in a section that depicts the rulers of several basin cities before and after their overthrow of Tepaneca rule (Figure 3.4). Before this time the kings of Tenochtitlan are depicted in quasi-Chichimeca, quasi-Tolteca costumes. They wear cloaks, but these are not the dyed cotton capes of the Neo-Tolteca. They are labeled as made of leather, but I would guess that maguey fiber was also used—in a reference to lower status and poverty. In the illustration regal costume and appurtenances change after the War of Independence and the ascendancy of Itzcoatl, signaling the change from dependency to independence. He and all succeeding rulers wear the royal costumes of full Tolteca—the turquoise-covered, pointed "crown" and the cotton cape either beaded with real turquoises or dyed blue— and they sit on woven reed thrones with backs.[8] In these aspects the change is probably from Chichimeca to Tolteca.

Sahagún's distinction between Chichimeca and Teochichimeca is rarely made in other alphabetic sources, and the term Chichimeca usually encompasses both categories—unacculturated barbarians and their acculturated descendants. In written sources problems in the usage of Tolteca and Chichimeca are different from those arising from the specific ethnic terms. Although generic in function, they can be found mixed with terms like Mexica in colonial sources as if they too were specific ethnicities. The Tolteca are made comparable in being given a migration period, and their polity, Tollan (Tula), is treated as if it had consisted of a single ethnic group (which is unlikely).

The term Chichimeca grouped various ethnicities of individual names whereas the term Tolteca grouped together the inhabitants of ancient cities in general, many of which had the name Tollan appended to another name. Alva Ixtlilxochitl (1975–1977:1:272–273 [1600–1640]), for instance, refers to a number of ancient ruins as Tolteca. When these terms were used metaphorically to characterize people living in late Aztec times, their connotations varied somewhat from their connotations vis-à-vis people in the past. In the present they were used most often to characterize differences related to hierarchical ranking, that is, class and relative political power. In short, they were paired to symbolize the contrast between those who were ascendant and those who were subservient (as in Figure 3.4) rather than between those who were civilized and those who were barbaric (Figure 3.3). In visual representations the costumes used to express the contrast between Tolteca and Chichimeca could vary greatly, depending on the intended message of the work and on the context. It could even be evident in a contrast between the presence of Toltec accoutrements and the absence of such, rather than the presence of anything markedly Chichimec, as in the case of the monument discussed below.

However, there were significant differences between the terms Tolteca and Chichimeca even when they were used generically. Differences in types of Toltec costumes worn are not a matter of progress through time, as in the case of the Teochichimeca and Chichimeca costumes. Rather, Toltec-related garb varies according to function—depending on whether a temple, palace, processional, or battlefield setting was to be evoked.

It is well known that nobles and commoners had contrasting prerogatives (see Berdan, this volume) and that their social comparability to Tolteca and Chichimeca corresponded with actual heritage in the Basin of Mexico and the near environs. However, symbolic usage of the accoutrements pointing to these differences sometimes contradicted such realities. For instance, in Tenochtitlan when warriors lost a battle, even though they were of noble (Tolteca) birth, their demotion was expressed in the wearing of the maguey capes of Chichimeca/commoners (Durán 1994:262 [1581]). Another contrast between symbolic usage and reality pertained to wealth. Although full Tolteca/noble status was linked to wealth, in actuality some commoners, notably merchants, gained great wealth, and some nobles did not. Other exceptions to the symbolic ideal in Tenochtitlan were commoners who became nobles through merit rather than birth (P. Carrasco 1971b:354), that is, descent from the ruler Acamapichtli (Calnek 1974:202–203), the conveyer of Neo-Tolteca royal blood to the Tenochca.

Although it seems that being Tolteca always trumped being Chichimeca, this was not the case. Both terms connoted symbolic ideas of positive and negative values. On the positive side, to be a Toltecatl in the present was to be a noble who lived in a city-state and had the prerogatives and the cultural attributes of civilized behavior. Tolteca were trained and skilled in the various arts, their specific occupations depending on talent, rank, and education, as well as birth. The high ruler, the *tlatoani*, could practice arts of different sorts and had an understanding of others. He also had the ability to rule other people in the hierarchical societies of city-state life, and this ability was bolstered by the sacred powers inherent in his noble birth; his sacred responsibilities were closely intertwined with political power. As the leader of a society reliant on agricultural production, he had to influence the deities who controlled the necessary resources (such as sun and rain) through the performance of petitions involving sacrifice.

On the negative side the person of Tolteca heritage might abuse his powers, perform immoderate or immoral acts, or forget the religious obligations that came with privilege. The last-mentioned was the case when a person of Tolteca birth esteemed the wealth-value of precious objects like jade and green quetzal feathers more than he esteemed what these items represented—the water and plants that supported the life of his polity. He forgot that his wealth and power were symbolic of sacred gifts and came with responsibilities. This is the point of a well-known cautionary tale about the last Tolteca ruler, Huemac, whose misunderstanding of the true meaning of the items of wealth led to the downfall of his society:

> Then Huemac played ball. He played with the tlalocs [rain gods], and the tlalocs said to him, "What do we win?" Huemac said, "My jades, my quetzal

plumes." And then to Huemac they said, "Likewise, you win our jades, our quetzal plumes." So they played ball. Huemac won. Then the tlalocs were… about to give Huemac an ear of green corn; and instead of their quetzal plumes, the shuck in which the green ear grows. But he did not take it. He said, "Is this what I won? Wasn't it jades? Wasn't it quetzal plumes?…" So the tlalocs said, "All right. Give him the jades, the quetzal plumes."… [In] Tollan, where there was intense heat, all the trees, the prickly pears, and the magueys dried up…. And when four years of hunger had passed, the tlalocs appeared in Chapoltepec…. And then a tlaloc spirit came out of the water and said…, "The Toltec[a] are to be destroyed" [Bierhorst 1992:156–157].

In the rest of the story, which is from the Leyenda de los Soles of 1558, the Mexica take over the sacred responsibilities of the Tolteca; they sacrifice a human being to the rain gods and subsequently receive from them rain and fertility.

Just as these negative features of being like a Toltecatl are less apparent in the data on the Aztecs, so too are the positive features of being like a Chichimecatl. When contrasted with the positive features of Toltecayotl, the negative features seem obvious. It meant being a member of the commoner classes with limited resources, wealth, and rights and a lack of political power above the calpolli level. In a symbolic sense it was also associated with political loss and humiliation. But there were positive aspects of being like a Chichimecatl. It referred principally to the fierceness necessary for fighting and challenging the status quo to conquer other peoples, as in the case of the barbarian ancestors (Davies 1980:162–163; Grillo 1998:70). It is for this reason that the Toltecized rulers of the Acolhua and Tepaneca areas fought to inherit the title Chichimecatecuhtli (lord of the Chichimeca), which first pertained to the early barbarian ruler Xolotl. Thus in contexts in which relative political power was evoked, the noble might call on his Tolteca heritage to indicate his dominance and ability to rule a stratified society. Yet in contexts in which the values of poverty and barbarian fierceness were exalted, he could call on his Chichimeca past. As Schroeder (1983) says in speaking of the Chalca, who shared this strong attachment to the barbarian past with the Acolhua and Tepaneca, "Chichimeca was just about the nicest thing you could say about anyone."

I have focused on the terms Tolteca and Chichimeca, as they have important visual correspondences in the Tizoc Stone. However, other generic terms existed, such as Huitznahua (southerners). The Huitznahua were the inhabitants of a calpolli in Tenochtitlan called Huitznahuac and are generally thought to be a distinct ethnic group or a faction of the original Mexica (Zantwijk 1985:53 and elsewhere). In a sense, this is true, but I suggest that the term referred to defeated forces in general, both human and divine, regardless of ethnicity. Other terms, such as Tlailotlaque—a group of painting specialists said to be from the Mixtec area—may be generic categorizations of people who practiced certain occupations rather than people of the same heritage, just as the term Tolteca was sometimes used. Also suspicious is the term Nonoalca (or Nunualca), referring to people who spoke with an accent or possibly to civilized migrants. Although scholars sometimes treat it as an ethnic term to designate people who migrated from Tollan/Tula to the Gulf Coast, its usage indicates that it actually may have referred to people originally of various ethnicities who were grouped together. According to Coggins (2002:71), "Like Itza, Toltec, Xiu, and Chichimec, the term Nunualca…did not describe ethnic identity, but rather referred to characteristics of groups of people" (see also Davies 1977:162–164; Proskouriakoff 1974:466). In Aztec times, however, as in the case of the Tolteca, groups like these could have been reconceived as ethnicities.

Nahuatl Terms of Identity: Gentile Nouns and Glyphs

As we have seen, people are labeled with names like Mexicatl or Mexica (plural), Toltecatl or Tolteca, and Acolhuacatl or Acolhua. These are called gentile nouns by Nahuatl specialists, and an understanding of their forms in spoken language and colonial glyphs is necessary for the analysis of the prehispanic monuments. In Aztec pictography one type of hieroglyph refers to a place, and another type refers to a person from a place or ethnic group. In colonial sources the glyphs representing places consist of a root word attached to temples/houses (as in Figure 3.2A, B, and D), or they consist of just the root (as in Figure 3.2C), or they have pictographic locative endings added to the root (as in Figure 3.7C, discussed below).[9]

According to Andrews, the gentile nouns were used to "signify national, tribal, or civic affiliation" (1975:331); he later defines them as referring to "regional inhabitant names, tribal-member names, clan-member names, dweller names, building-steward names, etc." (2003:503). He avoids the word *ethnic*, using *tribe* and *clan* instead. The basic notion is that they are designations of group membership, either with or without a specific locative referent—in other words, ethnic or civic groups. A member of a polity was indicated by combining the root of the polity name with the suffix *-tlacatl* (person) or one of its derivatives, *-tecatl*, *-ecatl*, or *-catl*, instead of the locative ending that indicated the place itself. (I use the most common form, *-catl*, to stand for the group.) Andrews's (1975:332) example of a polity member is Mexicatl (spelled by him Mēxihcatl), which derived from the place-name Mexico or Mēxihco (the cities of Mexico-Tenochtitlan and Mexico-Tlatelolco combined), and the plural was Mexica (Mēxi'ca' or Mēxihcah). The singular term would be translated into English as "person from or inhabitant of Mexico." The source of an ethnic name was (presumably) not a place-name. Andrews's example is Otomitl, referring to a member of the Otomí (plural) ethnic group. The same form was used for other types of identity, for instance generic identities (Toltecatl, Chichimecatl, and Huitznahuatl) and administrative identities (Tlacochcalcatl), the latter actually having a locative base in a particular civic building.

The distinction between place glyphs and gentile glyphs is made pictorially on two folios of the Codex Mendoza (Figures 3.5 and 3.6). In the column on the right of Figure 3.4 depicting a portion of folio 2v, four pictographs repre-

quauhnahuac. pu

mizquic. pn

cuitlahuac. pu

xochimilco. pu

A **B**

FIGURE 3.5.
Differentiation between place glyphs and gentile glyphs derived from place glyphs, from page with conquests of Acamapichtli, folio 2v of the Codex Mendoza (1541–1542, Bodleian Library, Oxford). (A) Pictographs depicting people from the places pictured in the column to the right, using heads of dead captives attached to the root of the place-name. (B) Pictographs depicting the place-names themselves, with burning temples attached to the same roots. Drawing by the author after Berdan and Anawalt 1992, vol. 4.

senting the roots of words (two different trees, a comma-shaped feces on a basin of water, and a field of flowers) are attached to symbols of burning temples to render the names of four captured places. These are revealed in the glosses as Quauhnahuac pueblo, Mizquic pueblo, Cuitlahuac pueblo, and Xochimilco pueblo. In the column on the left the artist attached the same four pictographic roots to the heads of sacrificed victims resulting from these conquests. The gentile terms for these captives are spelled out on folio 42r (Figure 3.6). Here three heads attached to other pictographic roots are identified by the glosses

FIGURE 3.6.
Glyphic configurations,
like those in the previous
figure, of people attached
to place-name roots with
glosses indicating that
they represent gentile
nouns, from the Codex
Mendoza, folio 42r, list
of tribute from Tepeacac
Province. Drawing by
the author after Berdan
and Anawalt 1992, vol. 4.

as Tlaxcaltecatl (person from Tlaxcala), Chululteca[tl] (person from Chollo-lan), and Huexotzincatl (person from Huexotzinco). The hieroglyphs in the left column of folio 2v would have been read the same way, to render Quauh-nahuacatl, Mizquicatl, Cuitlahuacatl, and Xochimilcatl. Gentile labels are seen also in historical sources such as the Codex Telleriano-Remensis (Quiñones Keber 1995) and migration pictorials such as the Codex Boturini (Galarza and Libura 1999). In the migration manuscripts the gentile glyphs refer to ethnici-ties whereas in the Codex Mendoza the nouns are titles referring clearly to rep-resentatives of captured places.

The different evidences relating to the gentile nouns in the Codex Mendoza lead to questions about the nature of the being that represented a place. All evidence from pictorial or prose manuscripts, including the Codex Mendoza, is colonial and thus edited in some ways according to Western notions. In the examples pictured in the Codex Mendoza, the representatives seem totally human. However, the evidence of a combination of sources indicates that the bearers of these titles conflated human and divine characteristics. The varying contexts of usage in both pictorial and verbal texts from the colonial period seem to indicate that some were human representatives whose names were known (rulers, warriors, and ambassadors), that others were generic representatives (office holders and others of unknown names), and that still others were supernatural beings (the patron deities of polities).

The referents of the gentile nouns and glyphs in colonial manuscripts are often generic in class, as in the Codex Mendoza examples. In real life an ordinary polity member bore the gentile name, but the same terms were used as titles for the highest level of representatives of a society, and these are often the referents in accounts of warfare (Berlin-Neubart and Barlow 1980:57–58; Bierhorst 1992:113; *Historia Tolteca-Chichimeca* as quoted in Rojas 1994:421–422).

The same term is used for even more powerful beings, the patron gods of polities. In a late modern ceremonial dialogue recorded in Tepoztlan in 1977, the warrior-protagonists representing a series of towns are called Yaotepecanecatl, Cuanahuacatl, and Tlayacanecatl, and they challenge a comparable personage who lives in the mountains above Tepoztlan, the Tepoztecatl (Karttunen and Céspedes 1982). These are known as pulque gods, as a group referred to as Totochtin (rabbits); Tepoztecatl, who occupied the temple called the Tepozteco on a volcanic ridge, was their leader. The titles have been recognized as locative names for deities who had other names. Tepoztecatl, for instance, was called Ome Tochtli (Two Rabbit) in other contexts (González 1928: 21; Seler 1990–2000:4:269).

The written sources give the sense that these were supernatural figures, and modern scholars think of them as just deities. However, given the evidence that the same sorts of titles were given to humans, I would argue that their names served as titles for the rulers who represented the gods and derived powers from them. The references and illustrations above plus the translation of the suffix -*tlacatl* as "person" all indicate that the being was conceived in anthropomorphic form, but they do not define its ontological essence as human in a modern Euro-American sense. In other words, despite the distinctions in postconquest contexts which make some bearers of the title more like deities and others more like humans, these spheres were not sharply separated in Aztec thought. Politically powerful people were closely linked to the patron gods of the polities they represented; when ascending to the office, they dressed as the patron gods and took on their powers to mediate between human society and the natural and supernatural forces of the territory. The deities, in turn, were the patrons of units from calpolli size to city-state to province and empire, with the one at the top, as in the human hierarchy, being the god of the polity's dominant group.

Aztec Views of Ethnicity Outside the Basin

When the Aztecs organized newly conquered territories or viewed unconquered areas beyond their near neighbors outside the Basin of Mexico, they often encountered people who were truly different—in their languages, cultures, and claims of heritage. We know something of how the Aztecs stereotyped foreign ethnicities (see Berdan, this volume), but it is much more difficult to see what strategies they applied to the home areas of these ethnicities.

According to present evidence, the empire had a pragmatic approach to meshing together very different areas into individual political units, and solutions varied according to the local situation when they entered a territory. Reorganization involved complex negotiations with collaborator-allies who aimed at gaining power over local rivals or with defeated lords who wished to maintain their positions, or it involved the imposition of imperial administrators who were outsiders to the area (see Berdan 1996:120–124; Berdan et al. 1996). The political and economic networks were generally the same, with a few exceptions in which the tribute collection point was different from the political capital (e.g., Smith and Berdan 1996:273; see also Berdan 1996:122–124).

The expanses covered by the imperial provinces represented configurations of conquered cities and their dependents, and the empire seems not to have been as sensitive to ethnic areas outside the basin as it was to those inside.[10] Unfortunately, published information is spotty, and the role of ethnicity has not been the focus of discussions of the whole empire. Because of limitations in our understanding of the etymologies of many place-names, it is unknown whether they derive from ethnic names. Yet some offer clues. An example is seen in one place glyph and its gloss in the Codex Mendoza. This is the hieroglyphic compound labeled Tollocan, which consists of a head on a hill (Tollocan) attached to a net and the hindquarters of a person (Matlatzinco or Matlatzinca)(Figure 3.7).[11] The inclusion of the net and hindquarters pictograph seems to signify that Tollocan was also called Matlatzinco, meaning "place of the Matlatzinca," the ethnic group that dominated the area, and it is called Tollocan-Matlatzinco in some sources (P. Carrasco 1950:65, 67, 91, 108; Durán 1994:265 [1581]; see also Berdan and Anawalt 1:221–222).[12]

As in the basin, the usage of the Matlatzinca glyph also points to an area where the capital changed on occasion. Tollocan was the seat of the Matlatzinca at the time to which the Codex Mendoza refers, but a later, colonial map of the area calls Calixtlahuaca the Matlatzinca center (Hernández 1950).[13] If this capital bore the ethnic designation as a second name, it is a clear recognition of the political importance of an ethnic group. Whether the name Matlatzinco was added in Aztec times or was a local designation predating imperial arrival is unknown.

Other problems concern Aztec categorization of different classes of people in foreign places, primarily foreign rulers and nobles. The commonality of Tolteca blood in a genealogical sense was emphasized in alliances and marriages in the basin and its near environs, but dealings with nobles of other heritages at greater distances led to an expansion of the notion of Toltecayotl to encompass people who were not descended from the dynasty of Tollan/Tula but who were comparable in their civilized urban antecedents and domination of their respective areas (Sahagún 1950–1982:10:187–188 [1575–1580]).

Further questions pertain to changes in the self-identity of central Mexicans when they moved to foreign areas. The published information on colonies is vague, for the most part (see Umberger 1996b for published sources). In

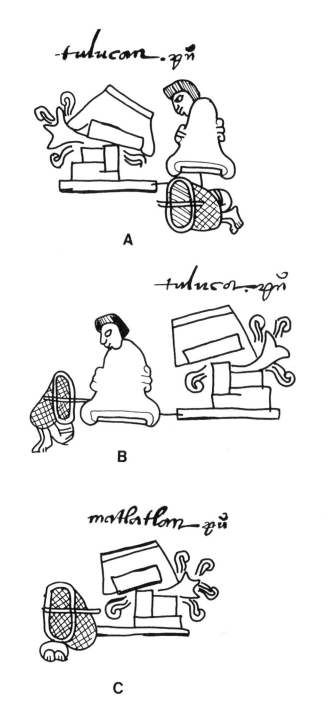

tulucan. pũ

A

tulucon. pũ

B

matlatlom. pũ

C

FIGURE 3.7. Hieroglyphs in the Codex Mendoza with a net (*matlatl*) sign. In the first two examples the significance of the net sign is not given in the glosses whereas in the third the gloss indicates that the net refers to the sound *matl-*. (A and B) Attached to place glyphs glossed Tulucan *pueblo* on folio 10v and 12r, conquests of Axayacatl. The combination of net (*matlatl*) and human hindquarters (*zintli*) probably indicates a double name, Tulucan-Matlatzinco, although the gloss does not say so. (C) Place glyph glossed Matlatlan *pueblo* on folio 10v. Drawings by the author after Berdan and Anawalt 1992, vol. 4.

their formation the ideal of division into calpolli of different groups was maintained as in basin cities, but the basis of section identity was the place of origin of a group in central Mexico. If the names that are considered ethnic in the basin are mentioned, it is because the place-name derived from that name. To what extent the barrio identities of people were retained is unknown. Alvarado Tezozomoc (1975:534–535 [1598 or early 1600s?]) gives the names of calpolli within Tenochtitlan that were the source of the noble colonists to Guerrero but says nothing about commoners or barrio identity. A map of the colonies around Tollocan (Hernández 1950) pictures how groups from different basin cities settled in separate areas, as also mentioned above. Information on the sources of colonists is not given for the Guerrero settlements, but there is an indication of long-term identity with basin city-states. In the 1940s some men near Oztoma identified themselves as descendants of colonists from Tlatelolco (Armillas 1944:166), who had settled there more than 450 years earlier. The division of these new settlements into groups from different basin territories may seem like a departure from the division based on ethnicity that seems to be the rule in the basin. However, the principle behind them may be the same. In both cases the primary consideration was place of origin, whether in a distant mythical or basin homeland.

Ethnicity in Historical Perspective

The above descriptions of ethnic patterns are idealized forms based on knowledge of how the Tenochca-Aztecs operated in central Mexico and regarded the rest of the world. What needs to be recognized is that these forms resulted from social and political changes over a period of more than 200 years (see Friedman 1992 on the importance of understanding historical changes in a group's usage of ethnic claims). Several important benchmarks had to have greatly altered Tenochca notions of heritage/ethnicity as well as those of the other groups in the Basin of Mexico. Probably the first was the consolidation of polities into units of more than one city-state and eventually the ethnic regions. The beginning date of this process is unknown, but the small expansionist empires of the fourteenth century—the Otomí, Acolhua, and Tepaneca empires—were involved. The process of defining territories continued and changed according to later events, especially upon incorporation of territories into the empire and their redefinition by the Tenochca (Brumfiel 1994a:95–96; Hodge 1996:20–23).

The introduction of the first Tolteca-style tlatoani, Acamapichtli, brought Tolteca blood and a Tolteca-derived class system to Tenochtitlan by the late fourteenth century. The War of Independence, in which the Acolhua and Mexica overthrew the Tepaneca between 1428 and 1431, reorganized relationships of dominance and subordination among these groups. Motecuhzoma I's expansion of the empire into distant places, the strengthening of class differences in Tenochca society, the rebuilding of the urban center in the style of ancient sites (López 1989; Umberger 1987b), and the activation of the charter myth of Huitzilopochtli's birth/rise at Coatepec consolidated ideas about Mexica political superiority and fortified them with ideas about values and duties inherited from revered ancient Tolteca. Finally, the 1473 Civil War, in which the Tenochca Mexica defeated their last rivals in the basin, the Tlatelolca Mexica, threw half the Mexica ethnic group into the arena of foreigners and enemies (on the Civil War, see Garduño 1997).

Despite the multifold changes in basin history over a period of more than 200 years, the development of a common culture among its inhabitants, and the complexities of the political and social organizations, it was still important to the Aztecs to maintain and organize symbolic differences among their regional groups. It seems to have been an aim of Aztec society to try to balance consolidating and divisive forces, and this tension between unity and disunity is evident in the imagery of the monuments, discussed in the next section.

THE IMAGERY OF IDENTITY ON LATE IMPERIAL ARTWORKS FROM TENOCHTITLAN

The interpretation of ethnic references in Aztec sculptures, constructed against this problematic background, is fraught with further difficulties, one being the dating of the sculptures themselves and another being the reading of the hieroglyphs of identity on them. Given the changing nature of ideas about ethnicity, the moment in history when a monument was made is crucial to its interpretation. The great monuments of Tenochtitlan are datable by rulers' name glyphs and hieroglyphic dates, archaeological context, imagery, and style to the time covered by the reigns of Motecuhzoma I and his successors, Axayacatl, Tizoc, Ahuitzotl, and Motecuhzoma II, between the years 1450 and 1521. These rulers, as the patrons of the monuments, controlled their imagery.

Monuments that illustrate Tenochca notions of identity most directly are those with anthropomorphic figures. Some have personal name glyphs, which identify them as specific historic beings; others represent the generic occupants of particular offices, with or without hieroglyphs; and still others represent anthropomorphic deity figures, again with and without hieroglyphs. In this last case deity figures are designated with the dates that indicate their calendar names or title glyphs that point to political patronage (see below). Sometimes their anthropomorphic forms can be understood as the result of their conflation with exceptional human beings, but this is not clear in all cases. In visual art we are accustomed to distinguishing between those who wear obvious costumes and those with naturally depicted supernatural elements. In the case of the former, we distinguish between everyday clothing and deity garb to define the beings who wear them. The problems inherent in these distinctions come from ethnocentric definitions of what it is to be human. Despite knowledge of prehispanic notions, we follow our sixteenth-century European-ate sources in interpreting figurative art in ways that are contrary to what we know. In Aztec thought, all humans were connected to supernatural forces in some way, and almost all the items they wore had inherent power.[14]

This aspect of anthropomorphic representation is especially clear in examples from the Tizoc Stone (Figure 3.8). The captive figures on it are apparently conflations of group leaders and patron gods. They are generic in not having specific names, but their high rank is indicated by their deity guises, details of costume, and context with a named Tenochca ruler. Their supernatural aspects are especially obvious in the representation of two as biological women rather than human males costumed like women (Figure 3.8, Captives 5 and 7). Likewise, the Tenochca ruler himself is depicted as not totally human in a late modern sense, even though identified as a historical figure by a glyph (Figure 3.9). Like the deity whose costume he wears, he lacks one foot and smoke emits from the ankle bone. This deity aspect is represented veristically, not as a costume part, and contradicts what we know about the historical person, who had both feet. These details along with obvious clothing parts, hair styles, poses, and glyphs all represent aspects of identity. Clothing pictures a mix of supernatural and political powers that allowed the wearer to operate in different settings in the Aztec world.[15] Stated another way, although the messages of monuments had primarily political purposes, those purposes were supported by religious powers.

The Tizoc Stone

The Tizoc Stone was one of the great sacrificial stones of the urban center of Tenochtitlan, and it manifests such political messages in the dressing, posing, and labeling of figures. By Tizoc's time, it had become the ideal for each ruler to commission one or two great sacrificial stones. They were considered both *temalacatls* (round stones) and *cuauhxicallis* (eagle vessels, with the eagle being the sun) because they were round and featured huge images of the sun on their upper faces. Each sacrificial stone was displayed at the city-state's center during the reign of the tlatoani who commissioned it, and it remained there until replaced by a new stone. It was then moved to a less prominent place. The victims immolated on these stones during public ceremonies were brought back to Tenochtitlan after imperial conquests in foreign areas (as in Figure 3.10), were donated by imperial provinces (as in Figure 3.6), or were taken in Flowery Wars against nearby enemies. Written documents indicate that seven

1   2   3   4   5

FIGURE 3.8. Tizoc Stone: rollout of figures on sides and solar disc on top. The numbering of the pairs of figures is traditional (e.g., Wicke 1976). It starts with (Pair 1) Tizoc and his captive and proceeds to the right around the cylinder, ending with (Pair 15) the conquest scene to Tizoc's immediate left. The captives in Pairs 5–12 appear to represent a block of Basin of Mexico polities; 13–15 and 1–4 may represent a block of polities outside the basin. Possible basin polities represented by captive figures are (5) Culhuacan; (6) Tenayuca; (7) Xochimilco; (8) Chalco; (9) unknown place, possibly Azcapotzalco city-state, if it is in the basin; (10) Acolhuacan; (11) unknown place, possibly Tepanecapan (Tepanec Province); (12) Tlatelolco (Tlaltelolco). Other polities represented by captive figures are (13) unknown place; (14) unknown place; (15) Cuetlaxtlan; (1) Matlatzinco; (2) Tochpan; (3) Ahuilizapan; (4) unknown place. The identified places in this block are outside the basin, so perhaps the entire group is outside. Drawings by the author.

| 6 | 7 | 8 | 9 | 10 |

FIGURE 3.9.
Conquerors on the Tizoc
Stone: (A) Tenochca-
Huitzilopochtli (Pair 1);
(B) one of fourteen
identical Tezcatlipoca
figures (Pairs 2–15).
Drawings by the author.

A   **B**

great sacrificial stones were made from about 1450 to 1512, but only three have been found: the Ex-Arzobispado Stone, the Tizoc Stone, and the so-called Calendar Stone. The Ex-Arzobispado Stone was carved probably before 1460 for Motecuhzoma I (Padilla et al. 1989; Umberger 1996a); the Tizoc Stone (Orozco y Berra 1877; Townsend 1979:43–49; Wicke 1976) was produced sometime before 1484 for Tizoc (Umberger 1998); and the Calendar Stone was carved before 1511–1512 for Motecuhzoma II (Beyer 1965; Umberger 1988).

The Tizoc Stone was made for use in two ceremonies anticipated by Tizoc (Figure 3.10), the first dedicating the pyramid base of his expansion of the Great Temple in 5-Flint (1484) and the second dedicating the completed temple in 8-Reed (1487) (Umberger 2002). Tizoc died before the second ceremony,

11   **12**   **13**   **14**   **15**

FIGURE 3.10. Events during which the Tizoc Stone was used, as depicted in the Codex Telleriano-Remensis (ca. 1562–1563, Bibliothèque Nationale, Paris): (A) Folio 38v, dedication ceremony and sacrifice of captives from Tzinacantepec (Matlatzinca area) at the completion of the pyramid base of the Tenochca Templo Mayor in 5 Flint 1484; (B) Folio 39r, sacrifice of victims from other areas to celebrate the completion of the whole temple in 8 Reed 1487. Note the gentile glyphs next to captive figures in Scene B. Drawings by the author after Quiñones Keber 1995.

which was conducted by his successor, but the monument's appearance indicates that he intended it for both events. The first ceremony celebrated his installation as ruler and featured the dispatch of victims he had captured during the conquest of towns in the Tollocan area. Victims from Tzinacantepec are mentioned in the gloss on folio 38v in the Codex Telleriano-Remensis (Figure 3.10A). A reference to this successful campaign is the primary scene on the Tizoc Stone, where Tizoc grasps the hair of a captive accompanied by a net pictograph indicating Matlatzinca affiliation (Figure 3.8, Pair 1). The second ceremony celebrated the completion and dedication of the temple that Tizoc had initiated in 4-Reed 1483, a date chosen because it was the anniversary of the foundation of the Triple Alliance in 4-Reed 1431. Tizoc intended it to celebrate at the same time Tenochtitlan's newly won control of the empire after victory in the 1473 Civil War with Tlatelolco. To this Ahuitzotl added the celebration of his own accession to the throne. The Telleriano-Remensis scene on folio 39r (Figure 3.10B) represents these celebrations, the captives being from Ahuitzotl's accession war.

Tizoc's intention for the monument to be used in the temple dedication is revealed in its emphasis on the expanse of the empire. It pictures Tenochca triumph over all other forces in important parts of the empire, even its Triple Alliance partners of Tepanec Tlacopan and Acolhua Texcoco. It is also apparent in the circular shape and the division of the monument into quarters by four solar rays and openings in the earth band below them. This four-part division represents the four corners of the world and echoes the layout of Tenochtitlan itself, which had four quarters divided by causeways, a layout that emphasizes the location of the city's temple precinct at the center of political and sacred space. During the ceremony, captives formed lines on the four streets/causeways as they approached the temple to be sacrificed (Townsend 1979).

On top of the Tizoc Stone is a central basin-like hollow for sacrificial blood, surrounded by the image of the sun. Around the sides fifteen pairs of figures, each consisting of a victor and a captive, signify all conquests until Tizoc's time (Wicke 1976); the captives are located between earth and sky bands. The upper band has stylized stars, and the lower band has crocodilian spines and four mouth bands lined with flint knives for teeth to symbolize the entrances to and exits from an underworld, conceived in zoomorphic terms. The setting is the empire conflated with cosmic space (Townsend 1979), and the time is the dawn of the day in the deep past when the sun of the Aztecs' Fifth Era first rose from the underworld. According to myth (Sahagún 1950–1982:Book 7:6–8 [1575–1580]), the gods assembled to wait for this new sun to appear but did not know from which direction it was to rise (thus the four possible underworld exits are emphasized). The sun finally rose in the east but stood still on the horizon. Since it lacked the energy to climb the vault of the sky, the assembled gods allowed themselves to be sacrificed by the wind god Ehecatl to give it strength; then Ehecatl blew on it. It began to move on the fourth day after its "birth"; the day was named 4-Movement, which gave the sun its name. The sustenance of the sun was afterward left to mankind, and the monument represents the Aztecs' inheritance of this duty to maintain the cosmos.

TOLTEC CONQUERORS, CHICHIMEC CAPTIVES

The monument conflates three time periods—the time of the birth of the sun, the time of the Tolteca and Chichimeca, and the time of contemporary imperial conquests of particular polities. The Tenochca-Aztec conquerors present themselves as human administrators in garb that combines the symbols of powers of two transcendent deities with parts from Toltec warrior clothing. These and the captives—foreign rulers dressed as their own patron gods—represent the assembled gods at the time of the first sunrise. But the captives are distinguished from the Tenochca in their non-Tolteca apparel. Here it becomes obvious that Tolteca identity equals political dominance, and the poses, clothing, weapons, and other paraphernalia reinforce a consistent and obvious contrast between winners and losers based on this idea.

The fifteen pairs of protagonists are posed identically, with the captor on the left grasping the hair of the captive on the right; and all carry implements of warfare, mostly atl-atls, weapons of the noble class which had solar associations. The fifteen captors are dressed identically, with the exception of the highlighted figure, the ruler Tizoc. Their costumes combine Tolteca parts—the butterfly-shaped breastplate, upright feather headdress, and triangular apron seen on the great atlantean figures at Tula—with the traits of the god Tezcatlipoca, the smoking mirror and detached foot emitting a plume (more smoke). Tizoc is the only figure on the monument labeled with a personal name glyph, a leg marked with wounds, which is to his upper left.[16] He also wears the hummingbird headdress and "starry sky" painted mask of the Tenochca-Mexica patron god Huitzilopochtli. (This mask and the sky band indicate that the figures are in darkness before the first sunrise.) The captors are unlabeled; there are no pictographs indicating places of origin, personal name glyphs, or titles.

In contrast, the fifteen captives, who have in common non-Tolteca articles such as plain loincloths to emphasize their difference from the Tolteca, have individualized costume parts as well as accompanying glyphs indicating their origins. What is seen here is the conflation of leaders and patron deities and a contrast between the winners, who are dressed as Tolteca, and the losers, who are not.

The two deities featured among the conquerors are Huitzilopochtli and Tezcatlipoca (Figure 3.9). Before the rise to dominance of Tenochtitlan, Tezcatlipoca had been the most powerful god in Aztec territory, and in this capacity he served as the patron of such important cities as Texcoco and Azcapotzalco (Alva Ixtlilxochitl 1975–1977:1:324, 351–353 [1600–1640]; Pomar 1964:163 [1582]). Despite the demotion that made Tezcatlipoca a subject of Huitzilopochtli, he was still honored as one of Huitzilopochtli's most powerful allies, and Huitzilopochtli was called a fourth Tezcatlipoca.

That Huitzilopochtli took precedence is obvious on the Tizoc Stone, where

FIGURE 3.11.
Drawings of glyphs
next to captive figures
on the Tizoc Stone.
The numbering starts
with Tizoc (Pair 1) and
continues to the right
around the monument
(as in Figure 3.8).
However, here the
glyphs are rearranged
to show the (probable)
grouping of references
to eight conquests inside
the Basin of Mexico
(Pairs 5–12) and seven
conquests outside (Pairs
13–15 and 1–4). See
glyph identifications in
Figure 3.8. Drawings
by the author.

the former is unique and identified with the ruler Tizoc and the latter is represented by multiple, identical, and unnamed images. Townsend (1979) has suggested that they represent the people who brought captives to the ceremonies during which the stone was used. More specifically, they may represent imperial generals who bore titles like Tlacochcalcatl and Tlaccatecatl, local collaborating rulers who retained or gained power over an area after Aztec arrival, or Aztec replacements in the absence of collaborators.[17] As in the case of the captives, the fact that these fourteen Tezcatlipoca figures lack personal names makes them generic officials rather than the specific occupants at a particular historical moment. Whoever they are, they are represented as serving the empire, and their identical appearance represents the virtue that explains the achievement of empire—coordinated action.

THE CAPTIVES, THEIR TITLE GLYPHS, AND THEIR DEITY GARB

As Wicke (1976) pointed out long ago, the hieroglyphs next to the captives were meant to point to different places of origin (Figure 3.11). I agree but would modify the idea that he shares with other scholars that they refer to place-names directly, that is, words with locative endings (e.g., Dibble 1971, Nicholson 1973, and others). Rather, all these pictographs should be read together with the figures to render something comparable to the gentile nouns discussed above. The reasons are the following. First, the lack of locative endings on the pictographs leaves room for alternate interpretations. Second, the pictographs are located like name glyphs next to the heads of the figures. Third, they recall the colonial manuscript glyphs with personages who represent places, but here accompanying full figures rather than just heads (and not attached to the figures by lines) (Figure 3.12).

I called them tribal glyphs in previous publications (Umberger 1998, 1999), but because the word *tribal* is problematic, limiting, and inaccurate, their designation as title glyphs is preferable. The only prehispanic examples known so

far are those on the Tizoc Stone and the Ex-Arzobispado Stone, and notions of their usage may change somewhat with added examples.

The Maya had two glyphs for titles with geographic references that are comparable in different ways to the Aztec glyph. One alludes to specific places and could be the title of a person who was not necessarily of the highest nobility. In contrast, the better-known emblem glyph was a title used only by rulers, and it had broader geographic associations, as it referred to the domain controlled by a dynasty. The size and center of power of this territory could change through time (Beliaev 2000; Mathews 1991; Mathews and Justeson 1984; Stuart and Houston 1994:3). The Aztecs do not seem to have had two glyphs of this type. The gentile glyph of colonial manuscripts resembles the emblem glyph in its reference to the breadth and variability of domains rather than the geographic specificity of city-state centers. But it resembles the other Maya title glyph in that it could refer to either a ruler of a place or someone lower in the hierarchy. Although the prehispanic Aztec examples represent only people from the highest levels of society, in practice people of indeterminate social levels could probably use it too, as seen above.

Even though the name *gentile title* seems appropriate, the word *gentile* itself is problematic because of its connotations in the English language. In addition, its use would imply that the prehispanic glyph form was totally comparable to the colonial form in usage and thus does not allow for possible differences reflective of the great changes in Aztec writing after the Spanish Conquest. The term *ethnic glyph* is also inappropriate as the examples seem to be derived from non-ethnic city names as well as those with ethnic names.

There are still many ambiguities in prehispanic Aztec glyphs, whether title or place glyphs, because differences between words are not "spelled out" by syllables or glossed the way they are in colonial sources and because phoneticism is rare on monuments (if it occurs at all). Primary among additional difficulties found in both colonial and prehispanic glyphs is our lack of knowledge of

FIGURE 3.12. Figure with *xochimil-* ("flower field") glyph on the Tizoc Stone (*right*, captive in Pair 7) compared with a similarly depicted captive in the Codex Mendoza (*left*). Both should be identified as bearing the gentile title Xochimilcatl. Drawing by the author.

the etymologies of many ethnic and place-names, which would help determine whether a pictograph is an ideograph or a phoneme.[18] Still, although there are problems with the specific interpretations of the glyphs next to the captives on the Tizoc Stone, their identification as title glyphs is reasonable.

The problems involved in specific interpretations of these glyphs are exemplified by discussions of the one depicting a dismembered arm (Figure 3.8, Captive 10). Even if we decide that this captive is from the Acolhua area in general (and this is the consensus among scholars), according to the evidence of the Codex Mendoza (Figure 3.2), the referent could be the Acolmecatl from Acolman, the Acolhuacatl from Coatlichan-Acolhuacan, or the Acolhuacatl from Texcoco-Acolhuacan.[19] My decision as to which is represented is based on their relative political importance and appropriateness. The Acolmecatl was either the imperial tax collector based in a city-state of relatively minor political status or the ruler of that place (or both) whereas the Acolhuacatl was the leader of the entire province. Because of the location of the monument in the imperial center of Tenochtitlan, it cannot represent a minor city-state, and because the figure is dressed as a god, it probably does not represent a tax collector. He must be the Acolhuacatl, who was located in Texcoco during imperial times.[20]

The same reasoning is behind the interpretation of the figure with the *matlatl* pictograph, the Matlatzincatl, who is the captive of Tizoc himself. There is even more evidence than in the former case to suppose that the referent represented a whole province, the Tollocan-Matlatzinco Province (Figure 3.7A and B). An alternative explanation is that he is the Matlacatl from the city-state of Matlatlan, a smaller polity (the place glyph is in Figure 3.7C). That the referent is Matlatzinco is supported by the Codex Telleriano Remensis depiction of the sacrifice of prisoners from Tzinacantepec, a place in that area, at the pyramid dedication of 1484. Written sources indicate that Tizoc's principal conquests during this time were a number of towns in this region.

The title glyphs accompanying figures indicate both the cities where their power was situated and the expanse of the polities that they controlled, whatever that was at a particular time. Inherent in this is the idea that some capital cities that did not bear the ethnic designation as a primary name probably had a secondary area-derived name. I would guess that in places such as the Chalca, Acolhua, Tepaneca, and Matlatzinca provinces, the province title was preferable to the city title to refer to a specific capital because of changes in location of the capitals over time. Stated in other terms, even though the glyphs on the Tizoc Stone seem to refer to a mix of polity membership and ethnic/province titles, like the gentile nouns and glyphs in colonial codices, in the end all references can be interpreted as relating to the member of a region or province, who controlled the province from a capital city.

The distinction between place-names and titles that I am emphasizing here is not as petty as it may seem. That the power of the politician who held the title often went beyond a single city-state is the obvious point, and its significance is made especially clear when one considers the glyphs that I interpret as referring to region or province titles. The territories controlled by the Matlatzin-catl and Acolhuacatl were much broader and more important than those con-trolled by the Matlacatl and Acolmecatl.

The regions on the Tizoc Stone seem to be divided into two groups, those within the Basin of Mexico and those without (as in Figure 3.11). I am following Wicke (1976) in my traditional ordering of the pairs of figures,[21] starting with Tizoc and his captive as Number 1 and proceeding to the right with Number 2. Numbers 6, 7, 8, 10, and 12 are usually identified as referring to places in the Basin of Mexico. Numbers 5 and 11, which are among them, one would suppose to be in the same vicinity. Of the seven others that are clumped together, four (15, 1, 2, and 3) can be identified fairly definitively as referring to places outside the basin, so the other four probably do too, although the two adjacent to the basin block could be unrecognized as from there also.

Most of the pictographs referring to basin places seem easier to analyze than those outside the basin because more is known about them and the com-plex interrelationships of place and ethnicity. Two of the titles (Culhuacatl and Xochimilcatl) probably refer to the head city-state, the province, and the eth-nicity simultaneously, so seem not to be problematic. A third title (Tenayucatl) is derived from a city-state name and seems not to have ethnic implications, as far as I know. In late Aztec history the city-state of Tenayuca was within a basin region with a different name, the Tepaneca region. (Of course, although Wicke [1976] demonstrated that the victories celebrated were those of all Tenochca rulers back to the War of Independence of 1428, it is still unknown whether the figures represent these polities at the time of their incorporation in the empire or during the 1480s.)

A fourth title (Tlatelolcatl) refers to the leader of a city-state of the same Mexica ethnicity as the conquering Tenochca. A fifth title (Chalcatl) refers to another basin region and either its head city before imperial conquest or the new one that was designated after conquest. The two final captives in the block of basin cities are accompanied by the dismembered arm glyph and a row of stones, respectively. As argued above, the first of these is probably the Acol-huacatl. Wicke (1976), following Barlow (1949:68), decided on Tecaxic for the second one. However, assuming that the figures stand for important places and because this is in the block of basin names, I suggest that he might be the Tepanecatl,[22] referring to that basin region. The final glyph among the basin conquests should also refer to the ruler of a basin place. It represents an ani-mal next to a hill with a top like a tipped cap, so I am tempted to identify it as referring to Azcapotzalco (ant hill place) as Azcapotzalcatl (Umberger 1998; see also Graulich 1992:6), but this is problematic as the animal looks more like a toad than an ant. If the identifications above are correct, the Tepaneca would be represented by one glyph derived from the ethnic/region name and two derived from important cities that seem not to have borne ethnic names (Azcapotzalco and Tenayuca), as far as we know, while other basin ethnicities (Colhuacan, Acolhuacan, and Xochimilco) are represented by just one figure. Apparently, some city-states were important enough to stand alone.

As for the glyphs referring to groups outside the basin, some seem to be easily identified but all are difficult to discuss because of lack of knowledge of the way in which imperial polities incorporated or overlapped with previously existing polities and ethnic areas. Easily identified are the figures representing the Tollocan Province to the near west of the Basin of Mexico (as discussed above), the Ahuilizapan city-state in central Veracruz (man splashing in pool), and the Cuetlaxtlan Province in central Veracruz (tied leather bands). The rabbit pictograph is always identified as representing the Tochpan Province in northern Veracruz.[23] The other three glyphs—the figure with a plume of smoke or mist, the figure with the sun on a mountain, and the figure with a tree growing from water—are not easily identified, but one would want them to be from important places to the near south, east, and north of Tenochtitlan, given that there were many attacks on these areas by Tizoc's predecessors. Among the figures representing provinces outside the basin, only the Matlatzinca title is clearly linked to an ethnicity.

In summary, the title glyphs include among them the representatives of polities with names that reflected claims of ethnic coherence. As argued above, these include the disputed Matlatzincatl, Acolhuacatl, and Tepanecatl, as well as the Culhuacatl, Xochimilcatl, and Chalcatl, whose places of residence are generally accepted by scholars (Figure 3.13). In all cases, whatever the source of the name, these titles are those of rulers who dominated regions, and on this monument they serve as terms more of polity membership than of ethnicity.

An important aspect of the captive figures is their deity clothing. Unfortunately, deities are dressed in many different types of costumes, so they are difficult to identify with specific names. Because Tizoc has the hummingbird headdress distinctive of the patron god of the Tenochca-Mexica and because both the leader of a group and the patron god could bear the same gentile title, the other figures must be comparable in representing a conflation of ruler with patron deity. But who are these rulers and patron gods? There are two ways of identifying them by names more specific than the locative names of the title glyphs. The first method, Wicke's (1976) iconographic method, is to examine their costume parts for clues that can be matched to named deity figures in central Mexican colonial codices. The second method is to use the names given in historical sources (Umberger 1998) and then ascertain why this personage is wearing the costume. If the first method is used, the deity parts of the Matlatzincatl figure are identified as those of one version of the Aztec god Tezcatlipoca whereas the second method would identify him as the god Coltzin, mentioned in historical sources as the Matlatzinca high god. A combination of the two methods would probably achieve the most satisfactory results, pointing to the multiple names of many of these deities. González (1928:21) noted that gods like the Tepoztecatl might have both calendric and locative names. In addition, deities could have many other names as time passed—revealing their different aspects and spheres of influence, as pointed out by such scholars as Nicholson (1971b). In the case of the Matlatzincatl the conquered ruler-god

FIGURE 3.13. Figures with ethnically derived titles from the Tizoc Stone: (A) Matlatzincatl (captive in Pair 1); (B) Culhuacatl (Pair 5); (C) Xochimilcatl (Pair 7); (D) Chalcatl (Pair 8); (E) Acolhuacatl (Pair 10); and (F) Tepanecatl? (Pair 11). Although the glyphs refer to ethnic groups, the reference is to the representative of the capital city of a polity. Drawings by the author.

was called Coltzin in his home territory, but he may have been categorized by the Tenochca as a version of their Tezcatlipoca.

Deities could be given further names, some unflattering, on changes in the political fortunes of their human representatives. Two examples from the Tizoc Stone are the Tlatelolcatl and the Matlatzincatl. During the conflict between Tenochtitlan and Tlatelolco the title Tlatelolcatl probably referred to both the ruler Moquihuix and the patron god of his city-state, who happened to be a second version of the Tenochca patron god, Huitzilopochtli. On defeat

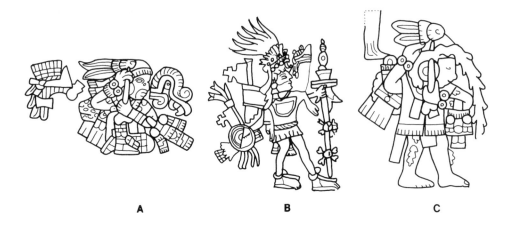

A   B   C

FIGURE 3.14. Tenochca rulers dressed as various deities: (A) Motecuhzoma II in costume combining references to Tepeyolotl and Quetzalcoatl (Hackmack Box, ca. 1506–1507, Museum für Völkerkunde, Hamburg); (B) Motecuzhoma II in costume of Xipe Totec (Codex Vaticanus A, in Anders et al. 1996:1:folio 85v); (C) Tizoc in priestly garb of Quetzalcoatl (Dedication Stone, ca. 1487, Museo Nacional de Antropología, Mexico City). Drawings by the author.

by Tenochtitlan both the ruler and the god went through name changes, most of them insulting and subordinate, such as Painal (messenger, lieutenant) and Huitznahuatl (chief loser) (Umberger 1998). The deity Matlatzincatl was called Coltzin in his home territory, and the image of this god was brought to Tenochtitlan at the time of Tenochca conquests in that area in the 1470s by a lord who, because of his alliance with the empire, was given special privileges. (This ruler, no doubt, claimed the same title.) In Tenochtitlan the deity may have been given a calpolli temple where he was called Tlamatzincatl as well as Coltzin (Durán 1994:269–270 [1581]; Sahagún 1950–1982:Book 2:171–172 [1575–1580]; Torquemada 1969:2:151 [1723]; Umberger 1996a:92).

Unfortunately, such precise information does not exist for the other deities represented on the Tizoc Stone. In these other cases Wicke's (1976) method produces other interesting results. One god that can be identified by his distinctive headdress is Otontecuhtli (Otomí Lord) (Figure 3.13F, Captive 11), a deity who seems to represent the Tepaneca Province, which had a large contingent of ethnic Otomí living in it. Wicke identifies others as additional versions of Tezcatlipoca, and if they bore one of his names as well as a local one, there are at least two possible scenarios: that the people of his home territory saw their deity as Tezcatlipoca or that he was categorized as the god by the Tenochca, as mentioned above.

The Symbolism of Identity on Other Tenochca Artworks

To further demonstrate the flexibility of identities on Aztec sculptures, I use artworks that provide variations in the representation of Tenochca and of foreign rulers. On the Tizoc Stone the Tenochca ruler is dressed as Huitzilopochtli, wearing the power attributes of Tezcatlipoca. However, this was just one of many powerful ruler guises that the Tenochca ruler took; he is said to have dressed in ceremonies as a number of other deities in addition to the city-state's patron (Broda 1976:40–41; Olivier 2003:223–224). In Aztec art various rulers are dressed in the guise of or identified with the deities Tepeyolotl (a variation of Tezcatlipoca), Xipe, and Quetzalcoatl (Figure 3.14).

If deities like Tezcatlipoca were represented as conquered by the Aztec god on some occasions, why is the Aztec king represented in their guises on other occasions? The different deity guises were worn at different points in the divinatory calendar, when the being was in power, and I suggest that there was a sequence in the calendar that reiterated the vicissitudes of "history," the rise and fall of previous gods, ending in the rise of Huitzilopochtli. This means that conquered deities were still respected (to greater or lesser degrees), and although their images were brought back to Tenochtitlan, they retained powers that were activated on particular occasions. It is apparent that deities defeated or incorporated after warfare were honored by the Tenochca, including the captured images brought back to Tenochtitlan. But in the end, Tenochca Huitzilopochtli triumphed and the foreign gods were treated in different ways: humiliated, as in the case of the conquered gods on the Tizoc Stone, or placed lower in the hierarchy of waxing and waning power, as in the case of the Tezcatlipoca victors.

A relevant depiction showing another aspect of Tenochca flexibility is on a monument of 1507 where there is a purposeful contrast between Tolteca and non-Tolteca costumes. On this sculpture, a monumental throne (Umberger 1984), the figures with the Tolteca triangular loincloth are animated deities with skeletal jaws, while the living figures above represent Huizilopochtli and Motecuhzoma (dressed as Tepeyolotl) as separate beings facing each other and wearing loincloths without the Tolteca apron (Figure 3.15). The hieroglyphic date on the roof of the temple behind them is that of the foundation of Tenochtitlan by the Mexica, so it seems that this ruler had himself depicted like the original Mexica ancestors before their acquisition of Tolteca culture and associated prerogatives and duties. This supports the idea inherent in colonial sources that the Chichimeca past was also valued.

The variety of identities that could be attributed to a non-Tenochca ruler is exhibited by a series of images of a single historical personage, Moquihuix, who lost the 1473 Civil War with Tenochtitlan. All these images were made in Tenochtitlan and identify him after his fall (unfortunately, we have no idea how he was represented in his home city-state while he was in power). Needless to say, these are all unflattering images. On no Tenochca monument is he named, but context makes it obvious that he is the referent. As seen above, on the Tizoc Stone the unnamed figure representing Tlatelolco, which could be Moquihuix, is a generic conflation of a warrior-ruler with the patron god of his city-state, and the term Tlatelolcatl refers to this conflation (Figure 3.16B). Because the god of Tlatelolco was another version of the Mexica patron god, this losing Huitzilopochtli forms an interesting contrast to the triumphant Huitzilopochtli represented by Tizoc. The Tlatelolcatl is depicted as having lost the rights of his Tolteca inheritance, but like Tizoc-Huitzilopochtli he has an atl-atl and a "starry-sky" mask, clues to his previous identity as a noble and as another representative of Huitzilopochtli; however, he lacks the definitive power attribute of the Mexica god, the hummingbird headdress, as well as the smoking

FIGURE 3.15. Tenochca self-representation as Teo-Chichimecs on front of temple on top of Teocalli of Sacred Warfare (ca. 1506–1507, Museo Nacional de Antropología, Mexico City); (B) Tolteca figures on pyramid base. Drawings by the author.

mirror and foot. In addition, his headdress may be a version of that worn by the "female" sibling who lost to Huitzilopochtli in myth, Coyolxauhqui (compare Figures 3.17A and B).

Other images made earlier, during or immediately after the Civil War, have been found in association with what I believe to be Moquihuix's funerary remains (Umberger 2007; Figure 3.17B, C, and D). These are a monumental image of Coyolxauhqui (the losing deity who wanted to rule the Mexica in myth), an image of a male deity of lower status than Huitzilopochtli on the face of the funerary urn, and a miniature image of a male Coyolxauhqui before defeat transformed him into a woman. The deity on the urn is a form of Tezcatlipoca, who, as seen above, preceded Huitzilopochtli as a powerful being in

A   **B**

FIGURE 3.16.
Winning and losing
Huitzilopochtli
figures from the Tizoc
Stone: (A) Tenochca-
Huitzilopochtli labeled
as the ruler Tizoc
by a personal name
glyph; (B) Tlatelolcatl-
Huitzilopochtli without
name glyph. Drawings
by the author.

preimperial history, so his appearance on Moquihuix's urn is another signal of the ruler's demotion in identity—a signal that he was no longer associated with Huitzilopochtli, the most powerful deity in the present.[24] That he had once been Huitzilopochtli may be signaled by the serpent in his hand, a reference to the *xiuhcoatl* (fire serpent) atl-atl unique to Huitzilopochtli (it is thus like the atl-atls on the Tizoc Stone referring to the previous Tolteca identities of the losers).

How do these images relate to questions of ethnicity? As stated at the outset, this variety of images of an ethnic patron deity, Huitzilopochtli, reveals the extent to which such images could be changed according to political fates. One wonders to what extent the other foreign god images on the Tizoc Stone were changed.

CONCLUSION

The evidence of prehispanic monuments, combined with the evidence of colonial written and pictorial manuscripts, provides a fuller picture of how identities of different sorts were manipulated for political purposes by the Tenochca Aztecs in the last fifty years before the Spanish Conquest. The colonial sources indicate that consciousness of ethnicity, based on descent from an invented group named for the regional territories of the basin, was part of Aztec identity, but also that such specific ethnicities are difficult to separate from other forms

FIGURE 3.17. Various images on Tenochca sculptures referring metaphorically to the conquered ruler Moquihuix: (A) as Tlatelolcatl-Huitzilopochtli on the Tizoc Stone; (B) as Coyolxauhqui on the Great Coyolxauhqui Stone, found in situ next to his possible funerary urn at the Templo Mayor, Tenochtitlan (ca. 1473, Museo del Templo Mayor, Mexico City); (C) as male deity figure, an aspect of Tezcatlipoca, on front of possible funerary urn of Moquihuix (1473, Museo del Templo Mayor, Mexico City); and (D) as a small male Coyolxauhqui on a greenstone pendant found in an offering cache below the Great Coyolxauhqui Stone (presumably 1473, present location unknown). Drawings by the author.

of identity, especially class and polity membership. Difficulties result from the intricate interrelationships of the categories of identity, the lack of differentiation between the Nahuatl terms that designate these categories, and their flexibility and manipulation. Only context, the particular circumstances wherein identities of different sorts were invoked, gives a clue to the political usage of different types.

Monuments made after about 1450, such as the Tizoc Stone, were used in state ceremonies before audiences of powerful people—foreign rulers and high administrators and warriors—as part of Tenochca strategies of intimidation. Because they celebrate the city's defeat of places, ethnicity is referred to only indirectly. But they reveal something that is only hinted at in colonial sources: that a person's identity could change with political rise and fall, and that generic categories rather than specific ethnicities were used to show these changes. Specific ethnic names appear only if they were in the titles of rulers, whereas it was the identity of rulers as Tolteca or Chichimeca that gives a clear and consistent message. The Tizoc Stone represents the Tenochca victors, the ruler Tizoc himself accompanied by fourteen unnamed imperial warrior-officials in archaic Toltec garb. There is no glyphic reference to their place or origin or ethnicity, this being unnecessary in a monument made for their city and representing it as the new Tollan at the center of the cosmos. The unity implied by the repetition of these costumes on all the victors is in contrast to the varied costumes of the losers, whose lack of coordinated effort was in part the cause of their downfall.

The defeated figures, the rulers of foreign territories, are identified by glyphs. It is among these glyphs that specific ethnic names are given, but when they are studied as a group it becomes apparent that the references are to areas controlled by the figures rather than to ethnic groups per se. In this respect they are actually polity membership terms. Among the rulers from the basin, four controlled the regions of Xochimilco, Acolhuacan (with the high ruler located in Texcoco), Chalco, and possibly the Tepaneca region (the ruler of Tlacopan?).[25] It seems that the Tepaneca region might have been represented additionally by the tlatoque of two traditionally powerful city-states within it: the Azcapotzalcatl and Tenayucatl. Also among the losers is the ruler of Tlatelolco, a city-state that was of the same Mexica ethnicity as the Tenochca. Outside the basin, only one title can be demonstrated to be derived from an ethnicity—the Matlatzincatl, who controlled an imperial province dominated by the Matlatzinca. This example is parallel to basin examples, such as the Acolhuacatl, who ruled the Acolhua region. Among the others, even in the cases of those whose graphemes can be identified as referring to the rulers of Ahuilizapan, Tochtlan, and Cuetlaxtlan, it is not known if these were names derived from ethnic groups or from citizenries without a dominant ethnicity. At any rate, the identification of the glyphs as referring to rulers of areas larger than single city-states recalls Marcus's (1983) observation that Mesoamericans thought in terms of rulers of domains rather than the nature or size of the domains at a particular moment in time (see also Smith 2000:587, 589).

Although the titles on the monument differ in their varied references and are thus difficult to understand, the intent of the costumes of the figures is clear. Above all, within this context Toltecayotl meant sovereignty. All these rulers were born to the Toltecized upper class, but that was not sufficient for rulership. The monument's imagery reveals that a person of noble birth, despite his genealogical heritage, could be symbolically stripped of that heritage.

Many other types of manipulation were used to indicate defeat on Tenochca artworks, as seen in a group of images that refer figuratively to Moquihuix, the losing ruler of Tlatelolco. Although on the Stone of Tizoc his defeat is pictured as a descent from Toltec to Chichimec status, the burial of his cremated remains next to the great sculpted image of the goddess Coyolxauhqui at the Templo Mayor indicates that even changes in gender could be implied with visual imagery. All these variations in the depiction of defeat were worked out with references to the supernatural powers of rulers, through their depiction either in the garb of (presumably) self-chosen patron deities or with a totally different assigned "patron" like Coyolxauhqui, chosen by the Tenochca for insulting reasons. The effective use of supernatural as well as political power was a determining characteristic of the ruler. On the Tizoc Stone the winners retain such sites of supernatural power as the smoking mirror and foot while the losers lack most of these. Their retention of the atl-atl, a weapon with solar associations, a seeming exception, points to the inability of defeated rulers to wield either form of inherited power effectively. They have failed their societies.

ACKNOWLEDGMENTS

I thank Steve Houston for information and bibliography on Maya glyphs and Barbara Stark and Elizabeth Brumfiel for careful readings and advice. I am also grateful to Barbara Stark and the other authors of this book for introducing me to the topic of ethnicity, for including me in this project, and for their insights.

4

Concepts of Ethnicity and Class
in Aztec-Period Mexico

Frances F. Berdan

CENTRAL MEXICO ON THE EVE OF THE SPANISH ARRIVAL WAS A MOSAIC of ethnic groups. Though the "Aztecs" dominated the region in an imperial fashion, the basic building blocks were numerous city-states (*altepetl*), which were often ethnic as well as political units (Lockhart 1992). This ethnic diversity was interwoven with a strong social class system, yielding a complex set of social and cultural arrangements. This chapter focuses on (1) identifying the sometimes elusive criteria and emblems indigenous peoples (particularly the Mexica) used to distinguish ethnic groups in late prehispanic times; (2) investigating the social relationships among these ethnic groups, especially in terms of community residence and social class; and (3) examining the political and territorial implications of these divisions and relationships. This discussion additionally serves as a springboard for understanding the changes in these cultural and social patterns wrought by the Spanish Conquest and continuing into modern times.

DOCUMENTARY SOURCES

This chapter relies heavily on historical sources. The documentary record is often biased and ambiguous, and the cultures themselves are loaded with contradictions and anomalies (see Chapter 1 for a discussion of such pitfalls). With few exceptions, our data on ethnicity in Aztec-period (roughly Late Postclassic) Mexico derives from colonial-period documentary sources. Fortunately, the most significant of these documents were based on native sources and informants, and the indigenous peoples were very heritage-conscious and history-oriented. This information also tends to be urban-heavy and largely from an Aztec point of view.

The major sources are the Florentine Codex (Sahagún 1950–1982 [1575–1580]) and *Primeros Memoriales* (Sahagún 1993 [1559–1561]) of the Franciscan friar Bernardino de Sahagún and the *Historia* (1994 [1581]) and *Book of Gods*

and Rites and the Ancient Calendar (1971 [1581]) by the Dominican friar Diego
Durán. Sahagún derived his materials in a rather ethnographic manner, questioning natives in the Nahuatl language. Although the questions were derived
from Sahagún's own cultural experience and background, the results (also
in Nahuatl) nonetheless reflect native views to a considerable extent. Durán,
though also speaking with living informants, based his *History* largely on the
mysterious "Crónica X," a native document, and his other works on various
"ancient pictorial documents" (Durán 1971:37–38 [1581]).

Both Sahagún and Durán wrote in the mid to late sixteenth century. Other
Spanish writers, such as Motolinía (1950 [1536–1543], 1971 [1555]) and Alonso
de Zorita (1963 [1566–1570]), discuss colonial conditions and interpolate most
of their preconquest information from their own colonial experiences. In these
and other Spanish sources the presentation of native values is often tinged with
Spanish opinions. It was popular, for instance, to consider the natives a lost tribe
of Israel, and some chroniclers (e.g., Durán) go to great lengths to establish this
identity. Not quite sure where to categorize these novel natives, Spaniards also
tended to describe them as "paradisiacal human beings"—noble yet savage—
while still recognizing them as part of a common humanity (Delgado-Gómez
1965:4, 17). In addition, indigenous information that may have been confusing
to the chroniclers is sometimes simply omitted. Motolinía, for instance, makes
a point of avoiding the history of ancient kings, explaining that "it seems unnecessary to tell of persons and names which can ill be pronounced or understood" (1950:25 [1536–1543]).

A few native chroniclers of the sixteenth century also put forth the history
of their city-states in some detail. For our purposes, most useful are the writings of the Texcocan Fernando de Alva Ixtlilxochitl (1965 [1600–1640]) and the
Chalcan Chimalpahin (Anderson and Schroeder 1997; Lockhart et al. 2006;
Schroeder 1991). These native nobles, having lost considerable power and writing under the pressures of a new regime, make unabashed efforts to establish
and affirm their hereditary rights and legitimacies; some of their discussion,
therefore, must be approached with caution.

Though providing only scattered and sparse information on native patterns of ethnicity, the few precolumbian pictorial codices nonetheless add
a touch of authenticity to our collection of pertinent sources on the subject.
For the Basin of Mexico, there are but two, the Codex Borbonicus (Nowotny
and Durand-Forest 1974) and, arguably, the Matrícula de Tributos (Berdan
and Durand-Forest 1980). The Matrícula is largely replicated in the later (and
better-preserved) tribute section of the Codex Mendoza (Berdan and Anawalt
1992), and together these sources offer tidbits of ethnic data, primarily embedded in patterns of tribute assessment, place-name glyphs, and some social representations. Other pictorials, though rendered after the Spanish Conquest,
also offer us some ethnic glimpses: for instance, the Codex Boturini (Corona
Nuñez 1964) depicts the travels and travails of the Nahua migrations, and the
illustrations accompanying the Sahagún corpus reveal some details of ethnic
identifications.

One may ask if archaeological investigations can augment the documentary record. Indeed, a good deal of work has been done on extracting ethnic data from archaeological sites (in this volume see especially Stark, Umberger, and a summary in Stark and Chance) but, alas, relatively little pertaining to the time and place under consideration here (see Bartel 1989). Archaeological research directed at questions of ethnicity includes the work of Brumfiel (1994a) in the Basin of Mexico, Stark (this volume) on the Gulf Coast, and Smith in Morelos (2000:589–590). The extensive material remains recovered from caches at the Tenochtitlan Templo Mayor (López Luján 2005) suggest some ethnically related materials in the deposits. Somewhat farther afield (in time), parallels come from the earlier site of Teotihuacan in the Basin of Mexico. So until additional concentrated archaeological efforts are made concerning the issue of ethnicity, we must rely primarily on the pictorial and textual records for this late time period. And taken together and divested of their biases and proclivities, the documentary sources yield some interesting insights into the meaning of ethnicity in pre-Spanish Mexican life. As Chance notes in Chapter 1, there is "cause for optimism."

CRITERIA FOR DEFINING ETHNICITY
IN CENTRAL MEXICO, A.D. 1519

Fundamentally, ethnicity, in its "soft" version, consists of a shared ancestry along with common cultural and religious traditions (see Grillo 1998:20 and Stark and Chance, this volume). Additionally, ethnic groups typically display visible and identifiable "emblems" of their group affiliation: language, food preferences, and clothing and other body adornments frequently serve as these overt identifying symbols (De Vos and Romanucci-Ross 1975:16). The use of ethnic categories provides people in complex worlds with one means of ordering their world; it serves as one dimension of their world view and also can affect individual behavior and political policies.

As discussed in Chapter 1, ethnic identity is not only "self-defined" but as often as not is defined by others. Ethnicity has significance only vis-à-vis recognized cultural differences with other groups and therefore pertains only in a multicultural context. In the Late Postclassic central Mexican world, one ethnic group frequently gained political and economic dominance in the society or region, thereby relegating other ethnic groups to a more subservient status. Thus the groups defined as "ethnic" also became woven into a hierarchical social class or caste system. This alerts us to be aware of not only those cultural features that ideologically or symbolically separate ethnic groups from one another but also the institutional factors that link them together into a broader social, political, and economic scheme (see especially Barth 1969).

A further complication in understanding ethnicity in Late Postclassic central Mexico involves dynamics and change: patterns of group separation, integration, dominance, and subordination tend to be unstable and even volatile. Furthermore, "ethnic identity is relative, and situational factors must also be taken into account"; and "the relevant traits are constantly changing" (Chance and Stark 2001:237, 238). Over time these dynamics may lead to ambiguities and blurring in ethnic and social categories. Such was the case in the central region of Mexico on the eve of the Spanish Conquest.

Although working in a different context (the Habsburg dynasty), Wheatcroft (1995:285) hit upon a particularly apt set of criteria for delineating distinctive group identity: common history, common interest, common enemies, and a common destiny. The first of these criteria looks to the past, and the last envisions the future; the remaining two link the group to the present in terms of internal matters (common interest) and external affairs (common enemies). To these dimensions, I would add two more. First, the primacy of place is a recurring theme in this volume and is a fundamental factor in group identity during the Late Postclassic period. Second, religion and ritual played significant roles in amplifying and accentuating ethnic identity. The flamboyancy and frequency of public ceremonial events at times displayed features of ethnic identity and stereotypes.

The Primacy of Place

Carochi (2001:219 [1645]) tells us, "From the names of provinces, cities, and settlements are derived the nouns signifying the natives and inhabitants of the said provinces, cities, and settlements." He is quite clear in stating that place is primary, person is derivative. Place, then, becomes the first dimension of identity. However, people do not always lead neatly sedentary lives, and those of Late Postclassic central Mexico were quite mobile indeed. The instability of city-state politics generated population movements as unpopular or dissatisfied groups fissioned off, founding new communities or becoming part of existing ones.

Examples abound. Consider, for instance, the aftermath of the fall of Colhuacan, when Azcapotzalco ascended to power in the Basin of Mexico: Colhua people dispersed to settle in other centers in the basin, including Cuauhtitlan, the Acolhuacan area, and even Azcapotzalco (Carrasco 1971a:465, 467; see also Carrasco 1999:134). Incessant wars and dynastic tiffs created displaced populations, along with colonization opportunities. A case in point is that of the war-devastated towns of Oztoma, Teloloapan, and Alahuiztlan (in the Aztec imperial province of Tepequacuilco), which were repopulated by settlers from the Basin of Mexico (Berdan and Anawalt 1992:2:80). In some cases, economic advantages were gained by moving to a new locale; this may have been the case with the Mixtec gold artisans who came to reside in Tenochtitlan (Smith 1996: 104), as well as the fine stoneworkers in Tenochtitlan, who reportedly originated in Xochimilco (Sahagún 1950–1982:Book 10, chap. 17 [1575–1580]). Unfortunate occurrences such as famine displaced many people at a time (Sahagún 1950–1982:Book 8:2, 3 [1575–1580]). Other unique events led to ethnic variety in a region; consider the case again of Oztoma, whose "Nahuatl speakers were left over from the time when Motecuhzoma's troops were stationed there"

(Berdan and Anawalt 1992:2:81). And the lengthy migrations of the Postclassic are well known, as groups of nomadic and seminomadic peoples migrated into central Mexico to share living spaces with resident sedentary populations. In addition to the usual (though sporadic) documentation of these events, toponymics offer some clues to these dynamics; Huexotla in the northeastern corner of Mesoamerica, for instance, contained small surrounding centers with the names Chololan and Tepehuan, suggesting immigrants from those locales or people displaying those identities (Berdan et al. 1996:293).

Among the people of central Mexico, the *calpolli* provided the paramount arena for an individual's social life, and the *altepetl* served as the fundamental social and, especially, political unit of organization. The altepetl (and its component calpolli), despite the frequently volatile nature of its internal politics, faced the world as a well-defined political institution. Many of them were multiethnic, but even among altepetl exhibiting the same general ethnicities there was incessant bickering and outright wars.

While altepetl were frequently multiethnic, the smaller calpolli more often exhibited a single ethnic composition. In multiethnic altepetl, individual ethnic groups tended to reside in separate calpolli, and it is here that ethnicity most likely took on its greatest significance (see Brumfiel 1994a; Carrasco 1971a:468, 471). At this level the ethnic dimension was combined with participation in common rituals surrounding a patron deity and his or her temple, a distinctive name linked to location or shared heritage, commonalities in historical traditions and legitimate leadership, and frequently a specialized occupation (see Lockhart 1992:16). For instance, Carrasco (1971a:468) observes, "Typical of Chalco were different ethnic groups occupying different wards within a given settlement and with a different ruler, each of whom had a distinct tecuhtli title." These overt expressions of distinctiveness, including titled leaders, would have served to reinforce the more fluid dimensions of ethnicity, grounding them in familiar social arrangements and institutions.

Common History

Elements of a shared cultural ancestry or heritage typically characterized altepetl and calpolli units. These historical and mythical links typically took the form of an origin story, adventurous peregrination, and founding legend, and often focused on a legendary leader and/or legitimized dynastic rulership (see Hicks 2001; Zantwijk 1985). The names of ethnic groups and of some locales (and, correspondingly, the names of the people residing there) sometimes derived from the names of ancestral leaders: for instance, the Tenocha (people of Tenochtitlan) were said to be associated with the early leader Tenoch; the Otomí derived from the legendary leader Oton; the Mazahua from their first leader, Mazatl tecuhtli (see Sahagún 1950–1982:Book 10:176, 184 [1575–1580], and Umberger, this volume).

Origin stories and founding legends provided the bases for the establishment and control of a territory by a group of people consisting of nobles and commoners, both ends of the social scale sharing this experience and calling forth a common past. Sahagún (1950–1982:Book 10:176 [1575–1580]) emphasizes this connection: "The name of the Otomitl comes from, is taken from, the name of him who first became the leader of the Otomí. They say his name was Oton. His children, his descendants, and his subjects were all called Otomí; a single one, Otomitl."

As to be expected, such histories focus on the experiences and feats of the leaders of migratory groups and rulers of city-states, providing an ancestral legitimacy for dynastic ascendancy and domination. Over time the notion of a common dynastic-focused heritage became somewhat blurred with the primacy of place, the altepetl. These politico-territorial units, complete with a dynastic ruler, also had their own complex dynamics: they rarely remained simply the homes of the original followers and their descendants. For instance, some altepetl accepted (or perhaps tolerated) migrants, who were outside the traditional shared ancestry of the original group (see Bierhorst 1992, Carrasco 1971a, Hodge 1984, and Schroeder 1991 for a profusion of examples). Often such groups were localized in calpolli, offering some exclusivity in terms of shared ancestries. In the end, however, residence in the altepetl generally overrode ethnic heritage in terms of one's daily life events and obligations.

Common Interest

As a defining dimension of ethnicity, common interest addresses the internal cohesive forces of the group. Several types and levels of common interest would have tugged at any person living in Late Postclassic central Mexico. These included household, calpolli, and altepetl loyalties; necessary or desired ties to a local lord or higher-level ruler; commonalities with fellow elites, fellow professionals, or fellow farmers; and frequently-expressed allegiances to a special or patron deity. Common interest also linked some communities at an imperial level: repeated involvement of already-conquered Basin of Mexico city-states in distant imperial wars yielded numerous social, political, and economic benefits to those that participated. How did ethnicity fare in this complex, dynamic realm of competing interests? I suggest that compared with these other demands and opportunities, ethnicity as a focus for common interest or action would find itself low on the list.

This does not mean that it was nonexistent or irrelevant. An element of ethnic pride, akin to altepetl and calpolli pride, may have been at work (Lockhart 1992:17). These feelings of attachment and loyalty were repeatedly reinforced through ceremonial events. Focus on patron deities at times transcended individual altepetl and represented broader ethnic allegiances: Otontecuhtli was the patron god of the Otomí, regardless of where they resided; Mixcoatl-Camaxtli was a Chichimec patron god; the Xochimilcas especially worshiped Quilaztli (Cihuacoatl); the Yopes to the south revered Xipe Totec; the Toloque and Matlatzinca worshiped a rather elusive deity, Coltzin. These patron deities had broadly ethnic, not just residential, associations. For example, the

Toloque and Matlatzinca "showed [Coltzin] honor in many ways. No others knew of him; no others glorified him; by themselves they celebrated the feast day" (Sahagún 1950–1982:Book 10:183 [1575–1580]). This element of religious and ceremonial exclusivity provided an overt expression of Matlatzinca-ness and would have helped weld them into a people sharing important commonalities. Throughout central Mexico at this time, common interests at the ethnic level may have been recognized generally and reinforced ceremonially, but it is likely that they were rarely activated during one's daily or yearly round.

Common Enemies

In the politically volatile climate of Late Postclassic central Mexico, it was common practice for one group to overtly set itself against another (or others) for purposes of political and economic advantage. Indeed, alliances and wars served as the defining dimensions of external relations for altepetl throughout the region. Inasmuch as ethnic identities were tied up in these polities, aspects of ethnicity also entered into these adversarial relations. But to what extent was an enemy defined by ethnicity? Lockhart (1992:20) speaks of "fierce rivalries and feelings of independence and superiority" in the region's "complex ethnic states" (resembling multi-altepetl confederations), implying that ethnicity was a factor in these conflicts.

It appears that in Late Postclassic central Mexican military politics, ethnicity played a minor role, bowing to factors such as economic gain, strategic advantage, and maintenance of political legitimacy. As the Mexica and their Triple Alliance allies conducted their wars of conquest, there appears to have been no particular ethnic considerations in their choices or treatments of adversaries. No special pattern, based on ethnicity, appears in a survey of tributary versus client subjects, with the exception that client city-states (as strategic provinces) tended to lie at greater geographic distances from the imperial core and likewise exhibited greater "ethnic distance." Some value judgments were involved, however. For instance, a battlefield captive from the ethnically close (Nahua) city-state of Atlixco, Huexotzinco, or Tliliuhquetepec (in the neighboring Puebla Valley) gained a Mexica warrior great renown and rewards; a captive defined as Huaxtec or another "barbarian" (Olmeca, Huixtotin, or Mixteca) brought his captor little or no recognition, even if as many as ten were taken (Sahagún 1950–1982:Book 8:77 [1575–1580]). This disparity may reflect differences in warrior incentives more than ethnic distinctions: wars with these "barbarians" were sporadic and infrequent at best whereas wars (especially of the "flowery" variety) with the Valley of Puebla peoples were common and fiercely competitive. On the ideological plane the hearty appetites of the gods apparently had a special craving for captives of recognizable culture (see below).

The matter of warfare brings up the business of battlefield booty. Distinctive warrior insignia, dripping with symbolism and worn on the battlefield, apparently became the property of the victors (although the precise disposition of this booty is not clear and may not have been the same in every instance). A well-documented case is that of the Mexica conquest of communities in the Pacific coastal region of Xoconochco. The merchant-conquerors apparently retained the rights to captured accoutrements (precious jewelry, feather fans, and clothing); the distinctive warrior regalia were presented to the Mexica ruler Ahuitzotl (Berdan and Anawalt 1992:2:116, 118–119). This insignia was the *quetzalpatzactli* and may have been distinctive to the people of the region (at least it was reportedly unknown among the Mexica before that time). Yet such insignia apparently was not so ethnically exclusive that it could not be adopted and used by another group. This quetzalpatzactli was "adopted" by Ahuitzotl (Sahagún 1950–1982:Book 9:6 [1575–1580]) and became a relatively common tribute item paid by imperial provinces at the time of the Spanish Conquest. Such martial symbolism apparently was not considered "immutable ethnic property" but could be appropriated and displayed by "outsiders" as well. This practice is reminiscent of the broad use of Huaxtec-style warrior insignia by the Mexica and their requirement that it be produced (or at least acquired) by non-Huaxtec imperial subjects for their tribute payments. The appropriation and display of such ethnically linked regalia and clothing (see below) could be interpreted as a demonstration of power, a conscious and advantageous manipulation of ethnic symbols.

Common Destiny

With an eye cast to a common destiny, an ethnic group envisions a future, even a mission of sorts. Such was the case with the Mexica: their very settlement of Tenochtitlan bespeaks of a destiny-driven people. Their long and arduous peregrination was far from random but was directed by their patron god, Huitzilopochtli (through his priests), always toward a distinct goal. That goal, the elevation of the Mexica to a position of prominence in central Mexico, motivated the Mexica to develop Tenochtitlan as the center of their cosmos and to actively undertake wars of conquest to glorify and elevate their position in the region.

In this sense of the future the Mexica were not especially different from other central Mexican groups, but their ability to take action pertinent to that vision apparently exceeded the efforts of others. Reliance on fate was a common characteristic of cultures of that time and place; it is possible that, relatively speaking, the Mexica exaggerated their perceived role in shaping or deceiving their fate. Fates could range from the personal (as in one's astrologically determined destiny) to the cosmic (as in the inevitability of the destruction of the Fifth Sun). In either case (and those in between) the Mexica strove to circumvent predetermined destinies: one's personal birth date (and attached fate) could be manipulated; human sacrifices could be enacted to ensure the continuation of the sun and its life-giving forces. This sense of a common destiny to enhance their political position and forestall these fates characterized the Mexica (especially) and accentuated their duties as "Mexica," in contrast to other ethnic groups. In turn, this active destiny orientation would have served to cement the Mexica as they pursued this common interest.

The Role of Religion

The people of prehispanic central Mexico were polytheistic, worshiping multiple deities and unabashedly borrowing each other's gods and goddesses. Yet the defined ethnic groups were accompanied by preeminent patron deities: Huitzilopochtli for the Mexica, Otontecuhtli for the Otomí, Xipe Totec for the Yopes, Camaxtli for the Tlaxcallans, and so on (see Carrasco 1971a). Hodge (1984:37) observes, "Each deity represented its group's culture and perhaps represented each group's elite lineage." These deities required special scheduled rituals in which the appropriate ethnic group figured prominently. However, since the gods were many and the rituals frequent, ethnic cooperation and ceremonial visibility seem inevitable (for instance, the role of Huaxtecs as companions to the goddess Teteo inan during the Mexica monthly festival of Ochpaniztli (Sahagún 1950–1982:Book 2:120, 122, 124 [1575–1580]). Indeed, Zantwijk (1985:261–266) argues for and documents these ethnic-related ceremonial obligations. So while specific religious beliefs and rituals accompanied ethnic groups, they also provided a forum for ethnic interaction.

The Dimensions Intertwined

These six dimensions, though presented separately here, were intricately intertwined in Late Postclassic central Mexican life. Feelings of rivalry and conflict (common enemies) were tightly woven with feelings of ethnic pride (common interest). Common interest and loyalty were reinforced by theatrical and participatory religious ceremonies. A group's fateful destiny was a continuation of its common ancestry. Such a destiny relied on internal cohesion (common interest) and external contrasts (common enemies). The links are multitudinous. And at the base of all was place.

LEVELS OF ETHNIC IDENTIFICATION
IN CENTRAL MEXICO, A.D. 1519

To this point, I have used the term Aztec off and on, but now it must be abandoned. Although Aztec is commonly used to refer to the people of central Mexico in the last couple of centuries prior to Spanish arrival, it is a generalizing misnomer and tends to mask the actual ethnic variation of the region. Aztec is often used synonymously with the inhabitants of the city of Tenochtitlan (now Mexico City), who more properly called themselves Mexica. But naming was no simple or static matter. According to Chimalpahin (Anderson and Schroeder 1997:69), "their [the Mexica's] names were Aztecs and also Mexitin. But now their name is said to [be] only Mexica. And later they arrived here taking as their name Tenochca." Even later, when high-ranking Mexica married into the esteemed Culhua ruling lineage, their name was revised yet again to

Culhua-Mexica to reflect this bonus of a "civilized" Toltec linkage. However, they did not abandon their earlier heritage, for they were also called Atlaca Chichimeca (Chichimeca who live on the water) in recognition of their Chichimeca background (Sahagún 1950–1982:10:197 [1575–1580]). Names reflected heritage, history, and self-identification and could change as a group's circumstances or goals changed.

The Mexica were originally a group of hunters and gatherers who along with several other named groups migrated from the northern deserts into the more lush valleys of central Mexico, most actively and persistently during the eleventh to thirteenth centuries A.D. These migratory groups, collectively called Chichimeca, established sedentary communities in central Mexico; among them were the Chalca of Chalco, the Tlaxcallans of Tlaxcalla, the Mexica of Tenochtitlan, and so on.

These Chichimeca settled with resident peoples, and hence we find the first broad division of peoples: Chichimeca and Tolteca, also rendered "barbaric" and "civilized" by Alva Ixtlilxochitl (1965:1:106 [1600–1640]). According to this source, Chichimecas included not only Nahuatl-speaking peoples of the Basin of Mexico but also Otomí-speaking peoples of the same region; Totonacs, Tepehuas, and Huaxtecs from the east coast; and Mazahuas and Matlatzincas living west of the basin. These groups were not uniformly "barbaric" but were further divided into Tamime and Teochichimeca (true Chichimeca; Figure 4.1). The former spoke a little Nahuatl or Otomí, were somewhat settled and grew maize as well as hunted game, but nonetheless wore only tattered capes (Sahagún 1950–1982:Book 10:171 [1575–1580]). The latter spoke a "barbarous tongue," hunted game, worked stones and feathers, wore clothing made of wild animal skins, and were pretty good at dispensing evil (Sahagún 1950–1982:Book 10:171–175 [1575–1580]). The Tolteca were considered settled peoples and descendants of a revered former civilization; according to Sahagún (1950–1982:Book 10:170 [1575–1580]), "All the Nahua, those who speak clearly, not the speakers of a barbarous tongue, are the descendants of the Tolteca." They included, among others, Culhua and Xochimilca from the Basin of Mexico, and Mixtecs and others from the south and east (Berdan 2005:9; Hodge 1984:82; Sahagún 1950–1982:Book 10:187 [1575–1580]). Late-arriving Nonoalca, associated with the Tolteca, settled in a separate calpolli of Amecameca in the southern Basin of Mexico (Hodge 1984:37). Of interest here is that there seems to be no particular pattern in terms of language affiliation or geographic location: people defined as "barbaric" and "civilized" were speaking a variety of languages, were dispersed in no special arrangement around the countryside, and exhibited mixed histories. For instance, the Xochimilca were also included among the Chichimec groups in the Aztec migration histories (Corona Nuñez 1964).

The term Chichimeca continues to appear in high-ranking titles throughout Aztec imperial history. Olko (2005:451) notes its particular Texcocan focus, emphasizing that it "expressed an essential part of the historical identity that was not perceived in terms of humble origins, but rather as a prestigious

FIGURE 4.1.
Teochichimeca (Sahagún
1950–1982:Book 10:
Figures 183, 184).
Courtesy University
of Utah Press.

affiliation." For Chimalpahin, the term Chichimeca also conveys considerable prestige in the formation of altepetl and dynastic histories: "The reference in 'Chichimeca teuhctli' is ultimately ethnic, 'Chichimeca lord,' 'lord of the Chichimeca,' but it is apparently no longer associated with a separate ethnic group or unit" (Schroeder 1991:172). It appears that by the time of the Spanish arrival, the terms Chichimeca and Tolteca were inoperable as ethnic categories and were used more metaphorically than practically: that is, someone described as a Chichimeca would be considered to display Chichimeca attributes, despite his or her actual cultural affinities or heritage; the same would hold for the term Tolteca. Both were loaded with prestigious and heritage-conscious symbolism.

A second broad division we find in the sources is between Chichimeca and "people to the east" (Sahagún 1950–1982:Book 10:197 [1575–1580]). This dichotomy divides up the world a little differently, separating peoples such as the Nonoalca and Olmeca from the Nahua, Otomí, and Purepecha of the high central valleys. Both these broad sets of divisions were based on perceived closeness of historical connections.

Beyond the gross divisions of Chichimeca/Tolteca and Chichimeca/people to the east, more specific categories of peoples are documented. So, for instance, Sahagún's informants note several culturally distinct peoples, including, among others, the Otomí, Matlatzinca, Ocuilteca, Maçauaque, Totonac,

Huaxtec, Tlalhuica, Tlappaneca, Mixteca, Michoaque, and Mexica (Sahagún 1950–1982:Book 10:176–197 [1575–1580]). Within the Basin of Mexico his informants mention several distinctly defined peoples, including the Tepaneca to the west, Acolhuaque to the east, Culhua to the southeast, and Chalcans, Mixquica, Cuitlahuaca, and Xochimilca to the south (Gibson 1964:14). There is some scholarly disagreement about the genesis and meaning of these larger groups within the Basin of Mexico. Gibson (1964) considers them to be the remains of tribal groups that migrated into the basin from the north and established themselves in geographically proximous altepetl. Brumfiel (1994a:95–96, 101–102) argues that such regional-level ethnicities emerged (through internal and/or external forces) in relation to the expansion of the Aztec state and that "ethnicity is itself shaped by political development." It is meaningful that these ethnicities appear more as categories with traits ascribed by the Aztec state (through predominantly Aztec sources) than as actual groups with their own sense of affiliation as ethnic entities.

Whatever the specifics of their genesis, all these more specific categories, with few exceptions, tended to cross-cut the most significant unit of organization in Late Postclassic Mexican life, the altepetl (but also see Chance on noble houses, this volume). Overall, these ethnic categories offered a way to identify different groups (usually from the documented Mexica point of view), and they were also charged with a mosaic of positive and negative attitudes. Although these attitudes might come into play in some interpersonal interactions (including some occupational "opportunities"—see below), general social and political decisions and behaviors showed little consideration for these categories. Elite intermarriages took place across ethnic groups, and over time the larger altepetl became multiethnic through immigration and/or conquest and subsequent resettlement (see Alva Ixtlilxochitl 1965 [1600–1640]; Berdan et al. 1996; Hodge 1984).

THE SIGNIFICANCE OF ETHNIC EMBLEMS

Our most significant sources of information, emanating from Nahua peoples who were politically dominant at the time of the Spanish Conquest, obviously take the point of view of those groups. The features used to identify these groups as ethnically distinct, then, are largely features attributed by the Mexica; our information is scant on the extent to which these (or other) attributes reflected how the members of those groups viewed themselves.

The Nahuatl language recognized the presence of "others" in the term *nepapan tlaca* ("diversas naciones de gentes"; Molina 1977:69r), yet the ethnicity of the Mexica of Tenochtitlan or the Acolhua of Texcoco (for instance) is barely mentioned or taken into consideration in discussions of the customs and characters of different groups (Sahagún 1950–1982:Book 10:168–197 [1575–1580]). In brief, the politically dominant Nahuas offer only one perspective from which attitudes are expressed; as with dialects, ethnicity is something the "other" people have. That baseline of specific values included virtues of moderation in manner and behavior, conservative dress and body adornment, hard work, courage, and respect for age and high social position (see Berdan 2005: 79–81). It is logical, then, that traits of excessiveness, vanity, laziness, cowardice, and disrespect would be held in contempt by these people. This is, indeed, what we find.

Cultural identity was overtly visible in emblems of language, clothing and other body adornments, hair styles, food preferences, and elements of technology. These attributes are summarized in Table 4.1. Groups were usually identified by clusters of these traits: so in Mexica ceremonies,

> if the song were to be intoned after the manner of Uexotzinco, they were adorned like men of Uexotzinco, and spoke even as they did; they were imitated with the song and in their adornment and their equipment.... Likewise, if a song were to be intoned after the manner of the Huaxtec, their speech was imitated, and their headdresses were taken, with which to imitate them in coloring their hair yellow; and the masks [had] arrow marks [painted] on the face, noses pierced like jug handles, teeth filed [to a point], and conical heads. And they [were clad] only in their capes [Sahagún 1950–1982:Book 8:45 (1575–1580); see also Stresser-Péan 1995:89, 91, for depictions of Huaxtecs characteristically adorned].

Together these overt emblems combined to yield a generalized image of each ethnic group. This is reminiscent of cases of staged deviance that highlight, in an amusing or theatrical display, the audience's control or "moral supremacy" over the significantly different "actors" (Savishinsky 1991). In the case of the Huaxtecs or Huaxtec impersonators, their inclusion in Mexica ritual offered the Mexica an overt and visible contrast with a group they considered less "refined" than themselves.

Language

The people of central Mexico used language as one means of segmenting their cultural world. From the dominant, prominent Nahua point of view, Nahuatl was the proper language, and indeed the term itself means "good speech." The Nahua valued flowery oratory and fine speech, and they denigrated even other Nahua who, according to their high standards, spoke the language imperfectly: "They speak a little [like] the Mexica, although not really perfectly,... they pronounce it somehow" (Sahagún 1950–1982:Book 10:175 [1575–1580]). The Annals of Cuauhtitlan (Bierhorst 1992:94) describe a Cuauhtitlan lord and his noble staff accommodated in a Huexotzinco palace: "They looked like Huexotzinca, and they went around the palace talking to each other as Huexotzinca." Non-Nahuatl-speaking groups, such as the Matlatzinca, Totonac, Yopime, and Olmeca, were considered to have "barbarous tongues" (Sahagún 1950–1982:Book 10:182, 184, 187 [1575–1580]).

TABLE 4.1. Characteristics Identifying Ethnicity in Aztec-Period Central Mexico (from the Mexica Point of View).

NAMED GROUP	LANGUAGE	CLOTHING	HAIR	FOOD	SUBSISTENCE/ TECHNOLOGY	OTHER
Tolteca	Nonoalca (Nahua peoples)	Blue capes, sandals	Like Nonoalca: shaved over foreheads (men)	Maize	Rich, cultivators & artisans	Devout, skilled, prudent, wise men, righteous
Tamime (Chichimeca)	A little Nahuatl or Otomí	Tattered capes	Men and women: long & parted in middle	Wild animals, maize	Somewhat settled; maize plots; hunting; bows & arrows; sold herbs	—
Teochichimeca	"Barbarous" tongue	Ruler: wild animal skins, feather fan; ruler's wife: skin shift & skirt. Yucca sandals. Others: deer, coyote, fox, squirrel skins	Men & women: long & parted in middle	Nopal, *tuna*, roots, cactus, honey, maguey, wild game and birds	Hunting; worked flint & obsidian & turquoise; knew herbs & peyote; tanned hides; glued feathers	Travelers, monogamous, became old (rarely sick); strong, lean, wiry, runners.
Nahua	Nahuatl (but not perfectly, like Mexica)	Elegant clothing, capes	—	Maize; distinctive food prep.	Cultivators, artisans	Able, devout, singers, feasters, prudent, industrious, adroit in speech, brave
Otomí	—	Men: capes, breech clouts, sandals; women: skirts, shifts. All good quality. Lip & ear plugs. Girls: cut short; women: forehead hair cut, rest worn long over shoulders; mature woman: hair bound about head	Small boys: cut short with tuft on back of head; men: foreheads shaven with long hair left in back	Good food & drink; maize, dried maize ears, beans, chile, salt, tomatoes, fruit tamales, cooked beans, dogs, gophers, deer, skunks, serpents, squirrels, mice, lizards, beetles, grasshoppers; *octli*	Cultivators, hunted game (rabbits, quail, deer), bored maguey; weavers of designs (but only maguey fiber)	Civilized. Untrained, uncouth, covetous, greedy; gaudy dressers, vain, lazy, shiftless, though great workers of the land (but did not gain more than needed at the moment)

Table 4.1. (continued) Characteristics Identifying Ethnicity in Aztec-Period Central Mexico (from the Mexica Point of View).

NAMED GROUP	LANGUAGE	CLOTHING	HAIR	FOOD	SUBSISTENCE/ TECHNOLOGY	OTHER
Matlatzinca (Toloque, Quaquata)	Barbarous tongue, but some spoke Nahuatl. They had the letter r.	Maguey fiber capes, breech clouts	—	Maize, beans, amaranth, fruit *atole*, popcorn, maguey wine (perhaps too much; Quatatl). No chile, salt	Adept with sling; agriculture	Strong, rugged, sinewy; presumptous, disrespectful (Quatatl); bewitchers; great workers of land; not well reared
Ocuilteca	Language not like Toloque	—	—	—	—	Like Toloque; bewitchers
Maçauaque	Distinctive (from Toloque)	—	—	—	Agriculture	Not well reared; old women paint faces and paste feathers on body; great workers of land; sinewy
Totonaque	Barbarous, though some spoke Otomí, some spoke Nahuatl, some spoke Huaxteca	Men: capes, breech clouts, sandals, necklaces, devices, fans. Women: shifts, skirts (embroidered): elegant. Commoners: blue skirts.	Cut, arranged well. Women commoners: hair strands braided with colored strips of cloth & feathers.	Cacao, herbs, tamales, tortilla (specialty), chile	Cultivated cacao, cotton, liquidambar, made reed mats & seats; women embroidered	Long-faced, broad-headed; humane, civilized; skilled in song & able in dance; women fair, tall, slender; imprudent, untrained
Huaxtec		Designed & good-quality capes; arm & leg bands, jewels, devices, fans. Women: skirts, shifts	Dyed diverse colors (red, yellow). Parted it. Men: hair hung over earlobes; tuft of hair at back of head. Women: braided with colored strips of cloth & feathers	Many different kinds of food grown there (not specified)	Cultivated *camotli*, cotton, many foods & flowers; used bow & arrows	Wide-headed, broad-headed; defects: men wore no breech clouts, perforated noses with palm leaves & decorated with stems & feathers; filed & darkened teeth; imprudent, untrained; much given to drunkenness

TABLE 4.1. (continued) Characteristics Identifying Ethnicity in Aztec-Period Central Mexico (from the Mexica Point of View).

NAMED GROUP	LANGUAGE	CLOTHING	HAIR	FOOD	SUBSISTENCE/ TECHNOLOGY	OTHER
Tlalhuica	Nahuatl	—		Maize, chile	Grew cotton, chile, maize	Imprudent & untrained, pompous, cowardly
Couixca	Nahuatl	—		—	—	Rich
Yopime	Barbarous tongue	—		—	Worked green stones	Painted themselves with red ochre; rich; untrained (worse than Otomí); wise
Olmeca (Uixtoti, Mixteca)	Barbarous tongue (also called Tenime, but also a branch of Tolteca); many spoke Nahuatl	Capes, *xicolli*, bark-paper breech clouts; women wore sandals, men wore precious sandals; rubber sandals		—	Grew cacao, rubber, flowers; acquired feathers; women embroidered; worked stones & metals; used bow, hatchet	Rich
Michoaque		Men: *xicolli*, wild animal skins	Shaved heads (Quaochpanme)	Dried maize, beans, amaranth, chia, gourds, fruit; prepared food in binges; unskilled with food	Artisans, made sandals; women: embroiderers	Men wore no breech clouts; enlarged ear & lip perforation; women wore short skirts & no tunics
Mexica	—	—	—	—	—	Uncouth (in migration)

Source: Sahagún 1950–1982:Book 10:165–197 [1575–1580].

FigURE 4.2.
Totonacs (Sahagún 1950–
1982:Book 10:Figure 195).
Courtesy University of
Utah Press.

There was apparently considerable bilingualism in central Mexico just prior
to the Spanish Conquest (see Berdan et al. 1996:Appendix 4). So there were, for
instance, Nauachichimeca who spoke a little Nahuatl, Otonchichimeca who
spoke some Otomí, and Cuextecachichimeca who knew Huaxtec as well as
their "barbarous tongue" (Sahagún 1950–1982:Book 10:175 [1575–1580]). Sahagún indicates that these persons were "civilized," settled, and had rulers. Here
language seems to provide one key to a lifestyle upgrade. We also see bilingualism among nobles of many city-states, perhaps reflecting administrative ex-
pediencies or elite intermarriage across ethnic boundaries. Such bilingualism
also spilled over into some elements of glyphic writing: the Códice de Xicotepec, for instance, depicts the name for the Totonac town Xicotepec using both
Nahuatl and Totonac elements in the same glyph (Stresser-Péan 1995:84–85).

Clothing, Warriors' Costumes, and Other Body Adornments

It has already been mentioned that one could identify a Tamime by his tattered cape or a Teochichimeca by his clothing of animal skins. In addition, the
Matlatzinca wore coarse maguey fiber capes, the Totonac wore elegantly embroidered clothing (Figure 4.2), and the Olmeca donned bark-paper breech
clouts. The Huaxtec scandalized (and fascinated) the Mexica by wearing no
breech clouts at all, as did the Michoaque, among whom the women wore
short skirts and no tunics (Bierhorst 1992:111; Sahagún 1950–1982:Book 10:189
[1575–1580]). In other aspects of bodily adornment, however, the Mexica believed the Huaxtec rather overdid it, much as the Otomí were considered vain
and gaudy dressers. Naturally, the Nahua themselves were "elegant with capes,
with clothes" (Sahagún 1950–1982:Book 10:176, 179, 183, 184, 185 [1575–1580]).
However, the Mexica were not so proud that they did not adopt a good thing
when they saw it. Gifts offered by conquered subjects and independent enemy
rulers at Mexica coronations and major religious ceremonies "could include
'local' items laden with profound symbolic messages related to the identity

FIGURE 4.3.
Cohuixca (Berdan and
Anawalt 1992:4:folio 37r).

of the givers" (Olko 2005:468). In addition, the imperial tribute lists are full
of capes and warrior costumes with ethnic-specific designs that were paid in
great quantities to the imperial overlords (Berdan and Anawalt 1992:3). On the
other hand, we are reminded of the story of the Chichimec ruler of the city-
state of Cuauhtitlan. As a reward for his loyalty, the emperor Motecuhzoma
Xocoyotzin offered this lord the costume and insignia of a Mexica warrior;
the lord refused, instead accepting gifts appropriate to a Chichimec (Hodge
1984:60).

Other features of bodily adornment characterized some groups. For instance, the people of Huexotzinco are portrayed wearing a stylized curved labret
(see Berdan and Anawalt 1992:3:folios 42r, 64r, 65r; Berdan and Durand-Forest
1980:11v; Quiñones Keber 1995:folio 43v; Stresser-Péan 1995:109), Chichimecs
are shown with cross-hatched face painting (Prem 1974:490r, 597r, 728v),
Otomí typically wore labrets made of stone (Sahagún 1950–1982:Book 10:177–
178 [1575–1580]), and at least some of the people of Morelos may have been
distinguished by metal nose ornaments (Brumfiel 1994a:99). Similarly, the
Coyuca people of the Pacific coast are depicted with a distinctive hair style,
the Cohuixca of Tepequacuilco are shown with black faces and a rod passing
over the ear (Figure 4.3), and a Totonac is depicted wearing a round blue lip
plug along with a large white ear plug and hair tied with a prominent red cord
(Berdan and Anawalt 1992:3:folios 13r, 38r, 6r, 8r, 37r; 21v; Berdan and Durand-
Forest 1980:9v, 9r, 3r). The prevalence and recognition of such overt symbols of
cultural identity should not be underestimated; the Mexica clearly recognized
their significance in sending out specialized merchants, *oztomeca*, to spy on
peoples in outlying regions; these merchants were disguised as the local people
in order to gain their confidence and obtain militarily pertinent intelligence.

In terms of technology, the Otomí were notable weavers (though only of

FIGURE 4.4.
An Otomí weaver
(Sahagún 1950–1982:
Book 10:Figure 190).
Courtesy University of
Utah Press.

FIGURE 4.5.
Ocuilteca cape (Berdan
and Anawalt 1992:4:folio
34r).

poor maguey fiber; Figure 4.4); the Totonac, Huaxtec, Olmeca, and Michoaque embroidered beautifully. These last two, along with the Yopime, were
also described as accomplished artisans (Sahagún 1950–1982:Book 10:165–197
[1575–1580]), as were the Mixteca. All these different groups not only ate, wore,
and used the products of their labors but also marketed and/or paid them in
tribute.

Particularly intriguing are the tribute payments to the Triple Alliance (or
perhaps to Tenochtitlan alone) in ethnically specific items, especially clothing and warrior costumes. For instance, three western tributary provinces
(Tollocan, Ocuilan, and Xocotitlan) all paid part of their tribute in distinctive Ocuilteca-style cloaks (Figure 4.5), glossed as *ocuiltecayo* in the Matrícula
de Tributos (Berdan and Anawalt 1992:3:33r, 34r, 35r; Berdan and Durand-
Forest 1980:34–45). Similarly, a style of cloak called *tochpanecayotl* was paid
by the people of the province of Tochpan (Berdan et al. 1996:292; Berdan and
Durand-Forest 1980:42). It is not clear how these specific cloaks were distributed or worn in the imperial capital(s).

More is understood about another ethnically specific item, the Huaxtec-
style warrior costumes. These styles, glossed *cuextecatl* in the Matrícula de

FIGURE 4.6.
Huaxtec military
costume worn by
a warrior who has
captured one enemy
in battle (Berdan and
Anawalt 1992:4:
folio 64r).

Tributos, shown in several colors and delivered by 19 geographically diverse
tributary provinces, were among the most common types of warrior costumes paid in tribute. Their distribution suggests that they were imperially imposed rather than just paid in local style (as may have been the case with the
Ocuilteca cloaks mentioned above). Interestingly, they were not paid by people
of the conquered Huaxtec provinces. Their common arrival in Tenochtitlan as
tribute could very well relate to the Mexica practice of rewarding a warrior's
second (and a priest's fourth) capture with such an outfit (Figure 4.6). Though
other tangible rewards were presented to warriors with initial captures, this is
the first and hence the most frequently given warrior costume awarded to non-
priests for enemy captures. One outcome of this practice (of tribute and subsequent distribution) was that a wide range of warriors, not just Huaxtec, were
wearing Huaxtec-style costumes on the battlefield. Here an ethnic style from
one group came into the service of social/military ranking of another, becoming recast as a socially linked symbol.

Distinctive clothing, tied to particular ethnic affiliations, was tenacious.
This tenacity is suggested by the clothing tribute of the Triple Alliance imperial province of Coayxtlahuacan, in present-day northern Oaxaca state (Berdan and Anawalt 1992:3:folio 43r; Berdan and Durand-Forest 1980:folio 12r).
Among the tribute of this rich province were three styles of cloaks: a quilted
variety with a black-and-white border, another with vertical red stripes, and a
third with vertical black stripes (800 of each annually). Each appears to have
been characteristic of specific regions (and groups) within the imperial domain: the quilted version was common in the northwestern corner of the empire, the red-striped ones were closely associated with the Ocuilteca peoples to

the west of the Basin of Mexico, and the black-and-white-striped cloaks were specific to peoples of the northeastern imperial realm. Yet each is found (and commonly enough to be rendered in tribute) in a province remote from its usual occurrence. This suggests rather strong connections between Coayxtlahuacan and these other imperial regions, most likely migrations and resettlement. Elsewhere I have suggested trade and marketplace as another explanation for the appearance of these styles in Coayxtlahuacan, but now I think that unlikely. The occasional region- or group-specific cloak may find itself traded outside its area of origin, but these quantities suggest local production by considerable numbers of weavers trained in the rendering of these specific styles (see Berdan and Anawalt 1992:2:104).

Hair Styles

An additional visible attribute in ethnic identification was hair style. To the Mexica at least, hair was not an inconsequential part of the body, since they considered the top of the head to be one of the body's major "animistic centers" (López Austin 1988:1:181–201), and the hair was an extension of this role. Also, like clothing, it is readily visible and a handy identifier. Hair style indicated marital status, warrior achievements, social station (from king to prostitute), mourning, elation, humiliation, and ethnicity. For instance, widows wore their hair loose, priests promoted to high political positions had their hair cut, other priests braided their hair with a red cord as a sign of victory and gladness, would-be priestesses allowed their short hair to grow, prostitutes wore half their hair loose and half wound about their heads, brave Cuachic (Shorn Ones) warriors had their heads shaved except for a small lock of hair above the left ear, lax warriors had their hair sheared, and kings wore their hair "as kings wore it" (Berdan and Anawalt 1992:3:folio 63r; Durán 1994:283, 287, 390, 454 [1581]; 1971:84, 138, 198 [1581]; Sahagún 1950–1982:Book 10:55 [1575–1580]). Hair styles were changed for different religious ceremonies, and the clipping or cropping of hair was also considered a beneficial curing strategy (Durán 1971:esp. 420, 443 [1581]).

Ethnic groups could be identified by hair style. The Otomí were particularly derided by the Mexica for their custom of shaving men's foreheads and leaving the hair long in the back. To the Mexica, whose valiant warriors cut that part of their hair, this style was not a positive symbol. On the other hand, the Mexica appear to have admired the elegant hairdos of the Totonac and Huaxtec women, who wore their long hair braided with colorful strips of cloth and feathers (Sahagún 1950–1982:Book 10:177, 184, 185 [1575–1580]).

Food Preferences and Technology

Some ethnic groups had distinctive food and technologies. Chichimeca were preeminent hunters and gatherers, although some of these desert dwellers were also "somewhat settled." The remaining groups discussed in detail by Sahagún's informants were sedentary cultivators, with maize their most notable crop. Yet the Mexica viewed these groups differently: the Otomí had "good food and drink," the Matlatzinca and their relatives used no chile or salt (both considered essential to the Mexica in proper food preparation) and perhaps drank too much pulque, the Totonac specialized in tortillas, and the Michoaque were "unskilled in food," which they prepared in binges. The Huaxtec definitely drank too much pulque to suit the Mexica. The Mexica, not surprisingly, had "distinctive food preparation." Differences in food preferences can be significant in identifying ethnic groups; Stark's observations (this volume) regarding changes in food preparation technology (especially the appearance of comales) suggest an archaeologically meaningful ethnic indicator.

Some ethnic groups were identified (at least by others) in terms of the use of specific, notable technologies (beyond that involved in food preparation). Thus the Matlatzinca made particularly clever use of nets and were adept with slingshots, the Chichimeca (being hunters and gatherers) characteristically carried bows and arrows, the Huaxteca used a specific style of slender bow and a "tipped arrow," and the Michoaque expertly fashioned objects from feathers, wood, and stone (Sahagún 1950–1982:Book 10:171, 182, 185, 188–189 [1575–1580]). Manufacture and use of distinctive objects, however, was complicated by the presence of lively trading and marketing activities in central Mexico just before the Spanish arrival. For instance, local styles of pottery manufacture could gain popularity elsewhere, as with the fancy Cholula polychromes that held the meals of the Mexica emperor Motecuhzoma Xocoyotzin, yet specific ceramic styles can also indicate local cultural traditions (Smith 2000).

Character

With these general characteristics and specific emblems in hand, the Mexica built notions of ethnic character. Their attitudes toward the neighboring Otomí were especially harsh. Mexica children, if they misbehaved, were admonished by being compared with Otomí: "Now thou art a miserable Otomí. Oh Otomí, how is it that thou understandest not?… Art thou perchance a real Otomí?… thou art a real Otomí, a miserable Otomí, a green-head, a thick-head, a big tuft of hair over the back of the head, an Otomí blockhead" (Sahagún 1950–1982:Book 10:178 [1575–1580]). The Mexica considered the Otomí untrained, uncouth, greedy, lazy, vain, and shiftless (Sahagún 1950–1982:Book 10:178–181 [1575–1580]). When the Mexica conquered the southern province of Coayxtlahuacan, they insulted the people there by calling them "Otomitillos" (little Otomís), although it appears that no actual Otomí lived in the area (Alvarado Tezozomoc 1975 [1598 or early 1600s?]:336; Carrasco 1979:303 [1950]). These strong opinions carried on into the colonial period, when the intoxicating pulque drink came in three grades: fine, ordinary, and Otomí (Gibson 1964:10).

Yet here we are faced with an anomaly. Although the Otomí did not meet Mexica standards for character and behavior, they were nonetheless considered "civilized" and great workers of the land, and they were sufficiently esteemed to be a designated warrior group in the Mexica military world. Similarly, the Mexica viewed the coastal Huaxteca as imprudent, untrained, and much too scantily dressed; yet Huaxtec-style warrior costumes were presented by the Mexica ruler to accomplished Mexica warriors. The Mexica seemed to have had no difficulty degrading a group on one dimension while elevating it on another. The Teochichimeca spoke a "barbarous tongue" but were knowledgeable of herbs; the Matlatzinca beat up people in nets but were adept with the sling; the Otomí were uncouth but good weavers; the Maçauaque and Matlatzinca were not well reared but were nonetheless great workers of the land. The Totonac and Huaxteca were untrained but were elegant dressers (when the latter dressed) (Sahagún 1950–1982:Book 10:165–197 [1575–1580]). Consider the Yopime (Tlapaneca): "These were completely untrained; they were just like the Otomí; yet they were really worse. These also suffered affliction. They dwelt in a land of misery; but nevertheless, [they were] knowers of green stones; [they were] people of wisdom" (Sahagún 1950–1982:Book 10:187 [1575–1580]). It seems that no group was viewed as all bad. This confounding of qualities may relate to Zantwijk's (1985:132) suggestion that there was no ethnic discrimination in central Mexico at that time.

Physical Attributes

The Mexica only rarely distinguished peoples by physical features. They did describe the Totonac as long-faced and broad-headed (and Totonac women as fair, tall, and slender), and the Huaxteca were also seen as broad-headed (Sahagún 1950–1982:Book 10:184, 185 [1575–1580]). Beyond these descriptions, a few peoples' physical attributes are mentioned only as they relate to their activities or homeland climate: the Teochichimeca were strong, lean, and good runners (being hunters and gatherers), the Matlatzinca were strong and rugged (living in cold lands), and the Maçauaque were sinewy (being hard workers of the land) (Sahagún 1950–1982:Book 10:174, 183, 184 [1575–1580]). The type of bodily adornment customarily used, including clothing, body paints, pasted feathers, ear and lip perforations, and filed teeth, seems to have superseded natural physical characteristics in defining "others."

ETHNIC RELATIONS: SEPARATION AND INTEGRATION

In central Mexico on the eve of the Spanish Conquest three criteria for group membership loomed large: community or city-state (altepetl) membership, social class, and ethnicity. Of these three, the least important appears to have been ethnicity, and ethnic groups seem to have been woven, with some flexibility, into the more basic territorial and social fabric. Nonetheless, ethnic opinions and stereotypes were certainly easily established and could have encouraged, discouraged, or textured interaction.

The Altepetl

In the context of the city-state, ethnic accommodation could be accomplished fairly neatly, as these centers were themselves divided into smaller territorial units (calpolli) and could quite readily accommodate migrant or displaced ethnic groups. Indeed, it appears that many city-states were multiethnic, and the different ethnic groups tended to be concentrated in distinct calpolli of those city-states (Hodge 1984). As Carrasco (1971b:360–61) observes, "The various ethnic components...form a series of settlements interspersed with other similar settlements of different affiliation." This arrangement had the consequence of maintaining ethnic identity, as these neighborhoods gained cohesion from not only common residence but also the worship of a common patron deity, presence of a school or schools, collective conscription for battle, and often a specialized occupation. We see similar ethnic-economic patterns in the nearby megacity of Teotihuacan, which flourished some one thousand years earlier (Rattray 1992).

Much as these ethnic groups may have been residentially separated in either time period, they were functionally integrated. They shared cooperative tasks on major building projects (Durán 1994:225 [1581]), exchanged specialized products and manufactures in marketplaces, established political and military alliances, trekked together to distant military engagements, and relied on one another for the performance of essential community-wide rituals.

Social Classes

Ethnicity was also integrated into the well-defined social class system. At the time of the Spanish Conquest, people were roughly divided into nobles and commoners, membership in either category being defined primarily by birth. The exalted noble ranks were legitimized through lineage, religious doctrine, and legal codes. Nobles maintained their status at least in part through elaborate sumptuary rules, including exclusive rights to certain types of clothing and adornment, particular ways of wearing clothes, and house sizes. The separation of nobles and commoners was quite marked: nobles and commoners were judged in separate courts, and behavior expectations were different depending on one's social station. Nobles and commoners also spoke the language differently, as Sahagún (1950–1982:Book 6:259 [1575–1580]) reminds us through the metaphor "Cease thy words. Speak not like a commoner."

As to be expected, nobles and commoners pursued different occupations, had different economic opportunities, and exhibited different standards of living. Nonetheless, there were cross-ethnic linkages. Elite intermarriage was the primary one: high-ranking individuals tended to marry other high-ranking individuals, and being of different and even distant city-states, they were sometimes of different ethnicities. Indeed, ethnic boundaries were constantly challenged in Aztec-period Mexico by this ever-common practice of elite marriages across altepetl and ethnic categorizations.

Social classes were reinforced by the profusion and demonstration of specific titles. These were most applicable, of course, at the highest rungs of the social ladder and tended to be the prerogative of the hereditary elite. Lesser titles or designations, such as those tied to specific warrior groups (eagle, jaguar, Cuachic, Otomí) or high-profile economic specialists (*pochteca, aman-*

teca, tolteca), served to highlight the achievements or professions of nobles or commoners. As with ethnically specific warrior regalia, the peoples of central Mexico seem to have had no qualms about adopting others' titles as their own. Consider the Otomí warrior group, integrated into the Mexica military order. At the highest level and just following the formation of the Triple Alliance, the Mexica ruler Itzcoatl assumed the title Culhua tecuhtli (Lord of the Culhua), the ruler of Tlacopan became Tepaneca tecuhtli (Lord of the Tepanecs), and Nezahualcoyotl of Texcoco was henceforth called Acolhua tecuhtli and Chichimeca tecuhtli (Townsend 1992:76). These exalted titles represent rule over more than just one's city-state, designating domination over an ethnically defined group of people. In the case of the Texcoco ruler, this included elevating the status of his ancient Chichimec heritage (also common in Chimalpahin's Chalco; Schroeder 1991); in the case of the Mexica king, it entailed validating his claim to Toltec descent through the Colhua line. Ethnicity seems to have been at the service of political expediency and social promotion.

Economic Dimensions

Another linkage was economic: many ethnic groups were known, even renowned, as specialists in certain activities or crafts, and these products came into high demand as tribute, consumer, or sumptuary goods. The exquisite metalwork of the Mixtec, the fine stonework of the Xochimilca, and the weavings and embroideries of the Totonac and Huaxtec come to mind. Some economic specialists, especially professional merchants and luxury artisans, not only carried some trappings of ethnic distinctiveness (specified patron deities, ceremonies, residence, adornments, and other customs) but also were emerging into a vague and dynamic social category intermediate between nobles and commoners (Berdan 2005). Inasmuch as these luxury artisans and professional merchants appear to have operated much along the lines of guilds, their ability to maintain exclusivity (in membership, knowledge, skills, and resources) was relatively great. Such specialized groups, especially embedded in a large and complex urban setting such as Tenochtitlan or Texcoco, might have maintained and even accentuated their distinctiveness where ethnicity was involved. Whereas elsewhere in Late Postclassic central Mexico considerations of ethnicity appear to have played second fiddle to other determinants of life, among some of the urban luxury specialists ethnicity may have played a consequential role in their adaptations vis-à-vis others.

Political Considerations

It should be kept in mind that different city-states were dominated by different ethnic groups: there were Mexica nobles and commoners of several ethnic groups in Tenochtitlan, Otomí nobles and various commoners in Xilotepec, Totonac nobles and various commoners in Cempoallan, and Huaxtec nobles and various commoners in coastal Tzicoac. We do not really find multiethnic clustering at the top of any one city-state's social strata; one or another ethnic group controlled a city-state's politics. But this was a highly dynamic, even volatile, moment in history. In the shifting power struggles some ethnic groups emerged as preeminent at one point, only to fall into hard times later on. Such was the case with the Otomí, who gained considerable power in the Basin of Mexico in the eleventh and twelfth centuries, only to lose that power and be demoted and deprecated by the later Nahua arrivals.

CONCLUSIONS: SOCIAL AND POLITICAL IMPLICATIONS OF ETHNICITY

So what can we say with some assurance about Aztec-period ethnicity in Late Postclassic central Mexico? First, there were recognized and culturally defined groups whose distinctiveness lay in defined locales, separate histories, special interests, traditional adversaries, historically specific destinies, and particular religious emphases, and whose overt emblems consisted of distinct languages, clothing, hair styles, food preferences, and details of technology. Of these general and specific criteria, place was primary.

Second, cutting across territorial dimensions were elements of both hierarchy and heterogeneity: social class and ethnicity. Of these two, social class emerges as the more meaningful dimension along which people established relationships and wended their way through the social milieu. Although peoples were categorized according to overt cultural criteria and common heritage, ethnicity does not appear to have been a strong determinant in ordering their lives or in directing social and political decisions. Late Postclassic central Mexican life was ordered by relationships of dominance and subordination, which were most prominently defined by social class and political control. Nonetheless, the stereotyping of certain ethnic groups (especially the nearby Otomí) by the politically dominant Mexica would have provided a clear cultural contrast and served to elevate and promote the interests and authority of the imperial rulership. And on another dimension the appropriation of ethnically specific symbols (e.g., warrior regalia and titles) by the Mexica served to advertise and even flaunt the preeminence of that imperial power.

Third, ethnicity was only a small player in ever-shifting power relations. True, value judgments were made about various peoples relative to those in political power. For instance, the imperial Mexica moral and behavioral codes provided the standards against which the Otomí, Huaxteca, and other groups were judged. At an earlier time in history, when the Mexica were humble migrants into the Basin of Mexico and the Otomí claimed some regional power, the Otomí viewed the Mexica arrivals as "evil" and "most perverse" (Anderson and Schroeder 1997:81). On a different scale, early colonial documentation contrasts the "polished people of good understanding" in urban sixteenth-century Teotihuacan with people of surrounding smaller dependent towns who were of "medium intelligence" or "well disposed but dull of understanding" (Hodge 1984:120). Yet these expressed attitudes did not seem to have major implications on the political, military, and economic stage of central Mexico. In other words, although negative attitudes were expressed toward and about certain groups (such as the Mexica toward the Otomí), these attitudes did not appear to have been embedded in social or political institutions. Such attitudes expressed a moral superiority, not a set of institutional imperatives or relations. For instance, the elaborate legal codes make no reference to ethnicity, although infringements on social class prerogatives clearly constituted seriously sanctioned offenses (Durán 1994:208–211 [1581]).

Fourth, Late Postclassic central Mexico was a competitive arena. In Chapter 1 the important point is made that "competition for resources and power is critical for ethnic maintenance." Yet the situation here was quite complex and multifaceted. City-states competed with one another for increasingly scarce resources, elites competed with one another for advantageous political alliances and marital arrangements, specialized producers competed with one another for a share of the economic pie. Competition along ethnic lines may have been felt, but it appears to have been effectively muted in the face of these other political, social, and economic imperatives. Nonetheless, as also observed in Chapter 1, this overall competitive scene provided the setting for "population movements and contacts," some of which took place along ethnic lines. Perhaps the ethnic groups most likely to have been maintained by competition were the urban "guild" luxury artisans; their ethnicity in these cases was reinforced by competition in the economic arena and an unstable (and potentially competitive) position in the social class arena.

Fifth, ethnic groups were dispersed about the landscape. This pattern had two major consequences: (1) territorial groups did not systematically develop a particular sense of unity based on their ethnicity and (2) many city-states were multiethnic. Within these city-states ethnic groups tended to be concentrated in specific neighborhoods (calpolli). There was, therefore, a sense of unity in belonging to a particular city-state (altepetl) but also a sense of physical separation in day-to-day activities. "Guilds" of certain luxury artisans, possibly immigrants and embedded in complex urban settings, may have been capable (and desirous) of maintaining their ethnic distinctiveness to a greater degree than did the general population.

Sixth, institutionalized discrimination and scapegoating along ethnic lines do not appear to have been issues. Indeed, the Mexica claimed that their gods preferred closely related Nahuatl speakers (such as Tlaxcallans) as sacrificial offerings, as they "will come to our god like warm breads, soft, tasty, straight from the fire" (Durán 1994:232 [1581]). More remotely related peoples such as the Huaxtec or Yopes were considered to be like "hard, yellowish, tasteless bread in [the god's] mouth" (Durán 1994:231 [1581]). And although it is not documented, one can hardly imagine an Otomí being palatable to such a god.

Seventh, the central Mexicans seem to have had little difficulty defining and accepting "good" and "bad" qualities for individual groups (see also Sandstrom, this volume). That is, while some groups were disparaged and denigrated, the

Nahua social system nonetheless allowed positive recognition for these same groups. So the untrained Otomí were also a cadre of highly respected warriors, and "Chichimec" was a common element in esteemed secular titles. Similarly, the Mexica were scandalized by the Huaxtecs' lack of attire and generally shameful behavior, but Huaxtec-style warrior regalia was highly valued, demanded from conquered provinces throughout the empire, and awarded to valiant warriors. On one dimension a single group may be deprecated; on another, validated and esteemed.

In all, this confounding of qualities helps explain apparent anomalies in central Mexican cultures and ethnic relations. Consider the Mexica themselves as the ultimate example. At some point in their hectic history the Mexica became sophisticated urbanites and relegated their "Chichimec-ness" to just one of many ingredients in their complex heritage. But they did not abandon it; they recast it. As 1519 Chichimecs, the Mexica were fierce and stalwart warriors, not desert dwellers wearing tattered capes, hunting game, and speaking a "barbarous tongue." An essential characteristic of their ethnicity was retained but became selectively defined and muted in favor of other emerging (Toltec) features that gained them political legitimacy in their expanding urban and imperial setting. These considerations help account for the apparent blurring and vagueness in ethnic categories and emphasize the dynamics of ethnic relations in central Mexico on the eve of the Spanish Conquest.

After that conquest some fundamental changes occurred in the arena of ethnicity. New economic, social, and political complexities faced the indigenous peoples, and many of their adaptations to these changes involved ethnic identities and an introduced concept, race. During the colonial period native peoples retained many continuities from the past but also made strategic adjustments to their new situation under Spanish rule. These important transformations are unraveled by John Chance in the next chapter.

5

Indigenous Ethnicity in Colonial Central Mexico

John K. Chance

T HE SPANISH INVASION IN 1519 AND THE SUBSEQUENT THREE CEN-
turies of colonization introduced new cultural and political economic contexts for the fashioning of ethnic identities of the indigenous peoples of central
Mexico. The political superstructures of the Aztec Empire and other, smaller
states were replaced by the colony of New Spain, predicated on European notions of government and how people ought to live. This change did not hap-
pen overnight, of course, and in some areas it took the Spanish decades to pacify local populations and introduce a semblance of colonial control. But even
in the Aztec heartland of central Mexico, which quickly became the center
of Spanish power and population, colonial rule provided considerable room
for the expression of aspects of traditional indigenous ethnicity. In rural settlements lacking significant Spanish population, the colonial experience was
in many respects one of indirect rule. The continuing strength of indigenous
communities, colonial goals of economic extraction, and weaknesses in Spanish political control led the colonial government to operate by appeasement in
many regions (Taylor 1979:168). Indigenous accommodation to colonial rule
took place, but there was also ample space for social and cultural continuity,
negotiation, and assertion of local prerogatives. Where the expression of ethnicity was concerned, there was an "ethnic dialectic" (Grillo 1998:117) between
ongoing practices of self-identification and new ethnic categories imposed
by the colonial government and Spanish elites. From this vantage point I assess recent work on indigenous ethnicity in Nahuatl-speaking colonial central
Mexico and present a case study concerning noble identity in Santiago Tecali
in the Valley of Puebla.

After 1519 the Nahuas of central Mexico surely found much that was familiar in the newly emergent colonial society. Both pre- and postconquest social
formations were hierarchically ordered, and subjects were accorded unequal
social statuses with different legal rights and privileges. Spanish policy, however, introduced several new features that had no precedents in Mesoamerican

culture. Spaniards and Indians were to live in separate communities, lead separate lives, and be subject to separate legal codes. As conquered subjects, Indians were regarded by the colonizers as inferior beings, ranked at the bottom of the colonial social order. The native nobility, as we shall see, occupied an ambiguous status. Indigenous nobles enjoyed special recognition and privileges, but in other respects they were still Indians—and hence inferior—in the Spanish view.

As offspring of mixed Spanish, Indian, and black African parentage began to appear, European concepts of race came increasingly into play. The colonialist image of Mexican society was codified in the *sistema de castas* (system of "castes") in which ethnic and racial strata were given legal definition, rights, and privileges along the lines of estates of nobles and commoners in Europe. The Mexican version was just as hierarchical but more complex, with Spaniards at the top, Indians at the bottom, and mestizos, mulattoes, and blacks in between (Chance 1978:126–127).

The study of indigenous ethnic identity in colonial Mexico has traditionally been a difficult topic, and the literature dealing with it is small. Sources written in Spanish by Spaniards and other non-Indians may reveal imposed categorical identities, but they typically give little indication of the self-identifications made by colonized populations. Fortunately, the situation has begun to change as ethnohistorians have learned to utilize a variety of indigenous-language documentation, written primarily in Nahuatl, Mixtec, Zapotec, and Maya. These sources were written by Indians for their own purposes, and they provide glimpses of the indigenous point of view in many areas of colonial life, insights that are difficult or sometimes impossible to detect in Spanish sources. As we shall see, studies employing Nahuatl sources have emphasized the persistence of aspects of indigenous ethnicity into late colonial times. However, there were significant changes in self-identification as well, particularly among some Indian elites.

To understand the expression of ethnicity in colonial Mexico, we must also take into account Indian interactions with non-Indians and with the colonial Spanish state, for these two areas formed important contexts in which identities were negotiated. To say that indigenous ethnicity in colonial Mexico was conditioned by domination is to state the obvious, though important questions have been raised about the degree of hegemony exercised by the state. My research on Santiago Tecali in the Valley of Puebla illustrates how active agency and political competition by one local indigenous elite produced a new form of ethnic expression in the eighteenth century.

ETHNICITY IN PREHISPANIC CENTRAL MEXICO

Ethnic identities are formed in historical contexts, and in order to understand ethnicity during the Mexican colonial period we must first look briefly at the situation that preceded it. Berdan (this volume) shows that in Aztec central Mexico in 1519 the terms Chichimeca and Tolteca as glosses for barbaric and civilized peoples no longer functioned as ethnic categories. She distinguishes three intersecting planes of self-identification: with the ethnic group, with the *altepetl* (city-state), and with one's noble or commoner class (or estate). All subregions and altepetl included people of diverse ethnic identities with different origins, cultural traditions, and roles in the division of labor (Carrasco 1971a:462). Hicks (2001:390–391) provides a list of 27 major ethnic groups in central Mexico in late prehispanic times. The names of the larger ones were frequently derived from their altepetl of residence (such as the Mexica, Acolhua, and Tepanec), although the states themselves were often named for the ethnic groups that established their ruling dynasties. Smaller groups, such as the Chimalpaneca and Huitznahuaque, were distinguished more by their historical traditions, which told of their earlier migrations from other places (García Martínez 1987:67; Hicks 2001). Some of the larger ethnic identities in the Basin of Mexico were regional in scope by the time of Spanish contact,[1] although as Berdan points out, there is some disagreement over whether these were remnants of peoples who had earlier migrated into the region or groups that emerged later in the context of Aztec rule (Brumfiel 1994a:94–96; Gibson 1964:22). What is clear is that by 1519, members of these ethnic groups, both regional and more circumscribed, lived in diverse altepetl, where they constituted two different kinds of ethnically distinct corporate groups: the *calpolli*, a landholding ward with distinctive economic, political, and ceremonial functions; and the *teccalli*, or noble house, which consisted of a group of related landholding nobles and their commoner dependents who tilled the soil. All these groups had a basis in shared ethnicity and were mindful of their own histories. All entered into coalitions with paramount rulers to establish the altepetl that were so characteristic of the region (Brumfiel 1994a:91–92). From this point of view, ethnicity was a means to build factions and engage in political action. As long as the most important political unit was the small altepetl, or petty kingdom, "ethnicity defined relationships within and between such communities" (Brumfiel 1994a:102).

Berdan notes that ethnicity was most significant at the calpolli level, yet even here it was less important than altepetl membership and the class divisions of nobles and commoners. However, we may regard identity with one's altepetl as itself a distinctive sort or level of ethnic identity. A broad view of Mesoamerica as a whole suggests that community of origin or residence was one of the most prevalent ethnic markers (Chance and Stark 2001). In Oaxaca, for example, many have observed that the most basic unit of ethnic identification was the kingdom or city-state, which was largely consonant with the local community (e.g., Chance 1990; Kowalewski 1994:127; Marcus and Flannery 1983; Oudijk 1998:38). Most Oaxacan polities were not ethnically segmented, and names of linguistic groups such as Zapotec or Mixtec did not always correspond directly to meaningful ethnic identities.[2] Likewise, among the Yucatec Maya, colonial indigenous-language documents indicate that the local political community, the *cah*, was the fundamental unit of identification (Restall 1997:13).

Much the same argument has been made for central Mexico, particularly by investigators who have worked with early colonial sources written in Nahuatl. Lockhart has stressed the fundamental ethnic importance of the altepetl, noting that in the Nahuatl sources "indigenous people are overwhelmingly categorized by altepetl grouping, each one separate. Any one altepetl has its friends and its enemies among the rest: from the point of view of each altepetl, all others are outsiders" (Lockhart 1993:14). At the same time, some of these sources also remind us of the continuing ethnic significance of the local calpolli and teccalli. For example, Reyes García (1977) and Liebsohn (1994:162, 181) have shown how the *Historia Tolteca-Chichimeca* and other sixteenth-century cartographic histories from Cuauhtinchan in the Valley of Puebla portray an altepetl identity fashioned from various component identities. The teccalli was especially prominent in polities of this region, where each altepetl was composed of multiple noble houses that maintained their own identities, territories, and rulerships. In general, however, at least in the western part of the central plateau, it appears that self-identification with the altepetl was gaining ground in the Late Postclassic as the Aztec Empire was politically consolidated.

Whether at the level of a regional ethnic group, the altepetl, or the constituent calpolli or teccalli, all these identities had in common a strong emphasis on a shared history derived from a common place of origin or residence. Members of a calpolli, for example, shared a common history because their ancestors came from a particular place, often after a long migration. Other local groups were sometimes composed of nobles who derived from an outside conquering group and commoners descended from a local subjugated population, as were many teccalli in the Valley of Puebla (Olivera 1978; Reyes García 1977). Identification with one's altepetl invoked the idea of common residence and common participation in a political order, as did the third level of broader regional identities. All these identities were distinctive in that they cross-cut the class system and do not seem to have invoked common descent lines or other notions of kinship. Rather, the central Mexican ethnic logic laid "claim to common history but not necessarily common blood" (Brumfiel 1994a:93). Altepetl and regional identities shared the same logic: all who belonged were one people, not because they were descendants of the same ancestors—they usually were not—but because they lived together in the same place and therefore shared a common history and common interests. The primary metaphors surrounding ethnic identity in central Mexico thus had more to do with *place* and *history* than with kinship or descent (see Berdan, this volume; Stark and Chance, this volume). Kinship ties and cognatic descent were not unimportant, especially among elites, but it was ethnic identity phrased in terms of common places and common histories that transcended class lines and made it possible for populations of nobles and commoners together to imagine themselves as unified peoples. With the advent of the European invasion, the most vulnerable of these ethnic identities were the regional ones. Perhaps created by the Aztec state, they would be undone by Spanish hegemony. The calpolli and teccalli also lost much of their significance, but the altepetl, in contrast, found new strength as an ethnic, as well as a political, entity.

INDIGENOUS ETHNICITY IN THE COLONIAL PERIOD

The ethnic significance of the local community—the successor of the altepetl in many parts of central Mexico—has been a staple of Mesoamerican ethnography since the 1920s (Redfield 1930). Wolf's (1957, 1960, 1986) model of the closed corporate community, a tightly knit Indian settlement with clear-cut social and ethnic boundaries, implies a strong ethnic self-identification with one's place of birth and residence. Although many aspects of this model are problematic in today's globalizing world, community identification remains important in much of indigenous Mesoamerica today, even in the face of heavy out-migration. Migration may change the nature of the community and how it is perceived, but identification with it is still highly significant in regions such as western Guatemala, the Chiapas highlands, and parts of Oaxaca that have produced regional political movements with marked ethnic characteristics (Fischer and Brown 1996; Monaghan 1995; Nagengast and Kearney 1990; Nash 1995; Watanabe 1992).

One historical feature of the closed corporate model which has been called into question is the formation of egalitarian colonial Indian communities as a response to colonial exploitation. Such pressures may have indeed served to maintain or even strengthen identification with the community, but research over the last few decades has shown that social divisions between elites and commoners remained salient (see Chance 1994 and 1996b for reviews). Although these inequalities diminished with the population decline of the late sixteenth and seventeenth centuries, they reappeared in reconstituted form in the eighteenth century. Many communities at that time were dominated by native elites who monopolized landholdings and access to local political offices. These studies have shown that a fine-grained ethnographic approach to the ethnohistory of particular localities is productive, and also that considerable differences existed from one community to the next. Rarely, however, have questions of ethnic identity been addressed. Part of the problem has been the traditional reliance on Spanish sources, which, when they mention matters of ethnicity at all, tend to emphasize identities imposed from above—such as the quintessential colonial notion of *indio*—and ignore or misconstrue the subjective aspects of indigenous self-identifications (Chance 1990:145). But our knowledge is improving as researchers have learned to interpret local, mundane documents written in the Latin alphabet by Indians and largely for other Indians. Wills and other notarial documents are the most abundant, but there are also court petitions and testimony and, in some places, early parish records. Studies employing such sources are most numerous for colonial central Mexico, where Nahuatl documentation from a variety of Indian communities has given us new insights into social identities.

The view of colonial indigenous ethnic identity emerging from the Nahuatl sources carries us well beyond the categories of *indio* and *español* imposed by the colonizers. These were not the most relevant categories for most indigenous people, and there is evidence for both continuity and change in self-identifications from the preconquest era. The most obvious change in the Basin of Mexico was the decline of the principal regional identities mentioned above. All of them had begun to fade by 1550 (30 years after the conquest) and most were gone by 1650, as the focus of ethnicity scaled down to the altepetl and its constituent parts: the colonial Indian community. Colonial court disputes, for example, involved only towns, never regional ethnic groups. The old regional ethnicities, particularly ones of moderate size like the Xochimilca, were reflected in Spanish-designed *corregimientos* (local political districts) and labor *repartimientos* (rotating labor drafts), ethnic separation in some *congregaciones* (resettlements), and the self-identifications of Indian migrants in Mexico City. But according to Gibson (1964:30–31), by the late sixteenth century knowledge of these ethnic divisions "was drawn mainly from Indian legend and historical records." The identities gradually faded into obscurity, victims of population decline and increased Spanish emphasis on towns (*cabeceras*) rather than indigenous regions as units of administration.

Gibson used primarily Spanish sources, yet recent works employing Nahuatl sources do not contradict this view. In her study of postconquest Coyoacan, for example, Horn (1997:20–21) notes that in the sixteenth century its citizens were aware of their Tepanec ethnicity and occasionally used the term in Nahuatl documents. But their primary identification was with the altepetl of Coyoacan itself. "The physical embodiment of altepetl identity inhered in the ruler's palace, the local temple, and the central marketplace. Yet altepetl referred above all to a people associated with a given territory" (Horn 1997:21). Within the altepetl each calpolli (or *tlaxilacalli*, a widely used term of similar meaning) had its own territory and sense of micropatriotism, and under the right conditions separatist tendencies could easily emerge. There were names of 100 different tlaxilacalli in Coyoacan in the sixteenth century, though some were parts of others and the standard number in administrative records was 24. Mexica and Otomí minorities lived in their own separate tlaxilacalli (Horn 1997:22). Depopulation and Spanish reluctance to grant official political status to sub-altepetl units, however, led to the gradual decline of the calpolli, tlaxilacalli, and teccalli in the seventeenth and eighteenth centuries, though they were sometimes visible in the process of community fissioning and barrio organization (e.g., Chance 1996a, 1998).

The Coyoacan example echoes Lockhart's (1992) extensive study of Nahua central Mexico, based almost entirely on Nahuatl documentation. Lockhart sees the altepetl as the fundamental locus of colonial, as well as prehispanic, ethnic self-identification. After the European invasion the altepetl gained in importance as it became the focus of sixteenth-century Spanish social engineering. The *encomienda*, rural Indian parishes, Indian municipalities, and initial administrative jurisdictions were all built on already existing altepetl

(Lockhart 1992:10, 14). Even the Spanish translation of altepetl as *pueblo* is apt, for pueblo means "people" and "each altepetl imagined itself as a radically separate people" (Lockhart 1992:15). From the indigenous point of view, the Spaniards initially entered into this scheme as just one more people, or player, in the network. In early Nahuatl sources "'we' and 'they' divides along altepetl lines, not between New Worlders and Old Worlders" (Lockhart 1993:14).

There is no reason to doubt that the indigenous peoples of colonial central Mexico and elsewhere in Mesoamerica knew that in the eyes of the Spanish they were indios and stigmatized as inferior beings. Of course, *indio* was also a legal status, impossible to avoid whenever indigenous people had contact with colonial civil and church authorities. This status was occasionally acknowledged directly by indigenous actors in documents written in Spanish. For example, in his will of 1604, Miguel de Santiago, of the Otomí village of Amanalco, stated, "I am an Indian of genuine stock because it pleased my Lord and God to make me an Indian, for which I am infinitely grateful" (quoted and translated in Gruzinski 1988:39).

Yet conspicuously absent in the mundane Nahuatl documentation, and in the Mixtec and Maya sources from the south as well, is any extensive use of the Spanish term *indio*. This was so despite the fact that other ethnic terms used by the Spanish were commonly adopted as loan words in indigenous languages. Lockhart (1992:115) found only two instances of *indio* in Nahuatl sources from the sixteenth century, and the term does not appear at all in Mixtec and Yucatec Maya documents (Restall 1997:13; Terraciano 2001:2). When writing for themselves in Nahuatl, indigenous central Mexicans "emphasized the narrow ethnicity of the local altepetl and calpolli-tlaxilacalli rather than broader ethnic categories. They tended to do so even when the contrast between indigenous and Spanish was specifically at issue" (Lockhart 1992:115). When it was impossible to avoid speaking of indigenous people generally, *nicantitlaca* (we people here) or *nicantitlaca ipan Nueva España* (we people here in New Spain) was used between 1550 and 1600, later replaced by *timacehualtin* (we macehualtin). *Macehualli* in Nahuatl usually refers to a commoner or dependent, but this ethnic usage included high-ranking people and sometimes non-Nahuatl speakers as well. Even so, it was used much less frequently in Nahuatl than *indio* was in Spanish (Lockhart 1992:115–116).[3]

It is worth noting that the Nahuatl language was not impervious to the penetration of Spanish concepts. Lockhart (1992:57) suggests, for example, that the meaning of *altepetl* in the seventeenth and eighteenth centuries may have been influenced by the Spanish concept of *pueblo*. Yet it seems clear that at the most basic level, colonial Nahuas never fully adopted the Spanish ethnic designation *indio* with its associated racial connotations. The idea of indigenes in general forming a biologically distinct ethnic group vis-à-vis Europeans or people of mixed heritage seems not to have been part of their world view. The native language sources focus our attention instead on the differences among altepetl and the continuing importance of place and history. The use of real or putative descent as a means of establishing ethnic solidarity became important for some Nahua nobles, as discussed below, but it was little employed by the Indian masses and not at all in the context of a generalized indigenous identity.

Identification with particular places, altepetl, and their subunits was, of course, relative, for people migrated and settlements and polities fissioned frequently. There was a pronounced tendency toward decentralization, and in the seventeenth and eighteenth centuries an increasing number of pueblos (which the Nahuas continued to call altepetl) were recognized as the population rebounded from its earlier decline (Horn 1997:228; Lockhart 1992:52). The new pueblos met Spanish requirements for population size and civil and ecclesiastic administration, but they continued to hold indigenous meaning and serve as loci for ethnic loyalties. The fissioning process embodied not the decline of the altepetl but rather its colonial fragmentation. The preconquest need for self-defense, which helped unify many altepetl, no longer mattered, "and the always existing forces in the direction of fragmentation could assert themselves more freely. Microethnicity was perhaps the strongest such force" (Lockhart 1992:27). The ethnic community as an organization of smaller ethnic units can best be understood in terms of Lockhart's cellular model, which he applies to various aspects of Nahua culture.

> The Nahua manner of creating larger constructs, whether in politics, society, economy, or art, tended to place emphasis on a series of relatively equal, relatively separate and self-contained constituent parts of the whole, the unity of which consisted in the symmetrical numerical arrangement of the parts, their identical relationship to a common reference point, and their orderly, cyclical rotation. This mode of organization can be termed cellular or modular as opposed to hierarchical, but it is by no means incapable of producing real, cohesive, lasting larger units [Lockhart 1992:15].

In colonial Nahua communities this mode of organization fostered distinct and competing identities among subunits but at the same time promoted the completeness and integrity of the whole. Certainly there were variations, which we are only beginning to understand. In Tlaxcala and the Valley of Puebla, for example, a case can be made that in the sixteenth century the altepetl was less salient than its constituent teccalli, or noble houses (Martínez Baracs 1998:50; see also Chance 1996a, 1998; Martínez 1984; Olivera 1978; Reyes García 1977). It is also necessary to distinguish early colonial from late colonial communities, for the political economies of these periods were quite different. In the jurisdiction of Tepeaca, for example, Perkins (2000:199) argues that late colonial community secessions owed more to Spanish jural concepts about the organization of the pueblo than to Nahua understandings of the altepetl. He regards this fissioning as contributing to the reconstitution of Indian *macehual* (commoner) class identity.

An interesting genre of indigenous-language documents that vividly illustrates the viability of community microethnicity in the late colonial period consists of the so-called *títulos primordiales*, or primordial titles. Examples have been found as far south as Oaxaca and Yucatan, though the best-studied documents come from the Chalco, Cuernavaca, and Toluca areas of the central highlands. These Nahuatl "titles" of the late seventeenth and eighteenth centuries were written to justify the rights of an altepetl to its territory in the context of population increase and competition for land. A combination of "corporate ideology, special pleading, oratory, and myth" (Lockhart 1992:416), the primordial titles show a surprising lack of awareness of the merging of indigenous and Spanish histories which they themselves document. The identity expressed in these sources is fundamentally indigenous and in the Nahua tradition. Wood (1998:203) has argued that they were written primarily for an indigenous audience by upwardly mobile males and probably reflect the views of local elites. Haskett (2005:21) offers a broader interpretation and suggests that the titles of Cuernavaca were presented publicly (perhaps as they are today in Ajusco, south of Mexico City) and therefore represented the views of not just the elite but the entire community. Impossible dates and appearances of individual Spaniards early in the sixteenth century are the norm in many of these documents, but to regard them merely as self-serving falsifications would be to miss the point. The altepetl is portrayed as a timeless and unchanging entity. Its people are different from all others and have always been so. No distinction is made between indigenous versus Spanish origins of customs or between preconquest and postconquest periods; all that matters is the local tradition. Though local Spanish colonists may be portrayed unfavorably, the coming of the Spanish king and the introduction of Christianity are seen as positive developments. In short, the primordial titles are the strongest expression we have of the Nahua altepetl identity in the late colony. Hostile outsiders may be either Indian or Spanish, and there is no hint at all of any broader ethnic awareness (Haskett 1992; Lockhart 1992:411–18, 1991:39–64; Wood 1991, 1998).

CACIQUE IDENTITY IN LATE COLONIAL TECALI

The growing body of studies based on Nahuatl documentation has opened new doors and given us a better understanding of colonial indigenous ethnic self-identification, particularly at the level of the altepetl. But colonial conditions also gave rise to another kind of indigenous identification in some parts of central Mexico and other areas of Mesoamerica which is not often recognized. I refer to the emergence in the eighteenth century of a very self-conscious group of Indian *caciques*, or nobles, in some Nahua towns.[4] The place of these individuals and their families in colonial Mexican society was profoundly ambiguous. They were quite numerous in some towns and virtually absent in others, but taken together their numbers were small relative to the large Indian masses and the significant numbers of people of mixed parentage, the mestizos and mulattoes.

Caciques that remained in Indian communities are usually treated as an embattled class that was but a pale shadow of its former self by the 1700s. There were indeed places that fit this view where indigenous nobles had lost much of their power and privilege and been relegated to the margins of indigenous society in the late colony. But there were other communities where cacique status remained important, even though its referents had changed considerably. I turn now to my own research on the indigenous elite of the altepetl (in the colonial period, first a *pueblo*, later a *villa*) of Santiago Tecali in the Valley of Puebla. The surprisingly large group of caciques in colonial Tecali was transformed, I argue, from a landowning class to an ethnic group during the eighteenth century (Chance 1996b). Most of my sources are in Spanish (wills, parish marriage records, censuses, and litigation records), for this was an acculturating group of people. Many caciques, especially the men, were literate in Spanish and operated comfortably in rural Hispanic society. Late colonial cacique identity and self-identifications were not unconnected with prehispanic antecedents, but they must also be understood in the broader social, political, and economic context of eighteenth-century New Spain. Nevertheless, cacique identity was no less "authentic" or "indigenous" than altepetl identity, for every ethnic identity, after all, is created in the context of interaction with others who are perceived to be different.

Located near the city of Puebla, Santiago Tecali remained an Indian community—a *república de indios*—with few Spanish residents during the entire colonial period; nor were there many self-identified mestizos or other non-Indians. Before the Spanish invasion Tecali had been host to a number of sharp ethnic and class divisions. From about 1175 to 1400 A.D. the region was dominated by Cuauhtinchan, a neighboring community subjugated and ruled by a series of Chichimec groups allied with the Tolteca-Chichimeca of nearby Cholula (Reyes García 1977:24, 119). Significant numbers of Mixtec and Popoloca speakers from the Coixtlahuaca region to the south also arrived in the twelfth century, recognizing the lord of Cuauhtinchan and settling in various places in the kingdom. Olivera (1978:73–74) believes Tecali was founded in the mid-fourteenth century by a dissident group of Chichimec nobles from Cuauhtinchan who subjugated the native Olmeca-Xicalanca inhabitants of the area. Henceforth Tecali joined Tepeaca, Quecholac, Tecamachalco, and Cuauhtinchan itself as a fifth *cabecera* (head town) in the Cuauhtinchan domain. Toward the end of the fourteenth century Tlatelolco, in the Basin of Mexico, became a power in the region, and the kingdom of Cuauhtinchan disintegrated. The Mexica took control in 1466, and Tecali remained as one of the same five cabeceras that were now incorporated into the Aztec tribute province of Tepeaca (Chance 1996a:108–109).

Tecali seems to have been formed from small ethnic settlements of Chichimecs, Mixtecs, Popolocas, Totomihuaque, and Cholulans who settled among the native Olmeca-Xicalanca. Only the Cholulans were organized into calpolli, however (there were 11 of them), and as in other parts of the southern Valley of

Puebla, the calpolli is rarely mentioned in the sources and played no significant political role. The fundamental political units of the altepetl of Tecali on the eve of the Spanish invasion were three teccalli (a fourth was founded when one of these segmented later in the sixteenth century), or noble houses, each with its own nobility. Together these teccalli had virtually exclusive access to the means of production. Most commoners were affiliated with a noble house and worked for particular lords in a well-developed network of patron-client relationships. Class and ethnicity overlapped considerably in Tecali's early years as the ethnically distinct Chichimec conquerors consolidated their grip on the new altepetl, becoming at once an ethnic noble estate and an economic class with privileged access to land and commoner labor. At the time of the Spanish Conquest some of the *estancias* (subject hamlets) of the noble houses contained people of Mixteca-Popoloca and Otomí origin, but they accounted for less than 2 percent of the population. Olivera (1978:135–36) posits a process of "nahuatization," beginning with the Mexica conquest and continuing after the Spanish invasion. This trend should be seen as just one part of the extensive spread of the Nahuatl language throughout much of central and eastern Mexico at this time, including the Gulf lowlands (see Stark, this volume).

There is no doubt, then, that in 1519 the fundamental social, political, and economic units that comprised the altepetl of Tecali were the teccalli, the noble houses. I concur with the view mentioned above that in this region, as compared with the Basin of Mexico, the noble houses carried more political weight than the altepetl. As the principal political entities, they were surely a primary focus of micropatriotism, with loyalties to the altepetl a close second. All sources indicate that ethnic ties with other teccalli in other communities were unimportant for nobles and commoners alike. The main problem at hand is how identity with the noble house was constructed in the early sixteenth century. Did it conform to the "soft" Mesoamerican pattern of ethnicity that placed the accent on place and history (see Stark and Chance, this volume), or was it construed in "hard" terms on the basis of kinship or descent?

The teccalli has been described as a lineage, whose noble members considered themselves to be patrilineal or cognatic descendants of the founder of the house (Carrasco 1976:21–22, 29). According to Carrasco (1976:32–33), some of the commoners subject to a teccalli may have been distantly related to the ranking lords while others were not, having been assigned to their lords as spoils of conquest or through administrative decisions. In contrast, I have argued on the basis of the Tecali case that the noble house was not a lineage or kin group but, as its name implies (teccalli in Nahuatl means "noble house"), can best be regarded as a "house" as defined by Lévi-Strauss (1982:174): a named, corporate body with an estate that it seeks to preserve intact through various, often contradictory, means. Tecali nobles traced descent patrilineally or cognatically from the *teuctli*, or head of the house, but I have argued that kinship and genealogy were not their primary preoccupations where house membership was concerned. The focus of attention was on establishing a tie to the house itself and its land and commoner labor force, not the descent line per se (Chance 2000:486, 496).

The supremacy of the political over the kinship aspect of the noble house in Tecali and its vicinity was embodied in the terms used to describe it in the Nahuatl language. In Tecali itself, it was designated by the term *tecpan* (palace). In neighboring Tepeaca, *tlatocayotl* (rulership) was used (Martínez 1984). A second sense in which the teccalli (tecpan) of Santiago Tecali was more like a house than a lineage lies in its integration of contradictory traits, as in Lévi-Strauss's definition. Eighteenth-century data show that the basic contradiction for nobles in Tecali was between descent from founding ancestors (lineality) and an equally strong emphasis on equal inheritance by all siblings from both parents (laterality). Late colonial noble landed estates, or *cacicazgos* (see below), remained intact despite this contradiction, and cognatic descent traced through males and females enabled some eighteenth-century nobles to claim rights in several cacicazgos simultaneously. Yet genealogical memory was shallow, not extending back more than three or four generations (see below). This is consistent with the language of late colonial noble wills from Tecali, which in all cases emphasized the landed estate (*cacicazgo*), not genealogy.

Finally, since the altepetl of Tecali originated in conquest, the commoners were connected to the houses not by kinship but through patron-client ties, as mentioned above (Chance 2000:495–497). As in any stratified society, we would expect that members of different social strata might construct their identities somewhat differently. Thus whereas descent or marriage ties were more relevant to a noble seeking to solidify his or her membership in a particular house, a commoner would have stressed the history of his or her family's ties of clientage to a particular noble family within the house. But what the noble and commoner shared was a common history through their affiliation with the house—a landholding political entity that ensured subsistence, administered justice, and provided protection from aggression from other houses. If we apply the house rather than the lineage model, it is reasonable to postulate that teccalli identities in Santiago Tecali did not differ fundamentally from those elsewhere in Nahua central Mexico.

If we include both nobles and commoners, as we must, Tecali provides another case in which identity with the teccalli conformed to the central Mexican ethnic logic that laid "claim to common history but not necessarily to common blood" (Brumfiel 1994a:93). Especially in the Valley of Puebla, micropatriotism and ethnic self-identification for nobles and commoners alike in the sixteenth century revolved primarily around the teccalli and secondarily around the altepetl. I would hasten to add that in many situations, ethnic identity in Tecali took a back seat to class identity, as it did elsewhere in contact-period central Mexico (Berdan, this volume). As Olivera (1978) has emphasized, the fundamental division that made the noble house possible in Tecali was the class bifurcation between *pipiltin* and *macehualtin*, nobles and commoners.

Much of this traditional sociopolitical structure survived the early conquest period but came under renewed attack by the colonial regime toward the end of the sixteenth century. In 1591 Spanish authorities, in a series of land grants, stripped the noble houses of their land rights and issued titles to 55 of their constituent noble members. The legal basis for Spanish-style private property and redefined class relations between nobles and commoners was thus established at this time, though Tecalenses tended to resist the redefinition of property relations and continued to think in terms of group tenure.

The seventeenth century brought population decline and impoverishment for nobles and commoners alike. With their traditional labor force much reduced, and with few Spaniards or mestizos interested in buying or renting their lands (better ones were available elsewhere), Tecali's elite struggled to maintain their position. Colonial records continued to identify nobles using the honorific *don* and *doña*, but the more formal term *principal*, a Spanish word that referred explicitly to elite status, was less common and was used rather erratically. After 1700, however, things began to change. The population was growing again, and the term *cacique*, long known in the area but rarely employed, came into common use to refer to all the descendants of the 55 original recipients of the 1591 land grants, now referred to as *cacicazgos*. Drawing on traditional status distinctions in Nahua culture and further promoted by recognition under Spanish law, the cacique sector steadily increased to a third (500 persons) of Tecali's population in the 1770s. This "status inflation"[5] occurred in the context of bitter conflicts with macehuales over land, and in winning most court cases, caciques found that their interests were best served by renting their extensive lands to Spanish ranchers and farmers, who were now actively seeking opportunities in the region (Chance 1998, 2003).

To be a cacique in eighteenth-century Tecali meant having rights to land and labor through kinship and marriage ties. It meant not being a commoner and hence freedom from royal tribute obligations. It also meant that one was recognized as a privileged Indian and not a mestizo. Some *mestizaje* (race mixture) had in fact occurred in Tecali by this time, but it had little impact on local ethnic categories. The town was still known as overwhelmingly Indian, and its inhabitants identified themselves accordingly. For indigenous nobles to openly recognize a mixed ethnic or racial heritage (as many could have) would have jeopardized their rights to land and municipal offices, which by Spanish law were restricted to "pure-blooded" Indians living in repúblicas de indios, recognized Indian towns. Although caciques never used the term *indio* when speaking or writing either Nahuatl or Spanish, they took great pains to present themselves as pure-blooded indigenous nobles. Cacique status thus involved ethnic as well as class characteristics, and as the number of recognized caciques grew, so did the cultural gap between them and the commoners.

At the same time, increasingly frequent challenges to the noble families' hold over land and labor coupled with economic diversification weakened the class unity of the caciques. Nobles who could no longer command privileged access to resources began to emphasize the ethnic, even racial aspects of their indigenous heritage. The result was that Tecali's elite was transformed, over a period of about 70 years, from a landowning class to an economically heterogeneous group defined more in ethnic terms.[6] Here, as in other parts of central Mexico at the time, local noble self-identification was asserted against a more restrictive legal categorization. Colonial law held that a cacique was the single individual owner of a cacicazgo and heir of a prehispanic *tlatoani*, or king (Gibson 1964:161). In Tecali, however, all descendants of the 55 grantees of 1591 called themselves caciques. This was a process of ethnogenesis in which the legal identity of cacique was redefined from below in Tecali and many other places. Though Gibson (1964:162) notes that there was confusion among Spanish officials, it is clear that self-identified caciques in Tecali and other Valley of Puebla towns such as Cuauhtinchan were able to win exemption from tribute.

As used in Tecali, *cacique* corresponded more to *pilli*, the general Nahuatl term for noble, than to the more singular *tlatoani*, king. Yet there was really no direct Nahuatl equivalent of the term *cacique* in Tecali in the eighteenth century. In earlier years the expression *pilli tlatoani* (noble ruler) occasionally turned up in wills, but the last known testament written in Nahuatl in the town dates from 1737. Thus much of the shift from class to ethnicity took place at a time when Nahuatl was receding as both a spoken and written language and Spanish was gaining ground. By the mid-nineteenth century most Tecalenses were bilingual and Spanish had become dominant.

Cacique identity in eighteenth-century Tecali in fact incorporated both indigenous and Spanish cultural elements. Descent was traced cognatically from founding ancestors, a pattern I have argued is basically Nahua (Chance 2000). Yet the founding ancestors invoked in the eighteenth century were invariably those who received land grants from the Spanish viceroy in 1591. Memory rarely extended any further back, and no one ever claimed descent from prehispanic forebears. The importance of descent as an ethnic marker in this context is noteworthy, as it represents a significant departure from the earlier accent on class over ethnicity in the sixteenth and seventeenth centuries, as we have seen. Though descent as an ethnic marker in earlier years remains problematic, it appears that as the noble houses weakened after 1591, so did the idiom of descent. Its revival in the eighteenth century occurred in a significantly different context: the Nahua concept of descent received new emphasis and was employed instrumentally in a new fashion. Claimants to cacique status in the eighteenth century sought privileged access to land and labor, but by then the old noble houses had long been defunct as viable political and economic units. Caciques now envisioned themselves in a more collective sense, as an ethnic group distinct from the macehuales because of their noble ancestry. In other words, descent was now being used to define divisions that had previously been conceptualized more in class terms. The use of descent in this late colonial context was also conditioned, I believe, by Spanish concepts of race and purity of blood that had become very prevalent by this time and were part of the legal code that governed the caciques' rights and privileges.

It has been argued that race in the sense of an organization of all people into ranked categories theoretically based on different biophysical traits was an idea that evolved in the colonies of the New World (Smedley 1998:691–694; 1999:16–18, 39–40). Unlike other terms for classifying people, *race* places emphasis on innateness and the inbred nature of what is being judged. The Spanish term *raza* was apparently used originally to designate a breeding line or stock of animals, such as horses. By 1611, at least, the term was also applied to people and had acquired the negative connotation of the existence of Moorish or Jewish ancestors in one's lineage. A dictionary of 1737 defined *raza* as "the caste or quality of origin or lineage" (Smedley 1999:39). Banton (1987:1–2) notes that the word *race* entered the English language in 1508 and during the sixteenth and seventeenth centuries was used in the sense of lineage. Only after 1700 did the term become joined with the idea of innate biological qualities (see also Brace 2005:17–36).

Whatever its history in Europe, the race concept and the value placed on racial "purity" were clearly present in early colonial Mexico as the framework of the *sociedad de castas* took shape in the seventeenth century. Cacique status was ambiguous in this scheme, for caciques were defined as Indians, though many of them were culturally closer to Spaniards and mestizos. They had to preserve their "Indianness" to hold on to their legal privileges, but they also had to distinguish themselves as fundamentally different from the macehuales, the Indian commoners. The frequent demonstrations of descent from sixteenth-century noble ancestors that filled late colonial land litigation cases in Tecali owed as much to Spanish racial hegemony as they did to indigenous concepts of descent. They are not unlike the Spanish court testimonies offered to prove the purity of one's blood, that is, the absence of Jewish or Moorish heritage.

It is not coincidental that Tecali's caciques began to emphasize their common ethnicity at about the same time that other altepetl in central Mexico were producing primordial titles that underscored Indian separateness from Spaniards in a different way. The continuing strength of both altepetl and cacique identity in the eighteenth century can be seen as indigenous responses to population growth and competition for land. Claims to cacique status in Tecali were forged in internal struggles over land with Indian commoners. In similar fashion, the authors of primordial titles faced external threats to their land base, often from Spaniards but from other Indian communities as well. Both forms of identity can be seen as part of a larger ethnogenesis, stimulated by resource competition, that affected parts of central Mexico and perhaps other Mesoamerican regions in the eighteenth century. Whether the ethnic arguments stressed descent or common residence, whether they drew on hegemonic Spanish ideas of racial difference or ignored (perhaps even challenged) them, they were directed above all at improving the life chances of people who considered themselves to be indigenous.

CONCLUSION

Colonial indigenous ethnicity in central Mexico demonstrated clear continuities with the prehispanic past as well as strategic adaptations to Spanish hegemony. The long history of the altepetl as an ethnic entity, the Spanish emphasis on the local community as a primary political unit, and the inherently unstable political alliances prior to Spanish contact all led to a weakening of regional ethnic identities after the conquest and a strengthening of identification with the local community. The subunits of the altepetl—the calpolli, tlaxilacalli, and teccalli—faded considerably after the sixteenth century, though never completely. Population decline and continuing adjustments to colonial rule in the early and mid-seventeenth century fostered a decline in indigenous ethnicity as communities turned inward on themselves. This trend was reversed in the eighteenth century, however, as an ethnic resurgence was stimulated by a commercializing economy, population growth, and competition for land.

Expressions of ethnicity in the late colonial years took different forms and reflected the growing cultural gap between indigenous commoners and elites. Identification with the altepetl or local community intensified, drawing on deep prehispanic roots but also affected by colonial exploitation and the Spanish notion of the pueblo. In some places, like Santiago Tecali, where communal solidarity was weak, longstanding class divisions became more overtly ethnic in character as acculturating cacique elites manipulated the dominant Spanish discourse on racial and ethnic distinctiveness for their own purposes.

In the larger scheme of things, the central Mexican case should lead us to be skeptical of definitions of ethnicity that have as a prerequisite the idea of a common biological inheritance. Ethnicity in Nahua central Mexico emphasized instead commonalities that derived from a shared place of origin or residence and common history. As Spicer (1971:174) recognized, symbols connecting a people with a particular territory (and language) are among the most powerful and widespread markers of ethnic identity, and this was the case in Mesoamerica (see also Zeitlin 1989). In Santiago Tecali, patterns of microethnicity changed significantly during the colonial era. Self-identification with the altepetl cum colonial community was a constant for both nobles and commoners while the noble houses declined after the close of the sixteenth century. It was not until the late eighteenth century that descent and the idea of biological origins became an unambiguous ethnic marker for the newly constituted cacique group. While caciques drew in part on the traditional Nahua notion of descent to define their ethnic distinctiveness, they also incorporated Spanish ideas about race. The rise of eighteenth-century cacique identity, like the appearance of the new Protestant identity in modern Amatlán, Veracruz, described by Sandstrom (this volume), was a response to a particular sort of political domination coupled with increased resource competition. With the dismantling of the colonial regime and the disavowal of legalized ethnic classification by the Mexican national governments after 1821, the terms of that political domination changed. Now lacking legal recognition from above, cacique self-identification in Tecali and elsewhere in Mexico lost much of its reason for being and began to fade.

ACKNOWLEDGMENTS

This work was originally presented at the 68th Anglo-American Conference of Historians, London, June 30–July 2, 1999, and again, in revised form, at the conference "Ethnicity in Mesoamerica," held at Arizona State University, February 1–5, 2005. I thank Frances Berdan for getting us all started, and I am grateful to her and other conference participants Alan Sandstrom, Barbara Stark, James Taggart, and Emily Umberger for their comments on the initial drafts of this chapter. Thanks also to the students in Stark's and my fall 2004 seminar on ethnicity in Mesoamerica at Arizona State University for their good ideas and many stimulating discussions.

6

Blood Sacrifice, Curing, and Ethnic Identity Among Contemporary Nahua of Northern Veracruz, Mexico

Alan R. Sandstrom

> *Culture is always defined in opposition to something else.*
> — Adam Kuper, *Culture: The Anthropologists' Account*

ETHNOGENESIS IS A CREATIVE PROCESS THAT IMPLICATES IMPORTANT cultural traits such as dress, productive activities, and features of religious ritual and world view. Ethnic identity is often created as a defense against domination by or competition with another group that possesses different socially shared traditions. I discuss these complex issues in the context of the ethnographic field research I am conducting among the Nahua people of northern Veracruz, Mexico. I hope to demonstrate that elements of Nahua culture are products of ethnogenesis—the creation of a collective ethnic identity. Northern Veracruz and the multiethnic Huasteca region of which it is a component is a natural laboratory for the study of ethnogenesis and interethnic relations.

I begin by exploring the nature of Nahua ethnicity, linking it to general processes of ethnogenesis found throughout Mesoamerica (see Stark and Chance, this volume). I then outline some key cultural principles of the Nahua, revealed by how they define and treat disease. Ritual cures illuminate much about the content of Nahua identity and relations with non-Nahua mestizo elites. Next I briefly describe a remarkable ritual that includes blood sacrifice and pilgrimage to a sacred mountain to appeal for rain. My family and I have been privileged to witness this elaborate crop-fertility ritual event on two occasions, in June 1998 and June 2001. I hope to link this example of ritual sacrifice to the way that Nahua cure disease, and to connect both types of ritual—crop fertility and curing—to fundamental processes by which the Nahua establish their ethnic identity (see Berdan, this volume). Ritual can be difficult to analyze, and I seek to demonstrate that we can gain insight into its fundamental nature by examining how ethnic groups interact with one another.

The Nahua speak the Nahuatl language, the most widely spoken (and the most studied) Native American language in Mesoamerica, with well over 1.2 million speakers (Kaufman 1994:34). Amatlán, the pseudonymous village that is the focus of this research, has about 600 inhabitants and is located in the hilly and tropical forested southern Huasteca on the Gulf Coast of Mexico, far removed from urban centers and transportation lines (see Ruvalcaba Mercado and Pérez Zevallos 1996 for an essay and extensive bibliography on the Huasteca, and Stresser-Péan 1979 for a detailed discussion). The 2000 Mexican census recorded 460,736 Nahua inhabitants in the Huasteca (comprising portions of six states; see Sandstrom 1995 for the region's boundaries). The Huasteca has the reputation in Mexico of being a rugged, lawless place much like the American frontier of the nineteenth century (Lomnitz-Adler 1992:51–55; Sandstrom 1991:63, 1995:184). Now all but about 10 percent of the inhabitants of Amatlán are bilingual in Nahuatl and Spanish. The remainder, mostly elderly people, speak Nahuatl monolingually. The villagers depend for their living on slash-and-burn horticulture and grow maize, beans, and squash as their staple crops. They also engage in temporary wage labor on neighboring ranches and increasingly in towns and cities. Until recently, they lived in thatch-roofed houses made from materials gathered in the forest and grouped in nonresidential patrilocal extended families, and they practiced a Native American religion to which had been added elements of Spanish Catholicism (on Mesoamerican kinship systems, see Chance 2000, Mulhare 2000, and Sandstrom 2000).

In the fall of 1997 I returned to the field after an absence of several years and noted important changes in Amatlán that bear on the question of ethnic identity.[1] In response to requirements of rural electrification, the village layout had been rearranged to conform to a gridlike urban model with houses located on lots along unpaved streets. In recent years houses are increasingly constructed from cement blocks with corrugated iron or concrete roofs, fewer people dress in the traditional clothing styles, and approximately half the 115 households have converted to one of several fundamentalist sects of Protestantism (see Dow and Sandstrom 2001; Sandstrom 1991:349–364). This last development was particularly puzzling. How could people have gone in just a few years from an essentially Native American religion, in which the earth, sun, water, hills, and the entire cognized landscape are the focus of sacred rites, to become Bible-reading, hymn-singing Pentecostals? As I will explain, I believe that ethnicity is implicated in this radical change.

ETHNIC IDENTITY AND NAHUA CULTURE

Ethnicity (or synonymously, ethnic identity) is a special kind of self-conscious identity shared by members of an ethnic group. The key features of ethnic identity, according to anthropologists, are, first, that members of ethnic groups believe themselves to share significant life experiences with other group members and, second, they believe their group traces back to primordial times. An ethnic identity is self-ascribed and ascribed by others. Ethnic identity is usually based on such cultural features as language, dress, religion, territory, and so forth, which the people view as their innate possessions and historical legacy. However, as described below, culture alone cannot be used to define an ethnic group. This is because individuals mediate ethnic identity through their interactions with others, and the mix of traits that come into play vary from situation to situation. Ethnic groups these days tend to occupy a position in society somewhere between the intimacy of the kin group and the anonymity of the state (see Maybury-Lewis 2002:47–79 on ethnicity in relation to states; Stark and Chance, this volume).

The worldwide phenomenon of the weakening of the nation-state, alongside many other causes, has led ethnicity to become a major factor in international politics over the past 30 years. The volatile situations in Africa, Sri Lanka, Indonesia, eastern Europe, and the Middle East testify to the increased importance of ethnic strife (e.g., see Huntington et al. 1996; Tambiah 1989). Ethnicity has also been an important factor in Mexico from the earliest times (Stark, Umberger, this volume). In my view, much of the dynamic of contemporary Nahua village life can also be linked to processes of ethnicity originating not solely at the local level but in the regional, national, and international areas as well.

The region surrounding Amatlán is inhabited by five different Native American groups as well as a Hispanic-oriented, mestizo elite that controls social, political, and economic resources. In addition to the mestizo and Nahua populations, there are substantial numbers of other indigenous peoples in the region, primarily Huastec, Otomí, Tepehua, and Totonac. Let me first characterize this complex situation from the perspective of the dominant group. Most urban Mexicans distinguish between mestizos—people of mixed Native American and European racial stock with a Hispanic cultural outlook—and *indios*, who are identified with the remnants of the indigenous races and cultures that existed at the time of the Spanish Conquest. In general, urban people recognize that mestizos share some indigenous cultural traits, but they believe mestizo culture is basically a rural or rustic version of the urban national Mexican identity. The term *indio* has pejorative connotations for most Mexicans and cannot be accurately translated into English simply as "Indian." Many urbanites consider Native Americans backward, partly because they are overrepresented in the lowest socioeconomic levels of Mexican society. The basic ethnic divide in northern Veracruz is between indios and mestizos. However, from an anthropological perspective, this commonly held distinction between people of mixed versus aboriginal race and cultural heritage is highly misleading (see Fuente 1967; Taggart, this volume).

An immediate problem is the use of the term *race*. Most citizens of Mexico are of mixed racial stock. People with Native American features, including straight black hair, dark brown eyes, brown skin, and relatively short stature, can be found at all levels of Mexican society. Because Native American features are observable throughout Mexican society, overt racial discrimination as experienced in parts of the United States is rare and would be difficult to maintain. *Indio* is a social category to which has been added a contradictory and inappropriate racial dimension. In effect, many people have conflated race, ethnicity, and social class. It is interesting to note that many anthropologists now advocate that the whole concept of race be abandoned because it is difficult to apply scientifically to actual human populations and because the concept historically has been so thoroughly misused. The situation in Mexico is a good example of how the concept can be misapplied by the dominant group (Fuente 1967:433).

Nor is this confusion totally eliminated if we focus on strictly sociocultural factors to distinguish Native Americans from mestizos. In one sense, virtually all Mexicans are mestizos, and scholars and writers sometimes say in the interest of solidarity, "We are a nation of mestizos." Indigenous cultures have influenced many aspects of urban national Mexico. In turn, there are no indigenous people today who have escaped the impact of modernizing Mexico. Nor can the criterion of language be used unambiguously to distinguish Native Americans from mestizos. Many rural mestizos speak indigenous languages bilingually. On the other hand, some indigenous people refuse to admit to census takers and other outsiders that they speak an indigenous language (Heiras Rodríguez 2005). Thus Native Americans and mestizos lie along a continuum, and defining just who belongs to which category is a matter of degree rather than kind.

The Nahua of Amatlán recognize the term Nahua but refer to themselves as *mexicaj*. *Mexicaj* is the name the ancient Aztecs from the capital city, Tenochtitlan, used for themselves. When speaking Spanish, the Nahua sometimes refer to themselves as *mexicanos* (and their language as *mexicano*). This term is ambiguous because all citizens of Mexico call themselves *mexicanos* but without the implication that they are identifying with an indigenous group. The Nahua call other Native Americans in general (as well as themselves) *masehualmej*, meaning "countrymen" or "farmers." The Nahua refer to other neighboring indigenous groups each by their own name in Nahuatl. For example, a Tepehua is called *tepehuatl* and an Otomí is called *otomitl*. A Nahuatl term for mestizo or any outsider is *coyotl* (plural, *coyomej*). The word refers to the small wild dog and has come into English as "coyote." The Nahua view this animal as a mischief-maker and backbiter as well as being clever and self-serving and find it appropriate to use as a general term for outsider. Paradoxically, *coyotl* can also mean "gentleman," and context is the only indication of which interpretation is appropriate. In Spanish, Nahua may use the term *rico* to refer to non-Nahua. We can observe that the Nahua themselves have names for each of the major ethnic groups and have a clear idea of stratification in Mexican society. It is important to note here that part of the confusion surrounding ethnic identity is the fact that it is highly situational. When speaking to other Native Americans, the Nahua identify as *mexicaj*. When interacting with mestizos, they may identify as *masehualmej*. In other situations they may identify themselves as inhabitants of Amatlán or the Huasteca region or, when dealing with foreigners, as Mexican nationals. The reference group is always shifting, depending on the circumstances at hand.

One feature of ethnicity in Mesoamerica that is often difficult for outsiders to understand is a lack of tribal identity. The Nahua do not stand against the Otomí as a group in the same way that, say, the Hopi stand in rivalry against the Navajo in the United States. Villagers may perpetuate stereotypes about neighboring Otomí, but they may have equally negative views of the people in the next village who are Nahua like themselves. The people of Amatlán often invite Otomí shamans and laypeople to participate in their rituals. They know that Otomí are different at some level, in language for example, but their syncretic beliefs and rituals are similar enough to allow them to recognize that Otomí and Nahua religions are fundamentally the same. Except for language, it is difficult to distinguish one indigenous group from another based strictly on cultural criteria. I am not certain, for example, that a future archaeologist could distinguish a Nahua village from an Otomí or a Tepehua village. As I have emphasized, the most significant social cleavage in the region is not among different indigenous groups but between Native American and mestizo. Schryer (1990) discusses the complexities of distinguishing class from ethnic group in the Huasteca region and shows how these relevant groupings are important for understanding historical developments and the contemporary situation there.

ETHNIC IDENTITY IN MESOAMERICA

Mesoamerican ethnicity presents puzzles for anthropologists and historians. Why is it that indigenous people in Mesoamerica have not developed ethnic identities to the same degree as indigenous groups in the United States? What historical processes account for the particular quality of ethnic relations in contemporary Mesoamerica? We have seen that the Nahua distinguish themselves from mestizos but do not tend to form bonds with other Nahua. In a related vein, why is it that indigenous peoples in Mesoamerica generally do not identify strongly with particular tracts of land as do some groups in the United States? Most Nahua seem perfectly willing to move to another community to take advantage of some opportunity, particularly if the extended family can move with them. People evince little loyalty to a specific tract of land even though the sacralized landscape plays an important role in traditional religion. For example, it is common for villages to fission, entire compounds moving to a new location that may be far distant. Answers to these questions can be found in the historical processes that underlie contemporary ethnicity in North America and Mesoamerica (see Chance, this volume).

Anthropologist Spicer (1962) studied patterns of cultural assimilation and the creation of ethnic identity in a number of Native American groups in the American Southwest and northwestern Mexico. He begins from the time each population was conquered militarily by the Spaniards, Mexicans, or North Americans. The scope of the study makes his findings useful in understanding other parts of Mexico and the world. He notes that Native American groups exhibited a diversity of reactions following contact, and he analyzes "the connections between the conditions of contact and the patterns of response" (Spicer 1962:17). He states that policies toward indigenous people were designed essentially to "civilize" by promoting assimilation into the European form of society. Each of these dominant groups, however, employed distinctive strategies for accomplishing this end. These different approaches, among many other complex factors, caused the indigenous people under each regime to respond in different ways.

To summarize briefly, United States policy was based on the creation of a reservation system with political control centered in Washington, D.C. Native Americans were to be assimilated into American society on an individual basis, and thus reservations as a whole were not incorporated into the national economy. This policy led members of each tribe to develop its own strongly separate identity based on a sacred attachment to specific tracts of land. In contrast, Spanish and later Mexican policy was predicated on gathering the indigenous people into new communities and then, under the direction of missionaries and other agents of change, easing the entire community into the local version of European civilization. Thus the focus of assimilation was on the community rather than the individual. Furthermore, the haciendas recruited labor from these population centers, and mixed groups of Native Americans were incorporated into the national economy as a temporary rural workforce. In the meantime, under laws of colonization, mestizo settlers were allowed to move into indigenous territory and eventually intermarried with local populations. The result has been that "tribal identification lapsed...even though the general identification as Indian continued" (Spicer 1962:573). In a process Spicer calls "suspended assimilation," the aboriginal populations of Mexico thus largely lost their separate group identities and replaced them with a generalized Native American identity. The analysis appears to explain very well the situation of ethnic groups in northern Veracruz.

FACTORS CONTRIBUTING TO NAHUA ETHNIC IDENTITY

The system of ethnic relations in northern Veracruz is complex and does not admit of easy generalizations. The fact is that no matter where we find people divided into ethnic enclaves, the situation is always complex and often elaborately ambiguous. What is perhaps unusual about northern Veracruz is the degree to which mestizos control the lives and fortunes of their indigenous neighbors. Mestizos occupy virtually all political offices in the region, own the large cattle ranches that provide temporary labor to people, control the court system, and manage the police, military, and various militias. Mestizos tend to lump all indigenous people together at the very bottom of the social pyramid.

Many mestizos (but not all) fail to recognize any difference among the various ethnic groups and generally do not acknowledge indigenous rights or dignity.

Relations between the Nahua and local mestizos are often hostile and seemingly always embedded in stereotypes and preconceptions. However, as might be expected, day-to-day interactions are complicated by a number of important factors and can appear to be based on cooperation rather than competition or domination. The Nahua rarely make prejudicial statements about mestizos in general. They usually speak about individuals. Thus they will say that such and such a rancher is known to be violently opposed to indigenous people whereas another is well disposed toward them. It is crucial that Nahua men be on good terms with a number of mestizo ranch owners so they can be hired as temporary laborers. In fact, individual Nahua often enter into ritual kinship relations with mestizo ranchers to formalize their close ties. They do so always as subordinates, however, and never as equals. The Nahua are motivated to pursue amicable relations with members of the dominant group because they must deal effectively with mestizo officials (particularly if they hold office in the community or *ejido*), and it is certainly in their interest to avoid dominant group violence. In addition, a number of Nahua, particularly younger people, migrate to cities and experience social mobility by entering into the mestizo world. Thus for a number of reasons it benefits the Nahua to keep the border between themselves and mestizos somewhat ambiguous and to prevent relations from deteriorating to the point where meaningful interaction is impossible (see Taggart, this volume). However, mestizos are superordinate outsiders, and the Nahua are well aware that most do not have their interests at heart and must be dealt with very cautiously.

ETHNIC IDENTITY AND CULTURE

Ethnicity is an important but elusive social phenomenon that defies attempts to isolate those features shared by all ethnic groups (Stark and Chance, this volume). As Barth (1969:14) has stated, "It is important to recognize that although ethnic categories take cultural differences into account, we can assume no simple one-to-one relationship between ethnic units and cultural similarities and differences. The features that are taken into account are not the sum of 'objective' differences, but only those which the actors themselves regard as significant." Thus, according to Barth, ethnic identity is actor-centered, it may vary among individuals, and individuals can modify it according to the situations they face. Because of these mutable features, as mentioned earlier, ethnic groups and cultures may not be synonymous (Berdan, this volume).

Barth (1969) is generally credited with alerting anthropologists to the study of ethnic phenomena. Trained in the British social anthropology tradition, Barth used the 1969 essay to criticize use of the concept of culture as a unit of analysis, preferring instead to focus on social structure and patterns of social interaction. However, the degree to which a set of cultural traits corresponds to an ethnic unit is an empirical question that can be clarified only through re-search. In his essay Barth hints that culture and ethnic group as analytical cat-egories overlap to a significant extent. In complex polyethnic systems, he notes, "the cultural characteristics of each ethnic group must be stable" (1969:19), and later he writes that "ethnic identity is associated with a culturally specific set of value standards" (1969:25). Barth asserts that he will discuss processes and factors that generate ethnic identity (1969:10, 18) but goes on to do so without implicating causation. For him, social factors condition behavior, although he hints that ecological conditions also structure people's responses. Barth's essay does little to help us understand what produces ethnicity or why it is of grow-ing importance in the world.

Twenty-five years ago Cohen (1981:307) remarked, "Ethnicity has already become the subject of such an extensive literature that there can hardly be any conceptual formulation about it not made by someone before." In my view, much of the ambiguity surrounding ethnic identity can be reduced if ethnic-ity is viewed simply as a creative response on the part of the members of one group to domination by or competition with members of another group. A situation in which ethnic groups coexist as equal partners within the same nation is at best extremely rare and probably impossible to sustain. In such cases in which ethnic groups are in a temporary precarious balance in the same society (see Tambiah 1989:339), there is almost always rivalry and competition over resources as one group tries to dominate another. Subordinate groups, such as contemporary Native Americans of Mexico, are likely to stress cul-tural differences between their members and those of the dominant group, or where salient cultural differences are lacking, to construct new ones. Ethnicity is a conscious process of differentiation whereby people foster a sense of be-longing to an in-group while simultaneously relegating others to an out-group. People augment or invent cultural differences in order to defend themselves against dominant-group exploitation or to construct an alternate social world in which they can succeed and prosper. People in the dominant position also constitute an ethnic group, but in Mexico as elsewhere, this identity is usually far less conscious or conspicuous, and the sense of solidarity is less well de-veloped than in the subordinate group. Dominant-group ethnicity is usually moribund compared with the conscious and active ethnicity of the people at the bottom of the social hierarchy. Subordinate groups of all kinds, including immigrants and members of lower economic classes and even prisoners, for example, may produce various cultural elements that are later taken up by the dominant group.[2]

My goal is to illuminate the degree of active participation of the subordi-nate group in the creation and maintenance of ethnic difference. It is obviously in the interest of the dominant group as well that subaltern groups be cultur-ally distinct. Such groups are more easily identified and their inferior position rationalized and justified if they differ culturally from the dominant group. I also do not wish to downplay the role that power and violence play in the suppression of one group by another in the context of ethnic divisions. During my years of residence in Amatlán, several people identified as troublemakers (primarily because they questioned the unequal distribution of resources) were murdered by local ranchers or militia members. (For a general statement on ethnicity and violent suppression, see Jimeno 1989; see also Taggart, this volume.)

Earlier chapters show the important role played by ethnicity in prehispanic Mesoamerica, but the conquest transformed many of the old arrangements (Berdan 1999; Chance 1999; see also Chance, Stark, Stark and Chance, this volume). Much ethnicity in contemporary Mexico traces most directly to the colonial period, when the large majority of indigenous people came under the domination of the Spaniards. As previously mentioned, it was the clear intention of Spanish authorities to have native populations become assimilated to a European way of life. But it is here that we enter the realm of paradox. By suppressing native populations and attempting to exercise total control over them, the Spaniards virtually guaranteed that Native Americans would respond by developing a separate ethnic identity that would allow them to endure and even thrive. Indigenous identity became a subtle and powerful force, a "weapon of the weak," to quote Scott (1985), employed by the downtrodden to resist domination and create meaningful lives for themselves.[3]

Many cultural features of the Nahua of northern Veracruz trace to the prehispanic period. This heritage includes elements of language, technology, living arrangements, religious belief, ritual, and world view (Mönnich 1976; Sandstrom 1989, 1991; Sandstrom and Sandstrom 1986). However, as implied above, it would be a mistake to assume that Native American identity based on these cultural traits exists in contemporary Mexico as a simple survival from the past. Nahua ethnicity is far from static. What counts here is the creation of difference, regardless of the origin of the culture trait in question. A look at how Nahua men and women dress illustrates the point. When in public, an indigenous man communicates his identity through his striking white costume, tire-tread sandals, and sheathed steel machete hung at his side. A woman proclaims her indigenous identity with her spectacularly embroidered blouse, colorful ankle-length skirt, and strips of bright cloth braided in her long hair. These symbols say "I am Native American" to all the world, and yet, paradoxically, each one of these elements is of Spanish origin. This fact implies that indigenous identity is not a passive remnant of prehispanic traditions that has survived in remote villages. Rather, it suggests that identity is actively and creatively pursued by villagers—what I have called an expression of "optimized ethnicity"—and that it is a rational response to the conditions of their lives (Sandstrom 1991:372). The shift in recent years to inexpensive manufactured clothing reflects changes in the nature of Nahua ethnicity, as discussed below.

British sociologist Stone (1996) writes that scholars have viewed ethnicity in one of two, basically incommensurate, ways (Stark and Chance, this volume). Some argue that ethnicity is primordial, that is, it represents cultural difference

that traces back to ancient times. In some cases these cultural roots are culti-
vated and paraded while in others they remain latent and appear only during
times of trouble or during certain special situations. Ethnic identity represents
continuity with the past, and contemporary ethnic groups are seen as holders
of the remnants of a culture that thrived in ages gone by. In this view the Nahua
are heirs to the great prehispanic civilizations, and their identity as indigenous
people perpetuates elements of those traditions. In the alternative view scholars who regard ethnicity as instrumental see it as consciously created by actors
to protect themselves from a dominant group or to create a sense of common
purpose in competition over resources. The perspective of instrumentalism is
based on methodological individualism and rational choice theory. Ethnicity
is a system of created difference with little importance placed on questions of
authenticity. Thus members of an ethnic group might create customs or traits
to distinguish themselves from those dominating them. What counts here is
the creation of difference regardless of the origin of such difference. The Nahua
community in my study retains sixteenth-century Spanish cultural traits such
as dress, and people use the traits to create a distinctive identity for themselves.
In a sense, as stated in the epigraph by Adam Kuper, Nahua culture and identity are clarified if viewed in relation to mestizo culture, and vice versa.

Although primordialism and instrumentalism would seem to be incompat-
ible explanations of ethnicity, I believe the differences between the approaches
are more apparent than real. In fact, while cultural authenticity may not be
paramount, people often choose to cultivate and perpetuate ancient traditions
from their perceived past in order to create difference. Though the Nahua of
Amatlán may wear dress of sixteenth-century Spanish peasants, they have actively preserved their ancient prehispanic rituals in the face of vehement disap-
proval by the Catholic church and secular authorities. Blood sacrifice, sacred
pilgrimages, and elaborate curing rituals, among other traits, serve to distinguish the Nahua from their mestizo neighbors and act as the basis of Nahua
ethnic identity. Thus the Nahua are instrumental is selecting and maintaining
their primordial customs.

One of the key problems for anthropologists working in Mesoamerica has
been to explain how it is that indigenous culture has persisted after 500 years,
despite often brutal policies designed by Hispanic elites to obliterate it. A number of theories have been proposed to account for this remarkable continuity. Redfield (1941) suggested that communities in Mexico fall along a folk-
urban continuum with small homogeneous Native American communities at
one end and the heterogeneous city at the other. Aguirre Beltrán (1979) contended that indigenous culture traits survive in "regions of refuge," remote areas inhospitable to capitalist development where ancient cultures persist as if
in a time warp. Wolf (1957) argued that prehispanic culture survives in corporate communities that have closed themselves to outside influence in response
to colonial domination. These approaches are variations on a similar theme,
namely, that indigenous culture survives because villages steeped in the past

and hermetically sealed against outside influences protect and nourish the ancient traditions. The unspoken assumption here is that once exposed to the invigorating influence of the city or the modernizing influences of the national and international economy, indigenous culture will self-destruct.

There are numerous theoretical and empirical problems with these formulations. One is found in observations by ethnographers that Native American villages closest to urban centers can be more conservative of ancient culture than villages farther removed. For example, French ethnographer Chamoux (1981) documented the persistence of indigenous culture in Teopixca, a Nahua village within walking distance from the provincial capital of Huauchinango, Puebla. American ethnographer Taggart compared Nahua from the Hispanic-dominated town of Huitzilan with Nahua in the remote village of Yaonáhuac, both in Puebla state. Surprisingly, he found that people in the remote village were less monolingual and more accepting of elements of Hispanic culture than were people living in closer proximity to the representatives of Mexican society (Taggart 1983:42–52). Reina (1966) studied the highly conservative community of Chinautla, which existed side by side with Guatemala City.

These observations from the field seem to contradict the formulations of Redfield, Aguirre Beltrán, and Wolf, as well as the prevailing view among Hispanic elites in Mexico that indigenous culture is weakly held and ready to disintegrate on contact with outside forces. The observations of Chamoux, Taggart, Reina, myself, and others reveal an important dynamic about the persistence of cultural systems in Mexico and perhaps in other parts of the world as well. Culture and ethnic identity, far from being the dead hand of the past, are actively pursued by people against other groups as an organized and effective form of resistance to domination and obliteration and as a strategy to marshal forces in the competition against other groups for scarce resources. If this perspective is valid, one would expect that indigenous culture and identity would be more strongly held by people in closer or more frequent contact with a dominant group. Native Americans more removed from direct domination would be freer to experiment with culture change and would be more likely to accept elements of Hispanic culture if they were seen as advantageous. The approach to ethnicity outlined here would explain why remote villages sometimes paradoxically exhibit greater willingness to borrow cultural elements from the Hispanic elite. Of course, not all indigenous communities resist, and different responses must be explained as the result of local conditions.

The factors causing ethnogenesis are to be found in the material and pragmatic conditions of people's lives, and researchers should strive to identify the empirical factors that lead individual creative acts to become shared by members of a social group (see Hobsbawm and Ranger 1983 on the creation of cultural traditions).[4] We must reject the assertions of scholars such as Romanucci-Ross and De Vos, who state that "relative priority must be given to the emotional, even irrational psychological features underlying one's social identity" (Romanucci-Ross and De Vos 1995:12). We must also reject their statement that ethnicity is "a subjective sense of loyalty based on imagined origins and parentage rather than something to be measured by objectively visible present cultural criteria or historical facts" (Romanucci-Ross and De Vos 1995:13). It is certainly true that the subjective views of cultural participants have to be taken into account and, one hopes, explained, but the dynamic of ethnic group formation cannot be reduced to the subjective states of the people involved. Clearly, these authors despair of establishing any objective knowledge of human behavior (see Kuznar 1997 for a defense of a scientific anthropology against similar philosophical positions).

Ethnicity is directly linked to the production of cultural difference. To oversimplify a bit, culture was originally conceived by Tylor (1871) as a self-contained "complex whole" that accounts for the diversity of behavior throughout the world. The collapse of the European colonial empires and the increased sophistication of method and theory in sociocultural anthropology have transformed how anthropologists view culture. Thanks to world system theorists and others, analysts now recognize that local cultures everywhere must be understood in relation to the universal spread of European industrial capitalism, an early example of which was the Spanish invasion of Mexico. Wallerstein (1974), Wolf (1982), and many others have extended this insight and made it fundamental to contemporary ethnography. Fried (1975), for example, showed that tribes traditionally studied by anthropologists are best viewed as secondary formations in response to penetration of Euro-American power. Even uncontacted peoples have been indirectly influenced by economic and social forces unleashed in Europe and the United States. The uncomfortable fact is that what anthropologists have been studying are not pristine cultures tracing back to prehistory, but secondary tribes organized in response to either direct or indirect colonial contact. According to Fried, we have few if any records of pretribal peoples. Culture as well as the ethnic identity linked to it increasingly appears to be a subtle and powerful strategy on the part of groups of people to survive social, economic, and political domination by outsiders or their proxies. In sum, in the competitive advantage and resistance to domination achieved through ethnic identity, we find the origin of many culture traits. Following Barth, we may not be able to equate culture with ethnic groups, but ethnic groups owe their existence to cultural differences.

Culture, however, is largely unconscious. People go through their lives mostly unaware or at best vaguely cognizant of what type of kinship system they belong to or what concepts of personhood or metaphysical beliefs about the nature of time are associated with their group. One of the few ways people can bring their own cultural traditions to consciousness is to observe people who have different traditions. By experiencing other cultures, it is possible for a person to look with a new perspective and become more aware of his or her own cultural traditions. This creative estrangement is what allows ethnographers to enter an alien community and comprehend and document customs that often lie outside the consciousness of the local people themselves. When people are conquered or dominated by an alien group or when they compete against an alien group, they not only become conscious of their traditions; they begin to manipulate, elaborate, and regularize them to exaggerate their differences with the hated and feared other. In Mexico the adjustment to domination may be measured by the extent that ethnic identity is established and maintained. Culture traits are born or elaborated out of such opposition.

NAHUA ETHNIC IDENTITY AND CULTURE

An example of the process of cultivating ancient cultural elements among the Nahua of Amatlán can be found in the beliefs and rituals surrounding the key spirit entity, 7-Flower (*chicome xochitl* in Nahuatl). The spirit 7-Flower and his twin sister, 5-Flower (*macuili xochitl*), are dual aspects of the maize spirit, the bringer and sustainer of life. The origin of these names is uncertain, but 7-Flower and 5-Flower were Aztec day or deity names that undoubtedly derive from the prehispanic era (Sandstrom 1998; see also Braakhuis 1990, 2001; Hernández Ferrer 2000; Leynes and Olguín 1993). Maize is intimately linked to human beings and the human body in Nahua thought, both physically and spiritually. A complex elaboration of pilgrimages, sacrificial offerings, rituals, myths, and beliefs has grown up around this spirit pair. Although ancient in conception, the 7-Flower complex in its current incarnation is relatively recent. Schryer (1990:182–184) reports that the 7-Flower cult traces to a revitalization movement that occurred in the 1940s in the state of Puebla, near the Veracruz border. In 1998 another revitalization movement in response to socioeconomic changes and the Protestant incursion was in the process of forming in a community neighboring Amatlán. A Nahua girl named Amalia Bautista claimed to be a reincarnation of 7-Flower. She was attended by hundreds (on occasion, even thousands) of followers, who surrounded her with marigold flowers, the sacred *cempoal xochitl* ("20-flower") in Nahuatl. Villagers contended that she has never been seen to consume human food but sustains herself by eating only flowers. Here is a superb example of a culture trait in the making.[5]

In a real sense the Nahua have adapted to life under mestizo domination by preserving, elaborating, and even flaunting their distinctive cultural elements in order to set themselves apart from their Hispanic overlords. This strategy in no way suggests that Nahua culture is a sham, pursued by con artists to fool mestizo elites simply to beat them out of scarce resources. Ethnic identity can serve people only if it is deeply felt—if the distinctions that separate one group from another are believed by people to be profound, irrevocable, authentic, and reflective of differences that are essential. In the end, ethnic identity is self-identity, and self-identity is linked to self-worth and ultimately to the meaning of a human life. Ethnic identity creates cultural differences, and it assumes critical importance when one group dominates another or when groups wish to separate themselves because of some perceived advantage. Otherwise, ethnic groups tend to disappear through assimilation.

Perhaps it required the collapse of the old colonial order for anthropologists to perceive culture in this way, but the seeds of discovery are apparent in the writings of earlier scholars. In any case, it would be an overstatement to assert that all aspects of cultures worldwide reflect Euro-American domination, but certainly the place these cultures occupy in modern nation-states is a key factor in understanding their internal structure and content. An important point is that in establishing their ethnic identity—that is, their cultural identity—the Nahua of Amatlán are unconcerned about the aboriginal authenticity of the aspects of culture they choose to regard as indigenous. In attempting to link the production and maintenance of cultural and ethnic differences to processes of domination and group competition, I am not arguing that such processes account for all the differences among groups in the ethnographic record. Culture and ethnicity are complex phenomena that are the product of multiple causes. For example, elements of culture and social organization of the Nahua of northern Veracruz can be partially understood in relation to the slash-and-burn productive system that sustains them. The internal workings of this system may have few or no direct links to ethnic group formation or to the positions of the various Nahua groups in Mexico. On the other hand, ecological adaptation may also be profoundly affected by group relations. Three examples from Amatlán illustrate the point. First, Nahua horticultural production is certainly implicated in the competition with mestizos and other indigenous groups over land resources. Second, land shortages in Amatlán resulting from competition with other groups have adversely affected the Nahua kinship system, a key element in their social organization (see Sandstrom 1991:182–188). Third, the level of Nahua technology is explainable to a certain extent as a strategy to avoid direct domination by mestizo elites. By not employing expensive fertilizers or machinery in their farming, the Nahua are effectively refusing to enter into debt relations with elites and thus retaining a degree of independence. Other groups, either in positions of dominance or as competitors for the same resources, are an important part of the overall environment in which the Nahua have to operate. Virtually no human group is completely isolated, and thus other people are always going to be important factors in the environment. The degree to which a culture is the product of ecological or other internal factors or the product of interaction with outsiders is a question that can be answered only by research in the field; see the similar point made by Barth (1969:12–13).

NAHUA RITUALS

I aim to link Nahua religious beliefs and practices with processes of ethnogenesis in order to clarify how competition over resources involves even the realm of religion and is indeed one of the major means by which Nahua define themselves in opposition to dominant groups (on contemporary Nahua religion, see Báez-Jorge and Gómez Martínez 2000, 2001; Gómez Martínez

1999a; Lupo 2001; Reyes García and Christensen 1976; Sandstrom 1991, 1992; Signorini and Lupo 1989; on Mesoamerican religion generally, see Monaghan 2000b).[6] Nahua rituals in this region of Mexico are complex affairs that entail adorning altars, depicting large numbers of anthropomorphic images of key spirit entities in cut paper, and dedicating valued commodities, especially animal blood. Paper was a sacred substance in prehispanic Mesoamerica, where it was used to adorn priests and statues, to make flags and banners, and as an offering in its own right. Sixteenth-century chroniclers documented that paper was cut into shapes and sprinkled with latex or blood as an offering to specific spirits; see the passage recorded by Bernardino de Sahagún (1976:Book 9:9–11 [1575–1580]) in the Florentine Codex; see also Barrera Rivera et al. (2001) for a description of a recent find in Mexico City of an Aztec cache containing paper offerings.[7] When I first entered this remote area in the 1970s, I had no idea that papermaking and its sacred associations survived there to such an extent. The answer to the intriguing question of why such a ritual complex would persist against overwhelming odds is clarified by the perspective developed in this chapter.

The key component of a ritual is the offering (*tlamanilistli* in Huastecan Nahuatl, *ofrenda* or *promesa* in Spanish), which the Nahua view as a kind of exchange with spirit entities. Spirits can be seen as metaphors for cosmic forces and processes of nature, and they provide such benefits for humans as rain, fertility, and health. For example, the Nahua conceive of spirits of the earth, spirits of the water, spirits of the seeds, and so on. Humans, in turn, create beautiful rituals and dedicate special offerings to the spirits. This exchange cycle represents the normal operation of the cosmos: in other words, the Nahua abide and the spirits provide. In this conception human beings are seen as dependent for their lives on precarious natural forces symbolically represented by spirit entities. In Burkhart's (1989) felicitous phrase describing the sixteenth-century Nahua world view, the earth is slippery and people must proceed with great caution. The spirits associated with natural forces provide the essentials for life so long as people respect the forces of nature as well as one another. The word for "respect" in Huastecan Nahuatl is *tlatlepanitalistli*, and for the Nahua it is the most important attribute of an authentic human being. One important way to demonstrate respect is to participate in the round of ritual offerings. The exchange function of rituals is quite conscious among most participants. Ritual specialists chant before the carefully arranged items, listing them and extolling their qualities. At major rituals helpers make a list of all participants along with the exact amount of money or goods they contributed so that the spirits will know precisely who demonstrates respect. What, then, interrupts this harmonious cycle and causes the problems of this world—climatic devastation, disease, and misfortune? In the delicate balance of goods and services circulated between the human and spirit realms, problems arise when acts of disrespect create obstacles.

Nahua curing practice and disease-prevention rituals are part of the same

FIGURE 6.1.
Ritual specialist
Encarnación (Cirilo)
Téllez Hernández
arranges a display as part
of a curing ritual. Note
the cut-paper figures that
represent disease-causing
wind spirits associated
with acts of disrespect.
The palm bundles are
symbolic brooms that are
rubbed on the patient to
remove polluting wind
spirits. A curing is called
an *ochpantli* in Nahuatl
and a *limpia* or *barrida* in
Spanish. The terms mean
"cleansing" or "sweeping
clean."

ceremonial complex and follow a basic pattern found in all Nahua rituals (see Gallardo Arias 2000). After first gazing in a crystal or casting kernels of corn to divine the origin or nature of the disease, the ritual specialist creates an elaborate altar and dedicates an offering to sacred cut-paper images of disease-causing wind spirits in an effort to remove them from the patient's body and surroundings (Sandstrom 1978; see Figures 6.1–6.7). The Nahua identify a number of causes of disease, including sorcery and soul loss, but at the root of most diseases are acts of disrespect, called *axtlatlepanita*. Disrespect encompasses such socially disruptive acts as gossiping, lying, saying malicious things, failing to make amends for planting in the milpa, sullying the earth through human activities, or neglecting to participate in rituals. Acts of disrespect attract the wind spirits, called *ejecamej* (singular *ejecatl*). Ejecatl spirits are the angry souls of villagers who died unpleasant or premature deaths. These aggressive spirits roam the villages seeking vulnerable people.[8] It is interesting to note that the person who engages in disrespectful behavior is often not the one to suffer from the resulting disease. Children or the elderly are more likely to fall ill because their life forces are less powerful than those of most adult men or women. This belief differs from the common assumption found in world or state-level religions that it is the sinner who pays for the sin. In contrast, Nahua religion demonstrates greater concern for the social good than the salvation of the individual (Sandstrom and Tsai 1996). Members of Nahua villages have an obligation to show respect in order to protect not just themselves but the whole community from wind-spirit attack. The Nahua often associate ejecatl spirits with filth or disorder. In essence, the dangerous winds are agents of pollution attracted to disruptions in the Nahua cultural order (Sandstrom 1989).

In a sense, all Nahua rituals, even those aimed at producing rain or increas-

FIGURE 6.2. Close-up of a curing display showing rows of paper figures representing wind spirits. The vine and marigold loop surrounding the display is used by the ritual specialist to remove wind spirits from a patient's body. The ritual specialist passes the loop over the patient a number of times to complete the cleansing (raising it seven times and lowering it seven times).

FIGURE 6.3. Close-up of a curing display showing blackened figures with lighted cigarettes in their mouths as a tobacco offering. These fearsome images portray *tlacatecolotl* (owl man) and his wife, who rule in *mictlan* (place of the dead). The brazier contains copal incense.

FIGURE 6.4. The central part of a curing display. Cups contain coffee and bread offerings. The curing specialist reaches for a candle before beginning his chant and dedication of the offerings.

FIGURE 6.5. The ritual specialist begins to pour out the offerings over the paper images of the disease-causing spirits. Each pathogen is attracted to its image and consumes the essence of the offering.

FIGURE 6.6.
Encarnación (Cirilo)
Téllez Hernández
dedicates the offerings
to images of the wind
spirits in a disease-
prevention ritual to
remove pathogens from
a spring where people
and cattle obtain water.

ing crop or human fertility, are cures, in that they correct an imbalance in the
cosmos by exchanging offerings and removing obstacles to the normal flow of
values between spirits and human beings. Acts of disrespect alienate key spirits
and cause them to withhold benefits, resulting in a broad class of misfortunes
ranging from illness or human infertility to natural events such as drought,
floods, and crop failure. Thus disease for the Nahua is defined much more in-
clusively than simple bodily injury or illness. Nahua rituals are fundamentally
similar to each other because they all seek to reestablish respectful relations
between humans and spirits. It is no surprise that the Nahua curing specialist (called a *tlamatiquetl*, literally a "person of knowledge") directs all rituals,
whether to alleviate physical illness or appeal for rain.[9]

One final symbolic association needs to be discussed before we turn to the
pilgrimage. As might be expected in the Mesoamerican culture area, blood oc-
cupies a special place in Nahua ideology. Most people are aware of the bloody
human sacrifices that horrified the Spaniards following their first contact with
the Aztecs. Blood contains *chicahualistli*, the animating force that supplies the
energy for living. It is literally the power or force of life—that which allows sen-
tient beings to move and feel. Chicahualistli comes from the foods that humans

FIGURE 6.7.
Ritual specialist Silveria
Hernández Hernández
sits before a display of
wind spirit images. She
is conducting a curing
ritual for a patient with
epilepsy.

eat but in particular from corn. And corn, in turn, acquires its energy from the sun, *tonatij*, the Nahua creator deity who animates the cosmos and illuminates the world. To offer blood by spreading it on paper images of spirits is to give the spirits chicahualistli, energy and power, and to motivate them to provide what humans need and desire. Thus paper images of water, thunder, earth, hill, wind, and seed spirits receive the precious substance in the expectation that once energized, these entities will restore the flow of benefits to humans.

PILGRIMAGE AND BLOOD SACRIFICE

I now turn to an elaborate pilgrimage and ritual sequence undertaken to appeal for rain and place this activity in the context of Nahua religion and processes of ethnicity. The destination of two recent pilgrimages is an unusual mountain, the basaltic core of an ancient volcano that rises abruptly nearly 2,000 feet from the surrounding countryside. Within sight of this enormous monolith, which lies about 25 miles from Amatlán near the Nahua town of Ichcacuatitla, Chicontepec, Veracruz, rise six other smaller volcanic formations. The major sacred peak, called Postectitla or simply Postectli, meaning "something broken" in Nahuatl, is the subject of many myths and legends, and it is visited regularly by pilgrims from all the neighboring indigenous groups. Postectli and the six lesser hills are among Mexico's most striking geological features. From certain angles Postectli does give the appearance of having been broken off at the top by some primordial cataclysm. Near its summit are two caves, one the home of thunder spirits and the other the dwelling place of *apanchanej*, the water spirit. At the peak the Catholic church has constructed a large cement cross to symbolize in a not-so-subtle way the conquest of Christianity over the Native American religions. For the Nahua, the summit is associated with *tonatij*, the sun spirit. In an interesting case of syncretism, the Nahua refer to the sun as Jesús, and they view the cross as a symbol of solar heat and power. Rejecting the church's definition of the situation, they have transformed a symbol of Spanish imperialism into an affirmation of their own belief system.

The pilgrimage to the sacred mountain and blood sacrifice is a ritual on a vastly different scale from a simple curing, and yet, as I suggested earlier, it derives from the same fundamental religious principles. Its purpose is to remove obstacles created by acts of disrespect. As mentioned above, we were able to witness the pilgrimage and associated rituals on two occasions. Including preparations, the events in each case lasted about 10 days. Typical of larger Nahua rituals, the preparations and offerings go on day and night with no pause for sleep aside from short naps. Throughout the entire period, including during the pilgrimage itself and the ascent to the summit, musicians continuously played the sacred melodies on guitar and violin. The musical pieces, repetitive and hypnotic as the hours stretch into days and nights, are called "flower songs" (or *xochisones* in the Nahuatl-Spanish expression) (see Hernández Azuara 2001; Sandstrom and Provost 1977). Ritual activity would increase dramatically from time to time, to be punctuated by periods of relative quiet and inactivity.

It is impossible to offer a complete description of an event so complex and filled with such richly layered symbolic acts, but here I briefly describe a few episodes from the pilgrimage in 2001. In response to drought conditions, the pilgrimage was organized by a widely respected Nahua ritual specialist named Encarnación Téllez Hernández, known locally as Cirilo. On Cirilo's altar in the tiny shrine attached to his house is a box made from tropical cedar. Inside is a collection of approximately 60 paper figures representing the life force or animating spirits of the seeds that Nahua farmers plant in the milpa. Each figure is dressed in a cloth outfit and is adorned with tiny necklaces, earrings, combs, and other accoutrements. During an episode early in the ritual, women opened the box and undressed the figures. They washed and dried the diminutive clothing and dressed each figure again and carefully placed it with the others in a new sisal carrying bag. All this activity was done in a slow and measured pace while the music played and individuals danced before the altar with smoking copal incense braziers. In Nahua myth the seed spirits represented by the paper figures were lured into the village from their cave home atop Pos-

FIGURE 6.8.
Encarnación (Cirilo) Téllez Hernández and other ritual specialists conduct a curing ritual to remove disease-causing wind spirits. The cleansing is held in anticipation of a blood sacrifice conducted as part of a pilgrimage to appeal for rain. Cirilo holds a smoking copal incense brazier, and others at his side hold sacred walking sticks.

tectli. The Nahua say that the seeds choose to remain in the community so long as they are treated well and not assaulted by acts of disrespect. Otherwise, they will return to their mountain home and the people will suffer starvation.

In another episode participants cleaned the altar in the shrine and placed fresh palm and flower adornments on it. Cirilo, along with other ritual specialists who had joined him, and a growing number of helpers, placed neat rows of paper images on cut-paper sheets called "beds," or *petates* (the Spanish word for palm sleeping mats, from the Nahuatl *petlatl*, singular). Several dozen of these mats were prepared and placed so that they completely covered the altar. In a related episode participants danced before the altar holding sheaves of palm and marigold adornments. This sequence served to dedicate the offerings to the spirits portrayed by the paper figures. In the middle of the night Cirilo moved outside the shrine to lay out on the ground a complex array of paper images of various colors along with offerings of tobacco, cornmeal, soft drinks, palm and flower adornments, cane alcohol, bread, and other items. Several ritual specialists stood alongside the array holding sacred walking sticks and smoking incense braziers, as well as the scissors they had used to cut the paper images. Each of the ritual specialists chanted individually to disease-causing wind spirits in order to keep destructive forces at bay during the ritual offering to follow (see Figure 6.8). This episode constituted a complete curing ritual encompassed within the larger observance. By removing wind spirits, the ritual specialists helped to eliminate the dangerous, disruptive potential of disrespectful acts and thereby protect the major offering and pilgrimage.

Several hours later the participants moved inside the shrine, where ritual specialists began the process of sacrificing a number of chickens and turkeys. In addition to other activities, this episode involved dancing, chanting, mock combat, and force-feeding the victims cane alcohol and soft drinks. At the height of the sacrifice, ritual specialists cut the throats of the birds with scissors and carefully sprinkled the blood on each one of the hundreds of paper figures arranged on the altar. The birds were later removed to be cooked and eaten by participants as part of the overall offering. In the early morning a procession made up of ritual specialists and musicians visited a spring in the village and dedicated an offering, which included bloody paper figures from the earlier sacrifice, to the water spirit *apanchanej* (literally, "water dweller" in Nahuatl) (see Báez-Jorge 1992; Gómez Martínez 1999b; Martínez de la Cruz 2000).

Throughout the proceedings male and female ritual specialists continued to cut paper figures while helpers made palm and flower adornments. Thousands of paper figures were produced, along with 3,000 palm and flower adornments. Not only did the paper for the sacred images have to be folded and cut, but various features such as the eyes, mouth, and cuts within the body had to be folded open. Once completed, the figures were carefully counted and arranged on the cut-paper mats, which in turn were stacked on top of one another to form thick books that were tied into a large bundle and then wrapped in a new palm mat. To be effective, Nahua rituals require a significant commitment of time, effort, and resources.

The trek to Postectli was proceeded by several days and nights of ritual activity, during which time we made preparations for the pilgrimage.[10] The pilgrims started out at noon and arrived in the dark at about 11:00 P.M. The walk took us cross country, far from roadways, skirting a number of remote villages and out-of-the-way settlements. We stopped briefly at springs and water holes along the way, where the ritual specialists left small offerings. The participants were led by a man who carried a beribboned sacred walking stick. Following at the rear, another man carried a smaller walking stick, thus setting off the moving sacred space. The walking stick is reminiscent of ones said to be held by 12 rain dwarfs—thunder spirits who are believed to transport water from the sea (Gulf of Mexico) to the cave on Postectli, from which vantage the water spirit distributes it to the fields. As these figures pass overhead, they strike their sticks, causing thunder and lightning. The colorful ribbons represent the rays of light at sunrise. Two women transported the dressed seed figures in sisal carrying bags as others, using tumplines, lugged carrying baskets filled with offerings. The procession consisted of nearly 70 people, ranging from children as young as 10 years old to women well into their seventies. As we walked along, it was remarkable to see people emerge from their houses bringing gifts of food, sugarloaf, flowers, and money so that we could include them among the offerings on the mountain. Some people had tears streaming down their faces as they presented us with these gifts.

On arriving at the base of Postectli, the pilgrims rested from their journey in the *xochicali* (Nahuatl for "shrine," literally "flower house") after eating the food prepared for them by local women. No one had slept properly for days. That evening the ritual specialists conducted yet another complete curing rit-

FIGURE 6.9.
Ritual specialists arrange
a display of images of
wind spirits just before
participants in the
pilgrimage begin their
ascent of Postectli.

ual, including the usual elaborate display of cut-paper figures and offerings to
the wind spirits. Following the curing, the ritual offering continued all night
with chanting, dancing, music, and blood sacrifice on paper figures arrayed
on the main altar. The crowd in the small building numbered more than 100
people. The ritual specialists spent hours finishing the task of cutting paper figures and arranging the offerings. It was another sleepless night of ritual activity
as everyone prepared themselves for the climb the next day.

Early the next morning the ritual specialists chanted together before the
main altar and then moved outside, where they laid out another array of wind
spirits and conducted another curing ritual. Some of the figures cut from white
paper had been blackened with charcoal from a fireplace. Helpers inserted
lighted cigarettes into the paper figures' mouths as a tobacco offering. These
images represented *tlacatecolotl* ("owl man") and his wife (*tlacatecolotl sihuatl*),
who are leading figures in *mictlan*, "place of the dead" (Báez-Jorge and Gómez
Martínez 1998, 2001). The offering was to prevent these harmful entities and
wind spirits from interfering with or benefiting from the rituals dedicated to
the sacred hill (Figures 6.9 and 6.10). Following this ritual, we loaded up the
offerings and lined up for the brief walk to the base of the mountain. The town

FIGURE 6.10.
Participants in the
pilgrimage approach the
curing display. Note the
ritual specialist holding
a sacred walking stick.
The woman just out of
the photograph to the
left carries a new sisal
bag containing sacred
cut-paper seed spirits
dressed in tiny outfits.

of Ichcacuatitla is situated beneath Postectli, but access to the trail leading to
the summit is about a mile away on the opposite side of the hill. The ascent begins gradually but soon becomes perilously steep. The pilgrims struggled up
the slope, made muddy and extremely slippery by the tropical downpour that
had occurred during the night.

About one-third of the way to the summit, Cirilo, the lead shaman for the
event, instructed everyone to rest at a flat place on the trail. There was an altar structure built up against the mountainside, and helpers cleared the area of
old ritual offerings and prepared to dedicate new ones. Meanwhile, the ritual
specialists conducted yet another curing ritual complete with paper images of
wind spirits and the full array of offerings (Figures 6.11–6.13).[11] As the curing
ritual was conducted off to one side, helpers laid out beds of paper figures on
the cleaned altar, decorated the arch with palm and flower adornments, and
created the beautiful space that defines a Nahua altar. Two chickens were sacrificed and their blood carefully sprinkled on the paper figures. People danced
before the altar as the ritual specialists chanted and the musicians played flower
songs on the guitar and violin. In one unusual episode Cirilo and his helpers
entombed a white chicken in a small depression in the rock face above the altar.

FIGURE 6.11.
About one-third
of the way to the
summit of Postectli,
Encarnación (Cirilo)
Téllez Hernández and
assistants construct
another curing display.
A major purpose
of the pilgrimage is
to neutralize acts of
disrespect, symbolized
by the paper images of
the wind spirits.

FIGURE 6.12.
Ritual specialists arrange
images of wind spirits
during the first stop en
route to the summit of
Postectli.

FIGURE 6.13.
Ritual specialists and
helpers view the curing
display before they begin
to chant and dedicate
the offerings.

The bird was buried alive with palm and flower adornments, soft drinks and beer, and other items as an offering to *mixtli*, the cloud.

We loaded up the supplies and proceeded farther up the rock face. It was hand-over-hand climbing for the next several hours. At about three-quarters of the way to the summit, we rested at another flat place and helpers immediately began to set up an elaborate altar (Figure 6.14). Each of the hundreds of paper figures received their blood offering as the participants danced and chanted before the decorated sacred space. A large cut-paper figure of *apanchanej*, the water spirit, dressed in a dark green cloth dress and highly decorated with jewelry and ribbons, was placed in a clay pot that was then paraded around. People placed candles and coins in the pot for luck and to increase religious merit. A small contingent of pilgrims then proceeded to carry additional offerings up the mountain to a small cave where *apanchanej* dwells. There Cirilo knelt before the opening and chanted as helpers arranged the offerings. Bloody paper figures on their paper sleeping mats were carefully placed in the cave entrance, and a chicken was killed and tossed into the cave as a final offering. Cirilo and his helpers then dedicated an offering to thunder spirits in a nearby cleft in the rock.

FIGURE 6.14.
An altar to beneficial spirits has been erected at the second stop on the way to the summit of Postectli. Note the two musicians standing in the background and bloody paper images on the ground.

After a brief pause the participants loaded up the remaining items and began the almost vertical climb to the summit. When we arrived, people immediately proceeded to construct four separate altars. A major one was dedicated to the cross. As mentioned, the cross represents the solar fire, the life-giving heat that animates the cosmos. Ritual specialists sacrificed chickens and laid an elaborate food offering atop the bloodied paper figures. Meanwhile, helpers fashioned a circular structure on the eastern side of the summit as an altar to the solar disk. Below this sun altar (slightly to the south), helpers constructed another altar, this time to the moon. Another small offering was laid out beneath the cement cross looming at the summit. Shortly after these offerings were dedicated, everyone undertook the arduous descent, and we arrived at the bottom many hours later. The ritual was officially ended, and the people expressed happiness that their efforts had been a success: the precarious balance between the spirit and human realms had been restored.

A religious observance of this complexity can be analyzed in a number of ways and at various levels of abstraction (see Sandstrom 2003 for a further interpretation). Here I briefly examine the ritual pilgrimage and offering at a very basic level to show the connection to Nahua ethnicity. The pilgrimage and blood sacrifice had two clear and fundamental purposes: first, to dedicate blood and other valued offerings to the spirit entities associated with the forces of nature on which the Nahua depend for their very lives; and second, to eliminate impediments to the flow of benefits between these spirits and the human community. The commitment in time, effort, and resources by the Nahua pilgrims and ritual specialists can clearly be seen in the manufacture of thousands of paper images and adornments and the number of altars laboriously constructed as part of the offering. Beyond the goods, the commitment extended to 10 days with little rest, a day-long hike over hot and hilly terrain, and a perilous climb up a 2,000-foot rock face carrying heavy loads of ritual offerings. Of greater direct relevance to the question of ethnic identity are the repeated efforts throughout the ritual to remove offenses that cause spirits to withhold their benefits. Eliminating these impediments was accomplished by conducting four complete curing/cleansing sequences at selected times during the 10-day observance. A curing was conducted prior to the first offering at the shrine in Amatlán, at the base of Postectli on the evening of the pilgrims' arrival, in the morning before their ascent, and at the first stop on the trail to the summit. Each curing episode was directed to wind spirits, represented in material form by hundreds of paper images. The curing rituals symbolically removed or neutralized the acts of disrespect that are so offensive to beneficial spirits. With these obstacles out of the way, Nahua ritual specialists were able to dedicate blood offerings to beneficial spirits in order to stimulate them to continue the flow of benefits.

While many local mestizos view the Nahua as uncultured and near savages, the Nahua obviously hold their stereotypes of the mestizos in return. They accuse individual mestizos of lying, being aggressive, saying malicious things, and stealing. According to the Nahua, it is largely mestizo acts of disrespect (*axtlatlepanita*) that cause the sickness, drought, and misfortune that plague them and other indigenous peoples of Mexico. I was told by one ritual specialist that it was the failure of rich people (*los ricos*, i.e., mestizos) to respect the earth that led to the devastating earthquake in 1985 that killed so many people in the Mexican capital. In Nahua opinion, though mestizos themselves do not have the power to produce such catastrophes directly, like all people they have the capacity to offend the spirits who possess such power.[12] The curing rituals are a symbolic means employed by the Nahua to neutralize obstacles to the flow of benefits from the spirit realm, obstructions largely put in place by the disrespectful acts of mestizo elites. I asked Cirilo as he was organizing the pilgrimage what he believed to be the cause of the drought. He answered without hesitation, "Because the rich people have polluted the earth and they have failed to respect the things of this world." The round of Nahua rituals, then, can be seen at one level as an expression of Nahua identity. More important, however, it is a strategy or an active mechanism that indigenous people employ to redress and counteract the misfortunes that mestizos inflict on them.

In and of themselves, the act of participating in traditional curing rituals and the undertaking of pilgrimages to Postectli constitute resistance to the mestizo definition of the world. No mestizo would participate in such rituals or pilgrimages. In the Nahua view, mestizos by definition do not abide by the processes and natural forces in the cosmos that make life possible and worth living. By not participating in ritual offerings, mestizos thereby fail to contribute to necessary exchanges with the spirits. To be Nahua is to understand the way the cosmos really works and to act accordingly; to be mestizo is to lack such understanding. The symbolic message of the curing rituals could not be plainer: domination by mestizos is the major cause of the misfortunes afflicting Nahua life and well-being.

This ritual complex is an important component of the religious and spiritual world of the Nahua as well as their Otomí and Tepehua neighbors. Anyone who is familiar with Mesoamerican culture history will recognize the continuity of practices rooted in the prehispanic past and the reflection of a world view radically different from the one introduced by the Spaniards. I do not claim that the pilgrimage and associated rituals are pristine and unchanged. On the contrary, over time they have been modified to address the tragedy of subordination to Hispanic elites. But I do see them as firmly based in indigenous Mesoamerican cultural traditions. Over the centuries the Nahua have resisted pressures to abandon their traditional beliefs and have asserted their identity as indigenous people against Spanish and mestizo dominant groups. They have used their cultural practices and identity as Nahua as an effective weapon of people in the untenable position of chronic weakness.

ETHNIC IDENTITY AND CULTURE CHANGE

This chapter has attempted to show that Nahua culture and ritual life are closely related to processes by which the people have created and maintained an identity as Nahua to resist domination by Hispanic elites in Mexico. What may seem on the surface to be distinct realms of experience, such as technology, dress, curing rituals, and sacred pilgrimages to appeal for rain, can all be seen as aspects of ethnicity. I have tried to make the case that key Nahua culture traits can be understood as creative attempts to generate and sustain difference in the face of colonial or other forms of domination or competition. The specific form that ethnicity takes depends on the historical experiences of the group and local conditions that affect the pragmatic concerns of people as they go about making a living and creating meaningful lives for themselves. Many of the familiar cultures of the contemporary world are not pristine social forms with origins deep in prehistory but rather formations arising in response to Euro-American expansion over the past half millennium. When different peoples meet, they are made aware of other customs and, as a by-product, become conscious of their own traditions. It is this same creative estrangement that has allowed anthropologists and other cross-cultural researchers to perceive their own largely unconscious social arrangements and shared beliefs and to gain insight into the phenomenon of culture itself.

Nahua rituals, regardless of purpose, share certain essential features. They differ from Hispanic beliefs and practices and thus define what it is to be Nahua in a mestizo-dominated world. To participate in ritual life is the strongest statement that can be made that one is a Native American and a person who respects the things of this world. Most mestizos, by definition in the Nahua view, do not respect the processes and natural forces in the cosmos that make life possible. More important, the rituals serve symbolically to remove and render harmless obstacles placed between people and the spirit forces that sustain them, placed there by mestizo (and even Nahua) acts of disrespect. Nahua rituals are filtering mechanisms that screen out dominant-group behavior that disturbs the equilibrium between the human and spirit realms. As such, these rituals sustain Nahua ethnic identity and remove alien elements that defile Nahua culture.

Clearly, ethnicity in its many manifestations is one of the most important social forces on the world scene today. Ethnicity has the power to tear nations apart and divide people into mutually hostile groups whose members do not recognize the humanity, much less the human rights, of out-group members. As in the case of the Nahua of Mexico, an ethnic identity also can protect the downtrodden and give the exploited a space in which to live their lives. In the end, I suspect that anthropologists and historians will locate the root cause of ethnic-group formation in political domination, resource competition, exploitation, and the need for subjugated groups to protect themselves from annihilation.

I conclude by illustrating how the perspective on ethnicity outlined here helps to explain puzzling changes that sometimes occur in subordinate populations. We have seen that the religious system in Amatlán is fundamentally Native American with an admixture of Spanish Catholicism. Therefore, I was quite surprised to observe the headway that fundamentalist Protestant sects have made in Amatlán and in other indigenous villages nearby since the 1980s. The missionaries and their converts are known generally by the Spanish label *hermanos*, "brothers," and the first converts appeared to be the poorer, less successful villagers. In an effort to uncover what was happening in Amatlán, I conducted interviews with several dozen men and women. Most people had a clear idea of what was happening and were more than willing to express their opinions.

Many of the villagers I spoke with agreed that the transformation could be traced to a period of several months between the end of 1982 and the late spring of 1983. During this time three major events occurred. First, the Mexican federal government approved an increase in per capita land allocations in the village. This policy meant that average household income rose in 1983. The second factor was the worldwide decline in oil prices in 1982, which led to the general collapse of the Mexican economy. Mestizo ranchers, who were hit harder by the depression than were small-scale horticulturalists, could offer little temporary work for the people. Suddenly, with more land to plant and potentially more income, the former symbiotic relationship between Nahua villagers and mestizo ranchers broke down. Young men were forced to search for work in the cities rather than on nearby ranches, and despite the depression, they discovered opportunities for higher-paying temporary wage labor farther from home. At this same time a third factor for change arrived in the form of Protestant missionaries, who moved in to take advantage of regional instability caused by the economic collapse (see Dow and Sandstrom 2001 on Protestant conversion in Mesoamerica).

By all accounts it was the young people returning from their temporary employment in the cities who provided the greatest and most conspicuous stimulus for change. It was not so much the new ideas they brought back or the money they were able to earn. Far more crucial was the fact that their act of leaving the region and finding work in urban centers had changed relations between the villagers and the local mestizo elite. As long as people were forced to search for work on ranches, being Nahua had its advantages. In the city, however, being Native American was a distinct liability, and this fact undermined the motivation to create or sustain an indigenous identity. The critical distinction between Nahua and mestizo originating in the distant colonial past and marked so well today by dress, language, motor habits, and religion no longer served the interest of many villagers. Obscuring the boundaries between Native American and mestizo poses little threat to the solidarity of the subordinate ethnic group as long as no alternative identities are available. In 1982, however, an alternative did become available, provided by the missionaries. The people first attracted to the new religion were unsuccessful by other villagers' standards and those who benefited least from maintaining their status as Native Americans.

Suddenly, a new option completely outside the range of traditional choices was opened for the marginal villagers. They no longer had to be either Nahua or rural mestizos—they now had the possibility of being *hermanos*. In essence, the Protestant converts are becoming a third ethnic group that owes little to its indigenous heritage or to the mestizo hierarchy. In an interesting affirmation of the past, however, it is Pentecostalism that has been the most successful among the Protestant sects finding converts in the Gulf Coast. Pentecostalism shares with the traditional religion the direct experience of the spirit order, an emphasis on curing, colorful and intense gatherings for worship, a relatively nonhierarchical power structure, and a number of other coincidental features.

Underlying the abrupt phenomenon of religious conversion are fundamental changes in the old economic and political arrangements. The now-easy flow of young people back and forth from the cities accelerated the abandonment of many traditional symbols of indigenous identity. Rapidly, in Amatlán as elsewhere, the old costume is being replaced by urban mestizo dress, the houses are being built with cement block and corrugated iron, and the village layout is made more urban-like to accommodate the electric and now telephone lines leading to each house. But not all Nahua are becoming Protestants. The people who continue to participate in the pilgrimages persist in embracing their traditions and use them to defend against exploitation, creating a reality that differs from that of the mestizos as well as the Protestant converts.

ACKNOWLEDGMENTS

An earlier version of this chapter was read at the symposium "Ethnic Identity in Mexico: Pre-Columbian to Modern Times" at the Anglo-American Conference of Historians, School of Advanced Study, University of London, in July 1999. I thank conference participants Frances Berdan and John Chance for their comments and also Pamela Effrein Sandstrom, Lawrence Kuznar, James Taggart, and Michael Smith for their critical remarks. A revised version was read at the Center for United States–Mexico Studies of the University of California, San Diego, in March 2001. I thank the American Council of Learned Societies, the American Philosophical Society, the Foundation for the Advancement of Mesoamerican Studies, Inc. (FAMSI), and Indiana University–Purdue University Fort Wayne for supporting the ethnographic research among the Nahua of northern Veracruz on which this study is based.

7

Nahuat Ethnicity in a Time of Agrarian Conflict

James M. Taggart

DEEP IN THE SIERRA NORTE DE PUEBLA, FORTY NAHUAT MEN INVADED a cattle pasture and planted a cornfield. They were members of the UCI, the Unión Campesina Independiente or League of Independent Farmers, an armed agrarian organization that appeared in the sierra in 1977. The pasture was called Talcuaco, meaning "land above the community," and was a blatant reminder, on the steep hills above Huitzilan, that mestizos had taken land that Nahuat had once used for growing corn and converted it to cattle pastures and coffee orchards. The Nahuat in the UCI collided with the ambitions of a prominent mestizo, who allegedly called in the army, which chopped down the UCI's cornfield. Seven years of conflict followed these events during which more than 200 women, men, and children, mostly Nahuat, died violently, and scores more left the village for good. The conflict seemed, at first glance, to pit poor Nahuat against rich mestizos, but ethnicity and ethnic relations are far more complicated.[1]

This chapter is about the subjective meaning of Nahuat ethnicity before and after this troubled period in Huitzilan's history. Ethnicity can mean many things in the Nahua and mestizo regions of Mexico, as Schryer (1990) has shown in his study of the nearby Huasteca of Hidalgo, where Nahuas were usually the subordinate group and mestizos the dominant one, as in Huitzilan. Schryer (1990:47, 245–256) raised some important questions about the meaning of ethnicity, questions that give one pause in concluding that the conflict in Huitzilan was as simple as it looked, at least from the surface. He discovered that Huasteca Nahuas did not apply the ethnic labels of *macehual* (commoner, indigenous person) and *coyot* (coyote, or mestizo) in ways that neatly accorded with other markers that anthropologists might use to classify people as indigenous or mestizo, such as language and dress. Ethnic and class boundaries often crossed rather than ran parallel in the land invasion and agrarian conflict in the Huasteca, which began six years earlier than in the Sierra Norte de Puebla. In some cases poor Nahuas invaded land owned by wealthy Nahuas, and some mestizos assumed Nahua ethnic identity to promote their careers in Huasteca politics.

For some Marxists, class is the real issue, and ethnicity is false consciousness that gets in the way of developing class consciousness.[2] However, Barth (1969) had in mind a more deeply inculcated notion of ethnicity when he recommended that the study of ethnic groups and boundaries shift from a focus on objective traits to an examination of how actors interpret their world. He wrote: "Since belonging to an ethnic category implies being a certain kind of person, having that basic identity, it also implies a claim to be judged, and to judge oneself, by those standards that are relative to that identity" (1969:14). To emphasize how an actor makes moral judgments is to treat ethnicity as an aspect of personhood grounded in the "practical religion," the standards that guide the conduct of an ordinary believer (Leach 1968:1).

I examine some of the ways ethnicity is a deeply inculcated part of the Nahuat subject by taking a close look at moral discourse. The Nahuat have a profound sense of morality, which parents teach children with a combination of love and punishment to form a subject (see Butler 1997). The Nahuat act as ethnic subjects when they apply the terms of their moral discourse to judge the behavior of mestizos. However, they tend not to make monolithic judgments, in part because their conception of ethnicity is not linked to race. Moreover, in response to the conflict that erupted over Talcuaco, the Nahuat have changed the meaning of terms that once had ethnic referents.

To understand Nahuat ethnicity in these ways, I relied on ethnographic observations, particularly oral narratives and oral histories, which I recorded in Huitzilan between 1968 and 1978 and again between 2003 and 2005. Dramatic changes, which affected the way Nahuat interpret their social world, took place during the seven years between 1977 and 1984, when violence raged through Huitzilan. Oral histories and narratives collected before (1968–1978) and after (2003–2005) reveal some of the ways the Nahuat changed their ideas about ethnic groups and boundaries because of conflict that arose over the Talcuaco milpa. My thesis is that the Nahuat changed their referents to terms in their ethnic discourse because they define ethnicity according to human activity rather than biological descent.

ETHNICITY AND CULTURE

Stark and Chance (this volume) define ethnicity as the sense of a "common heritage" that can take a variety of forms depending on the culture. For the purposes here, I use Geertz's definition of culture as an inherited system of meaning by which people make sense out of their experience (Geertz 1973:59). Barth (1969:14) and De Vos (1975:16) defined ethnicity as a sense of self that arises in a particular cultural setting when a subject encounters people of another culture. Sandstrom (1991) demonstrated convincingly that Nahua ethnicity is grounded in the meaning of corn, has great antiquity, and is based on a deep, personal identification between a man and the corn plants he cultivates in his milpa. Men and women literally internalize corn when they eat it, and it becomes their blood and thus their bodily essence. Sandstrom's work is a good place to start because Nahuat ideas about their "common heritage" have a lot to do with their association between planting corn and human procreation.

KINSHIP, PLACE, AND ETHNICITY

When some Nahuat of Huitzilan describe their origins, they tell the myth of two brothers: one stayed home to cook meals, and the other went into the forest to plant a cornfield, or *milpa*. The act of planting the milpa created both corn plants and people who are the ancestors of the Nahuat who live in Huitzilan today (Taggart 1983:207–208). The myth provides a notion of a distinctive common heritage and thus is one reason for concluding that the Nahuat have a notion of their ethnicity. The mestizos also have their own myth of common origins, which asserts that they or many of their ancestors came from Tetela de Ocampo, the former district capital on the highlands to the south of Huitzilan. However, a careful examination of the subtle differences between the Nahuat and mestizo conceptions of ethnicity reveal some very important differences, some of which emerged during the conflict that engulfed Huitzilan from 1977 to 1984. One consequence of that conflict is that the Nahuat but not the mestizos changed the referents for some of their most important ethnic terms for the opposite group.

Throughout my earlier fieldwork the Nahuat used the pejorative term *coyot* (coyote) for mestizo, but when I returned to the village in 2003–2005, I found that some Nahuat had radically changed their referents for this term. For mestizos then as now, once a Nahuat always a Nahuat, no matter how well one speaks Spanish, dresses in mestizo clothes, and acts like a mestizo. As Chance noted (this volume), mestizos inherited the notion of purity of blood from the Spaniards, which they express by equating ethnicity with race. The notion of ethnicity as race rests on biological metaphors, which have a deep grounding in European culture, including the notion of biological kinship.

Scholars have reached different conclusions about the relationship between kinship and ethnicity: some see the two as essentially the same (Keyes 1981) because both deal with the notion of descent; others prefer to keep them separate. Brumfiel (1994a) separates kinship from ethnicity in her interpretation of the ancient Aztec state, and her work serves as a point of departure for considering Nahuat kinship and ethnicity in Huitzilan. Brumfiel (1994a) argues that the Aztec state was organized on the basis of ethnicity rather than kinship because it was stratified, and social stratification and kinship are contradictory principles of social organization. She does not define kinship but appears to assume it is a biological relationship defined by a genealogy in which those who share the same blood are eligible to inherit rights in a family estate.

Marxist scholars from the time of Engels (1972 [1942, orig. pub. 1884]) have argued that allocating rights to some but not all kin undermines the unity of the kin group. However, ancient Nahua "reckoned descent bilaterally" (Berdan 1982:66), and societies with bilateral descent have a variety of ways of restricting rights and obligations to some but not all eligible relatives. An example is the Maori *hapu*, a bilateral descent group with restricted rights and obligations accorded to certain relatives who carried out exchanges and met residency requirements (Firth 1959).

However, kinship and ethnicity are related in many ways, particularly if one considers how talk about kinship resembles talk about ethnicity and how marriage can maintain ethnic boundaries as well as regulate relations between ethnic groups (see Leach 1954). It will help to recognize some of the ways that talk about kinship is like talk about ethnicity if one considers that both are expressions of culture as a system of meaning. Schneider (1984) proposed finding the culture in kinship by distinguishing between the European tendency to think of kinship as "being" and the idea of kinship as "doing," as found in some non-Western cultures such as Yap in Micronesia. Kinship as being refers to the idea that one is born a kin by virtue of the "facts of biological reproduction," and kinship as doing refers to the notion that one can make kinship by human activity.[3] Some scholars have applied Schneider's distinction to the study of ethnicity.

For example, Astuti (1995) argues that the Vezo of Madagascar do not have a concept of ethnicity because they define who they are by what they do; they do not think of themselves in terms of being and consequently do not have a notion of common origins. Astuti (1995:476) explains that for the Vezo to assert common origins would be to accept the views of Sakalava kings who have attempted to assert their political domination: "Because 'history' was carried in one's genealogy, 'surveying people's ancestors' was a means of transforming previously autonomous people into subjects of the monarchy by subsuming them into the general history of the kingdom."

For the Nahuat, the situation is different because they interpret many aspects of their social world in terms of being as well as doing, which provides them with a sense of their common origins but also gives them a notion of ethnicity that is more flexible that than of the mestizos, which is based on biological descent or race. The myth of the primordial brothers lays claim to the Nahuat as the original inhabitants of the valley of Huitzilan and justifies maintaining cultural autonomy relative to the mestizos, who arrived in Huitzilan much later, during the memories of some of the older Nahuat who were alive between 1968 and 1978. The Nahuat of Huitzilan consider themselves the descendants of the primordial brothers mentioned in the myth, and by virtue of their common descent, they apply the term *icniuh*, "relative in my generation," to all Nahuat in the community. They have personal genealogical knowledge to regulate marriage, which they prohibit with any icniuh who is a known blood relative. For most Nahuat, personal genealogical knowledge is shallow, and so the marriage prohibition usually extends to second or third cousins.

The "being" part of Nahuat identity is also apparent in beliefs about animal companion spirits, which Gossen (1994) considers the metaphysics of Meso-american personhood. According to the belief, every person has an animal companion, or *tonal*, which roams the wild. If something happens to a person's tonal, then the person will die. A person is born with a tonal but does not know what it is, although many claim to have figured out their companion through dreaming. There is some notion that the animal companion is the key to one's character, and many report that they dream of deer, an animal admired for its beauty. However, reports of other, less attractive animal companions include the horned owl, or *cuauhxaxaca*, a harbinger of death. Inheriting an animal companion is perhaps a legacy of the ancient belief that one's fate is linked to one's birth date, which often included an animal sign. Berdan (1982:84) notes that Aztec children "were frequently named after the day of their birth, especially children of commoners."

Nevertheless, the Nahuat also emphasize doing when talking about the social world, which is one reason they changed the referents to some of their terms of ethnic discourse and the mestizos did not. The Nahuat emphasis on doing is apparent in their talk about their connections to particular named localities or places. The Nahuat of Huitzilan today, like Nahuas in other parts of Mexico and the ancient Nahuas of the prehispanic and colonial periods, were organized into what Sandstrom (2000) calls toponymic groups and Chance (this volume) refers to as microethnicities (see also Schryer 1990:63–66). When a man I shall call Mazat (deer), a Nahuat who told many myths and provided a great deal of insight into his culture,[4] defined his social position in Huitzilan, he first of all pointed out that he was born and raised in the locality of Calyecapan (in the "last house" in the community). At one time in the recent past, Nahuat of Huitzilan took as surnames the names of the localities where they were born instead of inheriting the surnames of their father and mother, as is the practice of mestizos.[5]

The importance of place is apparent in the way Nahuat talk about kinship in terms of being and doing. For example, Mazat described his kinship tie with a man I shall call Itzcuinti (dog), whose house was the headquarters for the UCI when it took over the Talcuaco pasture. Mazat said: "He was our relative. From where I came, he was from where my grandmother came, from where my father came. We were from one stalk."[6] Mazat used the word *tactzon*, which is a combination of *tac-ti*, or "torso," and *tzon-ti*, or "head of hair" (Karttunen 1983:256, 318). Mazat defined *tactzon* as the stalk of a plant because he, like the ancient (López Austin 1988:1:162) as well as contemporary Nahuas (Sandstrom 1991), identifies the human body with the corn plant. Regarding the ancient Nahuas, López Austin (1988:1:162) notes that the word *tonacayo* (the whole of our flesh) "is applied to the fruits of the earth, especially to the most important one, corn, thus forming a metaphoric tie between man's corporeal being and the food to which he owed his existence."

At first glance, it might appear that the Nahuat and mestizos think of kinship in similar ways because Mazat appeared to invoke the image of a family tree when talking about his kinship tie with Itzcuinti. However, Mazat's image of the stalk alludes to some of the ways he and other Nahuat think about kinship as doing as well as being. Mazat was alluding to the equation between planting and procreation, which runs through many of his stories and is in the origin myth mentioned earlier. Planting is a form of work, or *tequit*, which is the word the Nahuat use for many forms of human activity. The notion that equates procreation with corn also appeared in the ancient myth of Tamoanchan in which Xochiquetzal gave birth to Cinteotl, the god of corn, after picking the flower from the tree in Tamoanchan, an act that probably referred to sex (Graulich 1997; Quiñones Keber 1995:29, 183). The ancient Nahuas also described conception with the phrase "The infant is seated in the womb" (*Ihctic motlalia in piltzintli*), which conveys an image very similar to planting a milpa by inserting kernels of corn in the moist feminine earth (López Austin 1988: 1:297).

Mazat's way of talking about kinship is related to his other ways of talking about social life. When referring to his field of social relations, he traced many connections to different ancestors in particular places, so that he has ties not only to the place where he himself was born but also to many other named localities. For example, Mazat was born in Calyecapan, and Itzcuinti was born in Talcuaco, but they have a connection to Taltzintan ("land at the foot" of Talcuaco) because their common ancestors were a brother and sister who were born in that locality. The sum total of Mazat's ties to people and places are what make him a Huitzilteco, or someone from the community of Huitzilan de Serdán. To consider oneself a Huitzilteco in this sense is perhaps the closest thing to a subjective notion of ethnic identity.

ICNOYOT

The doing that is involved in kinship and ethnicity also consists of many activities that include but are not limited to inculcating and creating ties of *icnoyot* (respect) within a family and a community. I have translated the term *icnoyot* as "respect," but the word has many different meanings, an understanding of which reveals some of the ways the Nahuat attempt to reconcile the apparent inconsistency between kinship and stratification. Mazat was born into a family that may have operated like the ancient *teccalli*, or noble house (see Chance 2000), and the equivalent to Mazat's noble lord, or *teuctli*, was his mother's brother, Bartolomé Hernández, who inherited a large (in Nahuat terms) landed estate that included a sugarcane field and press.

Bartolomé passed his estate to his only son, Domingo Hernández. Inheritance tends to favor males, and so Mazat and his brothers, as the sons of Bartolomé's sister, were at the margins of this extended family. They were the workers who cut the sugarcane and worked the press to make loaves of brown sugar. However, the potentially disruptive effects of stratification within the family in

Calyecapan were mitigated by the emphasis on respect, or icnoyot. The word *icnoyot* can refer to the idea that one should take into consideration the feelings of others and avoid acting egotistically. Parents go to great lengths to inculcate icnoyot in their children with a mixture of love and punishment to form the subject, and when a Nahuat judges himself or herself in terms of this value, he or she is acting as an ethnic subject.

The word *icnoyo(t)* appeared in Molina's 1571 dictionary (1966:346), where it was defined with the adjectives "compassionate" (*compasivo*) and "pious" (*piadoso*). Mazat explained that an *icnot* is a person who has respect, or icnoyot, as well as love (*tazohtaliz*) and compassion (*teicneliliz*) toward others. The inculcation of icnoyot by a combination of love and punishment is the process by which the Nahuat ethnic subject forms in the family.[7] Inculcation of icnoyot is what Geertz (1973:52) might regard as establishing the "control mechanism of a culture." The Nahuat interpret the behavior of other Nahuat and mestizos in terms of the morality of icnoyot, which, therefore, is part of their ethnicity (see Barth 1969:14).

Women frequently have the responsibility of teaching icnoyot to young children, and so I asked Antonia, a Nahuat woman I knew well, to explain what icnoyot meant to her in a conversation that began when I remarked, "Many children today don't have respect."[8] Antonia replied: "No. They act badly. Extremely so. Even though you hit them, they don't listen."[9] In her response the key word was *ilapaqui*, and when I asked Antonia what it meant, she replied, "Fight."[10] Her husband, Juan, added, "Fight with their siblings."[11] The converse of the *ilapac*, or disrespectful person, is the *icnot*, or respectful one. Antonia's son explained the meaning of icnoyot: "It means not acting inconsiderately. One just listens. If one does something [bad] to someone, he/she stops doing it."[12] Mazat had explained that a person who is an icnot has compassion, or teicneliliz. Antonia declared that to raise a child who is an icnot and consequently has teicneliliz is an act of love, or tazohtaliz. She said: "Well, if you engender a child, you love him. And if you do not engender him, you don't love him."[13] By *engender* Antonia meant form, socialize, or educate.

Antonia and other Nahuat engender their children with a combination of love and punishment. Parents show love to their children in different ways. Antonia's husband, Juan, said that the kin term for "father" means love: "*tahueh* means he who loves another."[14] Eduardo, Antonia and Juan's son, declared that he tells his children that he loves them: "I'll say, 'I love you, papá.'"[15] Antonia shows love to her children and grandchildren with caresses and hugs. Men interpret women feeding them as acts of love. When Mazat explained how he knew that his mother—now deceased—loved him, he said: "Because she was waiting for me with my tortillas. She begged me to eat. If I arrived, she'd bend down to say, 'Eat, while they're hot.' I knew she loved me. Because once she leaves you, she doesn't say 'Eat.' You'd always arrive, and she'd say: 'Drink coffee. Eat.' If I'd go, she'd say, 'Don't be long. Come soon. Come back soon.' So then one sees she loves you."[16]

The same woman who shows love to her children, however, also can dish out harsh punishment for disrespectful behavior. When I asked Antonia how she taught icnoyot to her children and grandchildren, she mentioned discipline first: "Well, one hits them so that they'll calm down, so they won't do bad things, won't fight."[17] She explained that she hits them with a *cuauhpitzac*, or switch, but only three times, never to excess and never to hurt them. Her son, Eduardo, explained that he also speaks to his children: "One speaks to them. One says, 'Don't fight with your brother because you'll hurt him. And he'll hurt you too.'"[18]

Applying Butler's (1997) reasoning to the Nahuat, we see that a child receives love and experiences moral anxiety or fears losing love when he or she behaves inconsiderately, or *telihuizti*. To reduce moral anxiety, a child must behave with icnoyot, meaning that one must listen to and obey parents and cease fighting with siblings. Above all, the child must develop compassion and be considerate of others, qualities found only in Nahuat who have parents who took the trouble to engender them because they loved them.

The inculcation of a conscience according to which one should not behave inconsiderately by fighting with siblings is consistent with the organization of Nahuat domestic groups, in which parents expect their married sons to "work for a common endeavor" (*ce cosa tequitih*) by pooling their labor to fill a granary and purse from which all members can draw according to need.[19] Mazat lived in an unusually stable extended family group in which he and his married brothers pooled their labor for many years until Mazat married and formed his own domestic group. He has replicated the extended family of his earlier years and currently lives and shares a common granary with his two married sons.[20] Mazat interpreted the events that took place following the appearance of the UCI as a colossal breakdown in icnoyot in his community.

Before the appearance of the UCI, the Nahuat in Huitzilan maintained icnoyot in their families and their community by avoiding acting superior, or *hueichihua*, and by carrying out rituals to spread human goodness (*cualtacayot*). Both ways are very important for holding the remnants of the teccalli together; when one person owns most of the land, he hires landless or land-poor relatives and neighbors to work on his family estate. Bartolomé and his son Domingo hired Mazat and his brothers, other kin, affines, and non-kin to cut sugarcane and produce the loaves of brown sugar in their sugarcane press. To mitigate against the serious accusation of acting superior, or hueichihua, Domingo spent a great deal of money sponsoring rituals that have as one of their ostensible purposes the sowing of icnoyot throughout the community.

The Nahuat also spend resources and energy on rituals to create ties of icnoyot with those who are not of the same stalk and with whom they do not share a connection to a particular named locality. There are many rituals that have this purpose, and the most often mentioned involve the flower tree, or *xochicuahuit*, which is efficacious for fastening people together by creating bonds of human goodness, or cualtacayot. The flower tree is used primarily to create ties of human goodness with the godparents of marriage and baptism, who become compadres. The efficacy of the flower tree rituals is one of the ways the Nahuat of Huitzilan, or Huitziltecos, distinguish themselves from other Nahuat who live in the Sierra Norte de Puebla. The Nahuat of Huitzilan say that they live in a ceremonial center because they alone possess this ritual adornment and know how to use it, giving expression to what is something like ethnic pride. Those who make this declaration are unaware that anthropologists have reported sighting the flower tree among other Nahuat, Otomís, and Totonacs living in the Sierra Norte de Puebla.[21]

Although many Nahuat in Huitzilan do not know that others have the flower tree, they are very much aware of linguistic and cultural differences between themselves and speakers of other Mesoamerican languages. The Totonacs live in the neighboring village of Zongozotla, to the northwest of Huitzilan, and the Nahuat identify language as one of the markers of Totonac ethnic identity. Totonac and Nahuat are mutually unintelligible languages, and the Nahuat represent the former as sounding like the barking of a female dog in a popular oral narrative from Huitzilan. They are also keenly aware of the differences between themselves and the Spanish-speaking mestizos, with whom they have more intimate contact in the biethnic community of Huitzilan de Serdán. Mestizos differ from Totonacs because they are the economically and politically dominant group and are in a position to confer ethnic identity on the Nahuat.

THE MESTIZOS

The mestizos' methods of reckoning social connections are fundamentally different from those of the Nahuat, and they resemble the European notions of biological kinship and ethnicity as race, which emphasize being rather than doing (see Chance, this volume). According to the European notion, one is born into a family, and although one can lose personal and family honor, one cannot lose one's biological connections. By the same token, one is born into an ethnic group, particularly when ethnicity is another word for race. From the point of view of many mestizos, once a Nahuat, always a Nahuat who will never become a mestizo even though he or she might learn to speak Spanish well and dress like a mestizo. One may try to pass from one ethnic category to another, but passing is difficult or impossible when others know one's ancestry. The mestizos' term for themselves, "the people of reason" (*gente de razón*), conveys cultural and possibly biological superiority.

The mestizo notion of ethnicity serves a number of purposes, including prohibiting sex and marriage between mestiza women and Nahuat men. Many mestizo men have sex with Nahuat women, but the mestizos do not confer social recognition on any of these relationships. Both mestizos and Nahuat consider the children who are products of these relationships to be Nahuat, but they view them in very different ways. Mestizos consistently refer to the children with their mother's surname to stress their illegitimate birth whereas the

Nahuat refer to the same person with the surname of the mestizo father. For example, Mazat's father-in-law, Juan, was the son of a wealthy mestizo, whose surname was Bonilla, and a Nahuat woman, whose surname was Pereañez. Mestizos referred to Mazat's father-in-law as Juan Pereañez whereas Mazat called him Juan Bonilla. Though Nahuat as well as mestizos attempt to protect their daughters from predatory men of all ethnic groups, mestizos take steps to isolate their daughters from the Nahuat community for fear they will adopt the rustic speech and behavior of their indigenous contemporaries and possibly marry a Nahuat.

The migration of mestizos into Huitzilan during the last decades of the nineteenth century and the earliest decades of the twentieth created new forms of ethnic difference. The Nahuat incorporated the mestizos into their quadrilateral conception of space by linking them in a variety of ways to the south, a cardinal direction with sinister connotations. The Nahuat also incorporated the mestizos into their webs of social relations with their notions of doing rather being, developing relations with mestizos that are "highly segmental, functionally specific and instrumental" and "circumscribed by well defined roles," to borrow a line from Colby and van den Berghe's (1969:157) study of an Ixil and Ladino community in Guatemala. The Nahuat idea of icnoyot and the mestizo notion of *respeto* are sufficiently similar to permit the creation of *compadrazgo* (ritual kinship) between Nahuat and some mestizo families. However, the overlap in meaning of *icnoyot* and *respeto* should not obscure the genuine differences between the two groups when it comes to talking about their experience.

MESTIZO AND NAHUAT INTERPRETATIONS OF HISTORY

Differences in how mestizos and Nahuat talk about Huitzilan's recent history provide an example of the way culture and ethnicity affect the two groups' interpretations of their experiences. Mestizo and Nahuat narrators of oral histories recalled and interpreted the conflict in their community in ways that resemble how they also talked about kinship and ethnicity. The historical event that was the focus of their attention was the conflict that erupted over the Talcuaco cattle pasture in 1977. Mestizos and Nahuat explained the conflict by emphasizing different aspects of Talcuaco's complicated history, which in some ways represents the history of ethnic relations in the Huitzilan.

It is helpful to know the names of the personalities who played key roles in the conflict in order to follow the mestizo and Nahuat oral histories. Juana Gutierrez was a mestiza who was an early owner of Talcuaco, and she married a man I shall call Bravo and started a branch of the Bravo family. Don Coyote is another mestizo who migrated into Huitzilan from the highlands, and he claimed ownership of Talcuaco because his daughter lived with one of the Bravo grandchildren. I have chosen the name Don Coyote because he resembled a coyote and acted like the character Coyote in a popular folktale that appears later in this chapter. In brief, the mestizos explained the conflict that erupted over Talcuaco as a land dispute between Don Coyote and the Bravo family, a dispute that included illegitimate landownership, which is like the concept of illegitimate birth when kinship is reckoned as a biological relationship and when ethnicity is treated as a racial category. The Nahuat interpreted the conflict as a problem of who did or did not work the land, which is consistent with talking about kinship and ethnicity as created through human activity (doing).

The Mestizo Version

A nephew of Don Coyote offered his view of the history of the conflict by presenting what he learned by investigating the land history of Talcuaco:

> One of the principal causes of the violence here in Huitzilan in the years at the end of the seventies, the beginning of the eighties, was precisely over the possession of some lands. As I told you. Many years ago there was a woman called Juana Gutierrez. That woman owned a lot of property, many plots of land, and when she died, she left all of her lands intestate. That is, she did not leave a will. Then that's the origin of the conflict because she had children, she had her husband, but she was the owner. The deeds, all of them, are in her name. And she did not bequeath her property to her children. Rather, her estate remained intestate, and her children took possession of those lands. Afterward her grandchildren followed suit. The plots that the people in the UCI invaded were all intestate from the estate of Juana Gutierrez. That's the way it is.

The nephew explained how Juana Gutierrez's grandson, Ruben Bravo, ended up with Talcuaco:

> Well, he acquired it in a violent manner because another cousin of his possessed it. Another member of the family. But since this man [Ruben Bravo], since he was a violent person, he snatched it from him. He snatched the plot, the property, and he was in possession of it. Then after they killed this man [Ruben Bravo], it remained in the possession of Don Coyote's daughter, who was Ruben's wife.

Don Coyote's nephew knew the details of Ruben Bravo's death, which occurred in 1960.

> He liked card games. Yes, yes, a lot. So then he had friends who were just as violent. So they met by chance in a bar in Zaragoza, in the city of Zaragoza, and they started to play cards and drink. And in the heat of their cups, they argued and the three of them died. There were three people. Those three had criminal records.[22]

Two surviving Bravos, great-grandsons of Juana Gutierrez, disputed Don Coyote's claim and so Talcuaco became the object of a dispute between two powerful mestizo families in Huitzilan. Meanwhile, the UCI appeared in the neighboring community of Pahuatla and invaded a plot of land owned by an absentee owner who lived in another *municipio*. A delegation of Nahuat from Huitzilan went to Pahuatla and asked the UCI leader, Felipe Reyes, for help in dealing with another Nahuat, whom I shall call Pedro Pistolero, who had threatened to kill them in disputes over women. Felipe Reyes apparently agreed to help the delegation and seized the opportunity to organize about forty Nahuat men from Huitzilan into the cooperative that invaded Talcuaco.

Thus the UCI stepped right into the middle of a dispute between Don Coyote and the Bravo great-grandchildren. Don Coyote allied himself with Pedro Pistolero and his family, and the Bravo great-grandchildren, who were among the wealthiest mestizos in Huitzilan, provided ammunition and some guns, including an AR-15 semiautomatic rifle, to the Nahuat in the UCI. Pedro Pistolero allegedly shot and killed Felipe Reyes, causing the UCI to disperse temporarily, but it regrouped and resumed cultivating the milpa on the slopes of Talcuaco. Then Don Coyote allegedly called in the army, which chopped down the milpa.

Mazat's Version

Mazat gave his story a different emphasis. Although he too began by talking about landownership and the genealogy of the Gutierrez-Bravo family, he turned to who worked the land. Mazat had knowledge of the history of Talcuaco because his godfather was a direct descendant of Juana Gutierrez and the brother of Ruben Bravo. This Bravo was not a gunfighter and preferred the company of Nahuat. He wore the Nahuat uniform of a white cotton shirt and loose-fitting trousers and huaraches, sandals with soles made from automobile tires. He spent most of his time working on his milpas with the help of his Nahuat workers. Mazat's version of the Talcuaco history began with Juana Gutierrez's daughter Lola, the person he remembered as the original owner. However, Mazat emphasized who worked and who planted or did not plant on Talcuaco rather than who owned the land. For Mazat, it is not who owns the land but what one does with it that matters.

> Well, as for that land, I remember that Lola had the land. She was an old woman then. She had that land. But afterward Ruben Bravo took it. Because that land wasn't a purchased piece of land. It was intestate. So then Ruben Bravo took Talcuaco for himself. But Ruben Bravo, as long as he was alive, he worked Talcuaco, and then he worked that land with Don Coyote. Then when they killed Ruben Bravo, Don Coyote took what was once Ruben Bravo's, and someone was still planting on it. It was my godfather who was planting on it. He borrowed it and paid rent and planted the land. But after they killed Ruben Bravo, Don Coyote took it for himself. He took it. He did not plant it. Then they fought over that land.[23]

The Nahuat and mestizo retrospective interpretations of the spark that set off the white-hot rage and wave of killings revealed further the ethnic differences related to doing and being, although it is also clear that the ensuing conflict did not reduce to interethnic warfare, for reasons addressed later. Most agree that the spark was the army's chopping down of the UCI's corn plants in 1978, but Nahuat and mestizos approached this event from different perspectives. The Nahuat spoke about work, and the mestizos about social position.

Mazat, for example, recalled when UCI leader Felipe Reyes appeared in Huitzilan and held a meeting in front of the church in the middle of town. Afterward, he said, about forty Nahuat men joined the UCI, probably because they believed the land should be worked and no one was working on Talcuaco in 1977.

> According to them, they came to divide up the land, to help the poor. A lot of people went to the meeting. They thought they really would help them. Well, after the meeting, they were emboldened to ask around about excess land. There was a man who wanted to stand up and look for where there was land that's called, well it's called "intestate," where whoever has it now does not have papers. Then the one who didn't have papers was not going to work that land, and so they took it.[24]

At the time, the Nahuat were experiencing tremendous land pressure. The main goal of many Nahuat was to grow enough corn to stock a granary for one year, and to achieve that goal required that they gain access to at least 1.0 hectares of the very best land. I did a census of Huitzilan in 1969 and discovered that the 2,273 Nahuat were organized into 438 domestic groups and owned only 97.3 hectares of private land. The entire municipio of Huitzilan also has a total of 336.2 hectares of ejidos shared with another community, but the vast majority of Nahuat have very small ejido plots that serve as house sites and average .20 hectare (Taggart 1975:32, 157). Many Nahuat have access to far less than the hectare of good land they need to feed their families and must rent land to plant corn, sometimes on plots far away from the community.

Mazat described several steps that led to what he called the rage, or *cualayot*, that begin when the Nahuat formed the corn-growing cooperative on Talcuaco under the leadership of Felipe Reyes and ended when Don Coyote apparently ordered the Nahuat *presidente municipal* to call in the army to chop down the Talcuaco milpa. Mazat made it clear that chopping down the milpa was the single most important reason the Nahuat in the UCI began killing in rage.

> Well, they worked Talcuaco. They planted corn and they probably intended to divide it up among the men who worked it, according to what they contributed to the crop. So then Pedro Pistolero and his brother attacked those men in the UCI. So they attacked Felipe Reyes. Well, they shot him. So

then, yes, those men in the UCI retreated. Some remained in town. Then they started working again. Those who had fled, afterward they were very emboldened. Afterward they came back. But the rich ones, Don Coyote's family, and the president, a Nahuat who went in with him, they brought the *federales*, the soldiers, to go after the UCIs. There were many who pursued them. Until one day, they broke up the milpa they had planted. They cut down the entire milpa. From there, yes, that's when the *cualayot* [rage] began.[25]

A mestiza witness, on the other hand, emphasized how members of the family of Don Coyote and the gunman, Pedro Pistolero, joined the army with machetes in hand and chopped down the Talcuaco milpa to humiliate the Nahuat in the UCI. Don Coyote's great-niece, who is very sensitive to class and ethnic inequalities in Huitzilan, recalled what happened when the army appeared in her community.

I was in Huitzilan. I don't remember exact dates, but yes, I do have in my memory the basic fact of, for example, the army coming into town. Yes. And the way Don Coyote's family became involved in the act of destroying the milpa. Using power to do so. There had not been any deaths, any wounded. Because at that moment the UCI did have arms and they displayed them at times. They used them that way. Those people walked through the streets of town with their weapons. They did not confront the army. Nevertheless, they put up what we might call passive resistance. And the army had to use force to get them out of there [Talcuaco]. Not by wounding anyone but... And the family of Don Coyote acted with arrogance by gloating about what happened. They thought they were triumphant after what took place. They gathered the youngest members of the family: the grandchildren of Don Coyote and some other boys, who worked for them who were from the family of Pedro Pistolero. Yes. There were three or four young men from that family. It's that they took an active part; they were physically there on the land when there was the eviction and the act of chopping down the milpa, destroying what was planted on the milpa. This was the spark. The indignation that caused in town! And it was the spark that caused the UCI to respond with violence.[26]

Don Coyote and his immediate family had a reputation for using racial slurs when speaking about the Nahuat and apparently intended to humiliate the Nahuat in the UCI in order to keep them in their place. They, like many other mestizos in Huitzilan, were very threatened by the Nahuat, who had armed themselves, carried out a land invasion, and then broadcast messages such as "Death to the rich" from a house just above Talcuaco. Before 1977 and the arrival of the UCI, the mestizos had maintained their dominance by controlling the economic and political life in the village and by regulating marriage, keeping Nahuat men from mestiza women.

At this point the struggle over Talcuaco appeared to be an example of the convergence between class and ethnicity: the landless Nahuat who had joined the UCI were pitted against the mestizo family of Don Coyote and his allies. To be sure, one of those allies was a Nahuat, Pedro Pistolero, but he was fighting on the side of Don Coyote because he had fought with and killed other Nahuat over a woman. It was mentioned that the Nahuat delegation that went to Pahuatla to ask the UCI for help had problems with Pedro Pistolero before the appearance of the cooperative in the Sierra Norte de Puebla. It is possible, even likely, that the Nahuat in the UCI who resumed cultivating their milpa on Talcuaco after the death of Felipe Reyes had formed a nativistic movement and were attempting to maintain their culture in the face of tremendous land pressure from the mestizos who settled in Huitzilan.[27]

FRATRICIDE, ETHNIC RELATIONS, AND NAHUAT ETHNICITY

The Nahuat in the UCI were well armed at this point, and they erupted in violence after the army chopped down the Talcuaco milpa. They killed numerous women, men, and children and drove many others out of the village. One man kept a running tally and counted nearly 300 dead in a community that had only 2,373 Nahuat and 275 mestizos just before the appearance of the UCI in 1977. Most of the dead were Nahuat, perhaps because they constituted nearly 90 percent of the population. Mestizo and Nahuat oral histories agree that most of the deaths occurred when Nahuat in the UCI shot other Nahuat whom they considered their enemies. Mazat described the deaths in the following way: "The UCI started killing. They became blind with rage. The UCI started spying. They spied. Until they just killed even if their victims did not have fault. They killed secretly [They shot their victims in the back]."[28]

There are many reasons why the Nahuat in the UCI targeted primarily other Nahuat rather than mestizos. One is that the Nahuat in the UCI regarded other Nahuat who refused to join the corn-planting cooperative as their enemies. They may have come to that conclusion because, as Good (2005) observed, the Nahua tend to equate work and love; those who work together love each other, and those who cease or refuse to work together do not love each other.

Another reason is that some mestizos put Nahuat in the line of fire by using them as their gunmen, sometimes providing them with ammunition and arms to fight battles with other mestizos who were their bitter enemies, and by placing them in strategic positions in the municipio government. This tactic enabled the *ricos* to appear uninvolved in the conflict, and in fact, many were. However, the degree of mestizo involvement in aiding and abetting the violence cannot be underestimated. In addition to the hostility between Don Coyote and the Bravo descendants, there was a serious dispute within Don Coyote's close extended family. Many years earlier Don Coyote wanted to kill one of his nephews for seducing and making pregnant several of his daughters, and this nephew allegedly collaborated with the UCI to attempt to kill three of his first cousins, who were also Don Coyote's sons. The UCI managed to wound one of those sons while he was drinking with the nephew. One member of Don Coyote's immediate extended family declared that it was a miracle that this nephew died in his own bed of natural causes. He was alluding not to the Nahuat in the UCI but to the nephew's enemies within his own family!

Despite the deep divisions within the mestizo community, the Nahuat ran risks in openly confronting members of the dominant group. The appearance of the army in Huitzilan and its role in chopping down the Talcuaco milpa in full view of the entire community was dramatic proof that Don Coyote had the backing of a very powerful and well-organized force that could easily annihilate the UCI. Many Nahuat in Huitzilan are heavily dependent on their mestizo employers, as was the case for Pedro Pistolero and his bitter enemy, a man I shall call Pancho Tahuel (*tahuel* means angry), who along with other Nahuat went to Pahuatla to consult with Felipe Reyes about getting some help in dealing with Pedro Pistolero. Pedro Pistolero worked with Don Coyote and allegedly shot and killed the UCI leader, Felipe Reyes. He also climbed up to Talcuaco and, along with Don Coyote's children and grandchildren, helped the army chop down the milpa. He was loyal to Don Coyote right to the end, when the UCI finally killed him. Pancho Tahuel, who allegedly killed Pedro Pistolero, had a very close relationship with some in Don Coyote's extended family, who had treated him with respect. He had worked for many years in the house another of Don Coyote's nephews, and he told the nephew's wife he would make sure that no harm would come to her children, and in fact, none did.

A further reason mitigating against interethnic warfare is that the Nahuat notion of ethnicity based on human activity (tequit) did not lend itself to blanket categorization of the mestizos as evil and deserving of ethnic cleansing. Although the mestizos and the Nahuat have critical things to say about each other, interethnic wars have not broken out in the Sierra Norte de Puebla. In the nineteenth century Pala Agustín Dieguillo and his Nahuat followers tried to resist non-Indian or mestizo encroachment into the nearby area of Cuetzalan del Progreso (Thomson 1991), but the main issue was the subdivision of public lands and their acquisition as private property by some of the gente de razón who had settled in the region. Thomson (1991:247) discovered that the gente de razón were divided and that during the height of the rebellion "an important faction" of them struck "an alliance with Pala Agustín's Nahuat rebels during the revolt of November 1869." Thomson (1991:257) concluded that Agustín's movement "stopped short of being a *guerra de castas* of the kind that gripped Yucatan throughout much of the second half of the nineteenth century and highland Chiapas between 1868 and 1870." [29]

THE CHANGING MEANING OF COYOT

One example of the flexible rather than monolithic meaning of Nahuat ethnic categories is the change in the meaning that some Nahuat gave to the word *coyot* (coyote), which before 1978 was a derogatory term for a mestizo. After the violence erupted when the army chopped down the Talcuaco milpa, some Nahuat reinterpreted the popular trickster tale "Rabbit and Coyote," which explained the meaning of the ethnic slur *coyot*. I did not detect any change in the meaning of the mestizos' words for the Nahuat, although there is now awareness that Don Coyote made a colossal error in humiliating the UCI. There is still a sense among the mestizos that once a Nahuat, always a Nahuat because the term *indio* is based on biological ancestry. In Huitzilan a macehual cannot become a "person of reason" by acting in a "reasonable manner" or demonstrating the power of reason. If anything, the violence that took place between 1977 and 1984 confirmed stereotypical notions of the Nahuat as appearing well mannered but actually seething with anger and likely to erupt into savagery.

We can see how some Nahuat changed the meaning of *coyot* by comparing versions of the popular folktale "Rabbit and Coyote" as told before and after the UCI period in Huitzilan. Coyote is a greedy carnivore in the version that Antonio Veracruz, a well-known Nahuat storyteller, recounted in 1973. Coyote runs into Rabbit when he wanders into an old woman's flower garden. Rabbit has been eating the old woman's flowers. She lays a trap by placing a wax doll over the hole through which Rabbit enters her garden. Rabbit, thinking the doll is alive, threatens to hit it if it won't let him pass. He strikes the doll, and his hand sticks in the wax. He strikes the doll again, and his other hand sticks in the wax. He kicks the doll until both feet are stuck in the wax, and the old woman lifts up the doll, pulls Rabbit out of the wax, puts him under a basket, and goes into her kitchen to sharpen a knife to butcher him for dinner. Along comes Coyote, who smells Rabbit and plans to eat him until Rabbit persuades Coyote to trade places because a *compadre* is going to take Rabbit to eat turkey, and Rabbit can eat only plants. Coyote takes the bait and climbs under the basket. Rabbit and Coyote have several encounters in which Coyote threatens to eat Rabbit, and Rabbit escapes by tempting Coyote with something better to eat.

I suspect that the great popularity of "Rabbit and Coyote" between 1968 and 1977, particularly in Huitzilan, was because it worked as a historical allegory, as a cautionary tale supporting the notion of respect (icnoyot), and as an expression of wish fulfillment. The story is a historical allegory because it describes Coyote as a greedy invader—he invaded the old woman's garden—much as the mestizos invaded Huitzilan and took Nahuat land, converting it to cattle pastures and coffee orchards around the turn of the twentieth century. The association between mestizos and meat is based on the Nahuat observation that mestizos are meat-eaters who convert milpas into cattle pastures. The Nahuat presented themselves in their myths as tortilla-eaters who, like Rabbit, have primarily a vegetarian diet. Coyote is also the Nahuat who fails to respect others, and "Rabbit and Coyote" is thus part of moral discourse because it teaches that no Nahuat should be greedy like Coyote. The greedy may perish, just as Coyote dies when Rabbit lures him into the final trap, once again with the promise of eating turkey meat at a fiesta. Coyote falls for the trick and waits inside a small wooden shack, or *jacal*, in the middle of a cleared field. Rabbit lights the debris surrounding the jacal, and Coyote perishes in the fire. The story is also wish fulfillment because some Nahuat wish the mestizos would disappear from their community.

Between 1968 and 1977 the story was what Scott (1985:163) had in mind when he described trickster tales as "the veiled cultural resistance of subordinate groups." At that time many Nahuat marked their moral superiority by contrasting their ethic of appetite moderation with the mestizos' rapacity. The Nahuat frequently mentioned the mestizos' greed for land and their unbridled desire for sex. Many Nahuat pointed out that mestizos took land by foreclosing on bills Nahuat had run up in stores, in some cases to buy *aguardiente*. The Nahuat also brought up mestizo men's unbridled appetite for sex by noting that many mestizo men had children with Nahuat women. One of Don Coyote's nephews alone reputedly fathered 60 children with Nahuat women. In Orpheus myths that circulated before the arrival of the UCI in 1977, Mazat depicted the devil as a mestizo, or coyot, who carried off a Nahuat woman and took her to the underworld, where he had sex by devouring her much as Coyote attempted to devour Rabbit (Taggart 1997:233–241). When depicting Coyote's appetite, another narrator used the verb *yecoa*, which means "to taste" as well as "to have sex" (Karttunen 1983:337).

Mazat retold the story of Rabbit and Coyote in 2004 to characterize the violence carried out by the Nahuat in the UCI between 1977 and 1984. In this version Mazat shifted the emphasis from Coyote as mestizo to Coyote as UCI to fit the historical changes that have taken place in his community. Moreover, Mazat characterized Coyote as a menacing *tecuani*, the human-eater in many Nahuat folktales.[30] His exegesis of "Rabbit and Coyote" is a shift from the way he characterized his community in stories he told before 1977. At that time he represented the mestizo migration into Huitzilan as a flood coming from the highlands to the south, the cardinal direction the Nahuat associate with sinister forces.[31] Mestizos posed the greatest threat to the Nahuat because they devoured land once used for growing corn and converted it to coffee orchards and cattle pastures such as Talcuaco. After 1977 a new threat to the Nahuat appeared that took the form of the UCI, which Mazat represented as a more menacing Coyote.

Mazat spoke from deep personal experience because the UCI had murdered his wife, Victoria, and had threatened to kill him, much as Coyote threatened to devour Rabbit. Mazat explained the meaning of "Rabbit and Coyote" by applying it to his oral history in the following way:

> For me,… well, Rabbit is very small, as I told you the other day, and Coyote is big. He's a human-eater. But although he is a big human-eater and Rabbit is small, the small one looks for a way to vanquish the big one. So then he looks for a way to win. Then, just as I told you the other day, one also knows how the UCIs came in, they felt like big human-eaters, they had guns, but there is also one who, even if he does not have anything, looks for a way to

win. Also, as I said, that story is wise about the way people are. It represents humanity because there is a great deal of everything in the world. There is conflict, there is rage, and with that, I think our ancestors made these stories because they knew how to do things, how to think. And they thought and that's how it was done. So then, for that reason, I think it means that as big as one might be, there is a way for the little one to win. That's what I think.[32]

HUEICHIHUA

Mazat accused the UCI of *hueichihua*, and the meaning and use of that term is very significant for understanding why the Nahuat turned on each other rather than the mestizos. I have heard the term used to refer with scorn to a young Nahuat woman who visited her family in Huitzilan after working in Mexico City. She returned to her natal village for the fiesta dressed in very fashionable clothing. In this context the term meant that she was upwardly mobile and turning her back on her culture. In other contexts it refers to anyone who goes against the ethic of icnoyot and acts egotistically by showing off wealth, power, or status. Mazat recalled how Pancho Tahuel, one of the UCI leaders, appeared in church and accused him of acting big, or hueichihua, because Mazat had not joined the UCI. It can also refer to anyone who curries favor with mestizos or those in position of power. To be hueichihua is a threat to the unity of siblings in an extended family household where brothers are expected to work for a common endeavor, or *ce cosa tequitih*, to fill a common granary and purse. It also is used for someone who refuses to share food from a granary with others, particularly children and grandchildren. One way a rich Nahuat like Bartolomé Hernandez or his son, Domingo Hernández, can avoid the charge of hueichihua is to sponsor rituals designed to fasten people together with bonds of human goodness, cualtacayot. However, as a sponsor he must display humility to avoid criticism. Mazat described the purposes of these rituals in the following way: "So we don't become unfastened. So we don't criticize each other. So we don't get angry with each other."[33]

Large, stable, extended families like the one in Calyecapan organized around Bartolomé Hernández are exceedingly rare in Huitzilan because so many Nahuat have lost their land to the mestizos. Even when they do exist, as in the case of Bartolomé Hernández's remnant of a teccalli, they are not a corporate lineage such one finds among the Tallensi in Africa (Fortes 1949). The Calyecapan group was not a corporation because the members did not have in common any rights in real or incorporeal property. With so few teccalli remnants, the majority of Nahuat in Huitzilan have created individual networks of ritual kinship with rituals designed to fasten compadres together with bonds of human goodness. With only loose networks tying them together, the Nahuat lack the social structure by which they can support their ethic of icnoyot, so they must deal with behavior they consider "to act big," or hueichihua, perhaps more often than they otherwise would were they to have lineages.

To judge another as hueichihua is part of a Nahuat's ethnicity in Barth's (1969:14) sense: "belonging to an ethnic category implies being a certain kind of person." The Nahuat judge others with the same standards they apply to themselves, and they regard some but not all mestizos as hueichihua who consider the Nahuat their social inferiors. When I began fieldwork in Huitzilan in 1968, many mestizos referred to themselves as the gente de razón, presumably because they considered the Nahuat to be people without reason. At that time many Nahuat referred to the mestizos as *razones* and *coyomeh* because of their tendency to use their "reason" to devour Nahuat land and ravish Nahuat women.

CONCLUSIONS

The Nahuat concept of ethnicity is based on a combination of being and doing. The being part is apparent when some Nahuat talk about themselves as the descendants of the two brothers, one of whom stayed home to cook and the other of whom cleared and planted a field in the forest from which sprouted both corn plants and people. The idea of planting people is an allusion to procreation, by which a man plants his seed in the womb of a woman, who gives birth to their children. However, talking about planting and cultivating a milpa as being on the same order as conceiving and rearing children also emphasizes human activity, or the doing part of Nahuat ethnicity. Both activities take place in specific locations throughout Huitzilan, and they are why the Nahuat say they come from the same stalk or trunk. The sum total of the ties the Nahuat have with each other in different localities within the Huitzilan area makes one a Huitzilteco, which is the closest thing to an ethnic identity.

When I first went to Huitzilan in 1968, I did not understand Nahuat ethnicity because I was accustomed to hearing people in my own country equate ethnicity with race. It came as no surprise that the mestizos considered themselves the "people of reason" and differentiated themselves from the Nahuat, whom they call "the humble people" (*gente humilde*), "little workers" (*peoncitos*), or the derogatory *nacos*, after Totonacos (Totonacs), the speakers of another Mesoamerican language to the north. Coming to Huitzilan right after the death of Martin Luther King, Jr., at the height of the U.S. civil rights struggle, I found mestizos' talk about ethnicity to be like the way whites talked about blacks in the United States, albeit with less obvious traces of racial bigotry. Nahuat ethnicity, however, was much harder to understand because it did not look like the equation between race and ethnicity I was used to. It appeared to me that the Nahuat did not really consider themselves an ethnic group, if one equates ethnicity with biological or blood kinship.

The changing meaning of ethnic terms, such as coyot, gave me further pause about Nahuat ethnic consciousness. Nevertheless, the Nahuat express their ethnic consciousness in ways that fit the less restrictive definitions of ethnicity and that are in accord with kinship based on doing as well as being. Many a Nahuat referred to himself or herself as a *macehual*, which Karttunen (1983:127) defines as a "subject, commoner, indigenous person, speaker of Nahuatl." A macehual is also someone who does work (tequit) that ties him or her to other people and places. Their memories of working for the same endeavor (ce cosa tequitih) and the love and respect co-workers come to share are the bonds that fasten them together and separate them from others. However, by working with a Nahuat and by guarding the memory of the experience, one can cross this ethnic boundary, much more easily than one can become a mestizo.

ACKNOWLEDGMENTS

The fieldwork for this chapter was carried out between 1968 and 1978 and from 2003 to 2005. The verbatim interviews on the violence that broke out with the invasion of the Talcuaco cattle pasture were recorded during the later period, and they form part of a larger study appearing in Taggart 2007. I received generous support from the Andrew Mellon Foundation, the American Philosophical Society Penrose Fund, and the National Science Foundation for the earlier fieldwork. Funds from the Lewis Audenreid Professorship in History and Archaeology of Franklin and Marshall College generously supported the later fieldwork. Many people from Huitzilan contributed to the current project, including Nacho Angel Hernández, Irene Aco, and Pablo Aco. I am very grateful to Frannie Berdan, John Chance, Alan Sandstrom, Barbara Stark, and Emily Umberger for inviting me to participate in a stimulating workshop on Mesoamerican ethnicity that took place February 2–5, 2005, on the campus of Arizona State University. I owe a special debt of gratitude to Barbara Stark for close editing of this manuscript and for herding this project to fruition.

8

Some Finishing Thoughts
and Unfinished Business

Alan R. Sandstrom and Frances F. Berdan

THE DIVERSE INDIGENOUS PEOPLE OF MESOAMERICA HAVE REPEAT-edly transformed and redefined themselves in response to tumultuous historical events that have unsettled life throughout the region. We conclude this book by summarizing and synthesizing how the contributors have traced ethnic identity among the Native American inhabitants of Mesoamerica, especially the Nahua, over a period of half a millennium. And since we recognize that this is not the last word on this subject (indeed, it is barely the first), we also consider some topics and themes that might derive from this undertaking. In the words of Jones (1997:104), "Ethnic groups are not neatly packaged territorially bounded culture-bearing units in the present, nor are they likely to have been in the past." Ethnic identity, used here interchangeably with ethnicity, is indeed an elusive, but eminently researchable, phenomenon.

THE MEANING OF ETHNICITY

Based on the contributors' definitions and usages, ethnicity includes, at minimum, the following list of elements. First, it is a special type of self-conscious identity founded on a belief that members of the group share an essence or set of experiences (biological or historical) along with ancestral connections that usually trace back to primordial times. In other words, ethnic identity is based on a shared state of being, or place in the world, grounded in similar historical experiences. Ethnic identity may be strong or weak, and it can originate as an imposition by outsiders, applied to a subordinate population that does not in fact constitute an ethnic group. In such circumstances, however, the subordinated peoples often react to their domination by forming an ethnic identity. Second, ethnic identity is expressed by cultural features such as language, dress, religion, occupation, and common territory. Third, ethnic groups always exist in relation to other ethnic groups within a larger political and economic system. They do not constitute complete cultures, and the essence or remembered experiences on which people base their identity can change over time in response to changing circumstances. This malleability means that members can base their ethnicity on descent from common ancestors at one period and at another time shift to ethnicity based on location with only vague reference to common descent. In the long run, flexibility and shifting meanings characterize ethnic identity regardless of where or when it is found.

As the chapters in this book aptly illustrate, the ways that people define their own group membership and the ways that outsiders define their membership are highly situational and responsive to changing contexts. People may hold multiple simultaneous identities and manipulate them according to the opportunities or circumstances they face. Virtually all social scientists who have examined ethnicity comment on its protean nature and how it represents a moving target for their analyses. And yet there is something essential about ethnic identity that gets at the heart of human society and the multiple ways that human beings define themselves and create meaning in their lives. Ethnic identity is played out in the subjectivities of people and simultaneously exists as a fact of human behavior observable and measurable by social scientists. Both emic and etic perspectives (and validations) are necessary if we are to explain this difficult-to-define phenomenon. Any advance in our understanding of the ways that people create and maintain ethnic groups will move us closer to the overall goal of describing and explaining the similarities and differences among the world's cultures as well as trajectories of change. This chapter reviews what we have learned from a multidisciplinary exploration of ethnic identity among the indigenous Nahua peoples of northern Mesoamerica and offers suggestions concerning where we should go from here in our research efforts.

THE VALUE OF MULTIPLE APPROACHES

No single field of study by itself is comprehensive enough to reveal all the complexities of ethnic identity. The authors in this book have approached the phenomenon from the perspectives of archaeology, art history, ethnohistory, and ethnography. Each of these fields covers a different (but overlapping) sector of the human experience and has developed its own methods and techniques for handling the special data that set it apart from other fields of inquiry. Each discipline and particular research strategy faces limitations but at the same time has a unique contribution to make.

Archaeology can illuminate cultural processes over deep time whereas ethnohistory reconstructs similar processes from documentary records. Art history provides insights into the aesthetic and symbolic worlds of past peoples, and ethnography gives us information on the range of contemporary cultural variation. These cognate disciplines together provide the critical and multifaceted perspective necessary to analyze a cultural and historical situation as complex as that found in Mesoamerica. However, each perspective entails gathering and analyzing different types of data that are often difficult to correlate. Archaeologists are increasingly recognizing the durable but often unobtrusive traces of ethnicity, and art historians are faced with sometimes ambiguous representations of the ethnic self and others that do not admit of straightforward interpretation. Ethnicity is generally poorly represented in the documentary record of Mesoamerica, and detecting it demands that ethnohistorians read between the lines. Ethnographers have their own problems in identifying patterns in the swirling complexities of people's behaviors and articulations. In a sense, all these specialists suffer from too much information deriving from rapidly changing contexts, and the difficulty is in sorting out what is relevant to ethnicity and what pertains to other dimensions of life. All too little of our data is unambiguous, but focused studies should yield valuable empirical information and enlightening insights.

THE DYNAMICS OF ETHNICITY

The century-long period preceding the arrival of the Spaniards saw the alliance between the city-states of Tenochtitlan, Texcoco, and Tlacopan grow into the Aztec Empire, the largest political system in the history of the region. The armies of the Triple Alliance moved out and conquered new territories and in the process incorporated many previously independent peoples into their expanding empire. As we have seen, groups of people continuously moved throughout the region either in search of new lands and a better political or economic situation or because they were forced or encouraged by military and political officials of the empire to relocate. State systems are always dynamic, but the Aztec Empire was especially energetic during its short period of military and political hegemony.

The inevitable result of these continuous processes of change was that people routinely came into contact with others from different cultural traditions. There were many opportunities for these interactions. As communities were conquered, some became incorporated into the rural estates of nobility to whom they now owed their labor and tribute. The situation was complex, as members of a single community may have owed tribute to several different lords of the land, a process described in detail by Gibson for the city-state of Cuauhtitlan (1971:390). Imperial tribute collectors, carrying the accoutrements, language, and other cultural trappings of the imperial order, were frequent (and characteristically unwelcome) visitors throughout the conquered domains. The process of meeting cultural others must also have been a feature of urban life throughout the region as rural people moved to the cities and urban dwellers moved from center to center, and there were considerable such movements.

Cross-cultural encounters must have been particularly common in markets throughout the realm. Professional merchants traveling to and from the imperial core carried not only merchandise but also their own cultural baggage. Cultural differences were clearly recognized by the ruling powers, for in some circumstances specialized professional merchants (*oztomeca*) entered restless districts disguised as locals. They must have acquired considerable cultural and linguistic knowledge to pull off such a deception. Large-scale professional merchant caravans would have appeared with some frequency in the many communities throughout central Mexico. Far more common were the regional merchants who plied their significant wares (such as foodstuffs, cotton, salt, and cacao) across ecological zones and into a variety of cultural orbits. Such mercantile contact (and consequent cultural exposure) was nothing new under Aztec dominion; it had characterized central Mexico since well before recorded time.

Language can be a critical element in ethnic identity, and this was undoubtedly the case in ancient Mesoamerica. Numerous languages were spoken in the region, many of which were historically unrelated. In this regard, it is interesting that Nahuatl, the language of the Aztecs, was becoming the lingua franca in large portions of Mesoamerica by the time of the Spanish Conquest. Ethnohistorians also believe that a process of "Nahuatization" was occurring in some areas in which Nahuatl was replacing more localized languages. This adoption of the dominant language was particularly characteristic of the elite in conquered communities. These processes may reflect simultaneous efforts: politically subordinated individuals sought to take better advantage of opportunities offered by the Aztec state, and dominant Nahuatl-speaking elites married local elites to further the interests of the empire. An intended or unintended consequence (on the part of the local elites or the state) would have been to reduce ethnic difference in the empire, at least at the more elevated political and social levels. The extent to which this occurred remains to be determined.

As we have seen in previous chapters, by the time of the Aztec Empire, Mesoamerica had become a mosaic of ethnic groups. There were many distinctive languages and cultures in the region, but settled life stretched back thousands of years and processes of diffusion produced similarities. These pan-Mesoamerican similarities included, in a general sense, the basic social and political order, religious systems and specific shared symbols, principles and types of architecture, and mythological tenets. Each culture, however, developed its own slant on these general features. Thus although significant differences among groups existed in the Mesoamerican culture area, a good deal was shared and would have been familiar to peoples who bumped against each other as the empire was being created and consolidated.

SOFT AND HARD VERSIONS OF ETHNICITY

Given the situation in Mesoamerica just before the Spanish Conquest, it would be easy to conclude that ethnicity might be the fundamental dynamic that accounts for events in the region. The tremendous meeting and mixing of peoples from related but different traditions must have set in motion forces that we can witness in the archaeological and historical record. This conclusion might also help explain the important role ethnicity plays among contemporary indigenous people in the region. It is commonly thought in Mexico today that such indigenous groups are simply remnants of those bygone days which have somehow survived with their ancient traditions intact. And yet from the previous chapters we can see that ethnicity, although significant, was simply not all that crucially important as a social force in prehispanic Mesoamerica. For example, we have no evidence from the prehispanic period that ethnicity compromised social statuses. Stark and Chance in Chapter 1 of this volume note that there exist hard and soft versions of ethnic identity. The hard version is based on putative kinship, that is, ideas of descent from common ancestors, and it can implicate biological or racial difference. The soft version is more general, based on nonspecific claims to ancestry or common history, but it does not implicate kinship. The evidence suggests that the people of prehispanic Mesoamerica exhibited the soft version of ethnic identity and that it was based more on place and historical experience than on unambiguous claims of descent. It is also clear that estate or social class relations (based heavily on kinship relations) rather than dynamics of ethnicity dominated the social scene on the eve of European intervention.

It would be fascinating and highly instructive to know precisely what people of the time thought about cultural or ethnic differences. We can get a substantial but not complete idea of indigenous views of these differences by probing the documentary record, by examining works of art, and by seeing how ethnic differences are viewed by indigenous people of today. We know that in prehispanic and early colonial times, chroniclers named many ethnic groups and furthermore that they held stereotyped views of the behavior and level of sophistication of these others (based predominantly on Aztec ascribed characteristics). We also know that membership in a calpolli, rights to work in certain specialized crafts, and membership in the nobility with its special perquisites were often based on ethnic group membership. As Umberger and Berdan point out in Chapters 3 and 4, respectively, it is clear that the Aztec state used ethnic stereotypes to divide dominated peoples, disparage specific groups (and hence elevate itself), and organize its subjects. In some cases the state simplified complex ethnic situations to facilitate its rule.

Yet ethnic identity was not seen by the prehispanic people as immutable and somehow reflective of the essence of a person or group. As Umberger points out in Chapter 3, artists working to enhance the prestige of the state often portrayed rulers as deities representing a particular ethnic group. She observes that artists, unlike the rulers themselves, could easily manipulate reality and change the ethnic designation (and even sex) of a ruler or significant figure if it served state interests. Negative stereotypes of groups were frequently tempered with positive portrayals, as when Otomí and Huaxtec people were generally disparaged but honors conferred on elite forces in the Aztec military were named after them. Chichimecs were thought to be barbaric, but urban elites liked to identify with their ruggedness and ability to fight effectively. Likewise, certain deities were often associated in the codices with specific ethnic groups, yet the conquering Aztecs readily appropriated some of these sacred figures as their own when it served their ends. People of Mesoamerica conceived of their gods not as paragons of good or evil but rather as mixtures of the two qualities. In similar fashion, prehispanic peoples likely did not conceive ethnic difference in terms of absolutes, as Berdan concludes in Chapter 4. Moreover, we find no evidence during the prehispanic period or among contemporary indigenous Mesoamericans that groups were or are distinguished by physical characteristics. Distinctions were made and continue to be made based on cultural attributes, not physical differences.

As the authors have shown, European ideas brought by the Spaniards about ethnic identity differed radically from the Native American conception. However, many contemporary peoples in the region continue to reflect ancient ideas about ethnic difference, and in most cases they appear not to have accepted the Spanish definitions of ethnicity. As Sandstrom and Taggart relate in Chapters 6 and 7, respectively, the Nahua of eastern Mexico recognize language and ethnic differences among Native American groups as well as between themselves and the Hispanic elites who dominate them. They use the Spanish word *costumbres* (customs) to talk about cultural practices, and there is no hint that these practices are viewed as somehow biologically innate or racially based. For example, the Nahua speak of church costumbres in the city that differ from their own, or of differences in costumbres among villages or other indigenous groups. They might say that Otomí costumbres differ from their own, but they do not thereby assert that the Otomí differ fundamentally from them. This is an important point. In fact, in northern Veracruz it is common for people from different Native American groups, speaking languages that are not mutually intelligible, to participate in the same ritual events. Religious pilgrimages to sacred mountains, caves, or springs often include people from various language and ethnic groups. In their own language the Nahua use the term *tlalnamiquiliztli* (in Nahuatl) or *talnamiquiliz* (in Nahuat) to approximate our word *culture*. The word, which may vary according to dialect, means "memory" or "remembered places and practices" and is used when discussing different ethnic or cultural traditions. Again, we find no hint that the remembered practices of different groups are innate to those groups, but instead we can say that the contemporary Nahua and other Native Americans see ethnic differences as rooted in the different histories each group has experienced. In sum, the contemporary perspective reflects the softer version of ethnicity described for prehispanic peoples.

The archaeological record in northern Mesoamerica appears to affirm the secondary role played by ethnic identity in the social life of the region. In Chapter 2 Stark is optimistic that researchers are learning how to recognize traces left by ethnic difference. Of course, many indicators of ethnic difference, such as language, do not survive to become part of the archaeological record.

Nonetheless, Stark notes some success in identifying ethnic enclave populations that lived within larger groups. The best method for studying ethnicity prehistorically is to focus on physical remains of individual household activities. By focusing on family-scale ritual, food, ceramics, and house architecture, archaeologists can identify groups whose behavior differs from that of the larger population. The assumption here is that differences in family practice are the product of enculturation and tend to persevere over long periods.

Archaeological data coupled with other lines of evidence from ethnohistory or art history show the greatest promise for clarifying relations in past populations. For instance, in Chapter 3 Umberger's illuminating analysis of the Aztec Tizoc Stone suggests that imperial approaches to groups both inside and beyond the Basin of Mexico were uniform; that is, closely related Nahuatl speakers were depicted in the same manner as more distant foreigners. Her detailed study of this same monument also supports the idea that these very place-oriented people conceived politico-territorial domains first and foremost in terms of their rulers. Both of these important points, combined with the ethnohistoric data, augment the suggestion that ethnic identity played second fiddle to other identification criteria among these Late Postclassic peoples. Stark holds out hope that new techniques, such as isotope analysis of bone taken from burials used to identify immigrants and migration patterns, may provide long-term information on ethnogenesis and what she calls ethnic-group fade-out. In her case study Stark presents evidence of the arrival of an ethnically distinct superordinate group in a populated area of southern Veracruz. Typical of the pattern found at other sites in Mesoamerica, the differences appear to be evanescent. There are, however, a few cases in the archaeological record in which ethnic enclaves seem to have persisted at least for several generations.

Why, then, was the ethnicity of prehispanic peoples so much softer than the harder version imported by the Spaniards? The Spanish view emphasized biological descent and kinship, with race as a concept. The only way to answer such a question is to have a theoretical understanding of what causes ethnicity in the first place and then to identify factors that foster its persistence. Much of the discussion of ethnicity in the previous chapters is influenced by a theoretical perspective based on the idea that ethnic groups form and persist in situations where people are competing for resources. The resources may be material, such as access to land, or they may be more abstract, such as political power. In certain circumstances, individuals may compete with each other for something of value, but in other situations individuals ally themselves with a group that has distinctive cultural features in order to achieve their ends. Circumstances that can lead to the development of an ethnic identity involve situations in which a migrant group enters a region where people with distinct cultural traditions already live, or alternatively, in which a group with distinctive cultural traditions of its own comes to dominate other groups with different traditions. There are undoubtedly other cases and circumstances whereby ethnicity gains salience, but domination and migration are of critical importance. It is our contention that ethnicity takes on characteristics of the harder version when lines are clearly drawn over the factor of resource competition.

Any groups of people who are in long-term competition with other groups will develop symbolic features that serve to distinguish themselves from the competitors. Clans and sports teams, like military units, fraternity houses, and political parties, in similar fashion symbolically distinguish themselves from each other and develop individual histories that underscore their uniqueness. Social classes at their simplest definition are groups of people who are in competition with other classes for social, political, or economic resources. Members of a social class develop speech patterns, food habits, dress, music, and other features in order to set themselves apart. But clans, sports teams, and social classes are not ethnic groups. Members of ethnic groups believe themselves—or are believed by others—to be descended from a common set of ancestors or from a generalized ancestral population. They are believed to share something significant with each other, and they use cultural features to distinguish themselves from members of other groups. What people in an ethnic group share may be a state of being or place in the world based on similar historical experiences. Ethnic groups are not complete cultures in and of themselves even though their members may think they are. As mentioned above, ethnic groups are often part of larger political-economic systems such as states or empires. Ethnic groups have boundaries, but these are often permeable and indistinct. Individuals use ethnicity in their strategies, and so ethnic identity is situational and constantly being redefined to meet new contingencies. One usually finds ethnic groups in a subordinate position relative to a dominant group that exhibits different cultural patterns. Members of a subordinate ethnic group maintain their identity to avoid dominant-group violence and create an alternative social world where they can make lives for themselves. It is important to recognize that in the strategic interplay between dominant and subordinate groups, members may actively create cultural differences to further distinguish themselves from members of other groups. The process of ethnogenesis is a sure sign that ethnic identity is hardening and that competitive lines are being drawn. For its part, the dominant group may create ethnic divides as it pursues its own interests. Dominant-group members also constitute an ethnic group, but they are often unaware of the fact. From their perspective, they represent the norm in opposition to the ethnic other.

Do different conditions or forces generate and maintain these different versions of ethnicity, and is resource competition in particular a critical factor in these processes? We might have expected that the intense competition over resources in prehispanic Aztec times would have led to the creation of hardened ethnic groups. But this was apparently not the case. Could the answer here relate to the nature of the Aztec political and social structure, particularly the complexity of competing cross-cutting loyalties among calpolli, altepetl, teccalli, and class lines? Might these arrangements, along with the general in-stability and fluidity of the imperial structure, have inhibited ethnic groups from forming strategies around specific resources?

ETHNICITY, SOCIAL CLASS, AND POLITICAL INSTABILITY

What we can witness in prehispanic Mesoamerica is the coming together of more or less distinct cultural groups that undoubtedly shared in a common Mesoamerican tradition. This process occurred under conditions of rapid yet uneven change. Polities throughout the region were characterized by instabil-ity, and even the militarily powerful Aztecs struggled to impose state control, in both core and peripheral regions of the empire. Although the various groups being incorporated into the Aztec Empire sporadically competed for land and political power, it appears that the political and social systems were not stable enough to lock ethnic groups into the long-term competition that would lead to ethnogenesis. People did not create cultural differences to set themselves apart from competing groups largely because of the geographic mobility of whole groups, as well as rebellions, forced relocations, elite intermarriages, flu-idity of alliances and wars, and other factors of change.

As Berdan points out in Chapter 4, the altepetl, or city-state, probably pro-vided the context for prehispanic ethnic identity, and Umberger's evidence from the great monuments reinforces this idea. Below that, the calpolli would have provided the focal point of local identity with a shared name and history, participation in specific rituals, occupational specialty, shared sense of destiny, common enemies, and unified traditional leadership. Such compartmentaliza-tion may have actually dampened ethnic competition and conflict because the calpolli were set up as relatively self-contained modules. Ethnic groups formed a mosaic throughout the region, but it was a shifting mosaic as each altepetl rose and fell in its fortunes in the constant jockeying for political position. It is possible that ethnicity may have been more important to people living in the context of the greater stability at the center of the Aztec Empire, while it was presumably less important in the shifting imperial periphery. Yet this remains to be established, offering fertile ground for future research. Berdan concludes that ethnicity in the Aztec Empire was of secondary importance (compared with class and political control) because of the heterogeneous social situation, the dispersed nature of ethnic groups, the unstable political context, and the high degree of mobility experienced by individuals and groups. It is interesting to note in this regard that prehispanic legal codes implicated class but not eth-nicity in determining sanctions and meting out justice.

In the archaeological record, as we have seen, researchers have uncovered evidence of an ethnic enclave that was apparently stable for a long period of time in the Classic-period city of Teotihuacan. The enclave was inhabited by people from Oaxaca, who retained their identity for several generations (see Spence et al. 2005). They made Oaxaca-style ceramics and enjoyed lives that contrasted with the people around them. It is noteworthy that these artisans continued to manufacture specific types of ceramics in the city long after they had gone out of style back in the homeland. Teotihuacan is exceptional in Mesoamerica because of its endurance over a relatively long period of time. Apparently, it provided the continuity and general stability necessary for more hardened ethnic groups to form. If resource competition is an important dimension here, one missing piece of information that would help clarify the roles played by such ethnic enclaves is the identity of the resource(s) over which they were competing. Was it political power or access to land or some form of tribute? Ethnicity requires people to expend effort and creativity to maintain identity in the face of pressures to conform to more dominant groups. What was it that motivated people to create and maintain their differences?

A key issue for prehispanic people during the rise of the Triple Alliance was the divide between the so-called Tolteca and Chichimeca identities. In the eyes of the Aztecs the Tolteca were a specific ethnic group whose capital, Tula, was the center of Mesoamerican power during the Early Postclassic period. The residents of Tula (probably itself a multiethnic city) represented sophistication and civilization in the minds of people of the time, and the nobility justified its exalted status by establishing and/or maintaining a direct connection to Toltec ancestors. As newcomers to the Basin of Mexico, the early Aztecs, who were themselves Chichimeca, took particular pains to marry into recognized Toltec lineages in order to establish their right to rule. The Chichimeca were bow-and-arrow hunters from the northern Mexican desert and represented the barbaric counterparts to the civilized Tolteca. Although they did not constitute a single group, the Chichimeca became classified as a distinctive ethnic group because of their common hunting-and-gathering lifestyle. As mentioned above, the people in Mesoamerica did not totally disparage the Chichimeca, and Aztec nobles asserted their pride in having a Chichimec ancestry. Nonetheless, based on information on the Aztec Tizoc Stone, Umberger concludes that the Tolteca-Chichimeca divide provides a politically useful distinction between dominant or elite (Tolteca) groups and subordinate (Chichimeca) ones. Though not clearly politically relevant, there was a similar division found less frequently in the chronicles between the so-called People to the East and the Chichimeca. These divisions, based initially on ethnic difference, over time began to refer instead to different and more general levels of civilization, with the Chichimeca occupying the primitive end of the continuum.

The arrival of the Spaniards in 1519 began a series of transformations that forever changed the ethnic landscape in Mesoamerica. During the first years, as the Spaniards began to set up their own government, daily life for many people probably changed imperceptibly. The dominant political power had been replaced, but people were accustomed to that type of change. Tribute still had to be paid, regardless of who was in power. As Chance points out in Chapter 5, two major differences were that now the indigenous population was segregated to a greater extent from the Spanish elites than they had been from their own rulers, and different legal codes were established for Spaniards and Indians. By the beginning of the seventeenth century, catastrophic declines in the native population and increased control by the Spaniards began to affect indigenous peoples dramatically, forcing them into a position of greater inferiority relative to the Spanish overlords.

The ethnic divide between Spaniard and Indian developed in the context of violence and domination, and sumptuary laws ensured that the division would be visible and enforceable. The Aztecs had also established elaborate sumptuary laws, which tend to be found where people at the top of the social hierarchy feel insecure about their position. At first the Spanish colonial class system may have been unstable, before it evolved into the more rigid system evident in later years. As Chance points out, traditional indigenous nobility occupied an ambiguous position in this emerging bipolar ethnic system. Many colonial documents are pleas on the part of former members of the prehispanic nobility who are trying to assert their rights and gain access to resources under the new system, or at least retain their anciently established traditional rights. In some cases they appear openly nervous and threatened by their "own" commoners (see Lockhart et al. 1986:79–84). It would be interesting to explore these complex dynamics, especially the possible impact of changes in access to private property (particularly land) and changes in the distribution of wealth among the differently defined groups.

At the time of the Spanish Conquest the two most important corporate groups in Mesoamerica were the calpolli and the teccalli. These two common-interest organizations entered into coalitions and formed the altepetl. Just as in prehispanic days, during the colonial period ethnic identity defined the relations both within and between each altepetl. Ethnicity was the primary basis on which coalitions were built in order to compete for political power. Thus from the perspective of the indigenous people, ethnic loyalty was directed to the calpolli and teccalli and then to the altepetl of which they were a part. As Chance sees it, ethnicity in the early colony was based primarily on place of origin and shared history. Any regional ethnic identity, say among Otomí, Nahua, or Zapotec, which was never well developed in prehispanic times, was further weakened under Spanish rule. Through time, as the lines of competition changed, the focus of identity shifted from the individual teccalli and calpolli to the altepetl or community as a whole. As clearly shown in the chapters by Sandstrom and Taggart, the community continues to be the primary basis of identity among the contemporary Nahua. Chance notes that the pejorative term *indio* rarely appears in the documents because, at least in the beginnings of the colony, the ethnic divide continued to be between the various altepetl and not between Indian and Spaniard. That, at any rate, was the understanding of the indigenous population. During this same time, descendants of the prehispanic nobility tried to create an identity system based on descent in order to justify their claims. Thus identity for the masses was based on place and history (the softer version) whereas for the indigenous nobles identity was based on kinship and descent (the harder version). To what extent were these patterns mirrored in other colonial situations?

ETHNICITY AND KINSHIP

Given the significance that is sometimes placed on ancestry and descent in Mesoamerican ethnicity, it is important that we have a clear idea of the nature of kinship relations among the indigenous peoples who inhabited Mesoamerica and continue to live in the culture area. Even a cursory review of kinship studies published about the region reveals that researchers have had a difficult time creating models of how systems of kin relations work. For the most part, indigenous peoples of the region lack the unilineal descent rules that produce lineages and clans so familiar to kinship studies of African cultures. Most groups in Mesoamerica practice bilateral descent and exhibit highly flexible rules governing postmarital residence, genealogical reckoning, and household structure.

An alternative to standard kinship models, proposed by Lévi-Strauss (1982), places the house rather than rules governing kinship relations as the focus of analysis. This relatively radical departure from more standard anthropological studies of kinship has been applied by Chance (2000) to colonial Nahua kinship systems and by Sandstrom (2000) to contemporary Nahua. Houses in house societies are viewed not simply as buildings but as estates with material and nonmaterial wealth. Land is the most common material wealth, and titles or names carry the bulk of nonmaterial value. Houses are elements of social organization, but they are tied to the physical structure and specific location of the headquarters. Most important, houses are the focus of social activity that includes kin and non-kin, and they may be based on contradictory principles of descent and affinity, patrilineality and matrilineality, or endogamy and exogamy. These contradictions are neutralized by the political nature of the house and by the common interest inhabitants have in the wealth associated with it. Without going into great detail, it is easy to see that organization of the house can be unstable; however, because of wealth held in common, its inhabitants are motivated to ensure that the house endures. This new conception of kinship better describes the teccalli as analyzed by Chance and the nonresidential patrilocal extended family among contemporary Nahua as discussed by Sandstrom. If kinship in Mesoamerica proves to resemble the house type, it would go a long way toward explaining the apparent flexibility of kin-related behavior and the fluid relationship between kinship and ethnicity. This topic is far from resolved and begs further study. Does this also point to the soft version of ethnicity? Do other early civilizations share these structural relationships?

ETHNICITY AND RACE

As the Spaniards consolidated power, they introduced a foreign element into Mesoamerica's ethnic mosaic, and that factor was race. As time passed, there was a growing population of people of mixed Spanish and Native American ancestry who came to be called mestizos. With the decimation of indigenous populations, rulers introduced African slaves to New Spain. These people eventually mixed with Indians and Spaniards, leading Spanish overlords to create the *sistema de castas* in order to consolidate their control over resources. The Spaniards devised a complex classification of people based on actual or supposed racial mixture and were concerned about maintaining pure blood lines (*limpieza de sangre*) for ruling elites. The changing position of the cacique in Santiago Tecali, discussed by Chance, is an excellent example of the transformation of the ethnic identity of a single group during the colonial period. The term *cacique* is an Arawak word introduced into Mesoamerica by the Spaniards and used to refer to indigenous rulers and their descendants. The word had been known in Santiago Tecali, but it did not come into common or widespread use until after 1700. Caciques had rights to land and labor and were free from tribute payment. They were not indigenous commoners nor were they considered mestizos, although in reality many of them probably were of mixed blood. In the documents caciques tried to justify their rights by claiming they were pure-blooded Indian nobles, but at the same time they scrupulously avoided the pejorative word *indio*.

Not surprisingly, caciques created ethnic and class differences between themselves and those they considered their inferiors. Ethnic identity and class superiority were strategies for maintaining access to important resources. Like the contemporary Nahua described by Sandstrom in this volume, the caciques in the eighteenth century used indigenous and Spanish elements in the creation of their identity. Over time the context for their inventions changed. Noble status no longer commanded the privilege that it once did, caciques were found in all classes, and they began to ignore class identity and emphasize instead ethnicity based on descent from colonial landowners and not the prehispanic ancestors. Here we see the influence of Spanish conceptions of race on the strategies of the caciques. At different times the caciques were in the uncomfortable position of justifying their privileges based on their Indianness while becoming increasingly ethnically Spanish to separate themselves from indigenous commoners. It was Mexican independence that put an end to the official categorization of people by race. The question remains how that social upheaval redefined the context of resource competition and its relationship to identity creation.

The form of racial identity found in the United States is unusual and can lead to confusion when we examine racial categories in other cultural and historical contexts. In the United States before the days of the civil rights movement, race was generally seen as an innate and immutable property of a person that had a direct effect on the character of that person. Race was destiny, and according to the "one-drop rule," even a single drop of African blood from a remote ancestor from Africa meant that the person was black. Though apparently the colonial Spaniards tried to impose a rigid racial classification of this type on the population, it soon broke down and became unmanageable. The mixed population found in Mesoamerica and throughout Latin America today makes such classification schemes impossible to sustain. Consequently, race is recognized throughout the region, but it is not generally viewed as immutable. The following anecdote illustrates the point. In 2004 anthropologist Lisa Chiteji, who conducted extensive field research in Belize, gave a talk on race and ethnicity to undergraduate students at Indiana University–Purdue University Fort Wayne. In a general sense, the students shared the widespread view that race is an innate biological attribute of people. Chiteji astounded the students when she stated that African-American basketball star Michael Jordan would be considered white in Brazil. To be wealthy and famous is to be white, and it has nothing to do with skin color or ancestry. The students were applying the definition of race found in the United States and were surprised to learn how much of our understanding of the phenomenon of race is a social construction. In Mexico today, racial definitions come out of historical circumstances that make Mesoamerica more like Brazil than the United States.

INDIANS, MESTIZOS, AND CONFLICT

In Chapter 6 Sandstrom emphasizes the ethnic divide between contemporary Nahua and the dominant mestizo elites of northern Veracruz. The Nahua recognize other neighboring indigenous groups such as the Otomí and Tepehua, and even have stereotypes about them, but they do not identify strongly as Nahua in opposition to these other groups. Their ethnicity is based largely on place, history, and social class, and in general they do not recognize race as an important factor in ethnic difference. Like the caciques of old, they too create their ethnic identity by combining indigenous and Spanish elements to set themselves apart from Hispanic elites. They use the term *coyotl* to refer to nonindigenous people, and *macehualli*, the ancient Nahuatl word for "commoner," to refer to any indigenous person. *Coyotl* and *macehualli* are clearly terms referring to people with different histories (i.e., *tlalnamiquiliztli* or *talnamiquiliz*, memories or remembered places and practices), but they also refer to differences in social class. The Nahuatl and Nahuat terms correlate with the Classical Nahuatl (sixteenth century) *tlalnamiquiliztli*, found in Molina (1977: 124v) as "memoria." Similarly, the term *icnoyotl* (respect), discussed by Taggart in Chapter 7, has its Classical Nahuatl parallel in *icnoua*, meaning "pious" or "compassionate," in Molina as well (1977:33v). It begs further research to determine if these terms carried the same meanings in similar contexts.

Nahua consider all Indians to be poor, regardless of their level of wealth. Being poor is part of what it is to be Indian. There are whole communities of people in the region who identify as mestizo but whose lifestyles are very similar to those of local indigenous people. Many of these people may even speak an indigenous language, but the Nahua still consider them to belong to the coyotl sector of the society. In general, the Nahua identify first as members of a specific community, then as macehualli, and finally as Nahua. They also have some identity with the municipality, state, region (such as the Huasteca or Sierra Norte de Puebla), and even less with Mexico as a whole. Just as we saw in the prehispanic period, however, contemporary Nahua do not have a strongly developed regional identity. Interestingly, they rarely speak badly about mestizos as a whole. If pressed, they might say something like the *coyomej* (plural of *coyotl*) are aggressive, arrogant, or self-serving. However, most people tend to judge individuals rather than make statements about whole groups. Here is an example of the soft version of ethnicity among Native Americans in the region, and it may resemble attitudes toward ethnicity present in Aztec times as well.

The unstable and situational nature of ethnic identity, combined with the need to find temporary wage labor on neighboring mestizo ranches, makes it advantageous for both Indian and mestizo to keep the border between them somewhat ambiguous and ill-defined. Social mobility exists in Mexico, and indigenous people may rise in class status but only if they leave their community and if they lose their identity as macehualli. Language is obviously a critical factor, and as a consequence fully bilingual young people are more likely to experience social mobility. The ethnic situation is complex in contemporary Mexico and throughout the culture area, but its roots lie in the prehispanic and colonial experiences of the people. The community of origin remains the primary source of identity, along with position in the local system of social classes. Mestizos may not always be rich, but Indians are always poor. In fact, when speaking of members of the Hispanic dominant group, the Nahua do not use the word *mestizos* but rather identify them with the phrase *los ricos*. Clearly, they see the ethnic divide as being based on differing historical experiences and differential opportunities in the class system.

Religious ritual is one of the major ways the Nahua described by Sandstrom create a sense of ethnic identity and common purpose. The Nahua world view in the southern Huasteca region is based on the idea that human beings receive a flow of benefits from spirit entities associated with a sacred cosmos. These benefits, such as rain, sunlight, and the procreative power of seeds, can be interrupted by human acts of disrespect. Disrespect can emanate from mestizos or Nahua alike, but it is more likely to be found in the behavior and attitudes of the dominant group. Curing rituals and sacred pilgrimages are designed to remove acts of disrespect and to restore the flow of benefits that make human existence possible. In a sense, these rituals remove mestizo traits and affirm Nahua values in a world out of their control. The rituals make the ethnic divide meaningful and clear: Nahua suffering is the result of mestizo domination.

In Chapter 7 Taggart provides an excellent example of the involuted and confusing nature of actual conflict situations involving Nahua and mestizos. At the same time, it highlights the power of fine-grained ethnography to reveal the subtle and nearly indiscernible differences between ethnic groups. Taggart focuses on language and shows how two ethnic groups bring a different understanding to the horrific slaughter that occurred in the Sierra Norte de Puebla community of Huitzilan in the late 1970s. Not surprisingly, the conflict began over access to land. But the struggle pitted Nahua against Nahua and mestizo against mestizo, and the ethnic lines were not clear-cut in the violent confrontation that ensued. Taggart demonstrates the ethnic divide in Huitzilan by re-counting Nahua versus mestizo views of the conflict. The mestizos saw the situation as a disagreement over an inheritance that escalated into a violent confrontation. The Nahuas, on the other hand, saw the roots of the conflict in lack of respect and disruption of community created when a group of Indians planted a cornfield together. Although sentiments in the conflict did not fall along strictly ethnic lines, a majority of the dead were Nahua, and Taggart's friends held generally negative views of the mestizo elites. He is able to locate the origin of Nahua ideas of respect and compassion in child-rearing tech-niques and in Nahua ideas expressed in oral narrations. Finally, he links the questions of ethnicity in Mesoamerica to the appearance of violent guerrilla groups in the region over the past several decades, underscoring the dynamic and ever-fluctuating nature of ethnicity and the extent to which it might be mobilized in traumatic times.

THE ELUSIVE NATURE OF ETHNICITY

It seems likely that the complex situation described and analyzed by Taggart is similar in many ways to the ethnic mosaic that existed throughout the region in prehispanic times. Ethnic groups definitely existed, and members of each group held opinions and stereotypes about their own and other groups. How-ever, actual historical events, whether wars, rebellions, or lesser conflicts, prob-ably did not line up along ethnic lines. Ethnic identity was a factor in a com-plex cross-cutting system of loyalties and treacheries that existed in a highly unstable and competitive environment. Ethnicity cannot by itself explain the political-economic system or events that the system generated, but any expla-nation of what happened must take into account ethnic differences.

Among the contemporary Nahua the shortage of land resources has pro-duced an excruciating situation that undermines the possibility of stability in many people's lives. Families split up, communities fission, and political orga-nizations disintegrate as desperate people invade ranch land or move to the cities to live in poor and dangerous neighborhoods. This intolerable circle of forces is played out in the context of a rapidly developing Mexico that is lurch-ing in the direction of modernization. As a collection of ethnic groups clus-tering at the lowest levels of national society, some eight million indigenous people are widely seen by elites as an anachronism and an obstacle to progress in the country. That view reveals the negative side of ethnicity. On the positive side, among indigenous peoples ethnic identity is a force that can be wielded to resist domination by Hispanic elites and a creative response to remedy an in-tolerable situation and effectively give people a sense of dignity and purpose.

In the unstable social, political, and economic conditions that character-ized the rise of the Aztec Empire, there were undoubtedly periods when eth-nicity was little more than a means to conveniently categorize people rather than a phenomenon involving actual people in organized groups. But in the give-and-take of competition over scarce resources, people have used ethnicity to create the basis for group action. We have presented evidence that ethnicity was sporadically used in this creative way in Mesoamerica. This feature of ethnic-based action means that systems of ethnicity can provide researchers with a window into the nature of the political and economic systems in which ethnic groups operate. In sum, the shape that ethnicity takes in a particular society, at a particular time and place, reflects the nature of the state in which it is found. We believe it is worthwhile to pursue research agendas that look for these regularities and patterns. In particular, we have noted various comparative questions that emerge better from the temporal and interdisciplinary panorama of these chapters than from any one discipline or time period.

From evidence presented in this book, it is clear that the Aztec state, much like other Mesoamerican superordinate political entities tracing deep into prehistory, suffered from a chronic inability to effectively dominate and control its populations. Aztec elites (and the armies they mustered) could certainly crush opposition, subdue rebellious provinces, threaten neighbors and more distant polities, and integrate peoples living close to the capital. But during their relatively short ninety-year hegemony they were unable to create a social system stable enough to give rise to more powerful and coherent ethnic groups.

With the coming of the Spaniards, a whole new set of variables was introduced into the region. At first the invaders could inflict only destruction, and beyond the ravaging effects of periodic major epidemics, the daily life for the average person in Mesoamerica probably changed little. Using the model provided by the recently centralized government of Spain, the conquerors solidified power and created a relatively strong central government. Spanish influence penetrated everywhere in the New World, and the nature of ethnic relations changed forever. The dominant group introduced the concept of race in consolidating its position at the summit of the social hierarchy and created a permanent underclass of indigenous people. For their part, the Native Americans in Mesoamerica solidified their identity as Indians in opposition to Hispanic overlords based on their community of origin and their shared history as a conquered people. Researchers are still learning how to recognize and understand the significance of ethnicity in the archaeological, documentary, and ethnographic records. By employing an empirical multidisciplinary approach, we are optimistic that the questions posed above can be systematically pursued and that more light will be shed on this most elusive feature of human social life.

Notes

Chapter 2. Archaeology and Ethnicity in Postclassic Mesoamerica

1. Gerstle (1987) argued for an ethnic enclave involving foreign political "hostages" at the Late Classic (A.D. 600–900) Maya center of Copán, which seemed to exemplify a persistent devaluation of the foreigners. Later analyses, however, treated the area as part of a range of statuses within and among patio groups (Hendon 1991).

2. Some small polities had only a head city and a small set of dependent towns or villages and can usefully be called city-states.

3. When I plot pottery types on these maps, I plot only rims for better visibility, but maps showing the occurrences of both rims and nonrims yield similar patterns.

4. The only ceramic griddles found earlier are made with a sandy, dark brown paste and exhibit a different, upturned lip profile compared with the buff comales; buff comales have a straight, nearly horizontal termination and a slight basal ridge akin to a ring base. Brown comales appear toward the close of the Late Classic period. Although occasionally recovered throughout the Blanco delta, they are concentrated at the east end, where the major center was Azuzules. This distribution contrasts with the concentration of Middle Postclassic ceramics and figurines to the west in the delta, nearer Sauce. Brown comales are seldom recovered within the formal architectural areas of Classic period centers, which indicates that rebuilding within centers likely did not occur late enough in the Classic period to incorporate fill containing brown comales. Because none of the brown comales were recovered at Sauce and few in its vicinity, brown comales are not associated with the Middle Postclassic period; instead, buff comales represent a new technological style for tortilla griddles in Middle Postclassic collections. Late Classic infiltration or settlement of new inhabitants who used the brown comales seems unlikely; these comales are not associated with other different ceramics. Nevertheless, despite the widespread occurrence of brown comales, they are concentrated toward the east, a distribution that may correspond to members of a different group with different food preparation practices scattered near Azuzules. At present there is insufficient evidence to decide if the brown comales represent an infiltration of immigrants or the start of a shift in foodways among some Late Classic families.

5. The two survey cycles employed slightly different lithic classifications. Variables included from the 1986–1989 survey projects are proximal prismatic blade segments (ground and not ground), medial and distal blade segments, indeterminate blade segments, whole prismatic blades, ridged pressure blades, plunging pressure blades, initial series pressure blades, irregular pressure blades, other pressure blades, and percussion blades. For the 1998–2002 survey project, the variables included are prismatic pressure blades (proximal, medial, distal, and whole), percussion blades (proximal, medial, distal, and whole), macro percussion blades (proximal, medial, distal, and whole), prismatic blades with platform reversal scars, blade shatter, second series blades, initial series blades, irregular pressure blades, ridged blades, secondary ridged blades, unidentified blades, and plunging blades.

Chapter 3. Ethnicity and Other Identities in the Sculptures of Tenochtitlan

1. I use the term Aztec to refer to the people, cultures, and productions of the Basin of Mexico collectively in imperial times and to the empire emanating from there and expanding into different parts of Mesoamerica after the War of Independence from the Tepaneca (A.D. 1428–1431). On the different usages of Aztec, see Barlow 1949, Berdan et al. 1996:4, Carrasco 1999:3–4, Nicholson 1971a:116, Smith 2000:582, and Umberger and Klein 1993:295.

   The people of Tenochtitlan and Tlatelolco shared the same island environment in Lake Texcoco and claimed the same Mexica heritage. Tlatelolco was sometimes a separate city-state and sometimes part of Tenochtitlan. Pictorial references to and alphabetic usage of the terms Mexica, Tenochca, and Tlatelolca vary accordingly in colonial sources.

2. On various concerns relevant to the definition of Mesoamerican and Aztec urban centers, see Cowgill 2004, Hicks 1982, Hodge 1984 and 1997, Marcus 1983, and Smith 2000.

3. As Smith (2000:587, 589) observed, Aztec citizenship was different from Greek citizenship, the source of our use of the word, because it was based on relations of subordination to nobles and not containment within territorial boundaries. Thus I use the term *polity member* rather than *citizen*.

4. The migrants are pictured and named by glosses in their region of origin in the Codex Azcatitlan: the Matlatzinca, the Tepaneca, the Chichimeca, the Malinalca, the Cuitlahuaca, the Xochimilca, the Chalca, and the Huexotzinca. The Mexica are not named but are pictured on a previous page. The reading of one glyph (a bow and arrow) as Chichimeca is debated by Smith (1984), who reads it as referring to the Tlahuica, the occupants of modern Morelos.

5. One of Xolotl's lieutenants was called Acolhua; perhaps he is the same one to whom Xolotl gave the town, or a relation.

6. Tenochtitlan was unusual among the Aztec city-states, as Hodge (1984:1–2) noted. Because it was on an island, it did not have the contiguous land tracts with outlying communities seen in other basin city-states. It did have small estancias in other territories or on islands in the lake, plus tracts of lakeshore agricultural areas to its south (see Carrasco 1999:93–96; Caso 1956).

7. Brumfiel (1994b) discusses further possible scenarios and hypothetical changes through time in Aztec central Mexico. One wonders to what extent ethnicity united commoner groups settled throughout the basin, and whether this was ever the basis for resistance.

8. On the blue capes, see Aguilera 1997 and Anawalt 1990; on other Toltec costume types depicted at Tula, see Anawalt 1985.

9. Figure 3.7C is an example of phonetic or rebus writing. The teeth (*tlantli*) refer to the suffix *-tlan*, which means something like "place of." For discussions of Aztec phoneticism, seemingly a colonial-period phenomenon in Aztec writing, see Nicholson 1973 and Prem 1970, 1992.

10. P. Carrasco (1950:106ff.) also notes the complexity of reconstructing political and other alignments in relation to ethnicity and ethnic areas (see also Berdan 1996:121–122).

11. Berdan and Anawalt (1992:1:219–220) translate Tollocan/Tulucan as "place where men incline their heads," an interpretation that derives from combining the etymology of the word Tulucan and the information of the pictograph.

12. Other examples in the Codex Mendoza of a foreign place whose glyphic names might allude to the ethnicity of inhabitants are found on folios 13r and 38r. These are two variant pictographs for the city-state Coyucac, which Berdan and Anawalt (1992:1:181) interpret as "in the place of the Coyuca [people]." The people of the place are referenced by the full figure of a woman with an elongated head attached to a cluster of signs that spells out the name phonetically and by just an elongated head, respectively.

13. On Tollocan Province, see also Durbin 1970, García Castro 1999, García Payón 1936, and Hernández 1988, plus materials in Alva Ixtlilxochitl 1975–1977 (1600–1640), Carrasco 1950, Chimalpahin 1965 (1606–1631), Hernández 1950, Quezada 1972, and Zorita 1963 (1566–1570). See the discussion of other Tollocan glyphs in Berdan and Anawalt 1992:1: 221–222.

14. On the sacred correspondences of different parts of the body, see López Austin 1988. On the inherent power of clothing parts, see especially Hvidtfeldt 1958 and Townsend 1979.

15. Not all forms of clothing are represented on monuments, only a limited repertory. Missing, for instance, are the items well known from colonial codices such as the blue cape or *tilmatli*, which was worn by rulers; the fitted warrior costume; and the chalk and feather adornment of conquered victims. This is probably a matter of different media, not a difference between prehispanic and colonial dates. See Anawalt 1981 on costumes in manuscripts.

16. The etymology of the name is unclear, but see Karttunen's reading in Umberger 1999: 95.

17. The warrior structures next to the Templo Mayor of Tenochtitlan were probably called Tlacochcalco and Tlacatecco, and the patron gods of these structures were Huitzilopochtli and Tezcatlipoca (Klein 1987:311–314). The top titles of governors in the empire held the comparable names Tlacochtectli and Tlacatecatl/Tlacatectli (Berdan and Anawalt 1992:4:folios 17v–18r), so it would not be surprising if these were the referents of the victorious figures.

18. See Prem 1970 and 1992 on the creative and unfixed aspects of Aztec hieroglyphs in glossed colonial documents.

19. Wicke (1976) believes it to be a reference to Coatlichan because of that town's designation at one time as Coatlichan-Acolhuacan. See text above.

20. I am aware that most scholars would object to the representation of one of the imperial co-rulers as a captive on a monument celebrating the empire, but the suggestion is supported by evidence that both co-capitals had fallen subject to the Tenochca by this time (e.g., Durán 1994:330–331 [1581]). This representation, of course, would have offended Nezahualpilli, the ruler of Texcoco when the monument was created.

21. These pairs are being reordered according to directional orientation by William L. Barnes (dissertation in progress).

22. In the Codex Xolotl, Acolhua and Tepaneca ethnicities are referred to with the same symbols, an arm in the case of the first and a stone symbol in the case of the second (Figure 3.3).

23. For the similar pictographs in the Codex Mendoza from which these places were identified, see Berdan and Anawalt 1992:1:Appendix E.

24. For the image on the vase found with it and probably containing Moquihuix's second-in-command, see Nicholson and Quiñones Keber 1983:94–97 and Umberger 2007.

25. The Cuitlahuac and Mixquic city-states/regions were probably not important enough to be pictured. The Otomí seem not to be represented either, seemingly because they did not control a territory.

Chapter 5. Indigenous Ethnicity in Colonial Central Mexico

1. Regional ethnic identities included the Otomí, Culhuaque, Cuitlahuaca, Mixquica, Xochimilca, Chalca, Tepaneca, Acolhuaque, and Mexica (Gibson 1964:22).

2. Terraciano (2001:318–344) posits a pan–Mixteca Alta Ñudzahui, or Mixtec, identity in the colonial period, though its applicability to preconquest times remains ambiguous.

3. Sandstrom (1991:xix) reports that *masehualmej*, which he translates as "countrymen" or "Indian farmers," is in common use today among Nahuatl speakers of northern Veracruz.

4. The term *cacique*, of Arawak origin, was adopted by the Spanish in the Caribbean in the early sixteenth century and subsequently applied to indigenous rulers and their descendants throughout the colonies.

5. Status inflation was quite common in both rural and urban settings in eighteenth-century Mexico and is probably characteristic of many multiethnic colonial societies. *Principales* accounted for over half the population of some colonial mountain Zapotec communities in Oaxaca in the late colonial period, while in the city of Oaxaca, despite extensive *mestizaje* (race mixture), the estate of *españoles* (including peninsulars and creoles) was larger than the population of mixed ancestry (Chance 1978:156; 1989:144).

In Tecali it appears that mestizaje contributed to the growth of the cacique group, since very few people self-identified as mestizos or mulattoes in parish and census records.

6. The caciques could also be characterized as an "estate," in that they comprised a hereditary group with distinct legal rights and privileges (Tönnies 1953; Nutini 1995:8; for a recent application to the Aztecs, see Hicks 1999). I find the estate concept less helpful here because it is rarely applied to post-eighteenth-century settings and lacks the broad comparative advantages of ethnicity.

Chapter 6. Blood Sacrifice, Curing, and Ethnic Identity Among Contemporary Nahua of Northern Veracruz, Mexico

1. Major periods of fieldwork in Amatlán include 1972–1973, 1985–1986, 1990, 1998, and 2006–2007. From 1985 on, my wife, Pamela Effrein Sandstrom, and son, Michael, participated in the research.

2. There are situations, such as apartheid South Africa and contemporary Israel, in which strong ethnic identity adheres to a group that dominates others socially, economically, politically, and militarily. It is interesting that in these cases the dominant group members identify themselves as the authentic minority in a large and overwhelming population of others. I suggest as well that ethnic groups are often similar to one another and that ethnic groups are often conflated with social classes. Ethnicity is not identical to class, but to a certain extent in any society, class differences express ethnic differences (see Berdan, Chance, this volume). Members of subordinate social classes create cultural differences to separate themselves from the dominant classes. For example, in the United States people in the working class often display a characteristic style of dress, occupy certain neighborhoods in the city, speak a distinctive dialect of English, and participate in the production of popular culture such as rock and roll or jazz music that comes to have class associations. Ethnic groups are different from social classes because they create distinctions based on a presumed common historical origin and presumed shared life experiences rather than simply on position relative to a dominant class or classes. But ethnic groups often occupy a specific position in the class hierarchy, and so they may appear to people in the dominant group to be equivalent to an underclass. Ethnogenesis, then, may be part of a larger process though which members of groups distinguish themselves for strategic purposes.

3. Skinner (1975:135) notes a similar historical occurrence in Africa: "European contact with and conquest of African societies created many more ethnic systems than had ever existed before on the continent."

4. Social scientists working around the world have noted the strategic value of ethnic identity in the day-to-day competition for resources. Despres (ed. 1975) edited a volume containing studies by several anthropologists who were able to explain ethnicity in their research areas as resulting from intergroup competition. In studying the San Blas Cuna of Panama, Holloman (1975:31; emphasis in original) writes, "The persistence of significant ethnic *organization* and of interethnic boundaries is always an indication that there is differential access to resources along ethnic lines, and that the assertion of ethnic identity has payoffs with respect to resource access and utilization." Whitten (1975:47), writing about the Canelos Quechua of Ecuador, states, "We must understand the expansion of Lowland Quechua ethnicity as a rational response to expanding opportunities in the money economy under the continuance of internal colonialism in Ecuador." In his analysis of ethnic identity in Peru, van den Berghe (1975:71) notes, "Throughout the world, the practical import of ethnicity is intimately linked with the unequal distribution of power and wealth." Despres (1975a:113–114) concludes his analysis of ethnicity in Guyana, "A system of ascribed ethnic statuses will…persist to the extent that the assertion of ethnic identities serves to confer competitive advantage in respect to environmental resources." Otite (1975:127) examines ethnicity in Nigeria and finds that "the coexisting and conflicting Hausa and Yoruba identities in the city of Ibadan were thus a function largely of the competition for the economic resources and products of the savannah and forest zones in Nigeria." Discussing ethnicity in Africa, Skinner

(1975:131–132) states, "Ethnic particularism most frequently occurs because one or more groups in the system, by remaining apart, derive tactical or strategic advantage in the competition for their societies' resources."

5. The religious movement surrounding Amalia Bautista has been studied by Quiroz Uria (2003).

6. After many years of research I am just beginning to understand some of the complex linkages and connections underlying Nahua world view and ritual. The difficulty of uncovering these features of Nahua culture underscores the benefit of long-term ethnographic research. It normally takes years of residence in a group for outsiders to understand what on the surface may appear to be simple features of the culture. Much of the information I present became available only in the past six years during our last two field trips to Mexico.

7. We know from a number of reliable sources that paper was a key item of tribute throughout Mesoamerica. Millions of sheets of paper flowed into the imperial capital each year. After the conquest the Spaniards outlawed the manufacture and use of paper by native peoples and brought individuals who were caught with paper before the Inquisition. In all of Mesoamerica the only place where paper continues to retain its sacred status and occupy a central place in ritual life is northern Veracruz and the surrounding region (see Sandstrom and Sandstrom 1986; Tolstoy 1991).

8. Here is a very good example of how analyzing material culture—the cut-paper figures—helped me to understand better the highly abstract Nahua beliefs about the causes of disease. It was because images of the wind spirits are cut with rib holes that I finally was able to ask the right questions and determine the identity of this important class of pathogens in Nahua thought.

9. An important point is that for the Nahua, rituals do not have the power nor are they designed to produce an empirical result directly. Cures do not create health; rather, they neutralize acts of disrespect that prevent health from being realized. The pilgrimage does not produce rain but rather restores the balance between the human and spirit worlds and thus removes obstacles to the normal flow of benefits, of which is included sufficient rain for the fields. Just as in the Western biomedical system a treatment may work perfectly well and yet the patient still dies, for the Nahua the pilgrimage may be a complete success and yet no rain is forthcoming. Understanding the indirect purpose of their rituals helps clarify why people persist in making elaborate offerings to the spirits in the absence of empirical evidence that they work. Even though Nahua rituals are not intended to produce direct results, those who participate are always delighted if they find empirical confirmation that the ritual has worked. While we were descending the sacred mountain Postectli in 1998, after making offerings to thunder and water spirits as described in the next section, a loud thunderclap took all of us by surprise. Our Nahua companions discussed the event excitedly, and many took it as a sign that the ritual was effective.

10. In 1998 and 2001 my wife, Pamela, and son, Michael, were present during the preparations and the ritual itself, and both climbed the mountain.

11. This sequence of photographs was taken during the pilgrimage of 1998.

12. It is interesting to note that an arroyo that loops through Amatlán has carried a significantly reduced volume of water for the past decade or so. People told me that they suspect ranchers upstream of pumping water out of the arroyo to irrigate their fields and pastures. In this case the *ricos* might literally be causing a water shortage and making the Nahua suffer new hardships.

Chapter 7. Nahuat Ethnicity in a Time of Agrarian Conflict

1. See Taggart 2007 for a more detailed account of the conflict that erupted in Huitzilan.

2. See, for example, Lorenzano 1998. Schryer (1990:22–22) points out that Marxists are divided on this issue.

3. In criticizing descent theorists, Schneider adopts some of the positions of the alliance theorists, who stress marriage exchange as the first principle of kinship organization.

Exchange theorists draw attention to making kinship by human activity or marriage exchanges.

4. Mazat's stories and life are featured in Taggart 1997, 2007.

5. Lockhart (1992:121) found evidence of toponymics in 1580.

6. "Topariente catca. Campa neh nihualliuh, yeh campa nohueinan catca hualliuh, notaht catca campa hualliuh. Ce tactzon ticen catca."

7. Inculcating icnoyot in this manner creates what Butler (1997) calls the "subject" that forms with the "bad conscience." The term *bad conscience* comes from Hegel and refers to the deeply learned ideas of right and wrong.

8. "Miaqueh conemeh axcan ahmo quipiyah icnoyot."

9. "Ahmo. Ilapaquih. Telzenca. Más cachi ticmacaz pero ahmo quicaqui."

10. "Motehuia."

11. "Motehuiah ihuan icnihuan."

12. "Quihtoznequi ahmo telihuizti. Zayo quicaqui. Como quichihuiliya, mocahua mochihuilica."

13. "Pos teh tacatilizquiya, teh tictazohta. Huan como ahmo tictacatilizquiya, ahmo tictazohta."

14. "Tahueh quihtoznequi quitazohta."

15. "Neh niquiliz, 'Nimitztazohta te tahueh.'"

16. "Porque nechchichixtoya ica notaxcal. Nechtatequihuiltitoya mah nitacua o ahmo. Como niehoc ya, pos a huetzi, 'Xitacua, mazo totonia.' Nicmatic nechtazohta. Porque ce tonal ahmo mitzcahuaz, ahmo xitacua. Siempre tiehoc, 'Xtayi in cafén. Xtacua ya.' Como nyo, 'Ahmo tihuecahuaz. Niman xihuiqui. Niman ximoquepa.' Entonces quitta teh tazohta."

17. "Pos ce quimaca para ma quicactiqui, para ahmo ilapaqui, ahmo tahtehui."

18. "Ce quinnonotza. Quili, 'Ahmo xitehui mocniuh porque hueliz ticocoz. Huan yeh no igual.'"

19. Many beliefs support the Nahuat "bad conscience," and some are regional variants of widespread notions such as the animal companion spirit, which has deep roots in ancient Mesoamerican culture (Gossen 1994).

20. See Taggart 1997:154–170 for a description of Mazat's domestic group during his early years. Clusters of related domestic groups in Huitzilan may derive from the ancient teccalli, or noble house, that Chance (2000:488) described as the "fundamental political subunit of the city state" in Puebla-Tlaxcala Valley. The teccalli was larger and more hierarchically organized than present-day Nahuat domestic group clusters.

21. See López Austin (1997:13, 15, 154), who cites the work of Aramoni Burgete (1990:177–178), Ichon (1973:299), and Knab (1991).

22. "Una de las principales causas de la violencia aquí en Huitzilan de los años, de los finales de los setentas, principios de los ochentas fue precisamente por la posesión de unas tierras. Le comentaba usted. Existía una señora hace muchos años que se llamó Juana Gutiérrez. Esa señora poseía muchas bienes, muchos terrenos y cuando ella murió dejó intestado todos sus terrenos. O sea no dejó testamento. Entonces allí fue el origen del conflicto porque tenía sus hijos, tenía su esposo pero ella era la dueña. Las escrituras, todas estaban en nombre de ella. Y no heredó a sus hijos. Sino que se quedó intestado y sus hijos poseyeron esas tierras. Después sus nietos así sucesivamente. Los terrenos que vinieron invadir la gente de la UCI, todos esos eran intestados de esa señora Juana Gutiérrez. Así es. Bueno él [Ruben] lo adquirió de manera violenta porque lo estaba poseyendo otro primo de él. Otro familiar de él. Pero como este señor, pos bueno como era una persona violenta, bueno le arrebató. Le arrebató el terreno, la propiedad y él la estuvo poseyendo. Después a este señor lo matan y queda poseyendo el terreno la señora [la hija de Don Coyote], que fue la esposa de este señor Rubén Bravo.... A él [Ruben Bravo], le gustaba mucho el juego de la baraja. Sí, sí mucho. Entonces tenía amigos que eran igual gente violenta. Entonces se encontraron por casualidad en un bar en Zaragoza, en la ciudad de Zaragoza, y comenzaron a jugar y a tomar. Y en el calor de las copas bueno discutieron y allí murieron los tres. Eran tres personas. Que los tres tenían antecedentes penales."

23. Taggart 2007:14–15: "Bueno non tal, achto niquelnamiqui quipiya tal yeh Lola, lamatzin catca. Yeh quipiya non tal. Pero zatepan, mocuili Ruben Bravo catca. Porque ne tal ahmo tacohual. Intestado. Entonces mocuilique za. Pero Ruben Bravo, mientras nemia, tequitia huan entonces yeh nihuan Don Coyote tequitiltiyah in tal. Entonces ihcuac quimictiqueh, de Ruben Bravo tecuili in tal, tatocaya oc. Yeh den notocay catca tatocaya. Yeh quitanehuaya quirentarohuaya in tal huan tatoca. Pero zatepa de quimictiqueh Ruben Bravo, yeh Don Coyote mocuili. Yeh mocuili za. Ahmo tatoac. Entonces huan ica non tal motehuitoyah."

24. Taggart 2007:14: "Huallayah segun yehhan quixexeloquih tal, quinpalehuitih pobres. Can non miaqueh tacayot motoquiayah. Moiliayah melauh quinpalehuitih. Bueno, zatepan de junta quinyolchicauqueh ma tahtantqueh can sobra tal. Yetoya ce tacat aquin quechiliznequi quitemohuaya can quipiya tal de non monotza, bueno ce tal quilia 'intestado' ca moquipiya aconi axcan, ahmo quipiya amat. Entonces ca non yeh ahmo quitoctequiliti ne tal huan quitecuiliqueh. Entonces para peuqueh tequitih."

25. "Bueno, yehhan tequitiyah. Quitocayah taol huan tac quinxehuiliayah tacah den tequitih, según que nin quimochihuayah tatoc. Tons ompa quintzintzacuilicoh non tacah. Entonces omba quitzacuilicoh. Pos quinmacaqueh. Entonces ompa quemah, tzinquizqueh nen tacah. Mocaoqueh. Zatepan todavía tequitih oc, Den non cholocah oc, zatepan cimi moyolchicauqueh. Zatepan huallaqueh. Pero ricos, nihin Don Coyote huan presidente, ihuan mocalaqui yehha. Entonces quincuitih federales, yehhan soldados, ma quintocaquih. Miac para quintocacoh. Hasta ce viaje quintepayanqueh mil den quitocah. Nochi quipatqueh mil. Ompa quemah. Ihcuac peuhque cualayot."

26. Taggart 2007:122–123: "Yo estaba en Huitzilan. No recuerdo con precisión fechas exactas pero sí guardo en mi memoria el acontecimiento fundamental que es, por ejemplo, la entrada del ejercito al pueblo. Sí. Y la forma en que la familia Coyote se integra ¿No? a la actividad esta de destruir la milpa. Haciendo uso, bueno, de la fuerza. ¿No? De la fuerza. No hubo en este momento ningún muerto, ningún herido. Porque en este momento la UCI así bien tenía armas y hacía en algunos momentos gala de ellas. Las usía. Porque la gente se paseaba por las calles del pueblo con las armas encima. No se enfrentaron al ejéricito por supuesto que se hicieron bien. No se enfrentaron al ejército. Sin embargo se pusieron alguna resistencia digamos pacífiica. ¿No? Y el ejército sí tuvo que hacer uso de la fuerza para que ellos salieran de allí. No hiriendo a nadie pero. Y la familia Coyote actuó con prepotencia, con burla de los sucedidos. Entiéndose triunfadora de los acontecimientos. ¿No? Y a ellos se unieron, los más jovenes de la familia. Nietos de don Coyote y algunos otros muchachos que trabajaron para ellos entre ellos la familia de Pedro Pistolero. Sí. Tres o cuatro jóvenes de esa familia. Que participaron actívamente, físicamente estuvieron allí en el terreno cuando fue desahuicio y la acción esa de tumbar la milpa, destruir el sembrado de milpa. Este fue el detonante. Sí. La indignación que este causó en el pueblo. Y el detonante para que se respondiera con la violencia que respondió la UCI."

27. There were several insurrections against gente de razón encroachment and the loss of land in and around the Sierra Norte de Puebla in the nineteenth century. They include the Nahuat protest against the privatization of communal lands in Cuetzalan from 1868 to 1884 (Thomson 1991) and the Totonac rebellion in Papantla during the era of Porfirio Díaz (Velasco 1979).

28. Taggart 2007:15: "Oncaya mauhcayot. Peuhqueh ya quinmimictiah. Peuhqueh ya quinixtacahuiqih. Peuhqueh mopihpiyah ya. Mopihpiyah ihcon. Hasta que ihcon quintamictiyah que mas ahmo tei itahtacol. Quichtacamictiqueh."

29. According to Rus (1983), the so-called Caste War of 1868–1870 in highland Chiapas did not involve Mayans attacking ladinos. If anything, the opposite was true, and the "caste war" in this part of Mexico was a fiction the elite of San Cristobal de las Casas circulated in an effort to keep the state capital in their city.

30. Karttunen (1983:218) defines *tecuani* as "wild beast," or more literally, "man eater."

31. Taggart 1983:67–75. See Hill 1995 for a similar spatial classification by Nahuatl speakers in Tlaxcala.

32. Taggart 2007:71: "Para nehha,... pues conejo cimi chiquitzin, como non tonal nimitzili,

huan coyote pues huei. Tecuani. Pero ihcon quemeh tecuani huei huan ne conejo chiq-uitzin, pero ne chiquitzin quitemoa quenin quitaniliz ne huei. Entonces quitemoa quen quitaniliz. Entonces como no nimitzili ton tonal no tamati quemeh axcan calacah non UCIs, mochiliayah hueihuei tecuanimeh, quipiyah arma, pero no yetoya ce mas ahmo quipiya tei huan quitemohuaya quenin para quitaniliz. No, que niquihtoa, que ne non cuento pues no tamati quemeh ce tacat yazquia. Quirepresentaroa tacat porque taltic-pac oncac miac, miac tataman. Oncac ne tehuil, oncac cualayot, huan ca non, que ne nimoilia que non totahthuan quichiuhqueh non cuentos porque no tamatiah quenieu quichiuhqueh, quenieu quinemiliqueh. Huan quinemiliqueh huan ihcon mochiuhtoc. Entonces por eso nehha nicnemilia que non quihtoznequi que mas cachi huei, pero tataniz ne cachi chiquitzin. Yeh non neh nicnemilia."

33. Taggart 2007:77: "Ahmo para timohuehuelozqueh. Ahmo para timihihtozqueh. Ahmo para timocualantizqueh."

References Cited

Square brackets after an entry indicate the chapters that cite the entry.

Adams, Kathleen M.

1997   Touting Touristic "Primadonas": Tourism, Ethnicity, and National Integration in Sulawesi, Indonesia. In *Tourism, Ethnicity, and the State in Asian and Pacific Societies*, edited by Michael Picard and Robert E. Wood, pp. 155–180. University of Hawaii Press, Honolulu. [1]

Aguilera, Carmen

1997   Of Royal Mantles and Blue Turquoise. *Latin American Antiquity* 8:3–19. [3]

Aguirre Beltrán, Gonzalo

1979   *Regions of Refuge*. Society for Applied Anthropology Monograph Series No. 12. Society for Applied Anthropology, Washington, D.C. [1, 6]

Alva Ixtlilxochitl, Fernando de

1965   [1600–1640] *Obras históricas*. 2 vols. Edited by Alfredo Chavero. Editora Nacional, Mexico City. [4]

1975–   [1600–1640] *Obras históricas*. 2 vols. 3rd ed. Edited by Edmundo O'Gorman. Serie
1977   de historiadores y cronistas de Indias 4. Universidad Nacional Autónoma de México, Mexico City. [3]

Alvarado Tezozomoc, Hernando

1975   [1598 or early 1600s?] *Crónica mexicana*. 2nd ed. Edited by Manuel Orozco y Berra. Biblioteca Porrúa, 61. Editorial Porrúa, Mexico City. [4]

Anawalt, Patricia Rieff

1981   *Indian Clothing Before Cortes: Mesoamerican Costumes from the Codices*. University of Oklahoma Press, Norman. [2]

1985   The Ethnic History of the Toltecs as Reflected in Their Clothing. *Indiana* (Berlin) 10: 129–145. [3]

1990   The Emperors' Cloak: Aztec Pomp, Toltec Circumstances. *American Antiquity* 55: 291–307. [3]

Anders, Ferdinand, Maarten Jansen, and Luis Reyes García

1996   *Códice Vaticano A. 3738* [with] *Religión, costumbres e historia de los antiguos mexicanos*. 2 vols. Códices mexicanos 12. Akademische Druck- und Verlagsanstalt, Graz, Austria; Fondo de Cultura Económica, Mexico City. [3]

Anderson, Arthur J. O., and Susan Schroeder (editors)

1997   *Codex Chimalpahin: Society and Politics in Mexico, Tenochtitlan, Tlatelolco, Texcoco, Culhuacan, and Other Nahua Altepetl in Central Mexico: The Nahuatl and Spanish Annals and Accounts Collected and Recorded by Don Domingo de San Antón Muñón Chimalpahin Quauhtlehuanitzin*. Vol. 1. Civilization of the American Indian Vol. 225. University of Oklahoma Press, Norman. [4]

Andrews, J. Richard

1975   *Introduction to Classical Nahuatl*. 2 vols. University of Texas Press, Austin. [3]

2003   *Introduction to Classical Nahuatl*. Revised ed. University of Oklahoma Press, Norman. [3]

Anthias, Floya
1998   Rethinking Social Divisions: Some Notes Toward a Theoretical Framework. *Socio-logical Review* 46(3):505–535. [1]

Appadurai, Arjun
1996   *Modernity at Large: Cultural Dimensions of Globalization.* University of Minnesota Press, Minneapolis. [1]

Aramoni Burgete, María Elena
1990   *Tlalokan tata, tlalokan nana: Hierfonías y testimonios de un mundo indígena.* Consejo Nacional para la Cultura y las Artes, Mexico City. [7]

Armillas, Pedro
1944   Oztuma, Guerrero: Forteleza de los mexicanos en la frontera de Michoacán. *Revista Mexicana de Estudios Antropológicos* 6:157–165. [3]

Arnold, Philip J. III, Christopher A. Pool, Ronald R. Kneebone, and Robert S. Santley
1993   Intensive Ceramic Production and Classic-Period Political Economy in the Sierra de los Tuxtlas, Veracruz, Mexico. *Ancient Mesoamerica* 4:175–191. [1]

Astuti, Rita
1995   "The Vezo are not a kind of people": Identity, Difference, and "Ethnicity" Among a Fishing People of Western Madagascar. *American Ethnologist* 22(3):464–482. [1, 7]

Báez-Jorge, Félix
1992   *Los voces del agua: El simbolismo de las sirenas y las mitologías americanas.* Universidad Veracruzana, Xalapa, Veracruz, Mexico. [6]

Báez-Jorge, Félix, and Arturo Gómez Martínez
1998   *Tlacatecolotl y el diablo: La cosmovisión de los nahuas de Chicontepec.* Secretaría de Educación y Cultura, Xalapa, Veracruz, Mexico. [6]

2000   Los equilibrios del cielo y de la tierra: Cosmovisión de los nahuas de Chicontepec. *Desacatos: Revista de antropología social* 5 (invierno): 79–94. [6]

2001   Tlacatecolotl, señor del bien y del mal: Dualidad en la cosmovisión de los nahuas de Chicontepec. In *Cosmovisión, ritual e identidad de los pueblos indígena de México,* edited by Johanna Broda and Félix Báez-Jorge, pp. 391–451. Consejo Nacional para la Cultura y las Artes, Fondo de Cultura Económica, Mexico City. [6]

Baines, John, and Norman Yoffee
1998   Order, Legitimacy, and Wealth in Ancient Egypt and Mesopotamia. In *Archaic States,* edited by Gary M. Feinman and Joyce Marcus, pp. 199–260. School of American Research Press, Santa Fe. [1]

Baker-Cristales, Beth
2004   *Salvadoran Migration to Southern California: Redefining El Hermano Lejano.* University of Florida Press, Gainesville. [1]

Banks, Marcus
1996   *Ethnicity: Anthropological Constructions.* Routledge, London. [1]

Banton, Michael
1987   *Racial Theories.* Cambridge University Press, Cambridge. [5]

Barlow, R. H.
1949   *The Extent of the Empire of the Culhua Mexica.* University of California Press, Berkeley. [3]

1952   Los tecpaneca después de la caida de Azcapotzalco. *Tlalocan* 3:285–287. [3]

Barrera Rivera, José Alvaro, Ma. de Lourdes Gallardo Parrodi, and Aurora Montúfar López
2001   La Ofrenda 102 del Templo Mayor. *Arqueología Mexicana* No. 48 (marzo–abril): 70–77. [6]

Bartel, Brad
1989   Acculturation and Ethnicity in Roman Moesia Superior. In *Centre and Periphery: Comparative Studies in Archaeology,* edited by T. C. Champion, pp. 173–185. One World Archaeology 11. Routledge, New York. [4]

Barth, Fredrik
1969   Introduction. In *Ethnic Groups and Boundaries: The Social Organization of Cultural Difference,* edited by Fredrick Barth, pp. 9–38. Little, Brown, Boston. [1, 3, 4, 6, 7]

Bartolomé, Miguel A., and Alicia M. Barabas (editors)

1990   *Etnicidad y pluralismo cultural: La dinámica étnica en Oaxaca.* Colección regiones de México. Instituto Nacional de Antropología e Historia, Consejo Nacional para la Cultura y las Artes, Mexico City. [1]

Baxandall, Michael

1985   *Patterns of Intention: On the Historical Explanation of Pictures.* Yale University Press, New Haven. [1]

Beliaev, Dmitri

2000   Wuk Tsul and Oxlahun Tsuk: Naranjo and Tikal in the Late Classic. In *The Sacred and the Profane: Architecture and Identity in the Maya Lowlands*, edited by Pierre Robert Colas, Kai Delvendahl, Marcus Kuhnert, and Annette Schubart, pp. 63–81. 3rd European Maya Conference, University of Hamburg, November 1998. *Acta Mesoamericana* 10. A. Saurwein, Markt Schwaben, Germany. [3]

Bentley, G. Carter

1987   Ethnicity and Practice. *Comparative Studies in Society and History* 29:24–55. [1]

Berdan, Frances F.

1980   Aztec Merchants and Markets: Local-Level Economic Activity in a Non-industrial Empire. *Mexicon* 2:37–41. [1]

1982   *The Aztecs of Central Mexico: An Imperial Society.* Holt, Rinehart and Winston, New York. [7]

1987   The Economics of Aztec Luxury Trade and Tribute. In *The Aztec Templo Mayor: A Symposium at Dumbarton Oaks, 8th and 9th October 1983*, edited by Elizabeth Hill Boone, pp. 161–184. Dumbarton Oaks Research Library and Collection, Washington, D.C. [3]

1996   The Tributary Provinces. In *Aztec Imperial Strategies*, by Frances F. Berdan, Richard E. Blanton, Elizabeth Hill Boone, Mary G. Hodge, Michael E. Smith, and Emily Umberger, pp. 115–135. Dumbarton Oaks Research Library and Collection, Washington, D.C. [3]

1999   Concepts of Ethnicity and Class in Aztec-Period Mexico. Paper presented at the 68th Anglo-American Conference of Historians, School of Advanced Study, University of London, June 30–July 2. [6]

2005   *The Aztecs of Central Mexico: An Imperial Society.* 2nd ed. Wadsworth, Thompson Learning, Belmont, California. [1, 4]

Berdan, Frances F., and Patricia Rieff Anawalt

1992   *Codex Mendoza.* 4 vols. University of California Press, Berkeley. [3, 4]

Berdan, Frances F., Richard E. Blanton, Elizabeth Hill Boone, Mary G. Hodge, Michael E. Smith, and Emily Umberger

1996   *Aztec Imperial Strategies.* Dumbarton Oaks Research Library and Collection, Washington, D.C. [3, 4]

Berdan, Frances F., and Jacqueline de Durand-Forest (editors)

1980   *Matrícula de Tributos (Codice de Moctezuma), Museo National de Antropología, Mexico (Cod. 35–529).* Codices selecti phototypice impressi Vol. 118. Akademische Druck- und Verlagsanstalt, Graz, Austria. [4]

Berlin-Neubart, Heinrich, and Robert H. Barlow (editors)

1980   [1948] *Anales de Tlatelolco: Unos annales históricos de la nación mexicana y codice de Tlatelolco.* Fuentes para la historia de México 2. Ediciones Rafael Porrúa, Mexico City. [3]

Beyer, Hermann

1965   Algunos datos nuevos sobre el calendario azteca. *México Antiguo* 10:261–265. [3]

Bierhorst, John

1992   *History and Mythology of the Aztecs: The Codex Chimalpopoca.* University of Arizona Press, Tucson. [3, 4]

Blanton, Richard E.

1978   *Monte Albán: Settlement Patterns at the Ancient Zapotec Capital.* Academic Press, New York. [2]

Blanton, Richard E., and Gary M. Feinman
1984   The Mesoamerican World System: A Comparative Approach. *American Anthropologist* 86:673–682. [1]

Bloch, Marc
1953   *The Historian's Craft*. Vintage Books, New York. [1]

Bonfil Batalla, Guillermo
1996   *Mexico profundo*. Translated by Philip Dennis. University of Texas Press, Austin. [1]

Boone, Elizabeth Hill
1991   Migration Histories as Ritual Performance. In *To Change Place: Aztec Ceremonial Landscapes*, edited by David Carrasco, pp. 121–151. University Press of Colorado, Niwot. [3]

Bourdieu, Pierre
1977   *Outline of a Theory of Practice*. Translated by Richard Nice. Cambridge University Press, Cambridge. [1]

Braakhuis, H. E. M.
1990   The Bitter Flour: Birth-Scenes of the Tonsured Maize God. In *Mesoamerican Dualism, Symposium ANT. 8 of the 46th International Congress of Americanists, Amsterdam, 1988 = Dualismo Mesoamericano, simposio ANT. 8 del 46o C.I.A., Amsterdam 1988*, edited by Rudolf A. M. van Zantwijk, Rob de Ridder, and Edwin Braakhuis, pp. 125–147. R.U.U.-I.S.O.R., Utrecht, Netherlands. [6]
2001   The Way of the Flesh: Sexual Implications of the Mayan Hunt. *Anthropos* 96:391–409. [6]

Brace, C. Loring
2005   *"Race" Is a Four-Letter Word: The Genesis of the Concept*. Oxford University Press, New York. [5]

Brass, Paul R.
1991   *Ethnicity and Nationalism: Theory and Comparison*. Sage Publications, Newbury Park, California. [2]

Braswell, Geoffrey E.
2002   Understanding Early Classic Interaction Between Kaminaljuyú and Central Mexico. In *The Maya and Teotihuacan: Reinterpreting Early Classic Interaction*, edited by Geoffrey E. Braswell, pp. 105–142. University of Texas Press, Austin. [1]

Bray, Warwick
1972   The City-State in Central Mexico at the Time of the Spanish Conquest. *Journal of Latin American Studies* 4(2):161–185. [2, 3]

Bricker, Victoria Reifler
1981   *The Indian Christ, the Indian King: The Historical Substrate of Maya Myth and Ritual*. University of Texas Press, Austin. [1]

Broda, Johanna
1976   Los estamentos en el ceremonial mexica. In *Estratificación social en la Mesoamérica prehispánica*, edited by Pedro Carrasco, Johanna Broda et al., pp. 37–66. Instituto Nacional de Antropología e Historia, Mexico City. [3]

Brown, Donald E.
1973   Hereditary Rank and Ethnic History: An Analysis of Brunei Historiography. *Journal of Anthropological Research* 29(2):113–122. [1]

Brubaker, Rogers, and Fredrick Cooper
2000   Beyond Identity. *Theory and Society* 29:1–47. [1]

Brumfiel, Elizabeth M.
1994a   Ethnic Groups and Political Development in Ancient Mexico. In *Factional Competition and Political Development in the New World*, edited by Elizabeth M. Brumfiel and John W. Fox, pp. 89–102. Cambridge University Press, Cambridge. [1, 2, 3, 4, 5, 7]
1994b   Factional Competition and Political Development in the New World: An Introduction. In *Factional Competition and Political Development in the New World*, edited by Elizabeth M. Brumfiel and John W. Fox, pp. 3–13. Cambridge University Press, Cambridge. [3]

Brumfiel, Elizabeth M., Tamara Salcedo, and David K. Schafer
1994 The Lip Plugs of Xaltocan: Function and Meaning in Aztec Archaeology. In *Economies and Polities in the Aztec Realm*, edited by Mary G. Hodge and Michael E. Smith, pp. 113–131. Studies on Culture and Society Vol. 6. Institute for Mesoamerican Studies, State University of New York, Albany. [2, 3]

Buikstra, Jane E., T. Douglas Price, Lori E. Wright, and James A. Burton
2004 Tombs from the Copan Acropolis: A Life-History Approach. In *Understanding Early Classic Copan*, edited by Ellen E. Bell, Marcello A. Canuto, and Robert J. Sharer, pp. 191–212. University of Pennsylvania Museum of Archaeology and Anthropology, Philadelphia. [1]

Burkhart, Louise
1989 *The Slippery Earth: Nahua-Christian Moral Dialogue in Sixteenth-Century Mexico.* University of Arizona Press, Tucson. [6]

Burmeister, Stefan
2000 Archaeology and Migration: Approaches to an Archaeological Proof of Migration. *Current Anthropology* 41:539–567. [1]

Butler, Judith
1997 *The Psychic Life of Power.* Stanford University Press, Palo Alto, California. [7]
2000 The Noble House in Colonial Puebla, Mexico: Descent, Inheritance, and the Nahua Tradition. *American Anthropologist* 102:485–502. [7]

Calnek, Edward E.
1974 The Sahagún Texts as a Source of Sociological Information. In *Sixteenth-Century Mexico: The Work of Sahagún*, edited by Munro S. Edmonson, pp. 189–204. School of American Research, Santa Fe, and University of New Mexico Press, Albuquerque. [3]
1976 The Internal Structure of Tenochtitlan. In *The Valley of Mexico: Studies in Pre-Hispanic Ecology and Society*, edited by Eric R. Wolf, pp. 287–302. University of New Mexico Press, Albuquerque. [2, 3]
1978 The Analysis of Prehispanic Central Mexican Historical Texts. *Estudios de Cultura Náhuatl* 13:239–266. [3]

Carochi, Horacio
2001 [1645] *Grammar of the Mexican Language, with an Explanation of Its Adverbs (1645).* Translated and edited by James Lockhart. UCLA Latin American Studies Vol. 89. Stanford University Press, Palo Alto, California. [4]

Carrasco, David
1982 *Quetzalcoatl and the Irony of Empire: Myths and Prophecies in the Aztec Tradition.* University of Chicago Press, Chicago. [3]

Carrasco, Pedro
1950 *Los otomies: Cultura e historia prehispánicas de los pueblos mesoamericanos de habla otomiana.* Publicaciones del Instituto de Historia No. 15. Universidad Nacional Autónoma de México, Instituto Nacional de Antropología e Historia, Mexico City. [3]
1971a The Peoples of Central Mexico and Their Historical Traditions. In *Archaeology of Northern Mesoamerica*, Part 2, edited by Gordon F. Ekholm and Ignacio Bernal, pp. 459–473. Handbook of Middle American Indians, Vol. 11, Robert Wauchope, general editor. University of Texas Press, Austin. [4]
1971b Social Organization of Ancient Mexico. In *Archaeology of Northern Mesoamerica*, Part 1, edited by Gordon F. Ekholm and Ignacio Bernal, pp. 349–375. Handbook of Middle American Indians, Vol. 10, Robert Wauchope, general editor. University of Texas Press, Austin. [3, 4]
1976 Los linajes nobles del México antiguo. In *Estratificación social en la Mesoamérica prehispánica*, edited by Pedro Carrasco, Johanna Broda, et al., pp. 19–36. Instituto Nacional de Antropología e Historia, Mexico City. [5]
1979 [1950] *Los otomíes: Cultura e historia prehispánicas de los pueblos mesoamericanos de habla otomiana.* Biblioteca Enciclopédica del Estado de Mexico No. 69. Biblioteca Enciclopédica del Estado de Mexico, Mexico City. [4]

1984   Royal Marriages in Ancient Mexico. In *Explorations in Ethnohistory: Indians of Central Mexico in the Sixteenth Century*, edited by H. R. Harvey and Hanns J. Prem, pp. 41–81. University of New Mexico Press, Albuquerque. [3]

1999   *The Tenochca Empire of Ancient Mexico: The Triple Alliance of Tenochtitlan, Tetzcoco, and Tlacopan*. University of Oklahoma Press, Norman. [3, 4]

Caso, Alfonso

1948   Definición del indio y lo indio. *América Indígena* 8 (4):239–247. [1]

1956   Los barrios antíguos de Tenochtitlan y Tlatelolco. *Memorias de la Academía Mexicana de la Historia* 15(1):7–63. [3]

Chamoux, Marie-Noëlle

1981   *Indiens de la Sierra: La communauté paysanne au Mexique*. Editions L'Harmattan, Paris. [6]

Chance, John K.

1978   *Race and Class in Colonial Oaxaca*. Stanford University Press, Palo Alto, California. [1, 5]

1989   *Conquest of the Sierra: Spaniards and Indians in Colonial Oaxaca*. University of Oklahoma Press, Norman. [5]

1990   La dinámica étnica en Oaxaca colonial. In *Etnicidad y pluralismo cultural: La dinámica étnica en Oaxaca*, 2nd ed., edited by Miguel Bartolomé and Alicia Barabas, pp. 145–172. Instituto Nacional de Antropología e Historia, Mexico City. [5]

1994   Indian Elites in Late Colonial Mesoamerica. In *Caciques and Their People: A Volume in Honor of Ronald Spores*, edited by Joyce Marcus and Judith Frances Zeitlin, pp. 45–65. Anthropological Papers No. 89. Museum of Anthropology, University of Michigan, Ann Arbor. [5]

1996a   The Barrios of Colonial Tecali: Patronage, Kinship, and Territorial Relations in a Central Mexican Community. *Ethnology* 35:107–139. [5]

1996b   The Caciques of Tecali: Class and Ethnic Identity in Late Colonial Mexico. *Hispanic American Historical Review* 76:475–502. [5]

1996c   Mesoamerica's Ethnographic Past. *Ethnohistory* 43(3):379–403. [1]

1998   La hacienda de los Santiago en Tecali, Puebla: Un cacicazgo nahua colonial, 1520–1750. *Historia Mexicana* 47:689–734. [5]

1999   Indigenous Ethnicity in Colonial Mexico. Paper presented at the 68th Anglo-American Conference of Historians, School of Advanced Study, University of London, June 30–July 2. [6]

2000   The Noble House in Colonial Puebla, Mexico: Descent, Inheritance, and the Nahua Tradition. *American Anthropologist* 102:485–502. [5, 6, 8]

2003   Haciendas, Ranchos, and Indian Towns: A Case from the Late Colonial Valley of Puebla. *Ethnohistory* 50:15–46. [5]

Chance, John K., and Barbara L. Stark

2001   Ethnicity. In *Archaeology of Ancient Mexico and Central America*, edited by Susan Toby Evans and David L. Webster, pp. 236–239. Garland, New York. [4, 5]

Chimalpahin Cuauhtlehuanitzin, Domingo F. de San Antón Muñón

1965   [1606–1631] *Relaciones originales de Chalco Amaquemecan*. Edited and translated by Silvia Rendón. Biblioteca americana 40; Serie de literatura indígena. Fondo de Cultural Económica, Mexico City. [3]

Coggins, Clemency

2002   Toltec. *Res* (Cambridge, Massachusetts) 42:34–85. [3]

Cohen, Abner

1981   Variables in Ethnicity. In *Ethnic Change*, edited by Charles F. Keyes, pp. 307–331. University of Washington Press, Seattle. [1, 6]

Cohen, Ronald

1978a   Ethnicity: Problem and Focus in Anthropology. *Annual Review of Anthropology* 7:379–403. [1, 2]

1978b   State Origins: A Reappraisal. In *The Early State*, edited by Henri J. M. Claessen and

Peter Skalník, pp. 31–75. New Babylon, Studies in the Social Sciences No. 32. Mouton, The Hague. [1]

Colby, Benjamin N., and Pierre L. van den Berghe
1969   *Ixil Country: A Plural Society in Highland Guatemala.* University of California Press, Berkeley. [7]

Collier, George A., with Elizabeth Lowery Quaratiello
1999   *Basta! Land and the Zapatista Rebellion in Chiapas.* Revised ed. Institute for Food and Development Policy, Oakland, California. [1]

Collier, Jane F., Bill Maurer, and Liliana Suárez-Navaz
1995   Sanctioned Identities: Legal Constructions of Modern Personhood. *Identities* 2(1–2):1–27. [1]

Comaroff, John L.
1987   Of Totemism and Ethnicity: Consciousness, Practice, and the Signs of Inequality. *Ethnos* 52:301–323. [2, 3]
1996   Ethnicity, Nationalism, and the Politics of Difference in an Age of Revolution. In *The Politics of Difference: Ethnic Premises in a World of Power,* edited by Edwin N. Wilmsen and Patrick McAllister, pp. 162–183. University of Chicago Press, Chicago. [1]

Cook, Scott, and Jong-Taick Joo
1995   Ethnicity and Economy in Rural Mexico: A Critique of the *Indigenista* Approach. *Latin American Research Review* 30(2):33–59. [2]

Corona Núñez, José (editor)
1964   *Antigüedades de Mexico Basadas en la Recopilación de Lord Kingsborough.* Vol. 2, pp. 7–29. Secretaría de Hacienda y Crédito Público, Mexico City. [4]

Cowgill, George L.
1988   Onward and Upward with Collapse. In *The Collapse of Ancient States and Civilizations,* edited by Norman Yoffee and George L. Cowgill, pp. 244–276. University of Arizona Press, Tucson. [2]
2004   Origins and Development of Urbanism: Archaeological Perspectives. *Annual Review of Anthropology* 33:525–549. [3]

Crespo Oviedo, Ana Maria, and Alba Guadalupe Mastache de E.
1981   La presencia en el área Tula, Hidalgo: De grupos relacionados con el barrio de Oaxaca en Teotihuacan. In *Interacción cultural en México central,* edited by Evelyn C. Rattray, Jaime Litvak K., and Clara Diáz Oyarzábal, pp. 99–112. Serie antropológica 41. Instituto de Investigaciones Antropológicas, Universidad Nacional Autónoma de Mexico, Mexico City. [1, 2]

Curet, Luis Antonio
1993   Ceramic Production Areas and Regional Studies: An Example from La Mixtequilla, Veracruz, Mexico. *Journal of Field Archaeology* 20:427–440. [2]

Curet, Luis Antonio, Barbara L. Stark, and Sergio Vásquez Z.
1994   Postclassic Change in South-Central Veracruz, Mexico. *Ancient Mesoamerica* 5(1):13–32. [2]

Daneels, Annick
1997   Settlement History in the Lower Cotaxtla Basin. In *Olmec to Aztec: Settlement Patterns in the Ancient Gulf Lowlands,* edited by Barbara L. Stark and Philip J. Arnold III, pp. 206–252. University of Arizona Press, Tucson. [2]

Davies, Nigel
1977   *The Toltecs: Until the Fall of Tula.* University of Oklahoma Press, Norman. [3]
1980   *The Toltec Heritage: From the Fall of Tula to the Rise of Tenochtitlán.* University of Oklahoma Press, Norman. [3]
1984   The Aztec Concept of History: Teotihuacan and Tula. In *The Native Sources and the History of the Valley of Mexico,* edited by Jacqueline de Durand-Forest, pp. 207–214. BAR International Series 204. British Archaeological Reports, Oxford. [3]

Delgado-Gómez, Angel
1965   The Earliest European Views of the New World Natives. In *Early Images of the*

Americas, edited by Jerry Williams and Robert Lewis, pp. 3–20. University of Arizona Press, Tucson. [4]

Demarest, Arthur A., and Antonia E. Foias
1993 Mesoamerican Horizons and the Cultural Transformations of Maya Civilization. In *Latin American Horizons: A Symposium at Dumbarton Oaks, 11th and 12th October 1986*, edited by Don Stephen Rice, pp. 147–192. Dumbarton Oaks Research Library and Collection, Washington, D.C. [1]

Despres, Leo A.
1975a Ethnicity and Resource Competition in Guyanese Society. In *Ethnic and Resource Competition in Plural Societies*, edited by Leo A. Despres, pp. 87–117. Mouton, The Hague. [6]
1975b Toward a Theory of Ethnic Phenomena. In *Ethnicity and Resource Competition in Plural Societies*, edited by Leo A. Despres, pp. 187–207. Mouton, The Hague. [2]

Despres, Leo A. (editor)
1975 *Ethnic and Resource Competition in Plural Societies*. Mouton, The Hague. [1, 6]

De Vos, George
1975 Ethnic Pluralism: Conflict and Accommodation. In *Ethnic Identity: Cultural Continuities and Change*. 1st ed. Edited by George De Vos and Lola Romanucci-Ross, pp. 5–41. Mayfield Publishing, Palo Alto, California. [3, 7]
1982 Ethnic Pluralism: Conflict and Accommodation. In *Ethnic Identity: Cultural Continuities and Change*, edited by George De Vos and Lola Romanucci-Ross, pp. 5–41. University of Chicago Press, Chicago. [1]

De Vos, George, and Lola Romanucci-Ross
1982 Ethnicity: Vessel of Meaning and Emblem of Contrast. In *Ethnic Identity: Cultural Continuities and Change*, edited by George De Vos and Lola Romanucci-Ross, pp. 363–390. University of Chicago Press, Chicago. [1]

De Vos, George, and Lola Romanucci-Ross (editors)
1975 *Ethnic Identity: Cultural Continuities and Change*. 1st ed. Mayfield Publishing, Palo Alto, California. [4]

Díaz Oyarzábal, Clara L.
1980 *Chingú: Un sitio clásico del área de Tula, Hgo*. Colección científica 90. Instituto Nacional de Antropología e Historia, Mexico City. [1, 2]
1981 Chingú y la expansión Teotihuacana. In *Interacción cultural en México central*, edited by Evelyn C. Rattray, Jaime Litvak K., and Clara Díaz Oyarzábal, pp. 107–112. Serie antropológica 41. Instituto de Investigaciones Antropológicas, Universidad Nacional Autónoma de Mexico, Mexico City. [1, 2]

Dibble, Charles E.
1971 Writing in Central Mexico. In *Archaeology of Northern Mesoamerica*, Part 1, edited by Gordon F. Ekholm and Ignacio Bernal, pp. 322–332. Handbook of Middle American Indians, Vol. 10. Robert Wauchope, general editor. University of Texas Press, Austin. [3]

Dibble, Charles E. (editor)
1980 *Códice Xolotl*. 2 vols. 2nd ed. Serie amoxtli 1. Instituto de Investigaciones Históricos, Universidad Nacional Autónoma de México, Mexico City. [3]

Dow, James W., and Alan R. Sandstrom
2001 *Holy Saints and Fiery Preachers: The Anthropology of Protestantism in Mexico and Central America*. Praeger, Westport, Connecticut. [6]

Doyle, Michael W.
1986 *Empires*. Cornell University Press, Ithaca, New York. [1]

Drennan, Robert D.
1984 Long-Distance Transport Costs in Pre-Hispanic Mesoamerica. *American Anthropologist* 86:105–112. [2]

Drucker, Philip
1943a *Ceramic Sequences at Tres Zapotes, Veracruz, Mexico*. Bulletin No. 140. Bureau of American Ethnology, Smithsonian Institution, Washington, D.C. [2]

1943b   *Ceramic Stratigraphy at Cerro de las Mesas, Veracruz, Mexico.* Bulletin No. 141. Bureau of American Ethnology, Smithsonian Institution, Washington, D.C. [2]

Durán, Diego

1971   [1581] *Book of the Gods and Rites and the Ancient Calendar.* Translated and edited by Fernando Horcasitas and Doris Heyden. Civilization of the American Indian Vol. 102. University of Oklahoma Press, Norman. [4]

1984   [1581] *Historia de las Indias de Nueva Espana e Islas de la Tierra Firme.* 2 vols. Edited by Angel María Garibay K. Biblioteca Porrúa 36–37. Editorial Porrúa, Mexico City. [3]

1994   [1581] *History of the Indies of New Spain.* Translated by Doris Heyden. Civilization of the American Indian Vol. 210. University of Oklahoma Press, Norman. [3, 4]

Durbin, Thomas E.

1970   Aztec Patterns of Conquest as Manifested in the Valley of Toluca, State of Mexico, Mexico. Ph.D. dissertation, University of California at Los Angeles. [3]

Durrenberger, E. Paul, and Gísli Pálsson

1996   Introduction. In *Images of Contemporary Iceland: Everyday Lives and Global Contexts,* edited by Gísli Pálsson and E. Paul Durrenberger, pp. 1–22. University of Iowa Press, Iowa City. [1]

Eder, James F.

2004   Who Are the Cuyonon? Ethnic Identity in the Modern Philippines. *Journal of Asian Studies* 63:625–647. [1]

Eisenstadt, Shmuel N.

1958   Internal Contradictions in Bureaucratic Polities. *Comparative Studies in Society and History* 1:58–75. [2]

1963   *The Political Systems of Empires.* Free Press of Glencoe, London. [1]

1964   Processes of Change and Institutionalization of the Political Systems of Centralized Empires. In *Explorations in Social Change,* edited by George K. Zollschan and Walter Hirsch, pp. 432–451. Houghton Mifflin, Boston. [2]

Emberling, Geoff

1997   Ethnicity in Complex Societies: Archaeological Perspectives. *Journal of Archaeological Research* 5:295–344. [1, 3]

Engels, Friedrich

1972   [1942] *The Origin of the Family, Private Property, and the State in the Light of the Researches of Lewis H. Morgan.* Ed. Eleanor Burke Leacock. International Publishers, New York. Originally published 1884. [7]

Firth, Raymond

1959   *Economics of the New Zealand Maori.* R. E. Owen, Wellington, New Zealand. [7]

Fischer, Edward F., and R. McKenna Brown (editors)

1996   *Maya Cultural Activism in Guatemala.* University of Texas Press, Austin. [5]

Flannery, Kent V., and Joyce Marcus (editors)

1983   *The Cloud People: Divergent Evolution of the Zapotec and Mixtec Civilizations.* Academic Press, New York. [1]

Fortes, Meyer

1949   *The Web of Kinship Among the Tallensi.* Oxford University Press for the International African Institute, London. [7]

Fried, Morton H.

1967   *The Evolution of Political Society: An Essay in Political Anthropology.* Random House, New York. [1]

1975   *The Notion of Tribe.* Cummings, Menlo Park, California. [6]

Friedman, Jonathan

1992   The Past in the Future: History and the Politics of Identity. *American Anthropologist* 94:837–859. [3]

Fuente, Julio de la

1965   *Relaciones interétnicas.* Instituto Nacional Indigenista, Mexico City. [1]

1967   Ethnic Relationships. In *Social Anthropology,* edited by Manning Nash, pp. 432–448.

Handbook of Middle American Indians, Vol. 6. Robert Wauchope, general editor. University of Texas Press, Austin. [1, 6]

Gailey, Christine W., and Thomas C. Patterson
1987   Power Relations and State Formation. In *Power Relations and State Formation*, edited by Thomas C. Patterson and Christine W. Gailey, pp. 1–26. Archeology Section, American Anthropological Association, Washington, D.C. [2]

Galarza, Joaquín, and Krystyna M. Libura
1999   *Para leer "La tira de la peregrinación."* [Includes reproductions of parts of the *Códice Boturini (Tira de la peregrinación)*.] Ediciones Tecolote, Mexico City. [3]

Gallardo Arias, Patricia
2000   Medicina tradicional y brujería entre los teenek y nahuas de la Huasteca Potosina. Tesis para licenciatura, Escuela Nacional de Antropología e Historia, Mexico City. [6]

García Castro, René
1999   *Indios: Territorio y poder en la provincia Matlatzinca: La negociación del espacio político de los pueblos otomianos, siglos XV–XVII.* Historias CIESAS. CONACULTA-INAH, Mexico City. [3]

García Martínez, Bernardo
1987   *Los pueblos de la sierra.* El Colegio de México, Mexico City. [5]

García Payón, José
1936   *La zona arqueológica de Tecaxic-Calixtlahuaca y los Matlatzincas*, Part 1. Secretaría de Educación Pública, Mexico City. [3]

Garduño, Ana
1997   *Conflictos y alianzas entre Tlatelolco y Tenochtitlán: Siglos XII a XV.* Biblioteca del INAH, Serie historia. Instituto Nacional de Antropología e Historia, Mexico City. [3]

Garraty, Christopher P., and Barbara L. Stark
2002   Imperial and Social Relations in Postclassic South-Central Veracruz, Mexico. *Latin American Antiquity* 13:3–33. [2]

Geertz, Clifford
1973   *The Interpretation of Cultures.* Basic Books, New York. [7]
2004   What Is a State If It Is Not a Sovereign? Reflections on Politics in Complicated Places. *Current Anthropology* 45:577–593. [1]

Gerstle, Andrea
1987   Ethnic Diversity and Interaction at Copan, Honduras. In *Interaction on the Southeast Mesoamerican Frontier: Prehistoric and Historic Honduras and El Salvador*, Part 2, edited by Eugenia R. Robinson, pp. 328–356. BAR International Series 327. British Archaeological Reports, Oxford. [2]

Gibson, Charles
1964   *The Aztecs Under Spanish Rule: A History of the Indians of the Valley of Mexico, 1519–1810.* Stanford University Press, Palo Alto, California. [3, 4, 5]
1971   Structure of the Aztec Empire. In *Archaeology of Northern Mesoamerica*, Part 1, edited by Gordon F. Ekholm and Ignacio Bernal, pp. 376–394. Handbook of Middle American Indians, Vol. 10, Robert Wauchope, general editor. University of Texas Press, Austin. [8]

Giddens, Anthony
1984   *The Constitution of Society: Outline of the Theory of Structuration.* University of California Press, Berkeley. [1]

Goldstein, Paul S.
2000   Communities Without Borders: The Vertical Archipelago and Diaspora Communities in the Southern Andes. In *The Archaeology of Communities: A New World Perspective*, edited by Marcello A. Canuto and Jason Yaeger, pp. 182–209. Routledge, London. [2]

Gómez Chávez, Sergio

1998 Nuevos datos sobre la relación de Teotihuacan y el occidente de México. In *Antropología e historia del occidente de México: XXIV Mesa Redonda de la Sociedad Mexicana de Antropología, 4–11 agosto 1996, Tepic, Nayarit, México*, 3:1461–1494. Sociedad Mexicana de Antropología, Universidad Nacional Autónoma de México, Mexico City. [1]

Gómez Martínez, Arturo

1999a Tlaneltokilli: La espiritualidad de los nahuas chicontepecanos. Tesis para licenciatura, Universidad Veracruzana, Xalapa, Veracruz, Mexico. [6]

1999b *El agua y sus manifestaciones sagradas: Mitología y ritual entre los nahuas de Chicontepec.* H. Ayuntamiento Constitucional de Chicontepec, Veracruz, Mexico. [6]

González Casanova, Pablo

1928 El ciclo legendario del Tepoztecatl. *Revista Mexicana de Estudios Históricos* 2:18–63. [3]

Good, Catharine

2005 "Trabajando juntos como uno": Conceptos nahuas del grupo doméstico y de la persona. In *Familia y parentesco en México y Mesoamérica: Unas miradas antropológicas*, edited by David Robichaux, pp. 275–294. Seminario Familia y Parentesco en México: Unas miradas antropológicas, Ciudad de México, February 11–12, 1998, Vol. 2. Universidad Iberoamericana, Mexico City. [7]

Goody, Jack

1966 Introduction. In *Succession to High Office*, edited by Jack Goody, pp. 1–81. Cambridge Papers in Social Anthropology No. 4. Cambridge University Press for the Department of Archaeology and Anthropology, Cambridge. [1]

Gossen, Gary H.

1994 From Olmec to Zapatistas: A Once and Future History of Souls. *American Anthropologist* 96:553–570. [7]

Graulich, Michel

1992 On the So-Called "Cuauhxicalli of Motecuhzoma Ilhuicamina": The Sánchez-Nava Monolith. *Mexicon* 14(1):5–10. [3]

1997 *Myths of Ancient Mexico.* University of Oklahoma Press, Norman. [7]

Grillo, R. D.

1998 *Pluralism and the Politics of Difference: State, Culture, and Ethnicity in Comparative Perspective.* Clarendon Press, Oxford. [1, 2, 3, 4, 5]

Gruzinski, Serge

1988 The Net Torn Apart: Ethnic Identities and Westernization in Colonial Mexico, Sixteenth–Nineteenth Century. In *Ethnicities and Nations: Processes of Interethnic Relations in Latin America, Southeast Asia, and the Pacific*, edited by Remo Guidieri, Francesco Pellizzi, and Stanley J. Tambiah, pp. 39–56. University of Texas Press, Austin. [5]

Gutiérrez Solana, Nelly, and Susan K. Hamilton

1977 *Las esculturas en terracota de El Zapotal, Veracruz.* Universidad Nacional Autónoma de México, Mexico City. [2]

Hall, Stuart

1992a New Ethnicities. In *"Race," Culture, and Difference*, edited by James Donald and Ali Rattansi, pp. 252–259. Sage Publications, in association with the Open University, London. [1]

1992b The Question of Cultural Identity. In *Modernity and Its Futures*, edited by Stuart Hall, David Held, and Tony McGrew, pp. 274–316. Polity Press, in association with the Open University, Cambridge, England. [1]

Haskett, Robert

1992 Visions of Municipal Glory Undimmed: The Nahuatl Town Histories of Colonial Cuernavaca. *Colonial Latin American Review* 1(1):1–36. [5]

2005   *Views of Paradise: Primordial Titles and Mesoamerican History in Cuernavaca*. University of Oklahoma Press, Norman. [5]

Hassig, Ross
1985   *Trade, Tribute, and Transportation: The Sixteenth-Century Political Economy of the Valley of Mexico*. University of Oklahoma Press, Norman. [2]
1988   *Aztec Warfare: Imperial Expansion and Political Control*. University of Oklahoma Press, Norman. [2]

Healan, Dan M., Robert H. Cobean, and Richard A. Diehl
1989   Synthesis and Conclusions. In *Tula of the Toltecs: Excavations and Survey*, edited by Dan M. Healan, pp. 239–251. University of Iowa Press, Iowa City. [1]

Hegmon, Michelle
1998   Technology, Style, and Social Practices: Archaeological Approaches. In *The Archaeology of Social Boundaries*, edited by Miriam T. Stark, pp. 264–279. Smithsonian Institution Press, Washington, D.C. [1]

Heiras Rodríguez, Carlos Guadalupe
2005   The Tepehua. In *Native American Peoples of the Gulf Coast of Mexico*, edited by Alan R. Sandstrom and E. Hugo García Valencia, pp. 211–230. University of Arizona Press, Tucson. [6]

Heller, Lynette
2001   Sources, Technology, Production, Use, and Deposition of Knapped Obsidian. In *Classic Period Mixtequilla, Veracruz, Mexico: Diachronic Inferences from Residential Excavations*, edited by Barbara L. Stark, pp. 159–170. Monograph No. 12. Institute for Mesoamerican Studies, State University of New York, Albany. [2]

Helms, Mary W.
1993   *Craft and the Kingly Ideal: Art, Trade, and Power*. University of Texas Press, Austin. [1]

Hendon, Julia A.
1991   Status and Power in Classic Maya Society: An Archaeological Study. *American Anthropologist* 93:894–918. [2]

Hendrickson, Carol
1991   Images of the Indian in Guatemala: The Role of Indigenous Dress in Indian and Ladino Constructions. In *Nation-States and Indians in Latin America*, edited by Greg Urban and Joel Sherzer, pp. 286–306. University of Texas Press, Austin. [1]

Hernández Azuara, César
2001   El son huasteco y sus instrumentos en los siglos XIX y XX. Tesis para licenciatura, Escuela Nacional de Antropología e Historia, Mexico City. [6]

Hernández Castillo, Rosalva Aída, and Ronald Nigh
1998   Global Processes and Local Identity Among Mayan Coffee Growers in Chiapas, Mexico. *American Anthropologist* 100:136–147. [1]

Hernández Ferrer, Marcela
2000   Ofrendas a Dhipak: Ritos agrícolas entre los teenek de San Luis Potosí. Tesis para licenciatura, Escuela Nacional de Antropología e Historia, Mexico City. [6]

Hernández Rodríguez, Rosaura
1950   Documentos relacionados con San Bartolomé Tlatelolco. *Memorias de la Academia Mexicana de la Historia* 9(1):233–250. [3]
1988   *El valle de Toluca: Epoca prehispánica y siglo XVI*. El Colegio Mexiquense, Ayuntamiento de Toluca, Toluca, Mexico. [3]

Hewitt de Alcántara, Cynthia
1984   *Anthropological Perspectives on Rural Mexico*. International Library of Anthropology. Routledge and Kegan Paul, London. [1]

Hicks, Frederic
1982   Tetzcoco in the Early 16th Century: The State, the City, and the *Calpolli*. *American Ethnologist* 9:230–249. [2, 3]
1994   Texcoco, 1515–1519: The Ixtlilxochitl Affair. In *Chipping Away on Earth: Studies in*

Prehispanic and Colonial Mexico in Honor of Arthur J. O. Anderson and Charles E. Dibble, edited by Eloise Quiñones Keber, with the assistance of Susan Schroeder and Frederic Hicks, pp. 235–239. Labyrinthos, Lancaster, California. [2]

1999   The Middle Class in Ancient Central Mexico. *Journal of Anthropological Research* 55:409–427. [1, 5]

2001   Ethnicity. In *The Oxford Encyclopedia of Mesoamerican Cultures*, Vol. 1, edited by David Carrasco, pp. 388–392. Oxford University Press, Oxford. [4, 5]

Hill, Jane

1995   The Voices of Don Gabriel: Responsibility and Self in a Modern Mexican Narrative. In *The Dialogic Emergence of Culture*, edited by Dennis Tedlock and Bruce Manheim, pp. 97–147. University of Illinois Press, Urbana. [7]

Hill, Robert M. II, and John Monaghan

1987   *Continuities in Highland Maya Social Organization: Ethnohistory in Sacapulas, Guatemala*. University of Pennsylvania Press, Philadelphia. [1]

Hirth, Kenneth

2000   *Archaeological Research at Xochicalco*. 2 vols. University of Utah Press, Salt Lake City. [2]

Hobsbawm, Eric J., and Terence O. Ranger (editors)

1983   *The Invention of Tradition*. Cambridge University Press, Cambridge. [6]

Hodder, Ian

1979   Economic and Social Stress and Material Culture Patterning. *American Antiquity* 44:446–454. [2]

Hodge, Mary G.

1984   *Aztec City-States*. Studies in Latin American Ethnohistory and Archaeology Vol. 3; Memoirs of the Museum of Anthropology No. 18. University of Michigan, Museum of Anthropology, Ann Arbor. [3, 4]

1996   Political Organization of the Central Provinces. In *Aztec Imperial Strategies*, by Frances F. Berdan, Richard E. Blanton, Elizabeth Hill Boone, Mary G. Hodge, Michael E. Smith, and Emily Umberger, pp. 17–45. Dumbarton Oaks Research Library and Collection, Washington, D.C. [3]

1997   When Is a City-State? Archaeological Measures of Aztec City-States and Aztec City-State Systems. In *The Archaeology of City-States: Cross-Cultural Approaches*, edited by Deborah L. Nichols and Thomas H. Charlton, pp. 209–228. Smithsonian Institution Press, Washington, D.C. [3]

Holloman, Regina E.

1975   Ethnic Boundary Maintenance, Readaptation, and Societal Evolution in the San Blas Islands of Panama. In *Ethnic and Resource Competition in Plural Societies*, edited by Leo A. Despres, pp. 27–40. Mouton, The Hague. [6]

Holtzman, Jon

2004   The Local in the Local: Models of Time and Space in Samburu District, Northern Kenya. *Current Anthropology* 45:61–84. [1]

Horn, Rebecca

1997   *Postconquest Coyoacan: Nahua-Spanish Relations in Central Mexico, 1519–1650*. Stanford University Press, Palo Alto, California. [5]

Houston, Stephen D.

1994   Mesoamerican Writing. In *The Encyclopedia of Language and Linguistics*, Vol. 5, edited by R. E. Asher and J. M. Y. Simpson, pp. 2449–2451. Pergamon Press, Oxford [3]

Howard, Alan

1990   Cultural Paradigms, History, and the Search for Identity in Oceania. In *Cultural Identity and Ethnography in the Pacific*, edited by Jocelyn Linnekin and Lin Poyer, pp. 259–280. University of Hawaii Press, Honolulu. [1]

Huntington, Samuel P., Fouad Ajami, Kishore Mahbubami, Robert L. Bartley, Binyan Liu, Jeanne J. Kirkpatrick, Albert Loren Weeks, and Gerard Piel

1996   *The Clash of Civilizations?: The Debate*. Foreign Affairs, New York. [6]

Hvidtfeldt, Arild

1958   *Teotl and Ixiptlatli: Some Central Conceptions in Ancient Mexican Religion, and a General Introduction on Cult and Myth*. Munksgaard, Copenhagen. [3]

Ichon, Alain

1973   *La religión de los Totonacas de la sierra*. Instituto Nacional Indigenista, Mexico City. [7]

Jameson, Frederic

1984   Postmodernism, or the Cultural Logic of Late Capitalism. *New Left Review* 146:53–92. [1]

Jenkins, Richard

1994   Rethinking Ethnicity: Identity, Categorization, and Power. *Ethnic and Racial Studies* 17(2):197–223. [1]

Jimeno, Myriam

1989   Conflicts and Strategies of Latin American Ethnic Minorities. *Current Anthropology* 30:264–265. [6]

Jones, Siân

1996   Discourses of Identity in the Interpretation of the Past. In *Cultural Identity and Archaeology: The Construction of European Communities*, edited by Paul Graves-Brown, Siân Jones, and Clive Gamble, pp. 62–80. Routledge, London. [1]

1997   *The Archaeology of Ethnicity: Constructing Identities in the Past and Present*. Routledge, London. [8]

Jonsson, Hjorleifur

2005   *Mien Relations: Mountain People and State Control in Thailand*. Cornell University Press, Ithaca, New York. [1]

Karttunen, Frances

1983   *An Analytical Dictionary of Nahuatl*. University of Texas Press, Austin. [7]

Karttunen, Frances, and Gilka Wara Céspedes

1982   The Dialogue of El Tepozteco and His Rivals, September 1977. *Tlalocan* 9:115–141. [3]

Kaufman, Terrence

1994   The Native Languages of Meso-America. In *Atlas of the World's Languages*, edited by Christopher Moseley and R. E. Asher, pp. 34–41. Routledge, New York. [6]

Kaufmann, Eric P.

2004   Introduction: Dominant Ethnicity: From Background to Foreground. In *Rethinking Ethnicity: Majority Groups and Dominant Minorities*, edited by Eric P. Kaufmann, pp. 1–14. Routledge, New York. [1]

Kaufmann, Eric P. (editor)

2004   *Rethinking Ethnicity: Majority Groups and Dominant Minorities*. Routledge, New York. [1]

Kearney, Michael

1996   *Reconceptualizing the Peasantry: Anthropology in Global Perspective*. Westview Press, Boulder, Colorado. [1]

Keyes, Charles F.

1981   The Dialectics of Ethnic Change. In *Ethnic Change,* edited by Charles F. Keyes, pp. 4–30. University of Washington Press, Seattle. [1, 7]

Kidder, Alfred V., Jesse D. Jennings, and Edwin M. Shook

1946   *Excavations at Kaminaljuyú, Guatemala*. Publication 561. Carnegie Institution of Washington, Washington, D.C. [1]

Klein, Cecilia F.

1987   The Ideology of Autosacrifice at the Templo Mayor. In *The Aztec Templo Mayor: A Symposium at Dumbarton Oaks, 8ᵗʰ and 9ᵗʰ October 1983*, edited by Elizabeth Hill Boone, pp. 292–370. Dumbarton Oaks Research Library and Collection, Washington, D.C. [3]

1993   Shield Women: Resolution of an Aztec Gender Paradox. In *Current Topics in Aztec Studies: Essays in Honor of Dr. H. B. Nicholson*, edited by Alana Cordy-Collins and

Douglas Sharon, pp. 39–65. San Diego Museum Papers Vol. 30. San Diego Museum of Man, San Diego, California. [3]

1994   Fighting with Femininity: Gender and War in Aztec Mexico. *Estudios de Cultura Náhuatl* 24:219–253. [3]

Knab, Tim J.

1991   Geografía del inframundo. *Estudios de Cultura Náhuatl* 21:31–57. [7]

Kowalewski, Stephen A.

1994   Communities in the Prehispanic Valley of Oaxaca. In *Factional Competition and Political Development in the New World*, edited by Elizabeth M. Brumfiel and John W. Fox, pp. 127–37. Cambridge University Press, Cambridge. [5]

Kubler, George

1973   Iconographic Aspects of Architectural Profiles at Teotihuacan and in Mesoamerica. In *The Iconography of Middle American Sculpture*, by Ignacio Bernal and others, pp. 24–39. Metropolitan Museum of Art, New York. [1]

Kunstadter, Peter

1978   Ethnic Group, Category, and Identity: Karen in Northern Thailand. In *Ethnic Adaptation and Identity: The Karen on the Thai Frontier with Burma*, edited by Charles F. Keyes, pp. 119–163. Institute for the Study of Human Issues, Philadelphia. [1]

Kuper, Adam

1999   *Culture: The Anthropologists' Account*. Harvard University Press, Cambridge, Massachusetts. [6]

2003   The Return of the Native. *Current Anthropology* 44:390–402. [1]

Kuznar, Lawrence A.

1997   *Reclaiming a Scientific Anthropology*. AltaMira Press, Walnut Creek, California. [6]

Laclau, Ernesto, and Chantel Mouffe

1985   *Hegemony and Socialist Strategy: Towards a Radical Democratic Politics*. Verso, London. [1]

Leach, Edmund R.

1954   *Political Systems of Highland Burma: A Study of Kachin Social Structure*. Harvard University Press for the London School of Economics and Political Science, Cambridge, Massachusetts. [2, 7]

1968   Introduction. In *Dialectic in Practical Religion*, edited by Edmund R. Leach, pp. 1–6. Cambridge University Press for the Department of Archaeology and Anthropology, London. [7]

Lem, Winnie

2002   Articulating Class in Post-Fordist France. *American Ethnologist* 29:287–306. [1]

Lévi-Strauss, Claude

1982   *The Way of the Masks*. Translated by Sylvia Modeski. University of Washington Press, Seattle. [5]

LeVine, Robert A., and Donald T. Campbell

1972   *Ethnocentrism: Theories of Conflict, Ethnic Attitudes, and Group Behavior*. John Wiley and Sons, New York. [2]

Lewis, Oscar

1951   *Life in a Mexican Village: Tepoztlán Restudied*. University of Illinois Press, Urbana. [1]

Leynes, Martín, and Enriqueta M. Olguín

1993   Cómo nació Chicomexochitl. In *Huasteca II: Prácticas agrícolas y medicina tradicional; Arte y sociedad*, edited by Jesús Ruvalcaba Mercado and Graciela Alcalá, pp. 115–139. Centro de Investigaciones y Estudios Superiores en Antropología Social, Mexico City. [6]

Lieberman, Victor

1978   Ethnic Politics in Eighteenth-Century Burma. *Modern Asian Studies* 12:455–482. [1, 2]

Liebsohn, Dana

1994   Primers for Memory: Cartographic Histories and Nahua Identity. In *Writing*

Without Words, edited by Elizabeth Hill Boone and Walter D. Mignolo, pp. 161–187. Duke University Press, Durham, North Carolina. [5]

Linnekin, Jocelyn, and Lin Poyer

1990   Introduction. In *Cultural Identity and Ethnography in the Pacific*, edited by Jocelyn Linnekin and Lin Poyer, pp. 1–16. University of Hawaii Press, Honolulu. [1]

Lockhart, James

1991   *Nahuas and Spaniards: Postconquest Central Mexican History and Philology*. UCLA Latin American Center Vol. 76; Nahuatl Studies No. 3. Stanford University Press, Palo Alto, California; UCLA Latin American Center Publications, Los Angeles, California. [1, 5]

1992   *The Nahuas After the Conquest: A Social and Cultural History of the Indians of Central Mexico, Sixteenth Through Eighteenth Centuries*. Stanford University Press, Palo Alto, California. [2, 3, 4, 5, 7]

1993   *We People Here: Nahuatl Accounts of the Conquest of Mexico*. University of California Press, Berkeley. [5]

Lockhart, James, Frances Berdan, and Arthur J. O. Anderson

1986   *The Tlaxcalan Actas*. University of Utah Press, Salt Lake City. [8]

Lockhart, James, Susan Schroeder, and Doris Namala

2006   *Annals of His Time: Don Domingo de San Antón Muñón Chimalpahin Quauhtlehuanitzin*. Series Chimalpahin. Stanford University Press, Palo Alto, California. [4]

Lomnitz-Adler, Claudio

1992   *Exits from the Labyrinth: Culture and Ideology in the Mexican National Space*. University of California Press, Berkeley. [6]

López Austin, Alfredo

1988   *The Human Body and Ideology: Concepts of the Ancient Nahuas*. 2 vols. Translated by Thelma Ortiz de Montellano and Bernardo Ortiz de Montellano. University of Utah Press, Salt Lake City. [3, 4, 7]

1997   *Tamoanchan, Tlalocan: Places of Mist*. University Press of Colorado, Niwot. [7]

López Luján, Leonardo

1989   La recuperación mexica del pasado teotihuacano. Instituto Nacional de Antropología e Historia, Mexico City. [3]

2005   *The Offerings of the Templo Mayor of Tenochtitlan*. University of New Mexico Press, Albuquerque. [4]

Lorenzano, Luis

1998   Zapatismo: Recomposition of Labour, Radical Democracy, and Revolutionary Project. In *Zapatista! Reinventing Revolution in Mexico*, edited by John Hollaway and Eloína Peláez, pp. 126–158. Pluto Press, London. [7]

Lupo, Alessandro

2001   La cosmovisión de los Nahuas de la Sierra de Puebla. In *Cosmovisión, ritual e identidad de los pueblos indígenas de México*, edited by Johanna Broda and Félix Báez-Jorge, pp. 335–389. Consejo Nacional para la Cultura y las Artes and Fondo de Cultura Económica, Mexico City. [6]

Marcus, George E.

1995   Ethnography in/of the World System: The Emergence of Multi-Sited Ethnography. *Annual Review of Anthropology* 24:95–117. [1]

Marcus, George E., and Michael M. J. Fischer

1986   *Anthropology as Cultural Critique*. University of Chicago Press, Chicago. [1]

Marcus, Joyce

1983   On the Nature of the Mesoamerican City. In *Prehistoric Settlement Patterns: Essays in Honor of Gordon R. Willey*, edited by Evon Z. Vogt and Richard M. Leventhal, pp. 195–242. University of New Mexico Press, Albuquerque. [3]

1989   From Centralized Systems to City-States: Possible Models for the Epiclassic. In *Mesoamerica After the Decline of Teotihuacan, A.D. 700–900*, edited by Richard A. Diehl and Janet Catherine Berlo, pp. 201–208. Dumbarton Oaks Research Library and Collection, Washington, D.C. [2]

Marcus, Joyce, and Kent V. Flannery

1983   The Postclassic Balkanization of Oaxaca. In *The Cloud People: Divergent Evolution of the Zapotec and Mixtec Civilizations*, edited by Kent V. Flannery and Joyce Marcus, pp. 217–226. Academic Press, New York. [1, 5]

1996   *Zapotec Civilization: How Urban Society Evolved in Mexico's Oaxaca Valley*. Thames and Hudson, New York. [1]

Martínez, Hildeberto

1984   *Tepeaca en el siglo XVI*. Casa Chata, Mexico City. [5]

Martínez Baracs, Andrea

1998   El gobierno indio de la Tlaxcala colonial, 1521–1700. Tesis de doctorado, El Colegio de México, Mexico City. [5]

Martínez de la Cruz, Rafael

2000   Apanchaneh: Señora del agua. Ritual y cosmovisión entre los nahuas de Chicontepec. Tesis para licenciatura, Universidad Veracruzana, Xalapa, Veracruz, Mexico. [6]

Mathews, Peter

1991   Classic Maya Emblem Glyphs. In *Classic Maya Political History: Hieroglyphic and Archaeological Evidence*, edited by T. Patrick Culbert, pp. 19–29. School of American Research Advanced Seminar Series. Cambridge University Press, Cambridge.[3]

Mathews, Peter, and John S. Justeson

1984   Patterns of Sign Substitution in Maya Hieroglyphic Writing: The "Affix Cluster." In *Phoneticism in Mayan Hieroglyphic Writing*, edited by John S. Justeson and Lyle Campbell, pp. 185–232. Institute for Mesoamerican Studies, State University of New York, Albany. [3]

Maybury-Lewis, David

2002   *Indigenous Peoples, Ethnic Groups, and the State*. 2nd ed. Allyn and Bacon, Boston. [1, 6]

McGuire, Randall H.

1982   The Study of Ethnicity in Historical Archaeology. *Journal of Anthropological Archaeology* 1:159–178. [1, 2]

Medellín Zenil, Alfonso

1960   *Cerámicas del totonacapan: Exploraciones arqueológicas en el centro de Veracruz*. Instituto de Antropología, Universidad Veracruzana, Xalapa, Veracruz, Mexico. [2]

Medina, Laurie Kroshus

1997   Development Policies and Collectivity in Belize. *American Ethnologist* 24:148–169. [1]

Metcalf, Peter

2001   Global "Disjuncture" and the "Sites" of Anthropology. *Cultural Anthropology* 16:165–182. [1]

Moerman, Michael

1965   Ethnic Identification in a Complex Civilization: Who Are the Lue? *American Anthropologist* 67:1215–1230. [1, 2]

Molina, Alonso de

1966   *Vocabulario nahuatl-castellano, castellano-nahuatl*. 2nd ed. Ediciones Colofon, Mexico City. [7]

1977   *Vocabulario en lengua castellana y mexicana y mexicana y castellana*. Biblioteca Porrúa 44. Editorial Porrúa, Mexico City. [4, 8]

Monaghan, John D.

1995   *The Covenants with Earth and Rain: Exchange, Sacrifice, and Revelation in Mixtec Sociality*. University of Oklahoma Press, Norman. [1, 5]

2000a   A Retrospective Look at the Ethnology Volumes of the *Handbook of Middle American Indians*. In *Ethnology*, edited by John D. Monaghan, with the assistance of Barbara W. Edmonson, pp. 1–6. Supplement to the Handbook of Middle American Indians, Vol. 6, Victoria Reifler Bricker, general editor. University of Texas Press, Austin. [1]

2000b   Theology and History in the Study of Mesoamerican Religions. In *Ethnology*, edited by John Monaghan, with the assistance of Barbara W. Edmonson, pp. 24–49. Supplement to the Handbook of Middle American Indians, Vol. 6, Victoria Reifler Bricker, general editor. University of Texas Press, Austin. [6]

Mönnich, Anneliese
1976   La supervivencia de antiguas representaciones indígenas en la religión popular de los Nawas de Veracruz y Puebla. In *Das Ring aus Tlalocan: Mythen und Gabete, Lieder und Erzahlungen der heutigen Nahua in Veracruz und Puebla, Mexiko = El Anillo de Tlalocan: Mitos, oraciones, cantos y cuentos de los Nawas actuales de los Estados de Veracruz y Puebla, México*, edited by Luis Reyes García and Dieter Christensen, pp. 139–143. Quellenwerke zur alten Geschichte Amerikas aufgezeichnet in den Sprachen der Eingeborenen Bd. 12. Gebr. Mann Verlag, Berlin. [6]

Motolinía, Toribio de Benavente
1950   [1536–1543] *History of the Indians of New Spain.* Translated and edited by Elizabeth Andros Foster. Documents and Narratives Concerning the Discovery and Conquest of Latin America, n.s., No. 4. Cortés Society, Berkeley, California. [3, 4]

1971   [1555] *Memoriales: O, Libro de las cosas de la Nueva España y de los naturales de ella.* Edited by Edmundo O'Gorman. Serie de historiadores y cronistas de Indias 2. Instituto de Investigaciones Históricas, Universidad Nacional Autónoma de México, Mexico City. [4]

Mulhare, Eileen M.
2000   Mesoamerican Social Organization and Community After 1960. In *Ethnology*, edited by John Monaghan, with the assistance of Barbara W. Edmonson, pp. 9–23. Supplement to the Handbook of Middle American Indians, Vol. 6, Victoria Reifler Bricker, general editor. University of Texas Press, Austin. [6]

Murra, John V.
1972   El "control vertical" de un máximo de pisos ecológicos en la economía de las sociedades andinas. In *Visita de la provincia de León Huánuco en 1562*, Vol. 2, by Iñigo Ortíz de Zuñiga, pp. 427–468. Universidad Nacional Hermilio Valdizán, Huánuco, Peru. [2]

Nagao, Debra
1989   Public Proclamation in the Art of Cacaxtla and Xochicalco. In *Mesoamerica After the Decline of Teotihuacan, A.D. 700–900*, edited by Richard A. Diehl and Janet Catherine Berlo, pp. 83–104. Dumbarton Oaks Research Library and Collection, Washington, D.C. [1, 3]

Nagata, J. A.
1974   What Is a Malay? Situational Selection of Ethnic Identity in a Plural Society. *American Ethnologist* 1:331–350. [3]

Nagengast, Carole, and Michael Kearney
1990   Mixtec Ethnicity: Social Identity, Political Consciousness, and Political Activism. *Latin American Research Review* 25:61–91. [1, 5]

Nalda H., Enrique
1981   Algunas consideraciones sobre las migraciones del postclásico. *Boletín Antropología Americana* 3:137–143. [2]

Nash, June
1981   Ethnographic Aspects of the World Capitalist System. *Annual Review of Anthropology* 20:393–423. [1]

1995   The Reassertion of Indigenous Identity: Mayan Responses to State Intervention in Chiapas. *Latin American Research Review* 30(3):7–41. [5]

Nicholson, H. B.
1971a   Major Sculpture in Pre-Hispanic Central Mexico. In *Archaeology of Northern Mesoamerica*, Part 1, edited by Gordon F. Ekholm and Ignacio Bernal, pp. 92–134. Handbook of Middle American Indians, Vol. 10. Robert Wauchope, general editor. University of Texas Press, Austin. [3]

1971b   Religion in Pre-Hispanic Central Mexico. In *Archaeology of Northern Mesoamerica*, Part 1, edited by Gordon F. Ekholm and Ignacio Bernal, pp. 395–446. Handbook of Middle American Indians, Vol. 10. Robert Wauchope, general editor. University of Texas Press, Austin. [3]

1973   Phoneticism in the Late Pre-Hispanic Central Mexican Writing System. In *Mesoamerican Writing Systems: A Symposium at Dumbarton Oaks, October 30th and 31st, 1971*, edited by Elizabeth P. Benson, pp. 1–46. Dumbarton Oaks Research Library and Collection, Washington, D.C. [3]

Nicholson, H. B., and Eloise Quiñones Keber

1983   *Art of Aztec Mexico: Treasures of Tenochtitlan*. National Gallery of Art, Washington, D.C. [3]

Nowotny, Karl Anton, and Jacqueline de Durand-Forest (editors)

1974   *Codex Borbonicus, Bibliotheque de l'Assemble Nationale-Paris (Y-120)*. Akademische Druck- und Verlagsanstalt, Graz, Austria. [4]

Nutini, Hugo G.

1995   *The Wages of Conquest: The Mexican Aristocracy in the Context of Western Aristocracies*. University of Michigan Press, Ann Arbor. [1, 5]

Offner, Jerome A.

1979   A Reassessment of the Extent and Structuring of the Empire of Techotlalatzin, Fourteenth-Century Ruler of Texcoco. *Ethnohistory* 26(3):231–241. [2]

1983   *Law and Politics in Aztec Texcoco*. Cambridge University Press, Cambridge. [3]

Okamura, J. Y.

1981   Situational Ethnicity. *Ethnic and Racial Studies* 4:452–465. [3]

Olivera, Mercedes

1978   *Pillis y macehuales*. Casa Chata, Mexico City. [5]

Olivier, Guilhem

2003   *Mockeries and Metamorphoses of an Aztec God: Tezcatlipoca, "Lord of the Smoking Mirror."* University Press of Colorado, Niwot. [3]

Olko, Justyna

2005   *Turquoise Diadems and Staffs of Office: Elite Costume and Insignia of Power in Aztec and Early Colonial Mexico*. Osrodek Badan nad Tradycja Antyczna w Polsce i w Europie Srodkowo-Wschodniej, Warsaw. [4]

Ong, Aihwa

1999   *Flexible Citizenship: The Cultural Logics of Transnationality*. Duke University Press, Durham, North Carolina. [1]

Onians, John

1988   *Bearers of Meaning: The Classical Orders in Antiquity, the Middle Ages, and the Renaissance*. Princeton University Press, Princeton, New Jersey. [1]

Orozco y Berra, Manuel

1877   El cuauhxicalli de Tizoc. *Anales del Museo Nacional de México* 1:3–39. [3]

Ortíz, Ponciano, and Robert Santley

1998   Matacapan: Un ejemplo de enclave teotihuacano en la Costa del Golfo. In *Los ritmos de cambio en Teotihuacán: Reflexiones y discusiones de su cronología*, edited by Rosa Brambila and Ruben Cabrera, pp. 377–460. Colección científica 366; Serie arqueología. Instituto Nacional de Antropología e Historia, Mexico City. [1, 2]

Ossa, Alanna

2000   Questioning Ethnicity in the Huasteca. Master's paper, Department of Anthropology, Arizona State University. [2]

Otite, Onigu

1975   Resource Competition and Inter-ethnic Relations in Nigeria. In *Ethnic and Resource Competition in Plural Societies*, edited by Leo A. Despres, pp. 119–130. Mouton, The Hague. [6]

Oudijk, Michel R.

1998   Zapotec Elite Ethnohistory Indeed. In *The Shadow of Monte Albán: Politics and*

Historiography in Postclassic Oaxaca, Mexico, edited by Maarten Jansen, Peter Krofges, and Michel Oudijk, pp. 37–44. Research School CNWS, Leiden University, Leiden, Netherlands. [5]

Padilla, J., P. F. Sánchez-Nava, and Felipe Solis Olguín
1989   The Cuauhxicalli of Motecuhzoma Ilhuicamina. *Mexicon* 11(2):24–25. [3]

Pasztory, Esther
1989   Identity and Difference: The Uses and Meanings of Ethnic Styles. In *Cultural Differentiation and Cultural Identity in the Visual Arts,* edited by Susan J. Barnes and Walter S. Melion, pp. 15–38. Studies in the History of Art 27. Center for the Advanced Study in the Visual Arts, National Gallery of Art, Washington, D.C. [1, 2, 3]
1993   An Image Is Worth a Thousand Words: Teotihuacan and the Meanings of Style in Classic Mesoamerica. In *Latin American Horizons: A Symposium at Dumbarton Oaks, 11th and 12th October 1986,* edited by Don Stephen Rice, pp. 113–145. Dumbarton Oaks Research Library and Collection, Washington, D.C. [2]

Patterson, Thomas C.
1987   Tribes, Chiefdoms, and Kingdoms in the Inca Empire. In *Power Relations and State Formation,* edited by Thomas C. Patterson and Christine W. Gailey, pp. 117–127. Archeology Section, American Anthropological Association, Washington, D.C. [2]

Perkins, Stephen
2000   The Nahua Teccalli of Puebla, Mexico: An Indigenous House Society Under Spanish Rule. Ph.D. dissertation, Department of Anthropology, Arizona State University. [5]

Pollard, Helen Perlstein
1994   Ethnicity and Political Control in a Complex Society: The Tarascan State of Prehispanic Mexico. In *Factional Competition and Political Development in the New World,* edited by Elizabeth M. Brumfiel and John W. Fox, pp. 79–88. Cambridge University Press, Cambridge. [1, 2]

Pomar, Juan Bautista de
1964   [1582] *Romances de los señores de la Nueva España: Manuscrito de Juan Bautista de Pomar, Tezcoco, 1582.* Edited by Angel Ma. Garibay K. Poesía náhuatl, Vol. 1. Fuentes indígenas de la cultura náhuatl 4. Universidad Nacional Autónoma de México, Mexico City. [3]

Pool, Christopher A.
1992   Strangers in a Strange Land: Ethnicity and Ideology at an Enclave Community in Middle Classic Mesoamerica. In *Ancient Images, Ancient Thought: The Archaeology of Ideology,* edited by A. Sean Goldsmith, Sandra Garvie, David Selin, and Jeannette Smith, pp. 43–55. Proceedings of the 23rd Annual Chacmool Conference, Calgary, Alberta. [1, 2]
1995   La cerámica del clásico tardío y el postclásico en la Sierra de los Tuxtlas. *Arqueología* 13–14:37–48. [2]

Pool, Christopher A., and Michael A. Ohnersorgen
2002   Archaeological Survey and Settlement at Tres Zapotes. In *Settlement Archaeology and Political Economy at Tres Zapotes, Veracruz, Mexico,* edited by Christopher A. Pool, pp. 6–31. Cotsen Institute of Archaeology, University of California at Los Angeles, Los Angeles. [2]

Prem, Hanns J.
1970   Aztec Hieroglyphic Writing System: Possibilities and Limits. In *Verhandlungen des XXXVIII Internationalen Amerikanistenkongresses, Stuttgart-München, 12 bis 18 August, 1968,* 2:159–165. K. Renner, Munich. [3]
1974   *Matrícula de Huexotzinco: Ms. mex. 387 der Bibliothèque Nationale Paris.* Akademische Druck- und Verlagsanstalt, Graz, Austria. [4]
1992   Aztec Writing. In *Epigraphy,* Vol. 5, edited by Victoria Reifler Bricker and Patricia A. Andrews, pp. 53–69. Supplement to the Handbook of Middle American Indians, Victoria Reifler Bricker, general editor. University of Texas Press, Austin. [3]

Price, T. Douglas, Linda Manzanilla, and William D. Middleton
2000 Immigration and the Ancient City of Teotihuacan in Mexico: A Study Using Strontium Isotope Ratios in Human Bone and Teeth. *Journal of Archaeological Science* 27: 903–913. [1]

Proskouriakoff, Tatiana
1974 *Jades from the Cenote of Sacrifice, Chichen Itza, Yucatan*. Memoirs of the Peabody Museum of Archaeology and Ethnology Vol. 10, No. 1. Harvard University, Cambridge, Massachusetts. [3]

Quezada, Noemí
1972 *Los matlatzincas: Epoca prehispánica y colonial hasta 1650*. Instituto Nacional de Antropología e Historia, Mexico City. [3]

Quiñones Keber, Eloise
1995 *Codex Telleriano-Remensis: Ritual, Divination, and History in a Pictorial Aztec Manuscript*. University of Texas Press, Austin. [3, 4, 7]

Quiroz Uria, Sitna
2003 El movimiento profético de Amalia Bautista: Religión y cambio socio-cultural en la Huasteca Veracruzana. Tesis para licenciatura, Escuela Nacional de Antropología e Historia, Mexico City. [6]

Rattray, Evelyn C.
1992 *The Oaxaca Barrio at Teotihuacan*. Monografías mesoamericanas No. 1. Instituto de Estudios Avanzados, Universidad de las Americas, Puebla, Mexico. [4]
1987 Los barrios foráneos de Teotihuacan. In *Teotihuacan: Nuevos datos, nuevas síntesis, nuevos problemas*, edited by Emily McClung de Tapia and Evelyn Childs Rattray, pp. 243–273. Instituto de Investigaciones Antropológicas, Universidad Nacional Autónoma de México, Mexico City. [1]
1988 Nuevas interpretaciones en torno al barrio de los comerciantes. *Anales de Antropología* 25:165–180. [1]
1989 El barrio de los comerciantes y el conjunto de Tlamimilolpa: Un estudio comparativo. *Arqueología* 5:105–129. [1]
1990 The Identification of Ethnic Affiliation at the Merchants' Barrio, Teotihuacan. In *Etnoarqueología: Coloquio Bosch-Gimpera*, edited by Yoko Sugiura and Mari Carmen Serra, pp. 113–138. Instituto de Investigaciones Antropológicas, Universidad Nacional Autónoma de México, Mexico City. [1]

Redfield, Robert
1930 *Tepoztlán: A Mexican Village*. University of Chicago Press, Chicago. [5]
1941 *The Folk Culture of Yucatan*. University of Chicago Press, Chicago. [1, 6]

Reina, Ruben E.
1966 *Law of the Saints: A Pokomam Pueblo and Its Community Culture*. Bobbs-Merrill, Indianapolis, Indiana. [6]

Renfrew, Colin
1986 Introduction: Peer Polity Interaction and Socio-Political Change. In *Peer Polity Interaction and Socio-Political Change*, edited by Colin Renfrew and John F. Cherry, pp. 1–18. Cambridge University Press, Cambridge. [1]

Restall, Matthew
1997 *The Maya World: Yucatec Culture and Society, 1550–1850*. Stanford University Press, Palo Alto, California. [1, 5]

Reyes García, Luis
1977 *Cuauhtinchan del siglo XII al XVI*. Franz Steiner, Wiesbaden. [5]

Reyes García, Luis, and Dieter Christensen (editors)
1976 *Das Ring aus Tlalocan: Mythen und Gabete, Lieder und Erzahlungen der heutigen Nahua in Veracruz und Puebla, Mexiko = El Anillo de Tlalocan: Mitos, oraciones, cantos y cuentos de los Nawas actuales de los Estados de Veracruz y Puebla, México*. Quellenwerke zur alten Geschichte Amerikas aufgezeichnet in den Sprachen der Eingeborenen Bd. 12. Gebr. Mann Verlag, Berlin. [6]

Rojas, José Luis de
1994   After the Conquest: Quauhtinchan and the Mexica Province of Tepeacac. In *Economies and Polities in the Aztec Realm*, edited by Mary G. Hodge and Michael E. Smith, pp. 405–431. Studies on Culture and Society Vol. 6. Institute for Mesoamerican Studies, State University of New York, Albany. [3]

Romanucci-Ross, Lola, and George A. De Vos (editors)
1995   *Ethnic Identity: Creation, Conflict, and Accommodation*. 3rd ed. AltaMira Press, Walnut Creek, California. [6]

Rouse, Roger
2002   Mexican Migration and the Social Space of Postmodernism. In *The Anthropology of Globalization: A Reader*, edited by Jonathan Xavier Inda and Renato Rosaldo, pp. 157–171. Blackwell, Malden, Massachusetts. [1]

Rus, Jan
1983   Whose Caste War? Indians, Ladinos, and the Chiapas "Caste War" of 1869. In *Spaniards and Indians in Southeastern Mesoamerica: Essays on the History of Ethnic Relations*, edited by Murdo J. MacLeod and Robert Wasserstrom, pp. 127–168. University of Nebraska Press, Lincoln. [7]

Ruvalcaba Mercado, Jesús, and Juan Manuel Pérez Zevallos
1996   *La Huasteca en los albores del tercer milenio: Textos, temas y problemas*. Centro de Investigaciones y Estudios Superiores en Antropología Social, Mexico City. [6]

Sahagún, Bernardino de
1950–   [1575–1580] *Florentine Codex: General History of the Things of New Spain*. 12 vols.
1982   Translated by Arthur J. O. Anderson and Charles E. Dibble. Monographs of the School of American Research No. 14. School of American Research, Santa Fe, New Mexico; University of Utah Press, Salt Lake City. [3, 4]

1954   [1575–1580] *Florentine Codex: General History of the Things of New Spain; Kings and Lords*, Book 8. Translated by Arthur J. O. Anderson and Charles E. Dibble. Monographs of the School of American Research No. 14, Part 9. School of American Research, Santa Fe, New Mexico; University of Utah Press, Salt Lake City. [2]

1961   [1575–1580] *Florentine Codex: General History of the Things of New Spain; The People*, Book 10. Translated by Charles E. Dibble and Arthur J. O. Anderson. Monographs of the School of American Research No. 14, Part 11. School of American Research, Santa Fe, New Mexico; University of Utah Press, Salt Lake City. [1, 2]

1969   [1575–1580] *Florentine Codex: General History of the Things of New Spain; Rhetoric and Moral Philosophy*, Book 6. Translated by Charles E. Dibble and Arthur J. O. Anderson. Monographs of the School of American Research No. 14, Part 7. School of American Research, Santa Fe, New Mexico; University of Utah Press, Salt Lake City. [2]

1976   [1575–1580] *Florentine Codex: General History of the Things of New Spain; The Merchants*, Book 9. Translated by Charles E. Dibble and Arthur J. O. Anderson. Reprint ed. Monographs of the School of American Research No. 14, Part 10. School of American Research, Santa Fe, New Mexico; University of Utah Press, Salt Lake City. [6]

1981   [1575–1580] *Florentine Codex: General History of the Things of New Spain; The Ceremonies*, Book 2. Translated by Charles E. Dibble and Arthur J. O. Anderson. Reprint ed. Monographs of the School of American Research No. 14, Part 3. School of American Research, Santa Fe, New Mexico; University of Utah Press, Salt Lake City. [2]

1993   [1559–1561] *Primeros memoriales*. Photographed by Ferdinand Anders. Facsimile ed. Civilization of the American Indian Vol. 200, Part 1. University of Oklahoma Press, Norman. [4]

1997   [1559–1561] *Primeros memoriales*. Translated and edited by Thelma D. Sullivan and H. B. Nicholson. Civilization of the American Indian Vol. 200, Part 2. University of Oklahoma Press, Norman. [3]

Sanders, William T.
1978   Ethnographic Analogy and the Teotihuacan Horizon Style. In *Middle Classic Meso-*

america: A.D. 400–700, edited by Esther Pasztory, pp. 35–44. Columbia University Press, New York. [1]

Sanders, William T., and Joseph W. Michels (editors)

1977   *Teotihuacan and Kaminaljuyú: A Study in Prehistoric Culture Contact*. Pennsylvania State University Press, University Park. [1]

Sandstrom, Alan R.

1978   *The Image of Disease: Medical Practices of Nahua Indians of the Huasteca*. Monographs in Anthropology No. 3. Department of Anthropology, University of Missouri–Columbia. [6]

1989   The Face of the Devil: Concepts of Disease and Pollution Among Nahua Indians of the Southern Huasteca. In *Enquêtes sur l'Amérique moyenne: Mélanges offerts à Guy Stresser-Péan*, edited by Dominique Michelet, pp. 357–372. Etudes Mésoaméricaines Vol. 16. Instituto Nacional de Antropología e Historia, Consejo Nacional para la Cultura y las Artes, Centre d'Etudes Mexicaines et Centroaméricaines, Mexico City. [6]

1991   *Corn Is Our Blood: Culture and Ethnic Identity in a Contemporary Aztec Indian Village*. Civilization of the American Indian Vol. 206. University of Oklahoma Press, Norman. [1, 5, 6, 7]

1992   Ethnic Identity and the Persistence of Traditional Religion in a Contemporary Nahua Village. *Journal of Latin American Lore* 18:37–52. [6]

1995   Nahuas of the Huasteca. In *Middle America and the Caribbean*, edited by James W. Dow and Robert V. Kemper, pp. 184–187. Encyclopedia of World Cultures, Vol. 8, David Levinson, editor in chief. G. K. Hall, Boston. [6]

1998   El nene lloroso y el espíritu nahua del maíz: El cuerpo humano como símbolo clave en la Huasteca veracruzana. In *Nuevos aportes al conocimiento de la Huasteca*, edited by Jesús Ruvalcaba Mercado, pp. 59–94. CIESAS, Mexico City. [6]

2000   Toponymic Groups and House Organization: The Nahuas of Northern Veracruz, Mexico. In *Beyond Kinship: Social and Material Reproduction in House Societies*, edited by Rosemary Joyce and Susan Gillespie, pp. 53–72. University of Pennsylvania Press, Philadelphia. [6, 7, 8]

2003   Sacred Mountains and Miniature Worlds: Altar Design Among the Nahua of Northern Veracruz, Mexico. In *Mesas and Cosmologies in Mesoamerica*, edited by Douglas Sharon, pp. 51–70. San Diego Museum Papers 42. San Diego Museum of Man, San Diego, California. [6]

Sandstrom, Alan R., and Paul J. Provost

1977   *Sacred Guitar and Violin Music of the Modern Aztecs*. Ethnic Folkways Records No. FE 4358. Folkways Records, New York; distributed by Smithsonian Folkways Recordings, Washington, D.C. [6]

Sandstrom, Alan R., and Pamela Effrein Sandstrom

1986   *Traditional Papermaking and Paper Cult Figures of Mexico*. University of Oklahoma Press, Norman. [6]

Sandstrom, Alan R., and Tsai Wen-Hui

1996   The Fate of the Soul in Chinese and Aztec Civilizations: A Comparative Study of Religious Ideology and the State. *Proceedings of the National Science Council Republic of China, Part C: Humanities and Social Sciences* 6(1):87–100. [6]

Santley, Robert S., and Philip J. Arnold III

1996   Prehispanic Settlement Patterns in the Tuxtla Mountains, Southern Veracruz, Mexico. *Journal of Field Archaeology* 23:225–259. [1]

Santley, Robert S., Clare Yarborough, and Barbara S. Hall

1987   Enclaves, Ethnicity, and the Archaeological Record at Matacapan. In *Ethnicity and Culture: Proceedings of the Eighteenth Annual Conference of the Archaeological Association of the University of Calgary*, edited by Reginald Auger, Margaret F. Glass, Scott MacEachern, and Peter H. McCartney, pp. 85–100. Archaeological Association, University of Calgary, Calgary, Alberta. [1, 2]

Savishinsky, Joel S.

1991   Free Shows and Cheap Thrills: Staged Deviance in the Arctic and the Bahamas. In

Deviance: Anthropological Perspectives, edited by Morris Freilich, Douglas Raybeck, and Joel S. Savishinsky, pp. 73–88. Bergin and Garvey, New York. [4]

Schele, Linda, and Mary Ellen Miller
1986   *The Blood of Kings: Dynasty and Ritual in Maya Art*. Kimbell Art Museum, Fort Worth, Texas. [1]

Schneider, David M.
1984   *A Critique of the Study of Kinship*. University of Michigan Press, Ann Arbor. [7]

Scholes, France V., and Dave Warren
1965   The Olmec Region at Spanish Contact. In *Archaeology of Southern Mesoamerica*, Part 2, edited by Gordon R. Willey, pp. 776–787. Handbook of Middle American Indians, Vol. 3, Robert Wauchope, general editor. University of Texas Press, Austin. [2]

Schreiber, Katharina J.
1992   *Wari Imperialism in Middle Horizon Peru*. Anthropological Papers No. 87. Museum of Anthropology, University of Michigan, Ann Arbor. [1]

Schroeder, Susan
1983   Chimalpahin and the Meaning of Chichimeca. Paper presented at the Annual Meeting of the American Society for Ethnohistory, Albuquerque, New Mexico. [3]
1991   *Chimalpahin and the Kingdoms of Chalco*. University of Arizona Press, Tucson. [4]

Schryer, Frans J.
1990   *Ethnicity and Class Conflict in Rural Mexico*. Princeton University Press, Princeton, New Jersey. [1, 6, 7]

Scott, James
1985   *Weapons of the Weak: Everyday Forms of Peasant Resistance*. Yale University Press, New Haven. [6]

Seler, Eduard
1990–   *Collected Works in Mesoamerican Linguistics and Archaeology*. 7 vols. 2nd ed. Edited
2000   by J. Eric S. Thompson, and Francis B. Richardson; Frank E. Comparato, general editor. Labyrinthos, Culver City, California. [3]

Siegel, Sydney
1956   *Nonparametric Statistics for the Behavioral Sciences*. McGraw-Hill, New York. [2]

Signorini, Italo, and Alessandro Lupo
1989   *Los tres ejes de la vida: Almas, cuerpo, enfermedad entre los Nahuas de la Sierra de Puebla*. Universidad Veracruzana, Xalapa, Veracruz, Mexico. [6]

Skinner, Elliot P.
1975   Competition Within Ethnic Systems in Africa. In *Ethnic and Resource Competition in Plural Societies*, edited by Leo A. Despres, pp. 131–157. Mouton, The Hague. [6]

Skoglund, Thanet, Barbara L. Stark, Hector Neff, and Michael D. Glascock
2006   Compositional and Stylistic Analysis of Aztec Era Ceramics: Provincial Strategies at the Edge of Empire, South-Central Veracruz, Mexico. *Latin American Antiquity* 17:541–559. [2]

Smedley, Audrey
1998   "Race" and the Construction of Human Identity. *American Anthropologist* 100:690–702. [5]
1999   *Race in North America: Origin and Evolution of a Worldview*. 2nd ed. Westview Press, Boulder, Colorado. [5]

Smith, Carol A.
1976   Exchange Systems and the Spatial Distribution of Elites: The Organization of Stratification in Agrarian Societies. In *Regional Analysis, Vol. 2: Social Systems*, edited by Carol A. Smith, pp. 309–374. Academic Press, New York. [1]

Smith, Michael E.
1984   The Aztlan Migrations of the Nahuatl Chronicles: Myth or History? *Ethnohistory* 31:153–186. [1, 2, 3]
1996   *The Aztecs*. Blackwell, Malden, Massachusetts. [1, 4]

2000   Aztec City-States. In *A Comparative Study of Thirty City-State Cultures*, edited by Mogens Herman Hansen, pp. 581–595. Filosofiske Skrifter No. 21. Kongelige Danske Videnskabernes Selskab, Copenhagen. [3, 4]

Smith, Michael E., and Frances F. Berdan

1996   Appendix 4: Province Descriptions. In *Aztec Imperial Strategies*, by Frances F. Berdan, Richard E. Blanton, Elizabeth Hill Boone, Mary G. Hodge, Michael E. Smith, and Emily Umberger, pp. 265–349. Dumbarton Oaks Research Library and Collection, Washington, D.C. [3]

Smith, Michael E., and Cynthia M. Heath-Smith

1980   Waves of Influence in Postclassic Mesoamerica? A Critique of the Mixteca-Puebla Concept. *Anthropology* 4(2):15–50. [2]

Smith, Michael E., and Lisa Montiel

2001   The Archaeological Study of Empires and Imperialism in Prehispanic Central Mexico. *Journal of Anthropological Archaeology* 20:245–284. [2]

Spence, Michael W.

1989   Excavaciones recientes en Tlailotlaca, el barrio oaxaqueño de Teotihuacan. *Arqueología* 5:81–104. [1]

1992   Tlailotlacan: A Zapotec Enclave in Teotihuacan. In *Art, Ideology, and the City of Teotihuacan: A Symposium at Dumbarton Oaks, 8th and 9th October 1988*, edited by Janet C. Berlo, pp. 59–88. Dumbarton Oaks Research Library and Collection, Washington, D.C. [1]

1996   A Comparative Analysis of Ethnic Enclaves. In *Arqueología mesoamericana: Homenaje a William T. Sanders*, Vol. 1, edited by Alba Guadalupe Mastache, Jeffrey Parsons, Robert S. Santley, and Mari Carmen Serra Puche, pp. 333–353. Instituto Nacional de Antropología e Historia and Arqueología Mexicana, Mexico City. [1]

Spence, Michael W., Christine D. White, Fred J. Longstaffe, and Kimberley R. Law

2004   Victims of the Victims: Human Trophies Worn by Sacrificed Soldiers from the Feathered Serpent Pyramid, Teotihuacan. *Ancient Mesoamerica* 15:1–15. [1]

Spence, Michael W., Christine D. White, Evelyn C. Rattray, and Fred J. Longstaffe

2005   Past Lives in Different Places: The Origins and Relationships of Teotihuacan's Foreign Residents. In *Settlement, Subsistence, and Social Complexity: Essays Honoring the Legacy of Jeffrey R. Parsons*, edited by Richard E. Blanton, pp. 155–197. Cotsen Institute of Archaeology, University of California at Los Angeles, Los Angeles. [8]

Spicer, Edward H.

1962   *Cycles of Conquest: The Impact of Spain, Mexico, and the United States on the Indians of the Southwest, 1533–1960*. University of Arizona Press, Tucson. [1, 6]

1971   Persistent Cultural Systems. *Science* 174:795–800. [5]

Stark, Barbara L.

1995   Introducción a la alfarería del postclásico en la Mixtequilla, sur-central de Veracruz. *Arqueología* 13–14:17–36. [2]

1999   Formal Architectural Complexes in South-Central Veracruz, Mexico: A Capital Zone? *Journal of Field Archaeology* 26:197–225. [2]

Stark, Barbara L. (editor)

1991   *Settlement Archaeology of Cerro de las Mesas, Veracruz, Mexico*. Monograph No. 34. Institute of Archaeology, University of California at Los Angeles, Los Angeles. [2]

2001   *Classic Period Mixtequilla, Veracruz, Mexico: Diachronic Inferences from Residential Investigations*. Monograph No. 12. Institute for Mesoamerican Studies, State University of New York, Albany. [2]

Stark, Barbara L., Lynette Heller, Michael D. Glascock, J. Michael Elam, and Hector Neff

1992   Obsidian Artifact Source Analysis for the Mixtequilla Region, South-Central Veracruz, Mexico. *Latin American Antiquity* 3:221–239. [2]

Stark, Barbara L., and Alanna Ossa

2007   Ancient Settlement, Urban Gardening, and Environment in the Gulf Lowlands of Mexico. *Latin American Antiquity* 18(4) (in press). [2]

Stavenhagen, Rodolfo
1975   *Social Classes in Agrarian Societies.* Translated by Judy Adler Hellman. Anchor Books, Garden City, New Jersey. [1]

Stein, Gil J.
2005   Introduction: The Comparative Archaeology of Colonial Encounters. In *The Archaeology of Colonial Encounters: Comparative Perspectives*, edited by Gil J. Stein, pp. 3–31. School of American Research Press, Santa Fe, New Mexico; James Currey, Oxford. [2]

Stone, Andrea
1989   Disconnection, Foreign Insignia, and Political Expansion: Teotihuacan and the Warrior Stelae of Piedras Negras. In *Mesoamerica After the Decline of Teotihuacan, A.D. 700–900*, edited by Richard A. Diehl and Janet C. Berlo, pp. 153–172. Dumbarton Oaks Research Library and Collection, Washington, D.C. [1]

Stone, John
1996   Ethnicity. In *The Social Science Encyclopedia*, 2nd ed., edited by Adam Kuper and Jessica Kuper, pp. 260–263. Routledge, London. [6]

Stone-Miller, Rebecca
1993   An Overview of "Horizon" and "Horizon Style" in the Study of Ancient American Objects. In *Latin American Horizons: A Symposium at Dumbarton Oaks, 11th and 12th October 1986*, edited by Don Stephen Rice, pp. 15–39. Dumbarton Oaks Research Library and Collection, Washington, D.C. [1]

Stresser-Péan, Guy
1995   *El códice de Xicotepec: Estudio e interpretación.* Gobierno del Estado de Puebla, Centro Francés de Estudios Mexicanos y Centroamericanos, Fondo de Cultura Económica, Mexico City. [4]

Stresser-Péan, Guy (editor)
1979   La Huasteca et la frontière nord-est de la Mesoamérique. In *Actes du XLIIe Congrès International des Americanistes: Congrès du centenaire, Paris, 2–9 septembre 1976* 9B: 9–157. Société des Americanistes, Paris. [6]

Stuart, David, and Stephen Houston
1994   *Classic Maya Place Names.* Studies in Pre-Columbian Art and Archaeology No. 33. Dumbarton Oaks Research Library and Collection, Washington, D.C. [3]

Sugiura Y., Yoko
2005   Reacomodo demográfico y conformación multiétnica en el Valle de Toluca durante el postclásico: Una propuesta desde la arqueología. In *Reacomodos demográficos del clásico al postclásico en el centro de México*, edited by Linda Manzanilla, pp. 175–202. Instituto de Investigaciones Antropológicas, Universidad Nacional Autónoma de México, Mexico City. [1]

Taggart, James M.
1975   *Estructura de los grupos domésticos de una comunidad de habla nahuat de Puebla.* Instituto Nacional Indigenista, Mexico City. [7]
1983   *Nahuat Myth and Social Structure.* University of Texas Press, Austin. [6]
1997   *The Bear and His Sons: Masculinity in Spanish and Mexican Folktales.* University of Texas Press, Austin. [7]
2007   *Remembering Victoria: A Tragic Nahuat Love Story.* University of Texas Press, Austin. [7]

Tambiah, Stanley J.
1989   Ethnic Conflict in the World Today. *American Ethnologist* 16:335–349. [6]
1996   The Nation-State in Crisis and the Rise of Ethnonationalism. In *The Politics of Difference: Ethnic Premises in a World of Power*, edited by Edwin N. Wilmsen and Patrick Mc Allister, pp. 124–143. University of Chicago Press, Chicago. [1]

Taylor, William B.
1979   *Drinking, Homicide, and Rebellion in Colonial Mexican Villages.* Stanford University Press, Palo Alto, California. [5]

Terraciano, Kevin
2001   *The Mixtecs of Colonial Oaxaca: Ñudzahui History, Sixteenth Through Eighteenth
        Centuries.* Stanford University Press, Palo Alto, California. [1, 5]
Thomson, Guy P. C.
1991   Agrarian Conflict in the Municipality of Cuetzalán (Sierra de Puebla): The Rise and
        Fall of "Pala" Agustín Dieguillo, 1861–1894. *Hispanic American Historical Review*
        71(2):205–258. [7]
Toland, Judith
1993   Introduction: Dialogue of Self and Other; Ethnicity and the Statehood Building
        Process. In *Ethnicity and the State*, edited by Judith Toland, pp. 1–20. Political and
        Legal Anthropology Vol. 9. Transaction, New Brunswick, New Jersey. [1, 2]
Tolstoy, Paul
1991   Paper Route: Were the Manufacture and Use of Bark Paper Introduced into Meso-
        america from Asia? *Natural History* 100(6):6–14. [6]
Tönnies, Ferdinand
1953   Estates and Classes. In *Class, Status, and Power: A Reader in Social Stratification*, ed-
        ited by Reinhard Bendix and Seymour Martin Lipset, pp. 49–63. Free Press, Glen-
        coe, Illinois. [1, 5]
Torquemada, Juan de
1969   [1723] *Monarquía indiana.* 3 vols. Introduction by Miguel Leon Portilla. 4th ed. Bib-
        lioteca Porrúa 41–43. Editorial Porrúa, Mexico City. [3]
Townsend, Richard F.
1979   *State and Cosmos in the Art of Tenochtitlan.* Studies in Pre-Columbian Art and Ar-
        chaeology No. 20. Dumbarton Oaks, Trustees for Harvard University, Washington,
        D.C. [3]
1992   *The Aztecs.* Ancient Peoples and Places Vol. 107. Thames and Hudson, London. [1, 4]
Tylor, Edward Burnett
1871   *Primitive Culture: Researches into the Development of Mythology, Philosophy, Reli-
        gion, Language, Art, and Custom.* J. Murray, London. [6]
Umberger, Emily
1984   El trono de Moctezuma. *Estudios de Cultura Náhuatl* 17:63–87. [3]
1987a   Antiques, Revivals, and References to the Past in Aztec Art. *Res* (Cambridge, Mas-
        sachusetts) 13:62–105. [1]
1987b   Events Commemorated by Date Plaques at the Templo Mayor: Reconsidering the
        Solar Metaphor. In *The Aztec Templo Mayor: A Symposium at Dumbarton Oaks, 8th
        and 9th October 1983*, edited by Elizabeth Hill Boone, pp. 411–449. Dumbarton Oaks
        Research Library and Collection, Washington, D.C. [3]
1988   A Reconsideration of Some Hieroglyphs on the Mexica Calendar Stone. In *Smoke
        and Mist: Mesoamerican Studies in Honor of Thelma D. Sullivan*, Vol. 1, edited by J.
        Kathryn Josserand and Karen Dakin, pp. 345–388. BAR International Series 402.
        British Archaeological Reports, Oxford. [3]
1996a   Art and Imperial Strategy in Tenochtitlan. In *Aztec Imperial Strategies*, by Frances
        F. Berdan, Richard E. Blanton, Elizabeth Hill Boone, Mary G. Hodge, Michael E.
        Smith, and Emily Umberger, pp. 85–106. Dumbarton Oaks Research Library and
        Collection, Washington, D.C. [1, 3]
1996b   Aztec Presence and Material Remains in the Outer Provinces. In *Aztec Imperial
        Strategies*, by Frances F. Berdan, Richard E. Blanton, Elizabeth Hill Boone, Mary G.
        Hodge, Michael E. Smith, and Emily Umberger, pp. 151–179. Dumbarton Oaks Re-
        search Library and Collection, Washington, D.C. [3]
1998   New Blood from an Old Stone. *Estudios de Cultura Náhuatl* 28:241–256. [3]
1999   The Reading of Glyphs on Aztec Monuments. *Thule: Rivista Italiana di Studi Ameri-
        canistici* 6–7:77–102. [3]
2002   Notions of Aztec History: The Case of the Great Temple Dedication. *Res* (Cam-
        bridge, Massachusetts) 42:8–108. [3]

2007   The Metaphorical Underpinnings of Aztec History: The Case of the 1473 Civil War. *Ancient Mesoamerica* 18:1–19. [3]

Umberger, Emily, and Cecilia F. Klein

1993   Aztec Art and Imperial Expansion. In *Latin American Horizons: A Symposium at Dumbarton Oaks, 11ᵗʰ and 12ᵗʰ October 1986*, edited by Don Stephen Rice, pp. 295–336. Dumbarton Oaks Research Library and Collection, Washington, D.C. [3]

Valdés, J. A., and Lori E. Wright

2004   The Early Classic and Its Antecedents at Kaminaljuyú: A Complex Society, with Complex Problems. In *Understanding Early Classic Copan*, edited by Ellen E. Bell, Marcello A. Canuto, and Robert J. Sharer, pp. 337–355. University of Pennsylvania Museum of Archaeology and Anthropology, Philadelphia. [1]

van Beek, Martijn

2001   Beyond Identity Fetishism: "Communal" Conflict in Ladakh and the Limits of Autonomy. *Cultural Anthropology* 15:525–469. [1]

van den Berghe, Pierre L.

1968   Ethnic Membership and Cultural Change in Guatemala. *Social Forces* 46:514–522. [1]

1975   Ethnicity and Class in Highland Peru. In *Ethnic and Resource Competition in Plural Societies*, edited by Leo A. Despres, pp. 71–85. Mouton, The Hague. [6]

van Schendel, Willem

1995   The Invention of the "Jummas": State Formation and Ethnicity in Southeastern Bangladesh. In *Indigenous Peoples of Asia*, edited by Robert H. Barnes, Andrew Gray, and Benedict Kingsbury, pp. 121–144. Association for Asian Studies, Ann Arbor, Michigan. [1]

Velasco, José Toro

1979   Indigenismo y rebelión totonaca de Papantla, 1885–1896. *América Indígena* 39:81–105. [7]

Wallerstein, Immanuel

1974   *The Modern World-System, Vol. 1: Capitalist Agriculture and the Origins of the European World-Economy in the Sixteenth Century*. Academic Press, New York. [6]

Watanabe, John M.

1992   *Maya Saints and Souls in a Changing World*. University of Texas Press, Austin. [1, 5]

Weiant, C. W.

1943   *An Introduction to the Ceramics of Tres Zapotes, Veracruz, Mexico*. Bulletin No. 139. Bureau of American Ethnology, Smithsonian Institution, Washington, D.C. [2]

Wheatcroft, Andrew

1995   *The Habsburgs: Embodying Empire*. Penguin, London. [4]

White, Christine D., Michael W. Spence, Fred J. Longstaffe, and Kimberley R. Law

2000   Testing the Nature of Teotihuacan Imperialism at Kaminaljuyú Using Phosphate Oxygen-Isotope Ratios. *Journal of Anthropological Research* 56:535–558. [1]

White, Christine D., Michael W. Spence, Hilary Le-Q. Stuart-Williams, and Henry P. Schwarcz

1998   Oxygen Isotopes and the Identification of Geographical Origins: The Valley of Oaxaca versus the Valley of Mexico. *Journal of Archaeological Science* 25:643–655. [1]

White, Christine D., Rebecca Storey, Fred J. Longstaffe, and Michael W. Spence

2004   Immigration, Assimilation, and Status in the Ancient City of Teotihuacan: Stable Isotopic Evidence from Tlajinga 33. *Latin American Antiquity* 15:176–198. [1, 2]

Whitten, Norman E.

1975   Jungle Quechua Ethnicity: An Ecuadorian Case Study. In *Ethnic and Resource Competition in Plural Societies*, edited by Leo A. Despres, pp. 41–69. Mouton, The Hague. [6]

Wicke, Charles

1976   Once More Around the Tizoc Stone: A Reconsideration. In *Actas del XLI Congreso Internacional de Americanistas, México, 2 al 7 de septiembre de 1974*, 2:209–222. Comisión de Publicación de las Actas y Memorias, Mexico City. [3]

Wilkerson, S. Jeffrey K.

1972   Ethnogenesis of the Huastecs and Totonacs: Early Cultures of North-Central Vera-
        cruz at Santa Luisa, Mexico. Ph.D. dissertation, Department of Anthropology, Tu-
        lane University. [1]

1987   *El Tajín: A Guide for Visitors*. Universidad Veracruzana, Jalapa, Veracruz. [2]

Wimmer, Andreas

2004   Dominant Ethnicity and Dominant Nationhood. In *Rethinking Ethnicity: Major-
        ity Groups and Dominant Minorities*, edited by Eric P. Kaufmann, pp. 40–58. Rout-
        ledge, New York. [1]

Winkelman, Michael

2001   Ethnicity and Psychocultural Models. In *Cultural Diversity in the United States: A
        Critical Reader*, edited by Ida Susser and Thomas C. Patterson, pp. 281–301. Black-
        well, Malden, Massachusetts. [1]

Winter, Irene

1977   Perspective on the "Local Style" of Hasanlu IVB: A Study in Receptivity. In *Moun-
        tains and Lowlands: Essays in the Archaeology of Greater Mesopotamia*, edited by
        Louis D. Levine and T. Cuyler Young Jr., pp. 371–386. Biblioteca Mesopotamica Vol.
        7. Undena, Malibu, California. [1]

1998   Affective Properties of Styles: An Inquiry into Analytical Process and the Inscrip-
        tion of Meaning in Art History. In *Picturing Science, Producing Art*, edited by Caro-
        line A. Jones and Peter Galison, pp. 55–77. Routledge, New York. [1]

Wolf, Eric R.

1955   Types of Latin American Peasantry: A Preliminary Discussion. *American Anthro-
        pologist* 57:452–471. [1]

1957   Closed Corporate Peasant Communities in Mesoamerica and Central Java. *South-
        western Journal of Anthropology* 13:1–18. [5, 6]

1960   The Indian in Mexican Society. *Alpha Kappa Deltan* 30:3–6. [5]

1982   *Europe and the People Without History*. University of California Press, Berkeley. [6]

1986   The Vicissitudes of the Closed Corporate Community. *American Ethnologist* 13:325–
        329. [5]

Wood, Stephanie

1991   The Cosmic Conquest: Late Colonial Views of the Sword and Cross in Central Mex-
        ican *Títulos. Ethnohistory* 38(2):176–195. [5]

1998   The Social versus Legal Context of Nahuatl *Títulos*. In *Native Traditions in the Post-
        conquest World: A Symposium at Dumbarton Oaks, 2nd through 4th October 1992*,
        edited by Elizabeth Hill Boone and Tom Cummins, pp. 201–231. Dumbarton Oaks,
        Washington, D.C. [5]

Wright, Henry T.

1977   Recent Research on the Origin of the State. *Annual Review of Anthropology* 6:379–
        397. [1]

Wright, Lori E.

2004   In Search of Yax Nuun Ayiin I: Revisiting the Tikal Project's Burial 10. *Ancient Meso-
        america* 16:1–12. [1]

2005   Identifying Immigrants to Tikal, Guatemala: Defining Local Variability in Stron-
        tium Isotope Ratios of Human Tooth Enamel. *Journal of Archaeological Science* 32:
        555–566. [1]

Wright, Lori, Douglas Price, James Burton, Jason Pursian, and Peter Rank

2002   Teotihuacanos at Tikal and Kaminaljuyú? Paper presented at the 67th Annual
        Meeting of the Society for American Archaeology, Denver, Colorado, March 20–24.
        [1]

Zantwijk, Rudolf van

1973   Politics and Ethnicity in a Prehispanic Mexican State between the 13th and 15th Cen-
        turies. *Plural Societies* 4(2):23–52. [1, 2]

1985   *The Aztec Arrangement: The Social History of Pre-Spanish Mexico*. University of
        Oklahoma Press, Norman. [2, 3, 4]

Zeitlin, Judith Frances
1989   Ranchers and Indians on the Southern Isthmus of Tehuantepec: Economic Change and Indigenous Survival in Colonial Mexico. *Hispanic American Historical Review* 69(1):23–60. [5]
Zorita, Alonso de
1963   [1566–1570] *Life and Labor in Ancient Mexico*. Translated by Benjamin Keen. Rutgers University Press, New Brunswick, New Jersey. [3, 4]

Authors

Frances F. Berdan is professor of anthropology at California State University, San Bernardino. She has conducted archaeological, ethnohistorical, and ethnographic research with a primary emphasis on Aztec culture. She has undertaken ethnographic research in the Sierra Norte de Puebla, Mexico, and is currently co-director of the Laboratory for Ancient Materials Analysis. Her publications include *The Aztecs of Central Mexico: An Imperial Society* (2nd ed., 2005), *The Codex Mendoza* (coauthored with Patricia Anawalt; 4 vols., 1992), *Aztec Imperial Strategies* (coauthored with Richard E. Blanton, Elizabeth Hill Boone, Mary G. Hodge, Michael E. Smith, and Emily Umberger; 1996), and *The Postclassic Mesoamerica World* (coedited with Michael E. Smith; 2003).

John K. Chance is professor of anthropology at Arizona State University. A past president of the American Society for Ethnohistory, he has written on issues of class, identity, and political economy in urban and rural settings of Puebla, Mexico, and colonial Oaxaca. He is the author of *Race and Class in Colonial Oaxaca* (1978) and *Conquest of the Sierra: Spaniards and Indians in Colonial Oaxaca* (1989).

Alan R. Sandstrom is professor of anthropology and chair of the Department of Anthropology at Indiana University–Purdue University at Fort Wayne. He is a cultural anthropologist with interests in cultural ecology, cultural materialism, economic anthropology, religion, ritual, and symbolism. He has conducted ethnographic research for more than thirty years among the Nahua of northern Veracruz, Mexico. His publications include *Corn Is Our Blood* (1991) and *Traditional Papermaking and Paper Cult Figures of Mexico* (with Pamela Effrein Sandstrom, 1986), along with three recent coedited volumes. He is editor of the *Nahua Newsletter*, an international publication covering the history, language, and culture of Nahuatl-speaking and related peoples in the Mesoamerican culture area.

Barbara L. Stark is professor of anthropology in the School of Human Evolution and Social Change at Arizona State University. She researches long-term changes (particularly economic, political, and settlement-pattern shifts) in Gulf lowland societies using the archaeological record. An example of her economic work is the assessment of the cotton industry over time (with coauthors, 1988). She has examined local settlement hierarchies (1999) and conducted residential investigations (2001). Among her publications are the edited volume *Classic Period Mixtequilla, Veracruz, Mexico: Diachronic Inferences from Residential Investigations* (2001).

JAMES M. TAGGART is the Lewis Audenreid Professor at Franklin and Marshall College and has done anthropological research in Mexico with Nahuat-speakers in the Sierra Norte de Puebla, in Spain, and in the Hispanic Southwest. His publications include *Nahuat Myth and Social Structure* (1983 and 1997), *Enchanted Maidens: Gender Relations in Spanish Folktales of Courtship and Marriage* (1990), *The Bear and His Sons: Masculinity in Spanish and Mexican Folktales* (1997), *Remembering Victoria: A Tragic Nahuat Love Story* (2007), and, with José Inez Taylor, *Alex and the Hobo: A Chicano Life and Story* (2003).

EMILY UMBERGER is professor of art history at Arizona State University. Her primary research areas are Aztec monuments, hieroglyphs, and history, and art in Spain and New Spain from 1500 to 1800. Recent works on Aztec historical thought include "Notions of Aztec History: The Case of the Great Temple Dedication" (2002) and "The Metaphorical Underpinnings of Aztec History: The Case of the 1473 Civil War" (2007). She also is one of six coauthors of *Aztec Imperial Strategies* (1996).

Index

Numbers in *italics* refer to figures or tables